Wentz

THE REV. ABDEL ROSS WENTZ, PH.D., 92, scholar, seminary president emeritus, church leader and author, died July 19 in Rockford, Ill. A professor of church history, he was associated with the Lutheran Theological Seminary at Gettysburg, Pa., for 40 years, served as its president (1940-51) and retired in 1956. He was then professor for two years at the Lutheran Theological Southern Seminary, Columbia, S.C. His career in education began in 1909, the year he was ordained and joined Gettysburg College as a professor of history. He held many offices in the United Lutheran Church in America, serving as president of the Board of Foreign Missions 1942-52. He was a longtime member of the Lutheran World Federation Executive Committee, served as its vice-president for seven years and was a member of the provisional committee which eventually formed the World Council of Churches. Dr.

Wentz was also on the American Bible Revision Committee which prepared the text for the Revised Standard Version of the New Testament. Among books he wrote is *The Lutheran Church in American History,* widely used as a seminary text.

A Basic History of

LUTHERANISM IN AMERICA

A Basic History

of

LUTHERANISM IN AMERICA

by
Abdel Ross Wentz

REVISED EDITION

FORTRESS PRESS   +   PHILADELPHIA

*Library of Congress Catalog
Card Number 64-12996*

6927C64   Printed in U.S.A.   UB763

PREFACE

The immediate purpose of this volume is twofold. It is intended to furnish an introduction to the history of the Lutheran church and Lutheran people in America. In this sense it is basic. It aims not merely to present facts but also to present an interpretation of the general course of events in such a way as to prevent the reader from losing the main thread in a webbed mass of details. At the same time it is intended to point the way for the more advanced student to carry his studies into greater detail and even into lines of special research. In this sense also it is basic.

The position of the Lutheran church in America rests upon a birthright. It is not an immigrant church that needed to be naturalized after it was transplanted from some European land. It is as old as the American nation and much older than the American republic. The Lutheran church in America is an integral and potent part of American Christianity. The people in the Lutheran churches of the land are a constituent and typical element of the American nation.

This reciprocal relationship between American culture and the American Lutheran church can be properly understood only in the light of the historical perspective. The church and the nation were born at the same time, grew up side by side, and developed by similar stages of progress.

This succession of parallels between church history and general culture is not an accident. There is a reciprocal relation between nationality and religion, between a man's conduct as a citizen and his conduct as a church member, between the political and the ecclesiastical history of a country. Certainly it is important that Lutherans should view their history in the framework of general American civilization if they are to take their rightful place in the Christian world of today and in society in general.

We must avoid the danger of abstraction that lurks in the study of church history. The life and work of the church must not be detached from the social and political environment in which it grew up. The purpose of every student of history should be to understand himself in the situation in which he finds himself. This determines our method of presentation. It is based upon an analysis of the facts of Lutheran history in America and a synthesis of those facts in a continuous line of interpretation down to our own day. The main purpose is to enable the reader to see the relation of the church's history to the history of society in general and so to interpret the main direction of events, particularly in the present day.

In this volume I have used the same method that was employed on a more limited scale in my *Lutheran Church in American History*. The framework for the interpretation of Lutheran church history continues to be the general history of America. Some of the materials of that earlier volume are included in this new and more detailed narrative. In accordance with our purpose to focus upon the situation of our own day, the scale of presentation grows larger as the narrative progresses. Moreover, in order that the attention of the reader might not be fixed entirely upon the church as an institution, I have sought to include in this account some of the social and cultural history of Lutheran people in America. This is the purpose, for example, of Chapters 6, 9, 14, and 20.

It is my hope that this volume may prove helpful to students of various grades in applying the light of historical perspective to the understanding and solution of current problems in the Lutheran church in America.

PREFACE TO THE REVISED EDITION

This new edition updates the narrative to July, 1963. The later chapters of the first edition, the index, and the bibliographies have been supplemented. A new part has been added, Part VII, which undertakes to estimate the period that began about 1950. In order not to increase the size of the volume, the highly important events of the last decade are presented only in outline. The Reverend Frederick K. Wentz, Ph.D., professor of historical theology at the Gettysburg Theological Seminary, was very helpful in the preparation of this new edition.

ABDEL ROSS WENTZ

Gettysburg, Pennsylvania
July 4, 1963

CONTENTS

Part I

IN COLONIAL TIMES

(1625-1740)

Growth of Local Institutions

CHAPTER 1

GENERAL BACKGROUND

The story of the Lutheran church in America is best told as a part of the great fabric of American history, for the religious life of a people is enmeshed in political and social life. The member of a church is the citizen of a state. Impulses and ideals that move him in the one capacity will influence his conduct in the other. Thus there are significant parallels between the nation's political history and the story of the Lutheran church in America.

The American beginnings of the church were diverse and disconnected, like the beginnings of the American colonies. If the church at first developed slowly, it must be remembered that 115 years elapsed between the discovery of America and the first permanent English settlement at Jamestown. From the date of that settlement, it was 169 years before the Republic was founded—and this is as long as the life of the nation to the close of World War II. The church, too, moved unhurriedly.

Population was sparse in the colonies. By 1660, it is estimated, there were not more than 60,000 people in the English settlements along the Atlantic seaboard. At the outbreak of the Revolutionary War over a century later there were not more than two and a half millions, considerably fewer, in all the colonies combined, than the active membership of the Lutheran church alone in this country today.

The institutions of the colonies were localized, without broad organization of church or state. Diverse, largely isolated, with little traffic or communication between them, the early settlements were like footnotes to European history. The nations of Europe in the seventeenth and eighteenth centuries were not only diverse in faiths, political attitude, and manners, but were also internally most varied. This pattern was transplanted to America and elaborated.

There were, furthermore, natural obstacles to keep the colonies apart. They were separated by great distances, measured in time. Rivers, mountains, and forests, savage beasts and savage men, prevented any easy common life among the colonists. Until the very end of the colonial period there was no sense of community of interest and little disposition to co-operate.

Strong ties still bound the colonies to Europe, however. Communication with the mother country by sea was easier than by land with neighbors, for the settlements were all oceanside or riverside, and no roads paralleled the shore. Even the English colonies, looking to the same source of control and guidance, were different in circumstances of origin, and grew under different influences of climate, crops, and trade. Political development and character were unlike.

Some colonies progressed towards diffusion of rights and privileges among all citizens, while others tended to centralize rights and privileges in the hands of a few. In some the democratic spirit was fostered by public schools and the printing presses, while elsewhere the aristocratic spirit flourished in private schools. Where industry was varied and labor free, wealth was distributed and movement of people easy. Where industry was simple and labor forced, wealth was concentrated and democracy stunted. The middle colonies, destined to be the home of the vast majority of Lutherans throughout this period, showed a partial blending of these tendencies.

The same diversity which characterized political and social life in the colonies produced the denominationalism that has always been such a prominent characteristic of American religious life. The earliest church history of America reads like a chapter from European church history. As the colonization of America represented many peoples of Europe, so religious life in the American colonies exhibited different kinds of European Christianity. The same religious customs that prevailed in the mother countries were practiced in the colonies: the same bigotry and superstitions, the same intolerance and intemperance, the same skeptical worldliness and gloomy otherworldliness. The colonies responded to the same high impulses that touched European Christianity from time to time and felt the waves of religious revival and decline that swept over the homelands. There was perhaps a more general diffusion of the spirit of missions than in Europe, owing

3

to the nearness of the heathen Indians, but lack of organization prevented any aggressive attack upon this problem.

Many of the colonists had crossed the ocean to escape intolerance in the Old World, but so completely were they saturated with European modes of thought that some of them upon reaching American shores set up their own established, and often intolerant, churches. In these colonies taxes were levied to purchase church property, to erect church buildings, and to support the pastors of the ruling church. Statutes were enacted to suppress vice and punish blasphemy, to promote the observance of the Lord's Day and to compel regular attendance at divine services. Strict laws were passed to prevent heresy and to quell dissent. In almost every sphere of life laws were made to regulate the citizen's personal conduct under a civil code severe in its penalties. The result in these colonies was a decided limitation on the exercise of free religious opinion. The unholy alliance between the state and some particular church was simply the heritage of the times.

To these practices Pennsylvania and Rhode Island were notable exceptions. Under the charter of Rhode Island no person was in any way disabled for any religious opinion. Under the proprietary government of Pennsylvania, liberty of conscience, freedom of worship, and eligibility to public office were granted to all persons professing to believe in Jesus Christ. To Pennsylvania, then, Lutherans came in largest numbers; elsewhere they were either persecuted or existed by tolerance rather than by right. Thus Pennsylvania became, if not the first, then certainly the chief home of American Lutheranism throughout colonial times.

CHAPTER 2

NEW NETHERLAND AND NEW YORK

The earliest Lutheran settlers in America came to the Dutch colony of New Netherland. This Dutch settlement on the Hudson, together with New Sweden on the Delaware, until 1664 prevented England from having a continuous colonial empire extending from French Canada to Spanish Florida. In 1623 the Dutch West India Company settled forty families at Fort Orange (now Albany) and in 1625 some 200 persons at New Amsterdam on Manhattan Island. These early Dutch settlers came chiefly for commercial purposes; in this respect they differed from the earliest settlers in most of the other colonies.

The established church in Holland was the Reformed. Under the administration of the Dutch West India Company that church was made the official religious organization in the settlements on the Hudson. But there were at the time large numbers of Lutherans in Holland—more than 30,000 in Amsterdam, and strong Lutheran congregations also in Rotterdam, Leyden, Woerden, and other Dutch cities. These Lutherans, some of them wealthy, co-operated with their countrymen in commercial enterprise in America, and some of them came to New Netherland with the other settlers in 1623 and 1625. But the Dutch West India Company, unlike the Dutch government itself, excluded all religions except the Reformed. The result was that the Lutheran settlers on the Hudson found themselves hindered in the exercise of their faith. They not only had to attend Reformed services but were obliged to have their children baptized and instructed by Reformed pastors. Efforts to cultivate their Lutheran faith in private services were met with severe measures of repression.

Many of the early settlers in New Netherland were Scandinavians and Germans who had been resident in Holland. In fact, the dominant element in the Lutheran congregation in New Amsterdam was not

Dutch but German and Scandinavian. The leading layman was Paul Schrick of Nuremberg. Besides those in New Amsterdam and Fort Orange, there soon were Lutherans at Loonenburg (Athens), Hackensack (Teaneck), Esopus (Kingston), and Bergen (Jersey City).

By the middle of the century the number of Lutherans in the colony had grown to such an extent, and their religious oppression had become so severe that they resolved to attempt an independent organization and strive for official recognition. They proceeded in orderly fashion. In 1649 they organized the Lutheran Church of New Netherland, the oldest Lutheran congregation in America still in existence. Then they appealed to the Lutheran consistory of Amsterdam to intercede for them with the directors of the West India Company. They renewed their request in 1653 with the petition that a Lutheran pastor be sent them. Not until 1657 did *De Oude Lutherse Kerk* ("The Old Church") in Amsterdam ordain and send to their persecuted brethren in the New World the young Johannes Gutwasser.

Reformed pastors set up a vigorous protest against Gutwasser. He was prohibited from holding services or performing ministerial acts and within two years was deported. A similar fate befell a successor, Abelius Zetskoorn, in 1662. It must be remembered that in the days of religious wars in Europe intolerance was rife.

Relief for the Lutherans came only with the surrender of the Dutch settlements to the English in 1664. New Amsterdam became New York and the English governor readily granted the petition of the Lutherans for permission to call their own pastor. Two calls were declined; the third was accepted, and in 1669 Pastor Jacob Fabritius arrived.

Earlier in 1669 a separate Lutheran congregation had been organized at Albany. Fabritius served both of these Dutch congregations. But he was a great disappointment to his long-suffering people, who for more than a generation had maintained their Lutheran faith and longed for a Lutheran pastor. Their first regular minister proved so despotic and irascible that in less than two years he was compelled to resign, in 1671, first in Albany and then in New York. Afterwards he took up work among the Swedish Lutherans on the Delaware.

As successor to Fabritius the consistory at Amsterdam sent over

6

Bernhard Arnzius, described as "a gentle personage and of very agreeable behavior." He was the only Dutch Lutheran pastor sent to New York, all others being Germans who had learned Dutch. Quietly and faithfully he administered the affairs of the two congregations for twenty years (1671-91), spending his summers in New York and his winters in Albany. When he was absent from either part of his charge, Pastor Arnzius appointed a lay reader to conduct the services. In New York the first Lutheran church building was erected in 1671 where Trinity Episcopal Church now stands. This first building was demolished in 1673, when the Dutch returned to power for a year, because it stood beyond the fortifications of the city and interfered with its defense. The congregation, compensated for its loss, built a second church in 1674.

Those were trying times in which Arnzius conducted his ministry. War between Holland and England brought changes of government in the colony. The Revolution of 1688, in which the Roman Catholic James II was overthrown by the Protestant William of Orange, kept the colonists in constant excitement. But the Lutheran congregation flourished, and when Arnzius died in 1691 the congregation in New York consisted of some thirty families and that in Albany of twelve.

During the last decade of the seventeenth century the pastorate was vacant, for the Lutheran authorities in Amsterdam insisted that the Lutherans of New York must now assume responsibility for securing their own pastor. In 1701 the New York congregation called Andrew Rudman, who had been ministering to the Swedes on the Delaware. He proved to be a man of constructive talents, but he remained in New York only a little more than a year. On November 24, 1703, in what was probably the first regular ordination in the New World, Pastor Rudman, as suffragan of the Archbishop of Uppsala, in Gloria Dei ("Old Swedes Church") in Philadelphia, in full Latin service with choir, ordained a German pietist of the Halle school, Justus Falckner, as his successor to serve the Dutch congregations in New York. This ceremony, at the beginning of a continuous Lutheran ministry in America, exemplified a fellowship among Lutherans of several nationalities, languages, and liturgical traditions.

Falckner's tremendous parish extended some 200 miles, from Albany to Long Island, and included settlements on both sides of the Hudson and in northern New Jersey. For twenty years Pastor Falckner, a

7

man of thorough education, deep spirituality and great vigor, ministered in Dutch to some extent, but mainly in German, as revealed by entries in his parish records. He appointed "readers" to conduct the services while he was absent in other parts of the parish. In addition to his abundant labors as pastor he found time to write and publish a handbook of Christian doctrine in the form of questions and answers. Upon his death in 1723, his older brother Daniel, pastor of the Raritan parish in New Jersey, for a time supplied both the Dutch and the German churches along the Hudson.

The rapid growth of the Palatine German element was spurred by events in Europe. When the armies of Louis XIV ravaged the Palatinate, many fugitives found temporary refuge in England, and there Queen Anne arranged for their transportation to the American colonies. In 1709 Joshua Kocherthal and a Lutheran congregation of sixty-one people settled the west bank of the Hudson at Newburgh. The next year three thousand more Palatines arrived in New York and were settled a hundred miles up the Hudson at the foot of the Catskills, where they suffered terribly from hunger and cold and from the avarice of governors. Some made their way westward into the Mohawk Valley and into the Schoharie Valley; some of these in 1723 pushed on south to the Tulpehocken region of Pennsylvania. Unceasingly Pastor Kocherthal ministered to the temporal and spiritual welfare of his scattered flock until his death in 1719. Then for several years these eight German parishes were added to the Dutch charge of Justus Falckner.

Falckner's successor was William Christopher Berkenmeyer. To this young theological student of Hamburg the Lutheran Consistory of Amsterdam had extended the call of the Dutch congregations in New York and Albany. After considerable hesitation he accepted and was ordained in Amsterdam. He reached New York in 1725, bringing with him a library for the congregation and funds for a new church building, contributed by friends in Germany, Denmark and England. Four years later the new Trinity Church was dedicated in New York. Since the parish of ten congregations which he had inherited from Falckner was too large for one man to cultivate successfully, he sent to Germany for another minister, resigned at New York, and took charge of the northern and more promising part of the field, making his home at Athens (then Loonenburg). The southern part of the field he placed in charge of Michael Christian Knoll, a native of Holstein, who had been ordained by the Lutheran pastors of London and had come to America in 1732. Two years later the Hamburg Consistory sent the young John August Wolf to have charge of the congregations at Raritan and other points in New Jersey.

Berkenmeyer was the most influential spirit among the Lutherans of colonial New York. A cultured man of impressive personality and strict Lutheran convictions, he was distinguished also by his organizing talent. In 1734 he prepared a church constitution which was intended to stabilize the individual congregations and to provide an effective administration for the whole province through the office of a superintendent. It was not long before Berkenmeyer had an opportunity to test the effectiveness of his plan. Pastor Wolf had become involved in serious difficulty with his congregations in New Jersey. There were questions about his charges for ministerial acts, his methods of preaching, his moral conduct. To adjust the difficulty Berkenmeyer in 1735 summoned the three pastors and lay representatives of the congregations to meet in a "Classical Assembly," a term imitative of the Reformed classis. This assembly at Raritan, after several tumultuous sessions, secured a short-lived agreement between Pastor Wolf and his reluctant parishioners, although in the end Wolf was exposed as a faithless and unreliable character. There is no record of any further meeting of the assembly. It did not develop into a permanent synod as Berkenmeyer had intended. The organization of a synod that would meet regularly, ordain ministers, legislate with authority, and provide regular oversight of congregations, waited for a new leader and a new day.

Pastor Knoll spent eighteen years of faithful labor in New York under difficult circumstances, for he was obliged to preach in Dutch to a congregation that had become predominantly German. The inevitable split came in 1750 when Christ Church was organized by some of the Germans under Pastor J. F. Ries. Worn out with the conflict, Knoll resigned from Trinity and went to Athens as successor to Berkenmeyer.

Berkenmeyer continued his ministry for a quarter of a century, until his death in 1751, eight years after Henry Melchior Muhlenberg had begun his ministry in Pennsylvania. But Berkenmeyer and his North German colleagues belong to a different school from that of

9

Muhlenberg and his Halle group of fellow-laborers. Berkenmeyer suspected Muhlenberg of pietism and laxity of practice, and the correspondence between the two sometimes savored of theological controversy. But that did not prevent Muhlenberg from coming to New York in 1751 and 1752 and saving the situation among Lutherans there.

CHAPTER 3

NEW SWEDEN

When William Penn in 1682 sailed up the Delaware River and selected the site for his city of Philadelphia, he chose a spot where stood a Swedish village and a Lutheran church. The Swedes had been there forty-four years when Penn arrived. They were part of the Lutheran settlement planned by Gustavus Adolphus, King of Sweden and Protestant hero of the Thirty Years' War, and carried through by Chancellor Oxenstierna, regent for the young Queen Christina.

The first settlers from Sweden landed from the ship *Kalmar Nyckel* in March, 1638, where Wilmington, Delaware, now stands. The colony grew with continued immigration and soon spread north and south on both sides of the Delaware. Here for nearly two centuries a succession of thirty-five devoted Lutheran pastors ministered to the colonists in at least six Swedish churches. Many of these immigrants had earlier come from Finland to Sweden and then came to America as Swedish colonists.

With a second expedition in 1639 came the Rev. Reorus Torkillus, the first regular Lutheran minister in America, eighteen years before Gutwasser reached New Amsterdam. Torkillus conducted services in a blockhouse that had been erected at Wilmington.

A few months before Torkillus died in 1643, a vigorous new governor, Johan Printz, had arrived with another minister, Johan Campanius. They brought instructions from Sweden to do missionary work among the Indians, to maintain worship and instruction according to the Unaltered Augsburg Confession and to exercise tolerance towards the "Reformed religion." When Printz moved the seat of government to his "palace" on Tinicum Island above Upland (now Chester, Pa.), Campanius built there in 1646 the first Lutheran church-building erected in America. There were now about five hundred people in the colony.

The Swedes purchased land from the Indians and lived peaceably with them, thus laying the foundations for the celebrated Indian policy of William Penn. Campanius faithfully carried on missionary work among the friendly Indians. During the six years of his stay in America he translated Luther's *Small Catechism* into their language. The composition of this catechism, the first Protestant work translated into an Indian dialect, antedated the publication in 1661 in New England of John Eliot's Indian New Testament, although it was not published for nearly fifty years.

Before Campanius returned to Sweden in 1648 Lars Lock had arrived to take his place. For twenty-two years he served the churches at Tinicum and Wilmington. The Dutch had always contested the rights of the Swedes on the Delaware, and in 1655 when domestic troubles arose in Sweden, Governor Pieter Stuyvesant of New Amsterdam took advantage of the situation to conquer New Sweden. Many of the Swedish colonists returned to Sweden after the Dutch conquest, and the colony was much weakened. Immigration and supplies ceased. Then in 1664 Dutch rule was supplanted by English.

Pastor Lock began in 1669 to conduct services in the blockhouse at Wicaco, north of the Schuylkill, now in the southern part of Philadelphia. For several years he had the help of Jacob Fabritius, former pastor of the Dutch church at New Amsterdam. But in 1677 Lock, sadly enfeebled, gave up his work entirely; five years later Fabritius became totally blind. Spiritually leaderless, the Swedish Lutherans were held together for some years by two laymen, Andrew Bengtson at Tinicum and Charles Springer at Wilmington, who conducted services and read sermons. But the parish weakened.

Efforts to secure a pastor through the Dutch were unavailing. Appeals to Sweden went unanswered until Andrew Printz, a nephew of the former governor, on his travels to America in 1690 saw the colonists' need, and on his return to Sweden interested King Charles XI in their plight. The king gave orders for the selection of ministers, for the publication of five hundred copies of Luther's Catechism as translated into the language of the Indians by Campanius, and for a large number of Bibles and other books desired by the colonists.

Three pastors were commissioned for service in America. Upon their arrival in June, 1697, Andrew Rudman took charge of Wicaco and Tinicum, Eric Björk became pastor at Wilmington, Jonas Aureen ministered first at Elk River in Maryland and later among the people east of the Delaware in New Jersey. Under the ministry of these pastors the Swedish settlements took on new life.

Soon the congregations began to build new churches. Two of these buildings with their interesting colonial architecture—Holy Trinity at Wilmington (1699) and Gloria Dei in South Philadelphia (1700) each known locally as "Old Swedes Church"—are still in active use by Episcopal congregations.

Influential among the successors of Rudman and Björk was Johan Dylander, pastor at Wicaco from 1737 to 1741, who ministered to the English and the Germans as well as the Swedes, and enjoyed a wide reputation as an eloquent preacher. From 1749 to 1756 Israel Acrelius, pastor at Wilmington, organized state conferences of the Swedish ministers, and to his very detailed *History of New Sweden* we are indebted for much of our knowledge of the settlement.

Greatest in the long succession of Swedish pastors was the learned and saintly Charles Magnus Wrangel. Arriving in 1759, he soon became the intimate friend and adviser of the patriarch Henry Melchior Muhlenberg, whom he helped to train Americans for the ministry. Wrangel's recall by the Swedish authorities in 1768 was deeply resented by the three thousand members of the Swedish congregations on the Delaware. After the Revolutionary War the Swedish archbishop recalled all his missionaries. The younger element in the vacated parishes called for services in English. Since their German brethren of Pennsylvania and New York could not supply them with American pastors for either Swedish or English service, the congregations accepted as pastors either Lutherans or Episcopalians—a transition which finally took them into the Protestant Episcopal Church.

That the Lutheranism of New Sweden failed to endure is to be explained by the shortsighted policy of the Swedish authorities. The American settlement was treated as a perpetual missionary outpost of the state church of Sweden. The pastors sent regarded themselves as temporary missionaries in waiting for better positions at home. The pastorates were mostly brief; there was no provision for a native American ministry or for securing the future independent development of a Swedish Lutheran church in America.

13

CHAPTER 4

PENNSYLVANIA

The earliest German Lutheran settlements in Pennsylvania were the result of adversities in Europe and advertisements of America. Among the German pietists and sectarians whom William Penn induced to settle near Philadelphia beginning in 1682 were some Lutherans. In 1694 an erratic preacher, Heinrich Bernhard Koester, gathered a few of these Lutherans together and held the first German Lutheran service in America. But this did not result in the establishment of a congregation.

After the turn of the eighteenth century a strong tide of German immigration set in. This was due to the long continued ravages of war in the Palatinate and the frequent changes of religion. Reports of the unjust treatment accorded the Germans in New York diverted the main stream of immigration to Pennsylvania. During the rest of the colonial period Philadelphia was the chief port of entry for Germans.

Since the majority of these Germans were Lutherans there were soon Lutheran congregations at Falckner's Swamp (New Hanover), Germantown and Philadelphia. Later congregations were organized at Providence (The Trappe), Lancaster, Earltown (New Holland), and Tulpehocken in the Lebanon Valley. The Lutherans at Tulpehocken came from New York in 1723, dissatisfied with the injustices of the authorities there. Under the guidance of friendly Indians, they had made their way three hundred miles along the Susquehanna. Their most distinguished member was Conrad Weiser, the famous Indian agent who was to be the father-in-law of Henry Melchior Muhlenberg.

Succeeding waves of German Lutheran settlers pushed farther and farther into the interior of Pennsylvania, dotting the colony with "preaching stations." In the fourth decade they crossed the Susquehanna and entered the valleys that lead southward to Maryland and Virginia. The high tide of German immigration into the colony came between 1735 and 1745; by the middle of the century there were at least 40,000 Lutherans in Pennsylvania.

These Lutherans brought neither teachers nor pastors with them. For a short time they were visited by the Swedish Lutheran pastors from the Delaware. But the Swedish settlement declined, and as the German Lutherans in Pennsylvania multiplied their pastoral needs became acute. In not a few cases they fell prey to unscrupulous itinerant ecclesiastics who took advantage of their unorganized condition to impose false and self-serving leadership upon them and nearly rob them of respect for the ministry and love for the church.

Yet several devoted pastors were active among them. One was Daniel Falckner, older brother of the Justus Falckner of New York. He was at first the American agent for a German land company. Apparently he organized the Lutherans of Montgomery County in a congregation at New Hanover about 1703 and ministered to them until 1708. He would thus be the first regular pastor of the first German Lutheran congregation in Pennsylvania. He then went to New Jersey and labored there for thirty-three years. For a few years after the death of his brother Justus, his field extended as far north as Albany.

Another pioneer preacher in Pennsylvania was Anthony Jacob Henkel, exiled to America in 1717, who became the progenitor of a long line of distinguished ministers, physicians, and businessmen. He came first to New Hanover, visited all the German settlements within reach, and went as far south as Virginia. He preached to the Lutherans in Philadelphia and Germantown, and may have founded the first congregations there. At any rate he replaced the old church at New Hanover, and encouraged the building of a church at Germantown.

In 1728, the year Henkel died, the Stoevers, father and son, both John Casper, arrived in Philadelphia. The father went on to Virginia and for several years ministered to the Lutherans there. The son remained in Pennsylvania. In the register of the ship that brought him to America he had called himself "missionary," and the word describes his work. He made his home first at The Trappe, afterward at New Holland, and finally in Lebanon County. For over fifty years as missionary, he traveled untiringly through eastern Pennsylvania and into

Maryland and Virginia. Wherever a few Germans had settled he held services, baptized their children, began a church record, and encouraged them to build a church. He never attempted a general organization. Indeed, for twenty years after Muhlenberg had organized a synod, Stoever held aloof, not joining it until 1768.

Another of the men who helped to prepare the way for Muhlenberg was John Christian Schulz. His stay in this country was very brief; he came in the fall of 1732 and left in the spring of 1733. But it was he who ordained the Stoevers, united the three congregations of Philadelphia, The Trappe, and New Hanover into one parish, and persuaded "the united congregations" to send him with two laymen on a "collecting tour" to Germany to secure more ministers and teachers and to solicit funds for churches and schoolhouses. From this mission Pastor Schulz never returned to America, but his enterprise resulted in the coming of Muhlenberg. The American delegation laid their appeal before Pastor Frederick Michael Ziegenhagen, the court preacher at London, and Professor Gotthilf August Francke at Halle. These authorities insisted on clear and definite arrangements in advance for the support of a pastor. Such arrangement the Pennsylvania congregations, though they embraced fifteen hundred families, refused to make, arguing that they could not support a man "in a life of luxury" and that they did not want "a covetous man" as pastor. The negotiations dragged on. But in 1741 Count Nicholas Ludwig von Zinzendorf, the Moravian, appeared in Pennsylvania posing as a Lutheran, holding interdenominational conferences, and assuming leadership among the shepherdless Lutherans of the colony. The Halle authorities were at last stirred to action. They called Henry Melchior Muhlenberg, and hurried him off to Pennsylvania. With his coming, the Lutheran church in America entered a new phase.

16

CHAPTER 5

FROM MARYLAND TO GEORGIA

While Pennsylvania was the chief colony of entry for Lutheran immigration during the eighteenth century, it did not retain all those who came but served as a distributing center to other colonies. These Lutherans from southwestern Germany were chiefly concerned to secure farm land, fertile, cheap, and in large amounts for themselves and their children. As eastern Pennsylvania filled up, and the best farm lands were taken, some of the immigrants left their first American homes and moved out toward other colonies southwestward along the fertile valleys beside the Blue Ridge and the Alleghenies. They formed the leading Lutheran congregations in colonial Virginia and the Carolinas, supplemented by immigrants who came directly from Germany through the ports of Baltimore and Charleston.

The governor of Virginia and the proprietor of Maryland offered cheap lands and other inducements to the sturdy German farmers of Pennsylvania to resettle in their colonies. As it was not yet permitted to settle on land west of the Susquehanna, some of the recent immigrants accepted these invitations. In the early 1730's there was a small community of Lutherans on Monocacy Creek near the present city of Frederick. For nine years beginning in 1734, the young Pennsylvania missionary, John Caspar Stoever, made semiannual pastoral visits to this community. A congregation was organized in 1738, the oldest in Maryland; in 1752 it moved into Frederick.

Another community of Pennsylvania migrants about the same time settled on the Conococheague Creek, north of the Potomac, about eight miles southwest of the present city of Hagerstown. Here Lutherans and Reformed united their efforts and built a log church. The Lutheran congregation had only the occasional ministry of the itinerant missionaries, John Nicholas Kurtz, John Caspar Stoever and

Charles Frederick Wildbahn until, a few years before the Revolution, it joined with a flourishing congregation that had been organized in Hagerstown in 1769.

Maryland A third center of Lutheranism in colonial Maryland was Baltimore. Shortly after its founding in 1730, several German families, mostly of Lutheran confession, took up residence there. The growing industries of the town began to attract immigrants, and by mid-century the Baltimore Lutherans outnumbered those farther west. In 1755 they persuaded Pastor Bager of Hanover, Pennsylvania, to include them in his circuit; in 1764 they built their first church; in 1765 they secured their first resident pastor, John Caspar Kirchner. With immigrants from Germany the congregation of "Old Zion" grew rapidly, but remained an independent, nonsynodical congregation for nearly two centuries.

Virginia In Virginia the oldest Lutheran congregation is Hebron in Madison County. In 1717 a group of Germans, among them a number of Lutherans from Württemberg, had settled in Orange County, twenty miles from Fredericksburg, as "redemptioners" of Governor Spotswood. When their term of service in the Governor's ironworks was completed in 1725, they moved west to Madison County, built a log church and organized a congregation. Other Lutherans came into the settlement from Pennsylvania; by 1737 they numbered over three hundred. John Caspar Stoever, father, was the first pastor of Hebron. In 1734 he and two laymen went to Europe and spent several years securing funds for a new church, some books for a library, and an assistant pastor, George Samuel Klug. Pastor Stoever died on the return voyage in 1739 and for twenty-five years Pastor Klug took his place at Hebron. In 1740 a frame church was built, parts of which remain to this day. The third pastor, John Schwarbach, came from the work of a catechist in Pennsylvania and served the congregation until the outbreak of the Revolution. Continued migration from Pennsylvania by way of the Cumberland and Shenandoah valleys resulted in the organization of a number of Lutheran congregations in Virginia, among them Winchester (1753), Woodstock (1772), Strasburg (1747), Rader's (1765), Pine Church (1774).

The first Lutheran effort at colonization in North Carolina was that of several hundred Palatines sent by Queen Anne in 1710. Their settlement at New Bern was virtually wiped out the following year by an Indian massacre. A quarter of a century later another group of Lutheran settlers from Pennsylvania came down the three-hundred-mile stretch of the Shenandoah Valley and settled in the central and western parts of North Carolina, where they found fertile lands. As their numbers were increased by additions from Pennsylvania, Lutheran congregations were organized among them: first, Zion (Organ) Church in Rowan County; St. John's in Cabarrus County; then congregations in the town of Salisbury and in the counties westward to the Blue Ridge. No pastors were secured for any of these congregations until 1773 when two laymen of Rowan and Cabarrus counties went to Europe and returned with Adolphus Nussman as their pastor and John Gottfried Arends as their school teacher. Pastors were furnished by the Consistory of Hannover until the Revolutionary War.

In South Carolina a few Palatine Lutherans had settled as early as 1732 at Purysburg on the Savannah. Other Lutherans remained in Charleston. In 1735 a German-Swiss colony pushed inland from Charleston and established itself at Orangeburg near the Edisto River. Soon the Lutherans among them organized a small congregation and in 1737 secured the services of John Ulrich Geissendanner, who had just arrived from Switzerland. German immigration enlarged the congregation and soon they built a church, the first Lutheran house of worship in the Carolinas, which stood until the Revolution.

From Orangeburg the settlements expanded westward to Lexington County, where Lutherans numbered 280 by 1750. Pastor John Martin Boltzius at Ebenezer across the Savannah in Georgia corresponded with them and sent them books, for they had neither pastor nor church building. In Charleston no Lutheran congregation was organized until the arrival from Europe in 1755 of John George Friederichs. The first church building was erected four years later. Before the Revolutionary War there were congregations also at Hard Labor Creek in Abbeville County, Amelia Township in Orangeburg County, and Indian Swamp in Barnwell County, fifty miles from Charleston. All these frontier communities suffered severely during the American Revolution.

Georgia, the last of the thirteen colonies to be founded, was the southern frontier of the English colonial empire in America. Established as a buffer against the Spanish in Florida and the French in Louisiana, it offered a refuge for persecuted Protestants. In 1733 General James Edward Oglethorpe founded Savannah. To this port in 1734 came the first shipload of Lutheran refugees from the Austrian province of Salzburg. For nearly two centuries these faithful followers of Luther had succeeded in maintaining their evangelical faith in a Catholic land in spite of terrible persecutions and hardships. But in 1731 the archbishop of the province, despite protests from the Protestant princes of Europe, had ruthlessly expelled them. The winter march of the pious Salzburg exiles and the joyous expression of their faith as they passed through the various countries of Europe constitute a historic record of the tenacity of that faith. Through the intercession of Dr. Samuel Urlsperger of Augsburg, the English people provided for the transportation of ninety-one of the Salzburgers to General Oglethorpe's new colony. There, at Ebenezer, twenty-five miles upstream on the banks of the Savannah, they settled with all the rights of English citizenship and with full freedom of worship. Dr. Urlsperger and Prof. August Hermann Francke of Halle had provided the emigrants with two young Halle instructors, John Martin Boltzius and Israel Christian Gronau, as pastors. Under their devoted leadership and wise management the settlement prospered. The following year, 110 more Salzburgers came, and additional shiploads in succeeding years brought the total population of the settlement to 1,200 by 1741.

The Salzburgers lived in peace with all their neighbors. They deprecated slavery and tried to Christianize the Indians. They cultivated silk, cotton, and indigo, made wooden ware, and ran mills. They erected churches and schools and an orphanage. Devoted to their pastors, they needed no secular authorities to maintain order or settle disputes. The famed evangelist George Whitefield and the founders of Methodism, John and Charles Wesley, who visited Ebenezer, were deeply impressed with the faith and piety of these Lutherans.

In 1744 Gronau died. Dr. Urlsperger sent to take his place another Halle man, Hermann Henry Lemke, who for nineteen years labored in the closest harmony beside Boltzius. Shortly after the middle of the century the settlement was augmented by three shiploads of Germans from Württemberg, and with them a third pastor, Christian Rabenhorst.

Troubles began only after the death of Boltzius in 1765 and Lemke in 1768. From Germany came a new pastor, Christopher F. Triebner, an impetuous and dictatorial man, who soon had the colony divided into factions. Henry Melchior Muhlenberg, summoned from Pennsylvania by the Salzburgers, restored peace among them.

But two years later the war for independence broke out and the Ebenezer colony fell victim to its frontier location. The Salzburgers were warmly sympathetic to the cause of independence, and one of their number, John Adam Treutlen, became the first governor of the state of Georgia. When the British invaded Georgia, they destroyed most of the property and rendered the town of Ebenezer desolate. Pastor Rabenhorst died in December, 1776; Pastor Triebner proved to be a Tory. Jerusalem Church, built in 1767, is all that remains today to indicate the location of this colonial Lutheran settlement. The people themselves were scattered to other settlements of German Lutherans in the Carolinas. There, and in Georgia, their descendants dwell today.

CHAPTER 6

THE RELIGIOUS LIFE OF THE LUTHERAN COLONISTS

The Lutheran people who came to the North American colonies took part in a thrilling episode of human history—the experiment of a free church in a free land. But this Protestant experiment shared by the Lutherans was, for them particularly, an opportunity, a hope for growth, rather than escape from ecclesiastical tyranny. Few of them were exiles. All brought with them their segment of the church of their homelands, and for many years remained derivative and dependent.

In the New World, the Catholic Spaniards' hope of endless conquest was shattered by their clumsy cruelty. The French Catholics carved out a huge empire, but, tangled in Europe, receded. The continent lay before the settlers from the Protestant lands.

The colonists who faced this challenge, unprecedented in history, brought courage and strength and initiative. Most of them bore also a zealous Christian faith.

The Lutherans among them were further distinguished. They came, for the most part, from countries which were not engaged in the competition for empire. They came not as agents, but as individuals and families, or in small bands, with purposes of their own.

There was much variety of religious doctrine and practice among the Lutherans of the various settlements. Even among the congregations of a single colony there was little uniformity of organization. This reflected their European origin, for the leaders of the church there, as followers of Martin Luther, had not sought uniformity. When these people and pastors came to America, where Lutheran diversity was compounded by variety of national origin and by colonial isolation, they produced a tradition of congregationalism that left enduring marks on the spirit of American Lutheranism.

From the beginning of their life in America, Lutherans have manifested comparative unity in faith, but have allowed themselves great variety of organization and practice.

Continued dependence on the church of the homeland was particularly marked among the Lutherans of Dutch New York and the Swedish Lutherans along the Delaware. Brought on the wave of commercial colonial enterprise that swept business and political leaders of seventeenth-century Europe, these settlers continued to be Europeans as far as possible in language, clothing, and food, in buildings and implements and industry, and in church.

The Swedish Lutherans on the Delaware received their ministers by appointment of the state church of Sweden, and conformed to the doctrine and liturgy of the home church. Governor Johan Printz enforced strictly the instructions of Queen Christina in 1642: "Above all things shall the Governor consider and see to it that a true and due worship, becoming honor, laud, and praise to be paid to the Most High God in all things, and to that end all proper care shall be taken that divine service be zealously performed according to the Unaltered Augsburg Confession, the Council of Uppsala, and the ceremonies of the Swedish Church; and all persons, but especially the young, shall be duly instructed in the articles of their Christian faith; and all good church discipline shall in like manner be duly exercised and received." The Council of Uppsala in 1653 had pledged the Lutheran ministers of Sweden to stand by "the pure Word of God, the Three Symbols, and the Unaltered Augsburg Confession," and this was the confessional position of the Lutheran pastor and the Lutheran congregations in the Swedish colony in America. The frontier did not change this.

In liturgy also the colonists followed the Swedish order. Building America's first Lutheran church at Tinicum in 1646, Governor Printz followed his instructions to "decorate the little church according to the Swedish custom." The Swedish order of service for "High Mass" as printed in the *Psalm-Bok* of 1614 was always used, so that the Governor could report to the regent in Sweden that "the service with its ceremonies are conducted as in old Sweden" and in the "good old Swedish language." The sacraments and the regular church festivals were carefully observed according to Lutheran custom, especially Christmas, Easter, and Pentecost. As there were no organs, the minister was obliged to lead the congregational singing and chanting. All devotional literature came from Sweden: hymnals, catechisms, books of sermons, Gerhard's *Loci Theologici*, Seckendorf's *History of the Reformation.* But in outlying settlements the people gathered for worship in private homes or barns, and laymen were appointed to read from a collection of sermons or simply from the Bible. Campanius made special efforts to reach these distant settlers periodically with Word and sacrament.

Similarly the Lutherans of New Netherland looked to the Lutheran Consistory in Amsterdam for ministers, devotional literature and spiritual guidance. But the Dutch Lutherans were always a minority group in that predominantly Reformed colony, and efforts to suppress them had taught them to struggle. Even in Holland the Lutheran churches maintained themselves without secular control or support. In America, often without pastors, they developed a high degree of initiative in ordering their religious affairs, cultivated the spirit of religious freedom, and moved more easily than many other colonists toward an independent church.

The Lutheran ministers who were sent to New Netherland by the Consistory at Amsterdam were pledged to teach in accordance with the entire Book of Concord. They called their first organization in New Netherland "The Christian Community Adhering to the Un-altered Augsburg Confession of Faith." But, for nearly a quarter of a century obliged to attend the services of the Dutch Reformed church, they unconsciously took over many of the customs of that church. In liturgy and in polity, like the Lutheran church in Holland, they closely resembled their Reformed neighbors. The only distinctive Lutheran element in the order of service was the requirement that the sermon be based on the Gospel appointed for the day.

In their congregational organization they followed the Reformed order and assigned a prominent place to lay elders. This lay leadership among the Dutch Lutherans distinguished them from other colonial Lutherans. The Swedish Lutherans on the Delaware brought their pastors with them and settled as congregations, as did the Salzburgers in Georgia. The Germans in Pennsylvania, Maryland, Virginia and the Carolinas first came and settled, then waited for missionaries from

Europe to come and organize them into congregations. But in New Netherland the Lutheran laymen organized themselves into congregations first, conducted services of worship, then sent persistent congregational calls for pastors. Indeed, if Berkenmeyer's constitution of 1734 had conceded more authority to the laity, instead of emphasizing the authority of council and pastors, and the final jurisdiction of consistories in Europe, that constitution might have produced a lasting synodical organization.

The Lutheran people in the Dutch colony were of various nationalities, for Holland had long been a refuge for the oppressed and the dissatisfied of other European countries. A large number were of German or Scandinavian origin. Most of these had first settled in Holland before coming to America. In America they used the Dutch language in their services of worship and their religious literature.

These Dutch Lutherans were mostly of the middle class, but all types were represented among them, from the wealthy nobleman to the humble peasant. Those who lived in the towns owned their homes and shops and the sites on which they were located; in the country the settlers remained tenants of the soil and owned the cattle and the improvements they had made. By occupation they were chiefly fur traders, merchants, and shopkeepers, but some of them were found in every occupation.

With the eighteenth century, Lutheran colonists began to come predominantly from the German territories, settling in or near coastal towns or pushing inland. The trader was in the background and the freehold farmer began to play the leading role. Now, in all the colonies, laity and clergy began to think of America as a permanent home, and timidly sank cultural roots instead of simply perpetuating European ways in this country. The German immigrants at this time, predominately from the Palatinate, came looking for new homes. They were not adventurers or businessmen. Mostly farmers, they expected to develop self-sustaining societies on American soil, alongside and in harmony with their Palatine brethren of the Reformed church. Often Lutheran and Reformed congregations occupied the same church building. But there was no dilution of loyalty to the Lutheran confessions. When Justus Falckner began his official register in 1703 he entitled it the "Church Book of the Christian Apostolic Protestant Lutheran Congregation Adhering to the Unaltered Confession of

Augsburg in New York." Five years later he wrote a text book on Christian doctrines which showed great zeal in combating the doctrinal errors of the Reformed.

The church constitution which Berkenmeyer drew up in 1734 and prescribed for all the congregations of the colony was called the "General Church Order for the Congregations Adhering to the Unaltered Augsburg Confession." Its first article pledges all the preachers in the congregations to regulate their teaching and preaching according to "our Symbolical Books" which are enumerated, and it is specified: "They shall not teach nor preach, either privately or publicly, anything against these, nor shall they use any phrases which contradict them." Berkenmeyer's staunch orthodoxy was made manifest also by his frequent warnings to the Palatine Lutherans against unionistic practices with their Reformed neighbors and by his refusal to associate with the Lutheran pastors who came from pietistic Halle. Kocherthal also regarded himself as a good Lutheran and called his official record the "Church Book of the Church of the Germans who Embrace the Augsburg Confession."

But in liturgical practice these German Lutherans of colonial New York showed the influence of their Reformed environment. In the order of worship for the principal service which Berkenmeyer made obligatory in all congregations, the absence of liturgy is conspicuous. Besides the sermon and the free prayer there is provision only for the singing of hymns, the readings of Scripture, and the benediction.

The meager church buildings of the seventeenth century, usually small structures built of logs, were replaced in the eighteenth century by larger and more substantial buildings, usually of stone. The pulpits were high and surmounted by sounding-boards.

Though Germans constituted the large majority in the Lutheran congregations on the Hudson, Falckner recorded that his members were "also Swedes, Danes, Norwegians, Poles, Lithuanians, Transylvanians, and other nationalities." Falckner, Berkenmeyer, and Knoll regularly admitted Negroes, both free and slave. (Slaves were pledged not to use their Christian profession to break their ties of obedience.) Indians also were evangelized and brought into the church. Pastor Sommer himself baptized eighty-four of them.

By occupation these Germans in New York were farmers. When the English government brought them to America and settled them along the Hudson they were under contract to make tar and naval stores. They had hoped to go to the fertile Schoharie region as their promised land, but they were in abject poverty and they were guests of the colonial government, and so they obeyed orders. But the Palatines had neither heart nor hand for manufacturing ship supplies. The enterprise on the Hudson was badly managed by the government authorities. The manufacturing scheme failed and the German colonists were subjected to more and greater hardships. In the end those who did not migrate to Pennsylvania secured titles to their lands on the Hudson, or in the Schoharie Valley, or along the Mohawk. They also secured agricultural implements, seed, cattle and horses, and, thus equipped to make their own contribution to the foundations of a stable social order and living on friendly terms with the neighboring Indians, they raised rich crops of grain and large herds of horses and cattle and began to cultivate the arts of peaceful civilization.

In the colony of Pennsylvania the people who constituted the first Lutheran congregations came from Germany in the early eighteenth century. Like the German Lutherans in New York, they came chiefly from southwestern Germany and in company with their Reformed neighbors. Their homes in the Palatinate and Württemberg had suffered the ravages of almost a century of devastating warfare. Under the government of the Quakers in Pennsylvania they were treated well and most of them went directly to the fertile soil stretching westward from Philadelphia to the Susquehanna and then to the foothills of the Alleghenies.

Most of these Lutherans came from communities where pietism had made its impression on both clergy and people. They sought to cultivate in every way possible a warmth of spirit and a devotion to the practical works of Christian love. Many a family had brought with them across the ocean copies of Luther's Bible, his Catechism, and a devotional classic used by the pietists, Arndt's *True Christianity*. Many of them had also brought their hymnbooks. Their eagerness for spiritual ministry, for preaching and the sacraments, made them victims sometimes of imposters and scoundrels, of ministers who had been unfrocked in Europe. But the great body of them continued to be steadfast Lutherans. Contacts with their neighbors of the Swedish and Finnish Lutheran churches helped to steady them.

The people of the frontier went great distances to hear preachers, receive the sacraments, or join in religious revival. Whitefield was amazed at the thousands of Germans who came many miles to hear him preach, even though most of them scarcely understood English. He wrote: "Some of the Germans in America are holy souls; they keep up a close walk with God and are remarkable for their sweetness and simplicity of behavior."

In the earliest organized congregations there were usually two orders of elected officers, elders and deacons, responsible respectively for the spiritual and temporal interests of the congregation. These officers directed all the affairs of the congregation. The pastor had no responsibility and little except personal authority in the organization.

Little is known of liturgical practices among the scattered German congregations in Pennsylvania during the first half of the eighteenth century. Until the first common liturgy was written and adopted in 1748 each pastor used the form of worship with which he was acquainted in Germany or which was provided in the hymnbook he happened to have.

The Falckner brothers and Anthony Jacob Henkel ministered in the pietist tradition. They knew how to hold edifying services in private homes, where there were few facilities for liturgy. Their only concern was to preach the Word and minister to the spiritual necessities of their brethren, and until there could be effective leadership and co-operative effort in liturgical practice, each pastor followed his own taste or convenience, and each congregation its own forms of worship.

In their every-day lives these colonial Lutherans of Pennsylvania were for the most part tillers of the soil. Many were weavers, tailors, shoemakers, bakers, and watchmakers, but the great majority of them were farmers and vinedressers. The circumstances of their emigration from Europe and the conditions that attended them during the first decades of their life on the edge of the American wilderness involved them in great poverty. But through the easy terms for securing good land, the native frugality of these Palatines and Württembergers, and the consummate agricultural skill which they had inherited from thirty generations of Europe's best farmers, their poverty was transformed into prosperity and plenty, though the colonial farmer could never be called wealthy. Unlike their English and Scotch-Irish neighbors they sought out the heavily timbered soil, laboriously cleared it, and then raised the abundant crops that only such soil could produce. They cared for the soil by regular fertilizing and by rotation of crops. They practiced good economy also in their raising and care of horses and cattle. Their large barns always attracted the attention of travelers. Their contemporary, Dr. Benjamin Rush, in his classic description of the manners of the German inhabitants of Pennsylvania, says that their rapid improvement in economic condition forms "such a monument of human industry and economy as has seldom been contemplated in any age or country," and he attributes these qualities to the early religious training of the people.

When the Lutheran farmer in colonial Pennsylvania had provided for his cattle and crops, he converted his temporary log house into a more commodious and permanent home. He quarried his own stone, sawed and seasoned his own lumber, and with his own hands and the help of his family, built his dwelling after the pattern of the home he had left in the Palatinate or in Württemberg. High up on the gable of his house he frequently declared his Christian devotion by inscribing a quaint proverb or a quotation from Luther's Bible or a stanza from his Lutheran hymnbook. The inside of the house was marked by plainness rather than elegance. These early Lutherans as a rule raised families of six or seven children, taught their children, boys and girls alike, that hard work is a virtue and idleness a sin, and brought them up in the nurture and admonition of the Lord.

The interesting dialect of German spoken by these farmers of Pennsylvania, a picturesque mixture of Frankish and Alemannic and English, has led many writers to regard them as ignorant and stupid. In recent years, however, much learned research has been applied to this sociological specimen of colonial times, his language and literature, his schools and churches, his religious and social practices, his superstitions and folkways, his music and his work, his architecture and art. It has now become clear, through a welter of printed materials of all sorts, that while these eighteenth-century Lutherans in Pennsylvania and their "Pennsylvania Dutch" neighbors of other churches did constitute a cultural island, theirs was not a culture of stupidity or ignorance. They were readers of books and papers. They were founders and supporters of schools. They insisted on having educated ministers. They produced a mass of literature themselves in that century. It was mostly the creative output of their religious leaders, descriptive accounts for European readers, or devotional writings for home consumption. The intelligence and culture of these Lutheran people was in no way inferior to that of other frontier communities, and today, after two centuries, the general historian gives them their proper place in the record of American civilization.

Among the Lutherans in the colonies south of Pennsylvania social conditions were very similar to those in Pennsylvania itself. Many of the settlers in the valleys that led to Maryland and Virginia and the Carolinas had come from the same general cultural background in Europe as the settlers in Pennsylvania, and many of them had been settled temporarily in that colony before migrating to the other colonies. They were industrious and thrifty farmers and avoided settling in towns. They regarded the barter and trade of the merchant as beneath them. The pastors whom they succeeded in securing for their congregations came as a rule directly from Europe and not always from pietistic background. Young Pastor Klug in Madison County, Virginia, was quite scornful of Muhlenberg and his pietistic colleagues in Pennsylvania. But the people themselves, in their daily pursuits and their mode of living, their body of customs and methods of agriculture, were quite like their fellow-Lutherans, their relatives and former neighbors in southeastern Pennsylvania. The services in their churches and the organization of their congregations varied little from those in the colony farther north.

The daily life of the Salzburger colonists in Georgia is of special interest. For a whole generation they lived a life of peaceful industry and prosperity and of relative isolation. They were not a large settlement. The new land where they settled did not resemble so closely the European land which they had left as was the case with the Palatine farmer of Pennsylvania and the other colonies, and the staple products of their fields and mills were not wheat and tobacco but silk and cotton and lumber. Because their individual holdings were not so extensive they could cultivate a more compact community life, both in industry and in worship. The patriarchal attitude of the pastors, their industrial supervision as well as their pastoral oversight, gave special character to their settlement. Several years after they arrived in Georgia, a visitor among them wrote: "New Ebenezer consists of about one hundred persons under the government of Mr. Boltzius, their pastor; they live and labor in a kind of community, and never commix or associate with strangers."

The Lutherans in Georgia had a congregational constitution before any other Lutheran group in America. This first German church order for use in America was prepared in Europe by Urlsperger, Ziegenhagen, and Francke; it followed closely the London Lutheran constitution of 1694 and the Amsterdam Lutheran order of 1597. The elders and deacons in every congregation were instructed as follows: "Touching the office and duties of the church elder, in regard to the ministers in the churches, the teachers in the schools, the whole congregation, and the money intrusted to them, it shall be indicated in the words of the printed London German Church Discipline given to us, altered, however, in several instances to accord with our peculiar circumstances." The ministers were pledged to the Augsburg Confession and the other symbolical books of the Lutheran church.

The Lutheran people in colonial times, from New York to Georgia, by their initiative and enterprise, by their diligence and Christian devotion, by their zeal for the ministry of the Word and the sacraments, helped provide the sturdy human materials from which the American nation was fashioned, and they planted strong foundations for a Lutheran church in America.

Part II

AT THE BIRTH OF THE NATION
(1740-1790)

Unity of Organization

CHAPTER 7

GENERAL BACKGROUND

When Muhlenberg came to America the colonial era in American history was beginning to draw to a close. The second half of the eighteenth century was a transition period. The civilization of North America was no longer entirely colonial and not yet fully national. The intermediate period was very significant both for the American people in general and for American Christianity in particular. The European settlements in America were shaking off the spirit of colonialism but they had not yet attained a homogeneous national life. It may be called a period of independence. The colonies were kindling the fires that would fuse them into a nation, and the Christian congregations were multiplying relationships that would organize them into church bodies. The prevailing spirit of independence cut the ties that had bound the colonists to European institutions, both political and ecclesiastical. To that spirit of independence Muhlenberg and his fellow Lutherans made their full share of contributions. This is better understood if we pause to examine the roots of the spirit of independence.

This new cultural frontier was compounded of at least three elements. One came from the Protestant Reformation of the sixteenth century, the Anglo-Saxon expression of Christianity. Luther had insisted upon the spiritual freedom of the individual Christian. This freedom awakened in the common man a sense of privilege and responsibility and brought a yearning for liberty in the widest sense of the word. In the organization of Christian forces the Reformation carries a divisive as well as a unitive element. It tends to foster individualism, because it sets up as the supreme religious authority the individual conscience enlightened and disposed by the Bible. In America this Protestant principle fostered the traditions of religious variety that

33

were planted here in colonial times, and it even produced new lines of dissent.

The second element in the spirit of independentism came from the Anglo-Saxon sentiment concerning the rights of free men. Long before American colonization began, this sentiment was shared in various degrees by all the nations of northern Europe. It received forceful expression in the Magna Charta and was cultivated through generations of history. On the American frontier force of circumstances raised this emotion to such a high pitch that it seemed a duty to resist any sort of encroachment on human liberty. It was stronger than any current of fear or awe that autocracy could generate. It helped to transform the colonial spirit of dependence into a high spirit of independence which made itself felt in both political and religious life throughout American history.

The third element that helped to produce the social climate of Muhlenberg's times was generated in the American wilderness itself. The mere lapse of time was having its effect. By the middle of the eighteenth century the imported culture of colonialism had begun to wither away and a native-born culture had begun to spring from its seeds. The rigor of frontier life and the standing of the freehold farmer had now made their impress on the character of the colonist. He had learned to support life directly from the American soil. He had acquired a sense of self-confidence. Gradually this self-consciousness led the colonies to cut the ties binding them to the mother country. Moreover, changes were rapidly taking place on all the fronts of civilization. There was growing activity in commercial, political and intellectual lines. The spirit of expectancy was abroad in the land. The new geography with its abundance of free lands furnished opportunity for a practical test of the political theory of social contract advocated by some European philosophers. This served to stimulate the tendency to independent thinking and voluntary organization.

In the sphere of religion the spirit of independentism led the churches to sever the ties that bound them to ecclesiastical tribunals in Europe. It led the Christians of America to organize on the basis of elective affinity, the religious counterpart of the social contract theory of politics. It led the several churches or religious groups to cultivate their separate existence. This was done by abandoning all fear or favor of the state and by fulfilling each its own sphere and function without regard to the spheres and functions of other groups. This planted the voluntary principle in American Christianity in distinction from a state-church or a national organization of a free church.

The growth of this voluntary principle to its full stature proceeded by several stages. The Great Awakening, usually associated with the name of Jonathan Edwards, served to invigorate the dissenters from the colonial establishments and to multiply the numbers of Methodists, Baptists, Quakers, etc. It gave a mortal blow to parish despotism and abolished the absolute rule of the Christian congregation over the entire community. The Revolutionary War severed the bonds with European institutions, both political and religious, and compelled American organization of the Methodists, the Protestant Episcopal Church, and the Roman Catholic Church. And it opened the way for the consolidation in America of religious groups whose polity had never tied them closely to European tribunals, such as Lutherans, Presbyterians, and Moravians. And the adoption of the American constitution and the setting up of the Republic placed in the fundamental instruments of government the clear principle of the separation of church and state.

It is clear, therefore, that when Muhlenberg came to America the times were fully ripe for his leadership. This is evident whether we look at the situation among the Lutherans who had preceded him to this country, at the developments among other Christians, or at the general political and cultural atmosphere of that second half of the eighteenth century.

CHAPTER 8

MUHLENBERG, THE ORGANIZER

When Professor Gotthilf August Francke at Halle in 1741 chose young Henry Melchior Muhlenberg for the work of the Lutheran church in America, he sent precisely the right man to bring about the organic unity of the parishes into the larger church, paralleling the federal union of the colonies into the American Republic.

The Lutherans, while still dependent upon Europe for missionary supplies, were becoming conscious of their own peculiar needs. Their numerical increase far outstripped the European supply of pastors and funds for churches. They needed only a leader with the proper talent of mind and heart to begin the process of integration that led the church out of its missionary and parochial epoch and created the independent and self-reliant Lutheran church in America.

Muhlenberg was thirty-one years old when he came to America. His training and experience had exactly fitted him for his work here. He had come from the electorate of Hannover and had received his theological education at the University of Göttingen. Then for fifteen months he had taught various branches in the Halle Orphanage. Meanwhile he had acquired facility in languages and in music.

For a while he entertained thoughts of going as a missionary to India, but he was prevailed on to accept a call to the country church of Grosshennersdorf in Saxony. Two years later, September, 1741, while on his way to his birthplace, he chanced to visit Halle. It was just at the time when the situation in Pennsylvania was engaging Francke's mind. The call from America was urged on the young pastor, and he promptly accepted it as a divine call. A fervent Christian and a firm Lutheran, strong in body and trained in mind, endowed with unusual tact and adaptability, a trained scholar, Muhlenberg brought to the task broad vision and talent for practical affairs.

36

Muhlenberg first landed at Charleston and spent a happy week among the Salzburg Lutherans at Ebenezer. He arrived in Philadelphia November 25, 1742, unannounced, as there had been no correspondence between the Pennsylvania congregations and the European authorities since 1739. He found the flock in Philadelphia confused and distracted, the majority following Zinzendorf while a minority had called the old vagabond preacher, Valentine Kraft, and were worshiping in a barn. At New Hanover, thirty-six miles northwest of Philadelphia, an unfinished log building was in use as a church, but the congregation was divided over the person of the ecclesiastical tramp and ex-druggist Empiricus Schmid. At The Trappe, nine miles south of New Hanover, Kraft had also imposed himself on the congregation. But in four weeks Muhlenberg was able to gain full possession of his field, withdrawing his congregations from the confusing influence of Zinzendorf and ridding his parishes of the imposters. On December 27, in Gloria Dei Church, Philadelphia, he was installed by Peter Tranberg, the Swedish pastor at Wilmington. The three churches known as "The United Congregations" now received him as their pastor.

Muhlenberg took as his motto *Ecclesia Plantanda*: the church must be planted. It was a splendid affirmation of an obligation that embraced not merely the three congregations but all the scattered Lutherans in Pennsylvania and other states, their permanent establishment, their abiding welfare, and their enduring witness to the gospel. This work of planting the church Muhlenberg began by opening a school in each of his congregations. Then the congregation in Germantown was added as the fourth church in his charge. He covered the field by alternating between the city and the country, week by week. The congregations grew and took courage. There was no salary for the pastor, only maintenance. His presence inspired new life and in the following summer, 1743, new churches were begun. In a few years suitable edifices were dedicated by all four congregations.

Meanwhile Muhlenberg's labors extended to other Lutherans. His spirit and the spirit of those who sent him was one of missionary expansion. Calls for help began to reach him from various quarters and wherever possible he responded, giving himself unreservedly to the work of catechizing, confirming, teaching, reconciling, establishing, building, preaching, and administering the sacraments. He rejoiced to see the people advancing in faithfulness and spiritual strength.

But Muhlenberg had many trials; the vast field with its pressing needs almost overwhelmed him. He needed helpers and sympathizers. He kept in touch with Halle and sent minute reports of his work in America. The fathers at Halle, in order to keep the mission cause before the people, published extracts from his letters and diaries. These publications, the famous *Halle Reports*, brought Muhlenberg reinforcements in men and money. As early as 1743, a layman, J. F. Vigera, came from the Ebenezer colony in Georgia and took charge of some of the schools. Another excellent teacher was J. J. Loeser. Muhlenberg's heart was greatly cheered by the arrival from Halle in January, 1745, of a pastor and two catechists, the Rev. Peter Brunnholz, John Nicholas Kurtz, and John Helfrich Schaum. They brought funds to help build new churches.

The two pastors divided the field, Brunnholz taking charge of the churches in Philadelphia and Germantown while Muhlenberg retained the country churches and general oversight of the field. The catechists were appointed as teachers in the schools. This arrangement made it easier for Muhlenberg to supply the means of grace to outlying districts and to undertake extended trips among the unorganized Lutherans. At the same time he gave notice that he had come to America to stay, for in April, 1745, he married Anna Mary Weiser. She was the daughter of the famous Indian agent, Conrad Weiser, whom he had learned to know two years before when he visited Tulpehocken to adjust difficulties among the factions in that congregation.

Tulpehocken

The work of "planting the church" now expanded rapidly. Outposts were established at Upper Milford, Saucon (in Lehigh County), Easton and Perkasie. Two journeys of 120 miles each were made across the Delaware to the Lutheran congregations on the Raritan in New Jersey in order to settle troubles stirred up by a clerical scamp. Lancaster called for help against the Moravian, Nyberg, who had taken charge of the Lutheran church there. That situation Muhlenberg saved by locating there Pastor John Frederick Handschuh, lately arrived from Halle.

In 1747 Muhlenberg journeyed to Frederick, Maryland, by way of Tulpehocken, Lancaster, York, Hanover, and the Monocacy.

Everywhere on this trip he found traces of Nyberg's pernicious influence. To the distracted churches his coming meant new life. He succeeded in reconciling jarring factions, encouraged organization, and brought the frontier congregations into closer relations with the older eastern parishes.

The greatest step forward in the work of "planting the church," the organization of a synod in 1748, was the most important event in Muhlenberg's career. In April of that year Muhlenberg, Brunnholz, and Handschuh held a conference and agreed upon a uniform liturgy, essentially the "Common Service" of the present day. It was to be submitted to the other pastors. Moreover, by August, St. Michael's Church in Philadelphia was ready for dedication and the occasion promised to bring together the representative men of the Lutheran church in America. Then, too, the Tulpehocken charge was strongly urging the ordination of Nicholas Kurtz to become their pastor. Here was abundant occasion for the organization of a synod. The dedication and ordination took place on August 25 and the organization of synod the following day.

This first synod consisted of six ministers and twenty-four lay delegates, in addition to the entire church council of St. Michael's. The ministers were Muhlenberg, Brunnholz, Handschuh, and Kurtz, with Hartwig of New York and Provost Sandin of the Swedish churches as advisory members. The lay delegates represented ten congregations. Muhlenberg occupied the chair and in his opening address emphasized the importance of a closer union among the congregations. The lay delegates reported concerning the efficiency of their pastors, and the pastors reported concerning the condition of their parochial schools. The common liturgy was examined and adopted. Congratulatory addresses were made by Hartwig and Sandin, and the synod adjourned to meet the next year in Lancaster.

This small beginning was the first step in the preparation for the independence of the Lutheran church of America. The synod, known at first as the "United Pastors" and their parishes as the "United Congregations," is today the Ministerium of Pennsylvania. Muhlenberg himself frankly considered the new organization an experiment. That it did not fail, like the parallel effort among his neighbors of the German Reformed congregations, was due largely to the fact that Muhlenberg conducted his experiment free from European control.

Embracing at first only ten congregations out of the seventy in Pennsylvania and adjacent colonies, it nevertheless grew rapidly and set the example for synodical organization in other colonies. It taught the Lutherans of America to lay aside the narrow parochial view and to take the larger synodical view, or as Muhlenberg himself said, to "understand the connection and interest of the whole." It created the spirit of self-reliance and aggressiveness that saved the church in times of danger.

Muhlenberg was the moving spirit of the newly formed synod, and from the time of its organization he had the oversight and care of all the churches. One of the foremost problems that engaged his attention was the supply of ministers. The number who came from Europe were inadequate to man the rapidly growing field. So Muhlenberg planned for a native ministry. The year after the synod was formed he bought forty-nine acres of land in Philadelphia on which to erect a school and seminary and a home for the aged. But wars interfered and the project was not accomplished. Nevertheless Muhlenberg gave his three sons to the ministry and took other theological students into his own home, where he maintained and taught them.

Meanwhile troubles in several congregations in the province of New York called for a peacemaker. Muhlenberg visited various congregations along the Hudson and in New York City. He was so impressed with the need in that city that he spent six months there in 1751 and three months the following summer. He had to preach in English, Dutch, and German, but he brought unity and new life to the distracted congregations. Much of his time was spent among the Lutheran churches of New Jersey. In 1753 he made another trip to the churches west of the Susquehanna as far as Frederick, Maryland. But permanent calls away from his Pennsylvania field, the president of synod could not accept.

The synod held no meetings from 1755 to 1759. The pastors were overwhelmed by the tide of Lutheran immigration. There was some opposition to the synod on the part of laymen and on the part of those ministers who had no connection with Halle. There were tremendous discouragements in the work and a growing conviction among the "United Pastors" that the authorities in Europe did not really understand the needs of their American "mission field" and were not making adequate efforts to supply those needs.

In the next decade conditions improved. The new provost of the Swedish churches, the learned and pious Wrangel, proved to be a valuable counselor and a warm personal friend. He encouraged Muhlenberg to revive the synod in 1760. Its organization was improved, the elements of a constitution were formulated, and never after that did synodical activity lag.

In 1762 a congregational constitution was adopted by St. Michael's in Philadelphia. This was highly important, for it embodied the results of many years of experience and observation among German, Swedish, and Dutch Lutherans, and it became the model for similar constitutions in other congregations.

By 1771 Muhlenberg reported eighty-one congregations under his care. Despite failing strength his travels continued. In 1774 he once more made the long trip south to Charleston and to Ebenezer. But other able men were arising to be his helpers and afterwards to take his place. The church was planted. People had been gathered into congregations and congregations had been organized into a synod. Buildings had been erected, stable constitutions provided, a community of interest established. American-born pastors were now filling American pulpits. Thus fortified, the church was prepared to withstand the shock of the Revolution and ready to resist the chilling blasts of rationalism and religious indifference that were soon to sweep over the land. The church was planted—let the nation be born.

In 1779 the correspondence with Halle was interrupted by the war. It was not resumed for more than a generation, and the church in America peaceably obtained its spiritual independence. An American hymnbook was ordered in 1782 and prepared under Muhlenberg's guidance. The liturgy and ministerial acts were printed. The synodical constitution was revised in terms of complete American control and democratic procedure. The American Lutheran church had been born.

Muhlenberg, the patriarch, lived until 1787. He received many honors in his lifetime and after his death, but his chief monument is the Lutheran church in America.

The years that cover the span of Muhlenberg's life in America witnessed not only the growth of organization but also a great numerical increase and geographical expansion of the church.

When Muhlenberg came to America the white population of the

country numbered less than three-quarters of a million. At the outbreak of the Revolution, when all immigration ceased for a number of
years, it numbered two and a half millions. A few years after Muhlenberg's death, when the first census was taken, it had grown to four
millions. The increase in the number of Lutherans in the land more
than kept pace with the increase in general population. When Muhlenberg arrived in Pennsylvania there were probably far less than twenty
thousand people in the colony who were in any sense Lutherans. But
two years after the organization of the synod the number had increased
at least threefold, and at the outbreak of the war it is safe to say that
seventy-five thousand of the one hundred and twenty thousand Germans in the colony were Lutherans. In other colonies also, though
not to the same degree as in Pennsylvania, the numbers of the
Lutherans were steadily growing. Of course, only a fraction of these,
perhaps one-seventh, were gathered into congregations.

Moreover, this growing Lutheran constituency was no longer in
1790 concentrated about the chief ports and main waterways near the
Atlantic. It had begun to scatter and spread into the interior.

Muhlenberg had been called to serve three congregations in 1742.
But so rapid was the growth of organization and the increase in numbers that already in 1771 he reported eighty-one congregations in
Pennsylvania and the adjacent provinces over which he was expected
to exercise some kind of oversight. And there were about thirty
Lutheran congregations in other parts of the country. Everywhere,
as enterprising Americans pressed into the interior, subduing the
hostile Indians, taming the wilderness, and beginning that long and
thrilling romance known as "the winning of the West," Lutherans
were in the van of that great movement carrying along with them
their faith and hope and beckoning for spiritual ministry to follow
them.

At the time of Muhlenberg's death there were not more than
forty Lutheran ministers of any kind in all America. There were
many noble spirits among them and several shining lights, such as
J. N. Kurtz and J. H. C. Helmuth, and Muhlenberg's sons-in-law,
Kunze and Schultze. But their number was all too few. Then, too,
the Halle type of minister no longer predominated so exclusively as
it once had. Moreover, Halle itself was changing. The teachers of
Muhlenberg's acquaintance had passed off the scene and the new

teachers were not so firmly Lutheran and evangelical nor did they inculcate the same religious fervor and warm Christian piety as the Franckes. All the more urgent was the need of providing a native American Lutheran ministry.

The project of establishing a theological seminary had vanished with the outbreak of the Revolution, and after the smoke of the battle had lifted, the times were not so favorable for such an enterprise, and a new generation of ministers had arisen unaccustomed to the heroic undertakings of a Muhlenberg. Only the organization of new synods covering the whole country and the gathering of these into a general body could furnish the background for such an undertaking. That time was soon to come. But for the present the Lutheran church in America was dependent on Europe for her ministry, even after the birth of the nation; and the supply of spiritual leaders from the native ranks, so necessary for the full maturity of the church, waited for a new period in general American history.

who were the Franke's

CHAPTER 9

THE LUTHERAN ELEMENT AT THE BIRTH OF THE NATION

Almost everywhere among the rank and file of people in the Lutheran church which Muhlenberg had organized, there was general participation in the spirit that prevailed in America during the second half of the eighteenth century. Muhlenberg himself reached the peak of his personal influence and activity about 1765. He started to turn over the leadership in church affairs to other hands just about the time political events in America began to move towards the Revolutionary War. At that time the field which he had begun to organize and cultivate extended from New York to Virginia. It embraced somewhat less than 15,000 Lutheran people, gathered into some 133 congregations and served by about 33 pastors. Three-fourths of them were in Pennsylvania, the largest of the thirteen colonies.

In Philadelphia, which was the largest town in British America and in which the most stirring political events were soon to take place, Lutherans constituted an important element in the citizenry. In numbers they were second only to the Presbyterians. With 500 heads of families in the city of 25,000 souls they were a political and social influence to be reckoned with. The two Lutheran congregations constituted a single corporation, Zion and St. Michael's. It was composed largely of artisans and mechanics, with only a few merchants, but they were alert and aggressive citizens and in 1769 when the corporation dedicated its second church building it was the largest religious edifice in the city.

In other towns also improved economic conditions after the middle of the century enabled Lutheran congregations to erect larger and more substantial church buildings and otherwise to give tangible evidence that they were constituent elements of American society. After 1765 the Lutheran population of the colonies began to branch out into more diversified lines of occupation. The preponderant mass of them were still engaged in agriculture, but now large numbers also were weavers, millers, carpenters, wagon builders, and tradesmen, and manufacturers of musical instruments, glass, iron and pottery. And in the country districts, where the great majority of Lutherans lived when the Republic was born, people were no longer required to give their entire attention to securing the necessities of life but could give effort to the improvement of their spiritual condition and could lift their sights to the stirring political events of the times.

In the American colonies the Lutherans had found an atmosphere different from that in which they had lived in Europe, and soon felt a distinct sense of release from many Old-World restrictions. Some of them used their newly found liberty to avoid all contact with organized religion, others were ready to submit patiently and devoutly to their ministers. But most of them did not want their church affairs to be ordered for them by superintendents and consistories. They were particularly averse to taxes imposed for the support of clergy and schools.

Many of the congregations had been organized and the churches built without benefit of clergy. The laymen naturally felt a proprietary interest in them and would be slow to recognize any higher religious authority than the congregation itself. Only a patient and skillful leadership among the clergy could prevent the Lutheran forces in the American colonies from splintering into fragments as they made the transition to the American principle of voluntary support in church life.

One of the fundamental principles of the German pietists of Halle had been to encourage laymen to participate actively in the government and services of the church. Those who desired to cultivate intensively their spiritual lives were accustomed to hold special meetings for the inner circle of the pious. The members of these pietistic groups were taught to make voluntary contributions to benevolent Christian causes, such as orphanages and schools, foreign missions, and Bible publication. In America there was ample room for the exercise of this tendency to organize on the basis of selective fellowship and for the practice of voluntary contributions to religious causes.

The spirit of independence among the laymen often irked their ministers. The laymen took seriously their responsibilities as owners of the church properties, and the clergy objected strenuously to the custom whereby congregations hired their ministers by the year. This was particularly true of those ministers who did not easily unlearn their European ways but hoped to continue the church-state relationship in which they had been trained. Many of the "church troubles" that Muhlenberg was called upon to settle grew out of the fact that the congregations asserted their independence while the ministers tried to maintain an Old-World relationship of pastor to people.

Excepting a few of these so-called "Old Lutherans," who remained Tory, the Lutheran element of the population was predominantly on the side of American independence. Here it is important to distinguish between the dominant attitude of the German immigrants before the middle of the century and afterward. So long as the newcomers were chiefly Mennonites, Dunkards, Amish, and Moravians, they were pacifist in temperament and not disposed to join in any measure of resistance to the British crown or to the colonial authorities. In Pennsylvania they consistently supported Quaker rule. But after 1750 the German "church people," as the Lutherans and Reformed were called, became much more numerous and more influential. They could no longer regard the Quakers in Pennsylvania or the Tory governments in other colonies as custodians of their liberties. Colonial governments had often left German farmers on the frontiers exposed to the terrible depredations of Indians; hence the Germans united with the Scotch-Irish, both in arms and in politics, to secure adequate defense of their homes. Tory governments were turned out. German farmers in the country districts and German artisans in the cities threw the balance of power to the revolutionary party and so helped to secure American independence.

That Lutheran ministers in general did not undertake leadership in political affairs was not due to any lack of private political opinions. It was because they regarded politics as outside a call limited to the welfare of souls. Muhlenberg himself set a good example in keeping politics out of the pulpit. He admonished his fellow-ministers that repentance and faith and godliness are the most direct means of strengthening the bonds of society and healing the body politic. His sons laid aside their clerical vestments before they put on the uniform of the soldier and the garb of the statesman, although Muhlenberg himself expressed his regret that they had "allowed themselves to be betrayed to the profane world."

Lutheran ministers, of course, prayed for their political rulers and lawmakers and for the peace of the country. They urged days of public prayer and penitence and services of thanksgiving. Muhlenberg himself preached a sermon of thanksgiving after the repeal of the Stamp Act, emphasizing obligation and loyalty due to the government. During hostilities Lutheran clergymen freely ministered to the needs of the men under arms. Most of them were sympathetic with the cause of American independence and rejoiced at the issue of events. But many maintained neutrality and made little effort to guide the political actions of their church members.

On the other hand, Lutheran laymen participated actively in the war of independence and the birth of the new nation. They did not normally look to their ministers for leadership in politics or other secular affairs. They formed their own opinions and determined their own course of action. After 1750 more than eighty-five per cent of them could read and write. Their schools had almost tripled between 1748 and 1765. And they had their newspapers. Before 1760 they formed their convictions largely from reading the *Berichte* of the Germantown Dunkard publisher, Christopher Saur. Muhlenberg in 1754 expressed to Franklin his regret that Saur's paper was stirring up so much insurgency both in church and in state affairs among Lutheran laymen. Later the *Staatsbote* of John Henry Miller, the Philadelphia Moravian, became the favorite newspaper of some 6,000 subscribers, from New York to Georgia. A vigorous champion of the American cause, it was militant against the Stamp Act, and after repeal continued to fire the American patriotism of German-speaking citizens by pointing out threats to their civil and religious liberties.

· Most of the Lutheran people in the colonies spoke German. They read the spirited articles in the *Staatsbote* and discussed them with their neighbors. They kept abreast of political events also by reading the charters and laws, the declarations and appeals, both of the colonial governments and of the Continental Congress. The older people among them were naturalized citizens and delighted in the privileges of living in America in contrast with the conditions in the Europe they had left. But most of them after 1760 had been born in America and identified themselves with every interest that was clearly American. They voted and acted not as Lutherans nor as Germans, but as heirs of the Protestant Reformation and as free men. They were moved by long-range considerations of their own liberty, peace and prosperity.

There were varieties of political loyalty among these Lutherans just as there were among other Americans. The frontier farmers were slower in their reaction against English rule than the people in the towns. They expressed their spirit of independence chiefly by voting against the oligarchies in the cities of the East. The mechanics and laborers in the cities, on the other hand, felt more quickly the restrictions imposed by English legislation and were more susceptible to the fiery harangues of the revolutionaries. On the question of ratifying the federal constitution, those whose interests were involved in mercantile, manufacturing or commercial pursuits, were favorable to ratification. This included the majority of Lutheran citizens in New York, Pennsylvania, Maryland, and Virginia. Those who feared the restrictions that a powerful Congress might impose on them, were opposed to ratification. This group embraced most of the farmers of Georgia and the upper districts of North and South Carolina. In some of the colonies, particularly Maryland and Virginia, Lutherans were dissenters from the established Church of England and saw in the struggle for American independence an opportunity to rid themselves of the establishment and its detested tithe. Everywhere Lutheran voters proved by their attitudes their fairly complete assimilation into American society in general.

During the struggle for independence some of the most determined and conspicuous supporters of the cause of liberty came from the ranks of Lutherans. Muhlenberg's oldest son, John Peter Gabriel, at the very outbreak of hostilities, divested himself of his ministerial robe in his church in Woodstock, Virginia, and as colonel of the Eighth Virginia Regiment went into action against the British in the campaign in the South. He soon became the right-hand support of his young Virginia friend, George Washington. Quickly he rose to the position of major-general. He fought with high distinction in a number of critical engagements during the war. After the war he was a member of the Executive Council of Pennsylvania, vice-president of the commonwealth, a member of the first, third and sixth Congresses, and United States Senator.

His brother, Frederick Augustus Conrad Muhlenberg, was also an ardent patriot. He attended the reading of the Declaration of Independence, was a member of the Continental Congress, twice speaker of the Pennsylvania legislature, president of the Pennsylvania convention which ratified the federal constitution, and speaker of the first and third federal Congresses.

Another distinguished Lutheran leader in the cause of American independence was John Hanson of Maryland. He followed his Swedish Lutheran father in the field of statecraft, was one of the leaders in planning united action of the thirteen colonies in resistance to the Stamp Act and other British measures, organized an American army in Maryland, was a member of the Continental Congress, signed the Articles of Confederation, and under that instrument in 1781 was elected the first "President of the United States in Congress Assembled."

Substantial contributions to the success of the American cause were made also by John Adam Treutlen, who was the first governor of Georgia and quartermaster general under Wayne during the war; Bodo Otto, surgeon general in charge of hospitals in the Continental Army; and Christopher Ludwig, a member of the Continental Congress, who became the baker general for the armies. The roster of officers under Washington includes many a Lutheran of German or Swedish descent. Peter Muhlenberg's Virginia regiment consisted mainly of German Lutherans. The Salzburgers organized three companies for active military service. Pastor Christian Streit served as a chaplain. The famous German Fusiliers of Charleston, South Carolina, came entirely from the Lutheran congregation there. A multitude of organizations among civilians for the support of the cause of independence received generous contributions of time and money from thousands of Lutheran men and women.

The break of the colonies with England made little change in the relations of the Lutheran churches in America. The German Lutheran congregations in the English colonies had no organizational ties with England or any of the German principalities from which they or their fathers had come. Many pastors had ties with Halle, but these ties were personal and spiritual. Very early in colonial America the Lutherans, unlike other churchly groups, had attained ecclesiastical adulthood. Their Reformed neighbors, for example, received financial aid from the Dutch government. The Methodists, the Episcopalians, and the Catholics achieved independent American organization only after the political ties with Europe had been severed. But the Lutherans from the beginning paid their own expenses, conducted their own benevolences, determined their own congregational organization and forms of worship, engaged their own pastors, and through their ministers did their own ordaining. There was no occasion for them to debate concerning the prerogatives of the fatherland or ties with the mother church. They were quite ready for adjustment to the political independence of the United States and the voluntary principle in church affairs.

Another thing that made it easy for Lutherans to join in the move for political independence of England was the fact that they had no strong organization themselves but were relatively independent of one another. In none of the colonies were they an established or favored church. Their polity was almost completely congregational. And the development of polity among Lutherans during the second half of the eighteenth century shows how completely they reflected the American spirit of independence.

At the outbreak of the Revolutionary War, Muhlenberg's synod dating from 1748 was the only semblance of Lutheran organization among the Lutheran parishes in this country. It was called by various names, such as the United Pastors, the Preachers' Conference, the Ministerial Conference, the United Reverend Ministerium. The organization claimed the attachment of less than half of the Lutheran congregations in the colonies. A large number of the pastors and a still larger number of laymen were suspicious of the synod. They thought of it vaguely as something like a European state-church that might begin to levy taxes on its members. They warned against synodical encroachments on the liberties of the people. The authority of the synod over Lutherans as a group was therefore very limited indeed. Even the strong personal influence of the overseer Muhlenberg could not make the synod a stronger bond among the congregations than was the Continental Congress among the colonies. Lutheran pastors and people were determined to enjoy their new liberties, in the church and in politics.

The synod did not even have a constitution until after the war. The constitution was adopted in 1778 and printed in 1781. It set up the first Lutheran "Articles of Confederation" among the pastors and congregations in this country. Printed in the very year that the political Articles of Confederation were adopted, it documented the independence of the Lutheran organization. It formulated the practices that had long been in acceptance, except that it made the president fully responsible to the Ministerium and made ordination a definite function of that body. It made the Ministerium an association of ministers, and laymen had no voice or vote in its synodical meetings.

But the political developments of the new nation soon made changes necessary in this ecclesiastical organization. The revision was made in 1792. It was a thorough revision, and many of the changes reflect the new political situation. The organization no longer embraced in its title "The Evangelical Lutheran Church in North America" but only "The Evangelical Lutheran Congregations in Pennsylvania and Adjacent States." The national Republic was organized according to states. The Protestant Episcopal Church was organized into dioceses by states in 1789. A separate Lutheran organization had been set up for the congregations in New York state in 1786. It seemed more truly American to recognize that the development of Lutheranism in the American Republic would also follow district organizations corresponding generally to states.

It is significant also that the new constitution adopted by the mother synod of American Lutherans, three years after the Republic began, admitted lay delegates of the congregations to the annual synodical meetings. They were seated with voice and vote on a parity with the ordained ministers. This provision was adopted at the request of the corporation of St. Michael's and Zion in Philadelphia, of which both Frederick Muhlenberg and his brother Peter were now lay members.

One of the new sections in the constitution of 1792 makes evident American ecclesiastical independence. Provision is made for only two officers, a president and a secretary; they are to be elected each year by a majority vote of all the pastors and lay delegates at the synodical meeting; their duties and powers are clearly prescribed. Then it is specified: "All ordained ministers are equal in regard to rank and title, excepting the officers spoken of before; they have therefore in their congregations no other superintendents but these officers, and these only in so far as this Constitution renders it incumbent on them to impart their views and advice to ministers . . . Every pastor may, as circumstances require, introduce regulations in the churches in his charge . . ." The last vestige of European control and European procedure is gone. The organization of Lutherans rested on democratic principles expressed in a constitution that safeguarded the independence of the congregation and the rights of the individual pastor and layman. Lutherans had now given complete expression in their corporate life to the fact that they are Americans.

' The people in the Swedish Lutheran congregations on the Delaware also felt the spirit of independence. As they shared the free spirit of their fellow Lutherans in Pennsylvania and other neighboring colonies, they grew increasingly restive under the detailed regulations sent to them from the mother church in Sweden. Their superintendent, Provost Wrangel, was prominent in the public events of Philadelphia and on occasion counseled his fellow Lutherans to take up arms in defense of the city. When he was recalled to Sweden in 1768 the younger members of the Swedish congregations openly expressed their dissatisfaction with the control exercised from Sweden.

Increasingly it was felt that American ecclesiastical interests could no longer be adequately supplied by consistories and bishops in Sweden, and demanded the right to choose their own pastors "from this side of the water." The break with the Swedish archbishop came in 1789. The congregations began to provide the means for their own support and proceeded to find pastors in America who were episcopally ordained and who used English. Wrangel himself had supplied several vacant Episcopal congregations with English services, and many of the Swedish Lutherans had learned to worship with their Episcopal neighbors. When the Church of England people in the colonies established themselves on an American basis as the Protestant Episcopal Church, the Swedish Episcopal Lutherans on the Delaware transferred their congregations to that communion.

Important Lutheran contributions to the writing of the federal constitution and the setting up of the Republic were made through several prominent individuals and exercise of the franchise in several critical areas. When the constitutional convention of the state of Virginia in 1776 incorporated into the organic law of that state the principle of religious equality, Lutherans joined Baptists and Presbyterians in agitating for the disestablishment of the Anglican Church, and this agitation did not cease until Virginia in 1785 adopted Jefferson's bill for religious freedom and thus became the first government in the world to establish by law complete separation of church and state. When that same principle was written into the proposed federal constitution and the commonwealth of Pennsylvania in 1787 assembled in convention to reject or ratify that constitution, ratification was finally achieved in this pivotal state only because Frederick Augustus Muhlenberg, as president of the convention, threw into the balance the weight of his own personality and the favorable sentiment of the great body of his fellow Lutherans in the state.

Turning from the field of political thought and action to the general social situation during the second half of the eighteenth century, we find Lutheran people active along many lines of benevolence and in protest against not a few of the current social practices.

The American Indians were still regarded as objects of Christian missionary activity by colonial Lutherans. The Lutheran ministers, particularly those who were trained at Halle, were imbued with the foreign missionary impulse and communicated it to the members of their congregations. In spite of the tremendous problems involved and the meager results attained, Lutherans, like other colonials, felt a sense of moral and spiritual responsibility toward the natives whose hunting grounds they were gradually occupying. One Lutheran layman in particular, Conrad Weiser, father-in-law of Muhlenberg, was well acquainted with the Indians and very influential among them. To his influence is attributed the fact that during the French and Indian War (1754-1763) the powerful Iroquois remained neutral and thus made it possible for the British to expel the French from the heart of North America. In that war most of the Indian tribes fought on the side of the French, and several horrible massacres were perpetrated on the frontiers. Moreover, the red man had now retreated farther into the wilderness and the white man's contacts with him were greatly diminished. As a result, the Indians came to be regarded in general by the whites as wild men and savage murderers, who had no permanent right to the lands and forests and streams needed by the white man. Lutheran ministers continued to preach that the surest way of dealing with the Indian menace was to convert him to Christian ideals of conduct. Occasional conversions among the Indians still took place, but the Lutheran reports to Europe no longer glowed with zeal for the soul of the American Indian, and the glory of persistent and effective missionary work among these "first Americans" during colonial days goes to the Moravians.

As to the attitude of Lutherans towards Negroes, they were quite ready to apply the means of grace to the needs of their colored neighbors. The congregational records include many a baptism of Negroes, both slave and free, and many an intercession for their liberation from slavery or their more humane treatment in their slave estate. The learned and devout Swedish Provost Wrangel in 1764 took special pains with a black man condemned as a murderer, induced him to accept Christ as his Saviour, carefully instructed him for baptism, administered both sacraments to him, and accompanied him to the place of execution. Muhlenberg also gave much time and energy to the evangelizing and baptizing of Negroes and mulattoes and to the improvement of conditions among the slaves. Like his fellow ministers, Lutherans and others, he usually mingled his ministry of grace to the Negro with a goodly portion of condescension from a superior to an inferior race. Lutheran laymen and clergy often expressed their sympathy with the poor slaves "for having been snatched from their homeland and sold into everlasting slavery in a strange land," as Muhlenberg put it. But they found in the very structure of the universe a basis for gradations among the races: "Even as the almighty and supremely wise Creator has made and ordered all things in beautiful graduated order in the animal, vegetable and mineral kingdoms, from the highest to the lowest and the greatest to the smallest, so too there is diversity in the political body of the human race."

Lutherans shared in the general revulsion against the horrors with which the commerce in slaves was carried on. They joined in frequent denunciations of the slave trade as such. As early as 1774 the politically active Lutheran of Maryland, John Hanson, helped to frame a resolution which was aimed particularly against the Boston Port Bill but which denounced the traffic in slaves and urged the colonies not to deal with nations engaged in the traffic. That resolution was adopted by the first Continental Congress. But the opposition of most

Lutherans to the slave trade did not prevent them from owning slaves themselves. Any religious scruples they may have had against slavery as an institution were often outweighed by economic considerations. Among the Salzburgers in Georgia slave labor was needed for the cultivation of the cotton fields, and it was argued: "If you take slaves in faith and with the intent of conducting them to Christ, the action will not be sin, but it may prove a benediction." Some of the Lutheran farmers who had denounced slavery in Pennsylvania changed their attitude when they moved to the South and became proprietors of larger estates.

Lutheran people furnished leadership along many lines of charitable and humanitarian activity after the middle of the eighteenth century. They co-operated actively in the work of societies organized to care for immigrants, to alleviate the terrible conditions of transoceanic travel and the dire needs of the immigrant on his arrival in America. These societies were particularly active in the ports of Philadelphia, Baltimore and Charleston. Orphans and widows always were special objects of kindly care. Among the very first institutions erected by the Salzburgers in Georgia was an orphans' home, which elicited the financial assistance of evangelist Whitefield and furnished the pattern for his own orphanage at Bethesda, near Savannah. Muhlenberg exerted himself on various occasions on behalf of orphans, both as individuals and as groups, although his plan for an orphanage in Pennsylvania was not realized until long after his death.

Lutherans often instituted special offerings for the poor, those in their own congregations and the poverty-stricken in general. Some congregations received regular weekly collections for the poor, the orphans, and the widows of the community. Not infrequently the congregational constitutions provided for the care of the poor and the orphaned and included "overseers of the poor" among the officers of the congregation.

The sick also received special attention. Many Lutheran pastors were able to combine medicine with their prayers. The University of Halle had compounded medical and theological science in the training of its ministerial students; thus for years Muhlenberg prescribed for the physical ills of the people in his parishes. The Lutheran pastors of Philadelphia and Lancaster and the people of their congregations showed more than ordinary courage during the terrible yellow-fever epidemics in Philadelphia from 1793 to 1799, by personal care of the patients and by gathering funds and provisions for the fever-stricken.

No needy group was beyond the interest of the devout Lutheran pastor, and scarcely a case of trouble or distress was called to the attention of the people in the pews without meeting a ready response in money or in kind or in personal effort. The poor and the sick, the orphan and the widow, the immigrant and the soldier, the prisoner and the underprivileged, all found among these Lutheran pastors and people loving hearts and helping hands that were true to the spirit of Spener and Francke and the benevolent institutions at Halle.

Some of the social customs that were current during and after the Revolution received sharp criticism from Lutheran pastors and people. Their outlook upon the world was generally conservative, like that of the Puritans in New England. They were opposed to expensive forms of entertainment. The theater they considered a corrupting influence. When plans were being made to erect a public playhouse in Philadelphia in 1766, Lutheran pastors there and elsewhere called on people to unite in a protest to the provincial governor. Card playing and dancing were considered wrong because they were a waste of time. Festivals were regarded as sinful because they led to indulgence and wasted money.

Many Lutheran people and their pastors frowned upon the custom of having big feasts in connection with funerals and baptisms. Beer, wine, and tobacco might be used in moderation to satisfy bodily needs, but drunkenness and other excesses were severely condemned. In 1765 Muhlenberg secured a court order to close an obnoxious tavern opposite the church at New Hanover, "where Satan conducted his school." Twenty-five years later the pastors of Lancaster joined in a general petition to the authorities to prevent the increase of taverns and fairs.

Lutheran people in general were opposed to extravagance of any kind and deserved their reputation for sobriety and frugality. They protested against the display of luxury in feminine dress. They regarded Sabbath-breaking as one of "the prevailing sins of the country." They were generally bitter in their opposition to Free-masonry, partly because it seemed to be a substitute for the church, and partly because their pastors believed it originated in the anti-Christian deism that swept over much of Europe at that time.

Lutheran pastors regarded their congregational schools as essential parts of the work of the congregation. Like Muhlenberg himself, they saw clearly that the daily school is often a more vital factor than the pulpit in molding the character of the people. Lutheran pastors believed firmly in the redeeming effect of well directed education. The call of the pastor included the ministry of teaching and responsibility for the congregational schools. Where no lay teachers were available the pastors themselves were obliged to teach their schools. In all cases the pastors determined the organization and curriculum of the school, and the teaching experience that most of them had gained under the system of ministerial training in Germany now stood them in good stead. Lay schoolteachers were chosen not only for their intellectual equipment, teaching skill, and fidelity to the confessions of the church, but for moral earnestness and warmth of spiritual life. The synodical organization from the beginning manifested concern for the congregational schools and received reports annually from the parishes about "the condition of the school."

During the war the congregational schools, particularly in the county parishes, received a setback because many of the best teachers enlisted in the army. But with the return of peace the number of congregational schools grew rapidly. This change is clearly reflected in the statistics of congregational schools. At mid-century, after the organization of the Ministerium, there had been 24 schools in the 70 Lutheran congregations of the several colonies. At the outbreak of the war the number of schools had increased to 64 and the congregations to about 100. But by the end of the century there were 139 church schools with at least 5,000 pupils in some 300 Lutheran congregations.

The constitutions of the congregations regulated the administration of the school. Often there were detailed codes covering the work of the teacher, the curriculum, and the discipline of the schools. These documents make it clear that the purpose of the schools was to train convinced and intelligent Christians, loyal and devout members of the Lutheran church who would be useful members of society and productive citizens of the commonwealth. Modern students of their methods regard them as superior to the average of that day.

The friendly appraisal of Dr. Benjamin Rush, contemporary analyst of the customs of the Pennsylvania Germans, applied to Lutherans generally: "They commit the education and instruction of their children in a peculiar manner to the ministers and officers of their churches; hence they grow up with prejudices in favor of public worship and the obligations of Christianity."

Next to the schools, the regular services of worship were the means of building practical Christian character. The subjective character of most of the hymns commonly used showed the pietist background of the pastors and their people. The emphasis in the hymns was on the individual personal experience of the worshiper rather than the objective facts of redemption. The people committed many of the hymns to memory and sang them with earnestness. Copies of the hymnbook were scarce and the selection of hymns was generally limited to those whose lines and melodies had been learned in the schools. Non-Lutherans were often impressed with the singing in the Lutheran churches, the large amount of it and the relatively high quality. In the liturgy recommended by the Ministerium to congregations in 1748, the congregation is directed to the singing of six hymns in each service of worship. Muhlenberg records more than one instance in which souls were converted, not by the sermon but by one or another of the hymns sung during the preaching service.

In liturgical practice also there were evidences of pietist influence. The liturgy that Muhlenberg and his colleagues had prepared in 1748 followed in the main the historic Lutheran order of worship with only a few features that showed the pietistic taste of its authors. But this liturgy was never printed; it was circulated only in manuscript form and did not succeed in bringing about uniformity in the practice of the pastors and congregations. There was a constant tendency throughout this period in the direction of less formality, less conformity to the church year, more extempore prayers with intercession for definite individuals, and more adaptation to circumstances. The liturgical part of the service of worship was shortened in order to permit more time for the sermon with its admonitions to a living Christian piety. When a liturgy was first published in 1786, it showed, therefore, a decided decline from the purer Lutheran service that Muhlenberg and his colleagues had prepared thirty-eight years earlier.

Pastoral instructions in the manuscript copies of the liturgy of

1748 make it clear that the sermon was to be regarded as the high point of the worship service, aimed at bringing the hearer to personal consciousness of conversion and daily manifestation of his converted state in practical living. Each sermon, whether in German, English, or a mixture of both languages, was expected to set forth in clear terms the way of salvation as taught in the Bible. The pastor was to feel personally responsible for the souls in his congregations: "The moral condition of church members should be investigated and should be used as guides in the preparation of sermons." He was to speak out against debasing practices and corrupting influences and to exhort his people to charity and missionary work. The style of the sermon was to be orderly and simple enough to reach the understanding of the largest number of hearers. At the conclusion of a sermon the pastor was to review its main points, and before beginning the Lord's Prayer "have an exordium" urging his hearers to repentance and more practical application of the sermon. Those who intended to come to the Lord's Supper were asked to announce their intention in person to the pastor a few days or weeks in advance so as to provide opportunity for a personal conference on the spiritual condition of the individual.

Thus the entire program of Lutheran congregations during the second half of the eighteenth century served the single purpose of stimulating vital Christian experience in the members and making them living witnesses to the power of the gospel. Their schools, in administration and curriculum, and their ministers, in the pulpit and in pastoral care of the people, aimed at regenerate hearts and positive Christian lives. In the critical decades of the beginnings of a free American republic, American Lutherans in their accommodation to the voluntary principle in church life, in the modifications they made during those decades in language and liturgy and synodical organization, in their zealous support of the cause of political independence, and in their loyalty to American principles of government, gave abundant evidence that they were constituent elements of American citizenry and integral parts of American society. For better or for worse, at the birth of the American nation these Lutherans had become American Lutherans.

Part III

IN THE YOUTH OF THE REPUBLIC

(1790-1830)

Cutting European Ties

CHAPTER 10

GENERAL BACKGROUND

The early years of the Republic saw the development of a new sense of nationality, born amid the debates on the Constitution and its ratification by the states. This growth of the American spirit with its attendant severance of European ties applied to intellectual and religious life as well as to the political and economic.

The national election of representatives to the federal Congress and the selection of presidential electors, the federal assumption of state debts incurred during the Revolution and the chartering of the United States Bank, the protective tariff and the encouragement of American manufactures, the use of federal funds for a program of internal improvements, Chief Justice Marshall's decisions interpreting the Constitution in the direction of greater federal authority, the Louisiana Purchase, the War of 1812, the Monroe Doctrine, and above all, the creation and admission of new states to the growing federal union—all these factors tended to strengthen the new government and foster the new national spirit. Despite the divisive effects of sectionalism, later to test the nation sorely, there did emerge by the time of President Monroe an "era of good feeling" in which the vigorous young nation became aware of new power and growth and a reaffirmation of independence from European ties.

Although American life continued to be predominantly agricultural, the growth of cities and towns and the rapid increase in population was striking. The exploration and settlement of the Midwest, the pushing forward of highways, canals, and later railroads characterized this period of energy and restlessness. New fertile lands to be had for the taking influenced American action and thinking and developed in the American people a "frontier psychology" and a feeling of "manifest destiny." A new national literature began with the *North American Review,* Niles' *Register,* and the writings of Washington Irving, James Fenimore Cooper, and William Cullen Bryant.

In the field of religious life the changes were no less striking. American independence brought about the disestablishment of state churches in Virginia and New England. Episcopalians, Methodists, Presbyterians, Congregationalists, and Baptists organized and reorganized as American church bodies. The loosening of European ties and the new national spirit gave rise to wholly new American denominations, e.g. Evangelicals, United Brethren, Disciples of Christ, Unitarians, Mormons—to mention but a few from this period.

But common opportunities and common problems brought about a surprising amount of co-operation. Common conditions of frontier life led to a widespread evangelical movement characterized by revivals that were not limited to any particular denomination but were shared alike by all. Traveling, circuit-riding preachers ministered to all they could reach; pulpits, pastorates, and church buildings were frequently shared by two or more denominations. In some instances even Catholics and Protestants co-operated in use of buildings and in ministrations.

American Protestantism is characterized by a multiplicity of denominational bodies fostered by the feeling for independence and freedom from all forms of ecclesiastical control. But a strong parallel feeling of interdependence and the necessity for Christian co-operation led at an early date to the association of individual members of various denominations in interdenominational organizations for the exercise of Christian philanthropy. The roster of these organizations and societies dating from the first half-century of the American nation is impressive: e.g. the American Bible Society (1816), the American Board of Commissioners for Foreign Missions (1810), the American Education Society (1813), the American Sunday School Union (1824) the American Tract Society (1825), the Seamen's Friend Society (1826), the American Home Missionary Society (1826).

German-speaking Protestants, chiefly Lutheran, Reformed, Moravian, and Mennonite, were somewhat slower than the various English-speaking denominations in responding to the quickening influences of the evangelical movement. This was only partly due to linguistic barriers. More largely it resulted from intrinsic conservatism in doctrine and practice. But they could not long isolate themselves from the new American impulse. Many now began to manifest intense fervor and zeal in the evangelical movement, with a resultant degree of confessional laxity that for a time threatened to obliterate the historic traits that had for centuries marked their individuality among Protestants. The insidious danger of unionism and loss of confessional standards soon called upon Lutheran leaders for decisive measures of education and conservation.

CHAPTER 11

WESTWARD EXPANSION AND NEW SYNODS

As the hardy Lutheran pioneer pressed forward with his family to the frontier, to engage in the great American epic of subduing the wilderness, he carried with him his long rifle, his ax, his Bible, and his faith. Soon calls began to come back from Lutherans on the frontier asking for spiritual help and inviting Lutheran pastors to come and minister to them.

For a long time it had been the custom of ministers who lived nearest to the frontier to undertake missionary tours on their own initiative, traveling into remote districts, preaching the Word and administering the sacraments. The pioneer work in the Lutheran church west of the Alleghenies was done by men who entered the field as "independent preachers," without synodical connection, to answer the call of Lutheran frontiersmen. Hundreds of flourishing congregations today trace their beginnings to such volunteer missionary effort.

The work of home missions, as we call it today, was officially undertaken by the Ministerium of Pennsylvania in 1804. The plan of the synod, as it went into effect in 1806, provided for the sending out of two or three men each year during the summer months. These traveling missionaries were members of the synod, were commissioned and paid by the synod, and rendered their reports to the synod.

Among the most eminent of these early home missionaries commissioned by the Ministerium of Pennsylvania for work in western Pennsylvania and Virginia, in Kentucky and Tennessee, in Ohio and Indiana were John Stauch and Paul Henkel, who labored westward from pastorates in the Valley of Virginia. Henkel, a remarkably

64

versatile man, during his long pastorate at New Market found time to be both author and publisher of hymnbooks and catechisms in English and in German, rear sons for the Lutheran ministry who carried on the family publishing firm, engage in extensive missionary travels and participate in the organization of three new synods, the North Carolina (1803), the Ohio (1818), and the Tennessee (1820).

Other energetic home missionaries of this period were John Michael Steck, who served in western Pennsylvania, and his son Michael John, who served in Ohio and was later one of the founders of the Pittsburgh Synod (1845). The famed Carl Friedrich Heyer, commissioned by the Ministerium of Pennsylvania in 1839 as the first American Lutheran missionary to India, spent his preparatory years in mission labors in an extensive field from western Pennsylvania to Ohio, Kentucky, and Indiana.

But the work of these indefatigable and self-denying servants of the church was weakened by lack of pastors to man the congregations they organized. New immigrants from Europe joined in the westward trek to free and fertile farmlands. The number of scattered Lutherans became too great for the infrequent ministration of traveling missionaries. If the church was to gather in her own and maintain her place in the spiritual life of her people, further synodical organization was necessary.

As early as 1773, Frederick Augustus Muhlenberg, then pastor in New York, had called a conference of all Lutheran pastors in that colony. But not until after the war, in 1786, did Henry Melchior Muhlenberg's son-in-law, John Christopher Kunze, succeed in formally organizing the second synod in America, the Ministerium of New York. Only three of the eight Lutheran pastors then in the state of New York and two laymen attended this organizational meeting in Albany; the next session was not held until six years later, in 1792. Growth was slow at first, but by 1807 there were fourteen pastors on the roll. Efforts to extend the work northward to Canada proved fruitless. The pastors sent there one after another left the Lutheran church for the Anglican (Episcopal) church. But westward through central New York the work of the synod grew successfully.

The third Lutheran synod to be formed was in the South. The Lutherans of North Carolina, feeling the need for an organization of their own to examine and ordain men to the ministerial office and to protect themselves from the tide of revivalism, met at Salisbury in 1803. There four pastors, among them the ubiquitous Paul Henkel, and fourteen lay delegates formed the Synod of North Carolina. This organization expanded rapidly to include congregations in South Carolina, southwestern Virginia, and eastern Tennessee. It sent out home missionaries to organize scattered Lutherans in those areas. By 1820 it numbered 26 ministers and catechists, about 60 congregations and over 6,000 members. Thus to Lutherans in the South this synod became truly a "mother synod."

The New York Ministerium and the North Carolina Synod had been formed without making a breach in the ranks of the Ministerium of Pennsylvania. They were constituted of congregations that lay outside the bounds of the Ministerium of Pennsylvania and with two exceptions their pastors had not been connected with the older synod. But the fourth synod to be organized was formed on the territory of the Ministerium itself.

As missionaries were sent out year after year to follow the westward advance of the American frontier, as they took up their permanent abodes farther and farther from Philadelphia and eastern Pennsylvania, it became increasingly difficult for these missionaries and pastors to make the long journeys necessary to attend meetings of the original synod. Still they longed to take counsel with their brethren and to have a part in deliberations for the general good. The Ministerium therefore had early established "Special" or "District" meetings at which the pastors and laymen of a particular region could meet as often as they desired for mutual edification and for counsel on certain subjects.

In 1801 the Ministerium had provided for seven such special conference districts. The Western District embraced all the territory west of Chambersburg. In 1812 the Lutheran pastors in Ohio organized their own conference and in 1817 asked permission to establish their own ministerium. They felt that this was necessary in order to secure candidates for the ministry and to stimulate interest among the congregations and bring about a more rapid development of their resources. The request was not granted, but permission was given to license candidates for one year. The next year the Ohio Conference quietly organized itself into the Synod of Ohio and Adjacent States and proceeded to ordain three men to the ministry. The first president of the new synod was the missionary John Stauch; the first secretary was Paul Henkel, who had traversed all Ohio in a two-wheeled cart. The new body numbered at first fourteen ministers and eight lay delegates.

The subsequent history of this body is complex. By mid-century certain elements withdrew to form other sectional synods in Ohio or to help form the Pittsburgh Synod. These elements eventually merged into the Ohio Synod of the United Lutheran Church. The original body, with name changed to the Joint Synod of Ohio and Other States, maintained a separate existence until 1930, when it merged with the Iowa and Buffalo synods to form the American Lutheran Church.

The Synod of Maryland and Virginia, organized in 1820, also grew out of a special conference of the Pennsylvania Ministerium. This conference had existed since 1793 but proved inadequate to meet the needs of a growing Lutheran population. When, therefore, the pastors of Maryland and Virginia asked permission to organize a new synod on their territory the Ministerium of Pennsylvania granted the request in view of the immediate prospect of a more inclusive fraternity to be known as the General Synod. The organization took place at Winchester, Virginia, in October, 1820.

Three months before that the Tennessee Synod had been formed by four pastors of the North Carolina Synod. The founders of this organization, two of whom were sons of Paul Henkel, could not agree with their synodical brethren on the question of licensing clergymen, and because of laxity in doctrine and practice in the older synods they strongly objected to the forming of a General Synod. So they withdrew and organized their own synod.

In 1824 another division took place in the ranks of the North Carolina Synod. This time in peace and brotherly love the pastors and churches in South Carolina withdrew and formed the South Carolina Synod.

The next year a number of pastors serving churches in Pennsylvania west of the Susquehanna River organized themselves, without the consent of the Ministerium of Pennsylvania, into the West Pennsylvania Synod in time to attend the meeting of the General Synod that year.

In 1829 the recently formed Synod of Maryland and Virginia amicably divided when eight pastors withdrew to form a separate Virginia Synod, the original body remaining henceforth as the Maryland Synod.

This progressive formation of new synods was evidence of the expansion of the church in this country. It was in reality a further development of Muhlenberg's organization and at the same time an expression of the new spirit of the times, the spirit of American aggressiveness and independence from Europe. It took place for the most part in peace and amity and it resulted in greater efficiency in the church as a whole, establishing new centers of light, and occupying new territories. This multiplying of synodical organizations logically pointed to some more inclusive union in the church that would unify the parts in the interest of conservation and would overcome the divisive and weakening effects that might have resulted from the formation of many separate synods.

CHAPTER 12

PROBLEMS OF FAITH AND LANGUAGE

With the steady expansion of her territory and the rapid increase in her numbers the Lutheran church in the early days of the republic was confronted with the age-long problem of men for the ministry. But even more serious were several problems growing out of internal conditions in the church. These sadly interfered with her peace and progress and at times even threatened her life.

First, there was the problem of rationalism. The close contact of America with France during the Revolutionary War left a deposit of rationalistic thought among Americans. Lutherans did not escape the infection, for the spirit of rationalism had crept into Halle and other German universities even before Muhlenberg's death.

In 1792 the constitution of the Pennsylvania Ministerium was revised. All references to the Lutheran confessions were stricken out. Candidates for ordination were pledged only to preach the Word of God in its purity, according to law and gospel as presented in the catechism and hymnbook. The constitutions of the congregations remained unchanged, but pronounced forms of rationalism were current in several districts of the Ministerium. There was no express antagonism to distinctive Lutheran doctrines but a general toning down of Lutheran convictions and many inconsistencies with sound Lutheran practice.

In New York the effects of rationalism were much stronger than in Pennsylvania. Following the death of the learned, devout, and influential leader, Dr. J. C. Kunze, in 1807, the presidency of the New York Ministerium passed for a period of twenty-one years to Dr. Fred Henry Quitman, who had come from Europe an avowed disciple of Professor John Semler, "father of rationalism" at Halle. In 1814 Quitman prepared and published, with the consent and approval of the synod, an English catechism as a substitute for Luther's. It denied the inspiration and authority of the Bible and the validity of the Apostles' Creed and the chief Lutheran confessions. A few years later he published a distinctly un-Lutheran liturgy and hymnal and succeeded in getting it officially accepted by the synod. Quitman was a man of commanding presence and great intellectual force, and his enormous rationalistic influence persisted for a generation. Yet, in the end, the opposition of a younger and more evangelical element produced a new English edition of Luther's Catechism which outsold Quitman's. Eventually the new leadership saved the day.

In North Carolina as early as 1788, Dr. John Caspar Velthusen's "Helmstaedt Catechism" had been published for American use and became known as the "North Carolina Catechism." It was full of the spirit of German rationalism. When the Synod of North Carolina was organized in 1803 its first constitution contained no confessional statement or reference to the great confessional writings of the church; in fact, the word *Lutheran* does not occur at all in this document. Quitman's rationalistic liturgy was officially recommended for use by the congregations. But these effects of rationalistic thinking died out more swiftly in North Carolina than elsewhere. A new constitution in 1818 made the synod the first since Muhlenberg's day to make official avowal of the Augsburg Confession. This new constitution further provided that only ministers ordained or licensed by an American synod could be admitted to the Synod of North Carolina.

The second problem that vexed the church in the youth of the Republic was unionism. The spirit of unionism was partly the off-spring of religious indifference. Rationalism had shattered confessional convictions, and points of difference among denominations were obscured. Motives of expediency also played their part—union with other church bodies seemed the line of least resistance. Even to the opponents of rationalism it seemed prudent to unite in the common cause of evangelicalism. For the Lutheran church it meant the decline of her denominational consciousness, and for a time the new American impulse to union threatened the very existence of the church in this country.

In New York the tendency was towards union with the Episcopal church. Even Dr. Kunze fell under the charm of the idea; in 1797 it was resolved that on account of "the intimate relation subsisting between the English Episcopal and Lutheran churches, the identity of their doctrine and the near approach of their discipline," the Ministerium of New York would not acknowledge a new Lutheran church in places where her members could partake of the services of an Episcopal church. Negotiations were begun looking toward organic union of the two bodies and episcopal ordination of the Lutheran pastors. The negotiations were not completed, but a number of individual congregations went over from the Lutheran to the Episcopal church. There was great need for closer union among the Lutherans themselves to stimulate their denominational consciousness and save the life of their church.

In Pennsylvania union was projected with the Reformed church. Many church buildings in the rural districts of that state had been erected by the common enterprise of Lutheran and Reformed people. In not a few instances the congregations worshiping in the same building were united under one church council and merely alternated their services between Lutheran and Reformed pastors. Lutherans and Reformed co-operated in managing the affairs of Franklin College at Lancaster and they had no compunctions about permitting a Catholic priest to be included among the trustees. The religious magazine founded by the Ministerium in 1812 made a special bid for Reformed and Moravian subscribers. In 1817 appeared the "Common Hymn-book" in German, which took the place of the Muhlenberg Hymnal, and which was endorsed by Dr. Quitman and recommended by both the Lutheran and Reformed synods in Pennsylvania. The next year active efforts were made to establish a joint theological seminary, for many ministers in both churches favored organic union of these two conservative, German-speaking bodies, influenced by motives of expediency growing out of intermarriage, propinquity, and a common language.

The North Carolina Synod reflected the unionistic tendencies of both Pennsylvania and New York. Union churches for Lutherans and Reformed were common, with common hymnbooks and catechisms in use among the congregations. In a book prepared to celebrate the tercentenary of the Reformation in 1817, Pastor Schober, one of the leaders of the synod, explained the articles of the Augsburg Confession in a Reformed sense and declared that among all the denominations of "those who worship Jesus as God there is nothing to prevent a hearty union." This book was endorsed and published by the synod. Moreover, the Lutheran synod fraternized closely with the Episcopal church in the South; both Episcopalians and Moravians officiated frequently for Lutheran congregations.

A third difficulty that impaired the progress of the church in this period was the language problem. The polyglot character of the Lutheran church in the world has been the cause of just pride to Lutherans, but the polyglot character of the Lutheran church in America has been the cause of many dark pages in her history. Muhlenberg, as we have seen, preached in whatever language the people could best understand, and for that purpose mastered and used three languages. The generation that inherited his spirit followed the same policy. Dr Kunze was active in preparing literature to meet the needs of the English-speaking parts of the church. But those who resisted the anglicizing current of the times were entrenched in the congregational and synodical organizations and the result was much bitter strife and great losses to the church.

The Ministerium of Pennsylvania in 1792 introduced the word "German" into its title. In 1805 at Germantown it took action forbidding the use of any other language than German in synodical sessions. But English-speaking members of the congregation of St. Michael's in Philadelphia, led by General Peter Muhlenberg, demanded that a third pastor be called who could officiate in English. Defeated by a narrow margin in a congregational vote, they withdrew and founded St. John's English Lutheran Church. Ten years later the controversy broke out afresh. It was carried into the courts, and this time the German party lost. The argument that seems to have convinced the court was based on the necessity of cultivating an American spirit and the futility of depending on the immigration of a "turbid current" of aliens for the future progress of any church. The times were not favorable to the maintenance of national distinctions within America.

Other sections of the church experienced the same trouble. In Lancaster, where Muhlenberg's youngest son, Dr. Henry Ernest, was a devoted pastor, eminent scientist and first president of Franklin College, his congregation, Trinity, refused to contribute to the synodical treasury until young men should be educated to preach in English. In the New York Ministerium English gained the ascendency more rapidly than in Pennsylvania and in 1807 became the official language of the body. Very similar was the course of affairs in the South.

Some of the arguments made in the course of controversies on the language question are amazing in retrospect. The Lutheran church, it was said, cannot exist apart from the German language. English is the language of the Episcopal and Presbyterian churches and is too shallow to furnish an adequate translation of Lutheran doctrinal and devotional literature. It was observed that children of German parents, as they learned to speak English, became frivolous and indifferent in matters of religion. Since much of the rationalism that made its way into the Lutheran church was clothed in the English language, many people regarded German as the bulwark of sound faith and evangelical theology. For example, the *Evangelisches Magazin*, established by the Pennsylvania Ministerium in 1812, had the twofold purpose of "conserving the German language and fighting rationalistic unbelief."

These persistent efforts to withstand the introduction of English, so contrary to the spirit of Luther and so opposed to the policy of the Muhlenbergs, alienated many, and drove thousands of young people into the churches of other denominations. Many Presbyterian, Episcopalian, and Methodist churches of today owe their origin to this fact.

Such were the internal problems with which the church had to deal in severing European ties. In the providence of God they were solved in course of time. Their proper solution meant the permanence of the Lutheran church in her own identity in this country. For eventually the bonds that tied American Lutherans to European rationalism were severed, religious indifferentism ceased, unionism vanished or ceased to threaten. Gradually, though reluctantly in many quarters, the use of English, as the language of the nation, came to be accepted in the church.

CHAPTER 13

A GENERAL ORGANIZATION AND
A SEMINARY

The times required a general organization, answering to the sense of unity and common brotherhood among Lutherans, to overcome the divisive effects of the synodical movement, to conserve the denominational consciousness, and to prevent absorption in more compact church bodies. Moreover, the acute need for more men and better trained men in the ministry called for common action.

The initiative came from the mother synod of Pennsylvania. In 1818 the New York Ministerium and the North Carolina Synod were the only other synods. But within the Pennsylvania Ministerium the Ohio Conference was taking steps toward organizing a new synod, and similar action seemed probable on the part of the Conference of Maryland and Virginia, the Conference of West Pennsylvania, and even the Lancaster Conference. Accordingly the Ministerium acted upon a suggestion that had been made seven years before by the Lutherans of North Carolina, who had felt the weakness of Lutheran organization as compared with that of the Episcopal church. It resolved that "in its judgment it would be well if the different Evangelical Lutheran Synods in the United States were to stand, in some way or other, in true union with one another." At the next meeting "A Proposed Plan" of union was adopted and ordered to be submitted to the other synods.

The convention for the organization of a General Synod was held at Hagerstown, Maryland, October 22, 1820. Representatives were present from four synods, Pennsylvania, New York, North Carolina, and Maryland and Virginia. Only Ohio and Tennessee were not represented. The pastors of the Ohio Synod objected to the general organization because they feared a hierarchical trend and the possible prevalence of the English language in the new body. The little Tennessee Synod also objected to the rule of majorities in general church affairs and to the fact that no mention was made of the Bible or the Augsburg Confession. The four synods organized themselves, however, and drew up a constitution. A year later, in October, 1821, three synods having adopted the constitution, all except New York, the General Synod of the Lutheran Church in the United States held its first regular convention at Frederick, Maryland.

The constitution and the proceedings of the first convention specified that the General Synod might propose to the district synods "books and writings such as catechisms, forms of liturgy, collections of hymns, or confessions of faith," but specifically disclaimed the "power of prescribing uniform ceremonies of religion." It provided for the organization of new district synods with the consent of the general body. The General Synod had power to advise on disputed points of doctrine or discipline when cases were appealed to it by individuals, congregations, or synods. It was also authorized to devise plans for seminaries of education and missionary institutions, to provide aid for ministers and their families, and to take measures to "promote the practice of brotherly love and the furtherance of Christian concord." This slight surrender of sovereignty by the individual synods and ministeriums aimed only at such a federation of Lutheran bodies as would prevent discord and schisms among them and provide the means and agencies necessary to foster the spirit of Lutheran unity, to occupy the field more efficiently, and to fortify the church's ranks against dissipation.

The first business convention of the General Synod in 1821 deferred the establishment of a theological seminary, for which plans were already being drawn, but recommended that the congregations be prepared for the enterprise and that books be gathered for its library. On the subject of home missions, it was recommended to the district synods that they send missionaries to answer "the earnest calls of the children of the church and others, resident on our frontier countries." From these and other actions looking toward the intensive occupation of the field and the supply of an educated ministry for the church, it was evident that the General Synod, even in its small beginnings, was organized for action and intended to face aggressively the tasks confronting the whole church.

The organization of the General Synod assured the independence of the Lutheran church in this country. It was fundamentally opposed to the schemes of union with the Reformed in Pennsylvania and with the Episcopalians in North Carolina and elsewhere. It operated as an emphatic protest against the rationalistic tendencies in New York and other parts of the church, and presented an effectual barrier to the further importation into the church of European deistic theology. It saved the church from becoming rationalistic as it became anglicized and Americanized. It maintained the historical connection with the fathers and stood for the confession of a positive faith. Its first constitution, it is true, did not mention the Lutheran confessions, else it would not have been adopted by the constituent synods. But before the end of this period, in the oath prescribed in 1825 for the professors in the theological seminary and in the model constitution for district synods drawn up in 1829, the General Synod was working vigorously toward a specific definition of the Lutheran faith. The General Synod was a medium through which new synods might minister to greater efficiency rather than weaken the church. It provided the means and agencies for prosecuting independent Lutheran educational, missionary, and charitable operations. Above all, it gave to the church in this country, even to those who did not at once become members of the General Synod, a nationwide outlook and interest and a sense of permanent citizenship in this Republic. As Dr. Charles Porterfield Krauth expressed it, "The General Synod was a declaration on the part of the Lutheran church in America that she had no intention of dying or moving, that she liked this western world and meant to live here."

Certainly the size of the General Synod in its infancy is no measure of its significance. The General Synod was the logical outcome of the process of organization begun by Muhlenberg in 1748. Theoretically the polity of the Lutheran church in America is congregational. But just as the common necessities of the congregations led to Muhlenberg's organization of a synod so, seventy years later, the larger exigencies of the church in this country led to a general organization. That it should have come into being in this period of our history is easily understood. As Washington and Jefferson and par-

76

ticularly Monroe had broken European bonds and announced to the European nations that our national policy was "America for Americans," so the organization of a General Synod proclaimed to the religious world that the Lutheran church in this country had reached its majority and announced the policy: "The Lutheran church for Lutherans." Both were the outgrowth of American independence and enterprise.

But the new organization encountered many difficulties. For many years its "general" character was more promise and policy than fact. After the organization meeting in 1820 the New York Synod waited sixteen years to join, since most of its members regarded the project of a general Lutheran organization as impractical and hopeless. Even the Pennsylvania Ministerium withdrew in 1823, because of the fears of congregations in the rural districts that the new organization would be nothing less than "an aristocratic spiritual congress," a union of church and state, that would rob them of their dearly bought liberties and impose on them the horrors of an ecclesiastical despotism. Theological seminaries were represented as useless and costly evils that would simply impose more taxes on the farmers. Moreover, it was felt that the General Synod would interfere with the cherished plans for union with the Reformed. In order to prevent further difficulties within the Ministerium the city congregations and the leaders yielded to the country districts, and thirty years passed before the Ministerium returned to the General Synod.

The withdrawal of the mother synod, which constituted more than half of the church, was a severe blow to the infant General Synod. The Ohio Synod, which had about decided to join, reconsidered and never came in. At this critical point, the General Synod was saved by S. S. Schmucker, then only twenty-four years old. Profoundly impressed with the need for a revival of confessional subscription and for an educated ministry in the church, he was particularly concerned to save the General Synod from dissolution. He succeeded in inspiring the discouraged synods and in 1823 prevailed on Maryland and Virginia, North Carolina, and Ohio to send delegates to a meeting. There was also a delegation from the Conference of West Pennsylvania, which did not sympathize with the attitude of the rest of the Pennsylvania Ministerium and which joined the general body in 1825 as the West Pennsylvania Synod. Thus the General

Synod and the ideals for which it stood were kept alive. Its significance went far beyond the numbers of the synods and ministers embraced in the initial organization, for as time passed it drew to itself most of the new synods, especially the English-speaking synods, as they were successively formed.

A principal objective of the General Synod was a theological seminary, for the permanence and independence of the church demanded that she be supplied with a learned and consecrated ministry trained in this country and by the church herself. It was vain to hope any longer for ministerial recruits from beyond the Atlantic, and perilous to depend on the schools of other denominations for the training of Lutheran ministers.

Muhlenberg's own project for a theological seminary had disappeared in the smoke of the Revolutionary War. Dr. Kunze had tried to establish a school for ministerial candidates first independently, then in connection with the University of Pennsylvania in Philadelphia, and afterwards in connection with Columbia College in New York. These undertakings failed, but Dr. Kunze gave private instructions to young men studying for the ministry. His students were the first English Lutheran pastors in America.

The Ministerium of Pennsylvania had hoped for much from Franklin College at Lancaster, operated in conjunction with the Reformed and Moravians, but it yielded no candidates for the Lutheran ministry. The theological seminary which it was proposed to establish jointly with the Reformed could not be realized. This synod also had to depend on private instruction for the education of its ministerial students, and from time to time it appointed pastors who were to be regarded as its official theological instructors. Likewise in North Carolina and Tennessee several efforts to begin a seminary had proved futile and candidates for the ministry were obliged to study privately under pastors.

A more promising attempt was made in New York State. Pastor J. C. Hartwick, minister at Rhinebeck and other places in New York, dying in 1797, left $16,000 to found an institution for the training of missionaries to the Indians. In 1815 in Otsego County the work of the institution was begun with Dr. E. L. Hazelius as professor in theology. The institution was not under synodical jurisdiction, and difficulties with the bequest and its remote location seriously hindered its work for many years. The curriculum was not purely theological, but general, and at first it did not reach a wide constituency.

But the church was growing. The home mission field was calling for more laborers. The men born and educated in Germany were gradually passing from the scene; no new supplies came from that source or were sought. The chief training of an American Lutheran ministry was in the parsonages of busy American pastors. Dr. Helmuth and Dr. Schmidt in Philadelphia trained many of the next generation of pastors. Dr. Geissenhainer in New York, H. E. Muhlenberg and his successor, Christian Endress, in Lancaster, George Lochman in Harrisburg, David F. Schaeffer in Frederick—all had private students continually under their care. Jacob Goering had as many as twenty-two such students in the course of his pastorate at York and elsewhere. In many cases the parsonages furnished the ministerial candidates as well as their training. F. D. Schaeffer instructed his four sons in theology, and Paul Henkel his five sons.

Many of the ministers trained in this way rose to eminence and usefulness in the church. But this method of ministerial education became increasingly burdensome to the busy pastors who undertook it and increasingly inadequate to the needs of the times. Education of proper range and depth was clearly the work of a special institution, and in that period such an institution called for the support of a general organization of the church. The founding therefore of the first official synodical Lutheran seminary in this country waited for the organization and action of the General Synod. It came in 1826. Andover Seminary had been established in 1808 in protest against the Unitarianism of Harvard. It was the first Protestant seminary in this country, but in less than twenty years seventeen such schools came into existence. S. S. Schmucker, having saved the General Synod from dissolution, wished to see the church establish her own seminary. He was concerned that the Lutheran church should be rescued from "her former lifeless and distracted condition," and to that end he believed that the church should revive confessional subscription to the Augsburg Confession and should found a theological seminary. He kept the subject before the church.

Through the Synod of Maryland and Virginia, of which he was a member, young Schmucker pressed the General Synod of 1825 to support the committee appointed at the organization meeting in 1820, with the result that it set the time for the opening of the seminary, elected Dr. Schmucker the professor, chose a board of directors, opened a book of subscriptions for the cause, selected agents to canvass the church in this country, and appointed Dr. Benjamin Kurtz to go to Europe to secure books for the library and funds for the endowment. At the same time the General Synod placed the seminary on the unmistakable basis of subscription to the Augsburg Confession by declaring: "In this seminary shall be taught, in the German and English languages, the fundamental doctrines of the Sacred Scriptures as contained in the Augsburg Confession." This was advanced confessional ground for those times.

The seminary was begun in 1826 at Gettysburg, chosen as most centrally located for the Lutheran synods then in the General Synod. The two older synods of Pennsylvania and New York were not in the General Synod at that time, but many of the prominent individuals in these older bodies co-operated in establishing the seminary. And the Pennsylvania Ministerium sent many of its students to the seminary and long afterwards transferred its interest in Franklin College to the college at Gettysburg.

Dr. Schmucker's talents and learning pointed him out as a teacher. He had studied under his father in York and Dr. Helmuth in Philadelphia, and had continued at the University of Pennsylvania and at Princeton. It was his experience at Princeton that impelled him to found a Lutheran college and a Lutheran seminary. Between 1820 and 1870, he led the General Synod, writing its organic documents and determining its policies. For nearly forty of these years he continued as head of the seminary, during which time about five hundred men were prepared for the ministry.

Dr. Schmucker's teachings later became the subject of violent controversy because they ran counter to the great changes then taking place in the church. But no one doubts that in his work for the establishment of an official synodical seminary he made a vital contribution to the Lutheran church in America, its independence and its prosperity. The seminary was tangible evidence that the Lutherans had broken through the narrow limits of synodical lines and had begun to contemplate the broader and deeper questions that arise out of the life of the Lutheran church as a whole.

CHAPTER 14

LUTHERAN PEOPLE IN THE YOUTH OF THE REPUBLIC

The vast majority of Lutheran people in America at the birth of the Republic were farmers. Large families were common among them. The sons, as they came to maturity, looked beyond the original homestead for new land to conquer, first with the gun and then with the plow. Good farming land became scarce and its cost high in the tidewater regions, and the new generation looked westward across the Alleghenies or southwestward to the valley called Cumberland, Shenandoah and Virginia, and to the uplands of the Carolinas. In many a Lutheran family, furthermore, there was a native restlessness inherited from the generation that had torn up its roots from the fatherland. Muhlenberg remarked early in his ministry about the migratory tendencies of his fellow-Lutherans in America. Renewed immigration after 1815 led to a search for elbowroom. The people of the East had heard about the rich resources of forests and fields and rivers beyond the Appalachians.

Many factors impelled the westward trek during the four decades following the setting up of the Republic. In 1790 only six per cent of the population lived beyond the western limits of the original thirteen states, while in 1830 more than 30 per cent lived on the new lands. Lutherans contributed their full quota to the migration and expansion.

The chief route westward, following the old military road cut by Forbes in the French and Indian War, started in New Jersey and ran through the Lutheran settlements of eastern Pennsylvania and Lancaster County, crossed the Susquehanna into York County, climbed the two Allegheny ridges of the Appalachian Mountains, passed through Bedford, and then wound down to Pittsburgh and the Ohio

River. Another good route, familiar to Lutheran families, had been blazed by Daniel Boone of Berks County, Pa., as early as 1769, from Baltimore to Cumberland on the Potomac and then across the mountains to Wheeling on the Ohio. For the Lutherans in the valley of Virginia or the uplands of the Carolinas there were several passages across the mountains into southern Ohio or Kentucky and Tennessee. Parts of these roads, improved through private capital, were called turnpikes and toll was collected from travelers.

Many of the migrants went on horseback, carrying their resources in their pockets. But the favorite vehicle of transportation, especially from Pennsylvania, was the Conestoga wagon, built especially for travel over mountains and streams and drawn by four horses. It is said that the drivers of the Conestoga wagons inaugurated the American custom of passing approaching traffic to the right instead of following the English rule of driving to the left. The adults in the family made much of the journey afoot, trudging alongside the wagon or driving a herd of cattle or sheep.

This migration was essentially individualistic, unlike the early American colonizations under the guidance and protection of powerful companies or semi-feudal proprietors. The movement across the Appalachians was a spontaneous swarming of individuals and families, each free to go or stay, free to choose a route and destination, and responsible to no one for success or failure. Once these men and women of zeal were planted in the new homes of their choice, they could be expected to continue their voluntary action and pioneering spirit in their religious lives.

Family life on the new frontier usually began in a crude hut along a river bank. As soon as temporary shelter had been erected, a small lot was fenced in with a worm fence constructed out of saplings. Then larger trees were girdled and killed, and the pre-empted tract was expanded. While the rifleman and fisherman of the family went in search of food, the women and children planted corn and potatoes, turnips, cabbage, and beans, in the rich soil of the river's edge. Before winter set in, a larger clearing was made, usually a short distance from the river or stream, and a more substantial cabin erected. Trees were felled, the logs were trimmed flat with a broadax, notched at the ends, and laid horizontally and slabs were overlapped to form the roof. The first floor consisted of two rooms, one of them with a large fireplace for cooking and heating. An inside ladder gave access to the loft under the sloping roof, the common sleeping-room, sometimes partitioned. The furniture was homemade and the pieces were few and simple. In some instances a bedstead or a chest of drawers had been brought along in the Conestoga wagon, a reminder of life "in the East."

Early crops consisted of corn and potatoes to feed the family, corn and oats to feed the cattle, and barley and rye for distillation and consumption or sale. Quantities were limited only by the manpower available for harvesting. The size of the new homestead varied with the policy of the federal government, but no farmer was far from vast tracts of untouched wilderness. To an industrious farmer with a growing family these lands were a constant invitation. Usually there was much confusion, much speculation, long delay in securing surveys, and much uncertainty as to titles. President Jefferson, a friend of the freehold farmer, believed that each individual or family should be limited to eighty or a hundred acres. In general this policy prevailed, discouraging landed aristocracy and promoting the democracy of the freeholder. It stimulated the process of social leveling already inherent in the physical hardships of the frontier, and begot a sense of equality in all social relationships, easily translated into religious practices. The Lutheran farmer on the new frontier had a sense of liberty and opportunity that his ancestors in Europe could hardly dream of.

Most of the leaders of the revolutionary Republic had intended merely to replace the Old-World aristocracy of blood and lineage with a new aristocracy of wealth and talents. In this they failed, largely because of the leveling influence of the rural sections. The Lutheran farmers were jealous of their rights as citizens of the Republic and suspicious of encroachment by the state or by the church. They were loyal to the Republic that the Muhlenbergs had helped to set up, but more than once they joined in demonstrations against threatened "seizure of power" by the federal authorities, until they could be reasoned into submission by their clerical leaders.

Lutherans on the new frontier, as soon as they had built a cabin and planted their crops, usually sought out others of their faith and language, often traveling twenty miles to find a neighbor. Journeymen of various trades traversed the whole frontier and brought news of the names and locations of other settlers. Sometimes old acquaintance was renewed in the West. Paul Henkel in his diary of missionary journeys to Ohio, and other missionaries, in vivid reports to their synods, record frequent meetings with families who had been their parishioners in the East.

The Lutheran people often gathered several families in a cabin for devotional meetings, and in some instances formed congregations and even built log churches before there was any prospect of securing ministers or regular services of worship. These devout Lutherans, seeing among their Methodist neighbors the itinerant preachers riding from the East, always cherished the hope that some Lutheran minister might be persuaded to come to the frontier for a few weeks or months to preach a series of sermons, administer communion, baptize children, admonish the careless, and hold memorial services for the dead. In the meantime intelligent laymen among them conducted simple services, read from Lutheran devotional books, and sent messages to ministers they knew in the East asking for help. Letters to the synods on the Atlantic seaboard appealing for trained leaders help to trace Lutheran expansion westward during the first forty years in the life of the Republic.

When volunteers or ministers appointed by the synods made the difficult journey to the frontier, they found many irregularities in religious affairs. Independent preachers of the gospel, self-appointed and self-educated, unordained and unsalaried, had wandered about among the shepherdless people and for a consideration preached to them and administered the sacraments. This sort of ministry was usually very primitive and crude. For example, baptisms were sometimes performed with plenty of water but without the use of a single word. Sometimes these itinerants proved to be reprobates and wrought much spiritual havoc among the people. But there were enough of the sincere and genuine "farmer-preachers" among them to provide the elements of real Christian ministry and to plant the roots of a church.

On the new frontier there were periodic recurrences of religious revivals. These were the result partly of the pietistic heritage of the settlers and partly of the new conditions on the frontier. The narrow range of their interests helped to give intensity to their religious emotions. The hardships and anxieties that attended the long struggle with the dark forces of the wilderness made Satan and divine wrath very real. The tinge of melancholy and the sense of loneliness furnished a psychological background for the upsurge of religious emotionalism. The freedom from restraint and the laxity in morals easily turned into a flood tide of moral enthusiasm. Perhaps more than anything else, the revivals fed upon the air of expectancy that hovered over the Christian people during the long intervals between the visits of ministers and missionaries.

Revivals frequently led to lurid extravagances. The camp meeting often encouraged the discard of all reserve and produced physical and moral results that were to become the subjects of psychological study. Methodist circuit riders, first, around 1799, gathered the people together from a wide area for preaching and administering the sacraments. Baptist and Presbyterian missionaries followed the pattern. People came from as far as a hundred miles or more, and by the thousands gathered in the woods for religious services that continued without intermission day or night for a week. Excited appeals made to throngs of people at night by the flickering light of the campfires often produced sobs or shrieks and sometimes "the jerks." Ministers of all denominations co-operated in the "meeting" and sometimes preached simultaneously.

Large numbers of Lutheran people attended these meetings, either out of curiosity or for more worthy reasons. The journals of Paul Henkel and the reports of other Lutheran missionaries to the frontier indicate that they could not overlook the opportunity that the camp meeting afforded to preach to the Lutheran people in large numbers. Occasionally the synods in the East warned their missionaries against participating in frontier revivals; camp meetings were branded as "deviations from our Lutheran ways." But the Lutheran people on the frontier generally did believe in religious revivals and did participate in these sessions of stimulated religious emotion.

Meanwhile, among the Lutheran people in the older settlements of the East, changes were slowly taking place. The primitive log cabins were exchanged for substantial frame buildings with glass windows, or more permanent houses of stone. Barns were rebuilt and made larger and more convenient. The quality of the live stock, horses, cows, sheep, and pigs, was gradually improved; rotation of crops was practiced and fertilizers were introduced. Only the farming implements and the house furniture continued to be crude and clumsy, and the clothing continued to be homespun.

Towns and cities were slowly growing in influence, but in congregational life there was little difference between the Lutheran people in the towns and those in the country. The outlook of the farmer was very much the same as that of the artisan and merchant. Foreign observers who visited America remarked about the nation-wide similarity of moral codes and religious practices and the lack of any urban-rural cleavage among Americans at this time.

At the beginning of the century public schools for all the people existed only in theory and elementary education was left almost entirely to the churches. In good Lutheran tradition, schools were maintained in connection with most of the Lutheran congregations. In 1802 we can count a total of 130 such schools, taught either by Lutheran pastors or by teachers under their supervision. Before 1830 the number of such schools had increased to about 300. The curriculum embraced reading, spelling, writing, and simple arithmetic, and, for those who were willing to endure it, the catechism and Scripture memorization. On the frontier the itinerant missionary, and afterwards the resident Lutheran minister, frequently conducted the semblance of a congregational school by expanding his catechetical instruction into the general field of reading and writing and memorizing of Scripture verses. Before the end of Jackson's administration the public school had been introduced.

In 1810 there were 366 newspapers in the Republic, 27 of them dailies. As Lutherans progressed in their transition from German to English in their family and community life and in their churches they shared in the benefits of these publications.

Means of communication were not lacking. When a farmer hauled his crops to the gristmill or to market in town, he met people from other communities and picked up papers and an occasional book, and returned home with materials to enlighten his family and neighbors. Many a novel or storybook was passed from farm to farm until it was illegible. Then, too, the itinerant craftsmen, the blacksmiths and tailors, the weavers and the cabinetmakers, the shoemakers and the peddlers with their stores on their backs, usually regarded it as part of their function to accumulate and purvey materials regarded as news.

Lutherans soon had their own denominational periodicals, first in

German and then in English. They reflect the main currents of interest and the religious conditions among the people. The first Lutheran periodical, the *Evangelisches Magazin,* was suggested by Dr. J. G. Schmucker of York, sponsored by the Ministerium of Pennsylvania, and edited by Dr. Helmuth of Philadelphia. It appeared quarterly and began with the last quarter of 1811. It carried about 250 pages of material each year. Most of the articles were written by Dr. Schmucker and Dr. Helmuth and reflected their pietistic background. The magazine was directed to the people in the pews. It carried much devotional material, synodical reports, letters from itinerant missionaries visiting the Western frontier, long accounts of foreign missions by the Lutheran churches of Europe, emotional appeals, tearful narratives, religious poetry, and urgent appeals for the preservation of the German language. It seems that Lutheran readers of that day were glad to read about life among their former neighbors who had gone west, about needy orphans in Europe, about deathbed conversions, about the burning of theaters, about instances of marvelous piety in children, and about the imminent end of the world. The *Magazin* attained a subscription list of 1,500 and was probably read by five or six thousand people. It continued to 1817, but during its last three years it appeared as an annual.

The first English magazine for Lutherans in this country was the *Evangelical Lutheran Intelligencer.* This was a monthly periodical authorized by the Synod of Maryland and Virginia and edited by Dr. David F. Schaeffer of Frederick, Maryland. It began in March, 1826, and continued for five years. Its pages, duodecimo in format and about twenty-five in each issue, indicate that many changes were taking place among the people in the Lutheran congregations. In spite of opposition, English had gained much ground as the language of worship. But this pioneer among English periodicals for Lutherans in America had only about half the circulation of its German predecessor, the *Magazin.* The new periodical was aimed at the needs and tastes of the rank and file of Lutheran people. Its general tone indicates that Lutheran readers had moved to a higher level of intellectual interest. Dr. Schaeffer had studied under Dr. Helmuth and inherited some of his pietistic tendencies, but assumed in his readers more theological interest and a broader intellectual range than Dr. Helmuth had earlier expected of his German readers. In addition to items of general interest, local and general church news, synod minutes, and devotional materials, there were doctrinal articles, Christian biographies, essays on Lutheran missions, and narratives of Lutheran history.

It may have been a result of the tercentenary celebration of the Reformation in 1817 that the reader of the *Intelligencer* ten years later was assumed to have a renewed loyalty to Martin Luther, to be interested in Philip Melanchthon, and to manifest the beginnings of antagonism to the "Romish Church" and the "errors of Popery." Moreover, English-speaking Lutherans seemed to be in need of warnings against the threats of Unitarianism and deism. It is clear that most of the people in the Lutheran congregations in this period were more devoted to general Christian causes than to specifically Lutheran causes. Such definite Lutheran organizations as the new General Synod and such distinctive Lutheran institutions as the young Gettysburg Seminary required spirited defense against obstinate critics.

The evangelical awakening that burned over the frontier during the early years of the Republic soon spread eastward across the mountains and became a nationwide revival movement to which Lutherans were not immune, particularly those who used the English language. Repeatedly the pages of the *Intelligencer* reported protracted meetings in Lutheran congregations, periods of special interest and emotional excitement in pulpit and pew, and sudden extraordinary growth in church membership. There was much debate as to the proper methods for Lutherans to use in stimulating these revivals. Sharp distinction was drawn between the traditional method of catechization and the high-pressure appeal to the emotions. One was called "respectable accessions to our congregations," the other was called "the new measures." But the alternate rise and subsidence of special religious interest and activity was generally accepted by American Christians, and Lutherans were no exception.

Another characteristic of the religious life of Lutheran people was the multiple organization of auxiliary "societies." The purpose of these groups within the congregations was to cultivate with special intensity certain phases of the Christian enterprise. Most of the Lutheran pastors and people in America were the heirs of the seventeenth-century pietistic movement in Germany, in which little groups were commonly organized within the congregations for the purpose of stimulating Christian activities, first Bible study, then welfare, and then missions. Lutherans as individuals had early joined the general Protestant organizations for the several forms of Christian work, such as the American Bible Society, the American Tract Society, and the American Sunday School Union. After the organization of the General Synod in 1820, Lutherans were organized locally for participation in these activities, particularly in the congregations of the synods belonging to the General Synod. Under the guidance of pastors, Bible societies, missionary societies and educational societies were organized to stimulate interest, provide information, and gather funds. The Bible societies bought Bibles and distributed them in neglected areas, particularly on the frontier, and often formed Sunday schools and Sunday school societies as adjuncts to the Bible societies. The missionary societies gathered funds to send itinerant missionaries to the frontier and to help build churches there. The education societies directed projects to secure funds for the support of students for the ministry. There were also tract societies and, later, temperance societies. Students in the seminary organized a missionary society among themselves, and during their vacations they were employed by the benevolent agencies, Lutheran or general, to form such societies in Lutheran congregations.

In some cases the membership of these groups was entirely of women and the organization was called by some such name as the Female Missionary Society or the Female Lutheran Society.

In time the several societies organized on a larger scale and supported distinctively Lutheran projects. These larger organizations followed state or synodical lines, but usually without official connection with the synods. The more general organizations were known as parent societies and the local groups as auxiliary societies.

The auxiliary organizations drew bitter criticism, just as the group meetings of pietists in Germany had done, and the meetings of dissenters in England. Opposition meetings were held in Pennsylvania, and German-speaking ministers denounced the benevolent societies as the work of selfish fanatics, indolent swindlers, and puritanical hypocrites who objected to innocent amusements on the Sabbath which were entirely consistent with "rational piety." These critics also included theological seminaries in their condemnation. From Tennessee came the criticism that such societies promoted too much co-operation with non-Lutherans. But the movement spread and before the end of this period benevolent societies were flourishing in six of the seven synods among Lutherans in America.

The promoters of the organizations denounced their critics with equal severity and lauded the societies as the best means of overcoming the obstacles which the German language had presented to the increase of the Lutheran church. The numerous friends of the benevolent auxiliary organizations hailed them as the inevitable moral result of genuine religious revivals, the best evidence of vital religion among the people, the nurseries of true piety, and the real pulse of the spiritual life of the congregation.

These societies are significant as an early form of lay activity in the Lutheran church in this country. On the colonial and on the western frontiers, laymen had taken the initiative in holding services of worship and securing regular ministers. But these societies, flourishing in settled congregations with their own ministers, supplemented services of worship, preaching, sacraments and catechetical instruction with special concern for the practical tasks of Christian benevolence. They enlisted women as well as men. These unofficial societies among the Lutherans in the youth of the Republic laid the base for the official stewardship of devotion and benevolence in the Lutheran churches and agencies of late years.

Of the forms of worship used in the congregations in this period there is little to record. Not much attention was given to liturgy. The service that had been devised by Muhlenberg and his colleagues in 1748 was not published until 1786 and then in sadly altered form. It was translated into English in 1795 but used only in some parts of New York State. In most of the congregations that used English the pastors were left to their own devices in their services of worship. In 1817 the New York Synod published a new liturgy, and the following year the Ministerium of Pennsylvania issued its own, but both reflected the relaxed confessional position of that time. They called for almost no participation in the worship service by the people in the pews. There was no Gloria in Excelsis, no Collect, no Creed, and no Gospel or Epistle for the Day. The liturgy opened with a brief Confession of Sins followed by a prayer and the Kyrie. Then came the reading of a "suitable selection" from the Scriptures, a hymn, the sermon, a free prayer, a closing verse, and the Benediction.

There is no evidence that these liturgies were widely used. The influence of frontier life did not favor formality in worship. Revivalists regularly decried "religion of forms" and lauded "religion of the spirit." Moreover, the influence of rationalism and the necessities of union services with nonliturgical groups militated against liturgical development. And so, for more than half a century after the beginning of the Republic, the services of worship in Lutheran congregations showed little acquaintance with the rich liturgical heritage belonging to the Lutheran church, and they made little use of the fine treasury of hymns cherished among the Lutherans in Europe. The positive developments along these lines waited for another period when the emotionalism and subjectivism of revivals had subsided, when American culture in general began to recover its esthetic perception and its sense of history, and when the church as an institution was more firmly established in the hearts of the people.

When the Republic was only a quarter of a century old, Lutheranism had an opportunity to stand forth as an architect of important parts of the structure of the young nation. The occasion was the three-hundredth anniversary of the Lutheran Reformation in 1817. Although denominational loyalty was still at low ebb among most Lutherans, the tercentenary was widely celebrated. Among Americans in general there was a feeling that the fundamental principles of the American Republic are related to the fundamental teachings of the sixteenth-century reformers. The celebration naturally showed the current tendency to emphasize the broad evangelical teachings common to all Protestants and to exercise restraint with reference to distinctive Lutheran teachings. It also reflected the rationalism of some of the leaders of the Lutheran church.

The New York Synod took the initiative and in 1815 invited the Pennsylvania Ministerium and the North Carolina Synod to help in a general North American celebration. The invitation was accepted and the co-operation consisted in holding simultaneous services of worship on Reformation Day, October 31, 1817, with special music and sermons or addresses on Reformation themes. In New York City two services were held, one in the Lutheran church in the morning when Dr. F. C. Schaeffer preached in German and a Reformed and an Episcopal clergyman assisted in the service; the other a three-hour service in the afternoon in St. Paul's Episcopal Church with at least 5,000 people present, when Dr. Schaeffer preached in English and a

Moravian and two Episcopal clergymen assisted, and special music was provided by the Handel-and-Haydn Society and an orchestra. The New York Synod used the occasion to publish two sermons by its President, Dr. Quitman, which, however, exalted reason with revelation as the sources of Christian truth.

In Pennsylvania the Ministerium invited other Protestant churches to help celebrate the festival: the German Reformed Synod, the Moravians, the Episcopal and the Presbyterian churches. Some of these accepted the invitation, but the initiative in every case seems to have been left to the Lutherans of each community and the people of the other denominations simply attended the special services in the Lutheran churches. In Zion Church in Philadelphia, the eloquent Dr. Helmuth preached and special music was rendered by soloists and choir and orchestra, accompanied by "the largest organ in the United States." The Protestant clergy of the city attended in a body. The large church was completely filled with the festive assembly. In York the choir of the Lutheran church presented a concert of music written especially for the occasion. With its festival program was printed the Augsburg Confession and a sketch of the Lutheran Reformation. The pastor, Dr. J. G. Schmucker, delivered the sermon. At Frederick, Maryland, both the sermon by Dr. David F. Schaeffer and the newly written hymn emphasized the fundamental accord of Zwingli and Calvin with Luther himself.

In North Carolina the celebration consisted of special services by the individual local ministers. The synod recognized the occasion by the publication of a book. The volume is a summary account of the Reformation and the progress of the Lutheran church during the three centuries. It was familiarly entitled *Luther*. The author was Gottlieb Schober, an ex-Moravian who had joined the North Carolina Synod. The little volume was in reality a plea for a general assembly of all Protestant denominations to which the several churches would send official delegates.

The celebration of the Reformation was inspired in part by the knowledge that on the very same day the Lutheran churches all over Germany would be celebrating. The formation during that year of the Prussian Union of Lutheran and Reformed churches by royal decree suggested a parallel union in this country. One of the results of the celebration of 1817 was a series of efforts to establish a joint theological seminary to prepare ministers for both the Lutheran and the Reformed churches. This project failed when the General Synod of the Lutheran church was organized and plans were made to establish a distinctively Lutheran seminary.

A further result of the tercentenary was a series of efforts to fashion a general union of the Lutheran and Reformed churches. It was argued that voluntary action of the two churches could be just as effective in a republic as a royal decree in a kingdom. For a number of years the two churches had been exchanging "fraternal delegates" as voting members at their conventions. At many places, especially in Pennsylvania, congregations of the two churches used the same house of worship. They practiced intercommunion. For five years preceding the tercentenary they had jointly supported the *Evangelisches Magazin.* They were using the *Union Hymnal* which was first published in the tercentennial year and passed through twenty-one editions. In the efforts at organic union that followed the celebrations of 1817, official committees were appointed by both ecclesiastical groups, and for nearly twenty years there was prospect of success. The Pennsylvania Ministerium withdrew from membership in the General Synod in 1823 partly because it feared that such membership would interfere with the proposed Lutheran-Reformed union Negotiations with the Reformed continued until 1836 when a new spirit began to manifest itself in American Christianity. The unhappy results of the Prussian Union became known in this country. At the same time the denominational consciousness of both the Lutheran and the Reformed church began to manifest itself again. So the plans for organic union of the two churches were quietly dropped.

One permanent result of the tercentenary was the increase of interest in Luther and the reformers, the gradual stimulus to Protestant loyalties, and the renewed fear and hostility toward Roman Catholicism. Yet the celebration of 1817 did not have such beneficent long-range effects as those of the Lutheran celebration in America of the quadricentennial of the Reformation.

Part IV

IN A PERIOD OF INTERNAL DISCORD
(1830-1870)

Sectionalism and Sectarianism

CHAPTER 15

GENERAL BACKGROUND

During the first quarter of the nineteenth century the national enthusiasm born of foreign aggressions and internal expansion reduced sectionalism and internal conflict, and the undeveloped West helped to maintain the American balance of power. But after 1830, as the nation expanded to continental proportions, the economic and social implications of the colonial diversity were brought into clear expression. After serving as a field of competition for eastern sections, the West became itself a substantial and separate section of the Union. The social landscape began to show wide diversities in every field of interest.

The manufacturing North, the cotton-raising South, the farming and wool-growing West, each slowly developed an awareness of self-interest and identity. The merchant aristocracy of the East, the planter aristocracy of the South, and the pioneer community of the West, grew constantly more conscious of their peculiar needs. The South began to protest against the protective tariff and the North demanded higher protection. The presidential election of 1824 brought forward the "favorite sons" of the sections as candidates, and the election was thrown into the House of Representatives. Despite these indications of germinating sectionalism, President Adams maintained throughout his administration the policy of a strong national government controlling the interests of all parts of the country. It was left to the administration of Jackson to raise the issue of slavery which hurled the country headlong into a new era. Not until now did sectionalism take slavery as its weapon and consciously oppose the principle of nationality.

The controversies over the annexation of Texas and the admission of California and Kansas, the congressional battle over the right of petition, the doctrine of nullification in the South together with the assertion of state sovereignty and threats of secession, the abolitionism of the North and the Underground Railway, the filibustering expeditions of the South—these gave evidence of deep cleavage between the sections. War, when finally it came, seemed "inevitable."

This was not a revolt of the South against the nation. It was a struggle between North and South over conflicting interests. Nor was this sectionalism healed immediately after the war. The South was treated like conquered territory. A new spirit of nationalism did not begin to evolve until 1870 with the proclamation of universal manhood suffrage. The United States now began that career of unrivaled nationalism on which it might have entered in 1840, had not slavery blocked the way.

During these years church history again moved parallel to politics. Sectionalism was matched by sectarianism. By 1830 the tendency toward union or co-operation among the churches had run its course. The evangelical impulse of the beginning of the century was differentiated and diffused among the denominations. Each had its own methods of doing Christian work, usually inherited from an honorable past and associated with godly and heroic fathers. They sought to serve the God of their fathers after the pattern given to their fathers. Loyalty to one's own church once more came to be regarded as a virtue, and this virtue was emphasized at the expense of love for all Christian brethren.

This brought about a new period in the history of American Christianity. The churches began to recover their historical perspective. There was an increasing interest in the study of church history. During the thirty years preceding 1830 only forty such works appeared, while in the next thirty years there were a hundred and fifty. Denominational histories greatly outnumbered general works.

The sense of mission that had invigorated the American church now indirectly infused new vigor into its component parts, but this time the pendulum swung to dogmatism in religion and ethics. Schism was almost regarded as a virtue, and the result was often an angry parting of allies, as well as internal discords, divisions, and strife.

The spirit of controversy and factionalism in American Christianity was reinforced by thought-patterns imported from Europe. The Church of England was being stirred by the Oxford Movement with its emphasis upon historic forms and its trend toward Rome. At the same time a large school of Lutherans in the churches of Germany were returning to orthodoxy, and the Scandinavian Lutheran churches were assailed by loud advocates of a return to seventeenth-century Lutheranism. Likewise, in the Roman Catholic Church in Europe this period is characterized by a revival of the Jesuits, whose activities led to the decree of the immaculate conception and on to the dogma of papal infallibility.

Heresy trials abounded, and party feeling, running high in every sphere, expressed itself dogmatically. Protestants not only withdrew from general Christian organization into their own churches and denominations, but even proceeded to further disputes and separations. The human spirit was highly sensitive and combative in all its interests. Acrimonious debates occupied pulpits, stages of theaters, and pages of public print. Preachers studiously cultivated a rhetoric of paradox and hyperbole so as to astonish their hearers, inflame their passions, and stir their prejudices. The great immigration that swept into the Mississippi Valley and beyond, fed the competitive energies of rival denominations which left permanent deposits in buildings and institutions to bear witness to the sectarian intolerance of this "Middle Age" of American Christianity.

Many new sects arose between 1830 and 1850 to contribute divergent currents to the stream of religious life. Such were Mormonism, Spiritualism, Millerism, and Adventism in its various subdivisions. Even so unlikely a place for controversy as the Unitarian denomination took up the sword against the Universalists and the pantheists in its own ranks. The Quakers had a friendly dispute on matters of doctrine and the Hicksites withdrew from the Orthodox. Among the older and larger churches all the distinctions of former times were recovered and intensified and in most cases internal divisions were born.

In the first place there was a sharp differentiation and even warlike antagonism between Protestants and Catholics. American Catholicism was reverting to her true historical position and soon ceased to have any dealings with Protestants. But Protestantism as such had also awakened and had begun an active war on her old enemy. Rome was fiercely denounced by tongue and pen. And it was not merely a battle of pulpits and pamphlets. Numerous acts of violence against Roman

Catholics were committed in various quarters. Monstrous slanders were circulated. The zeal of the anti-Romanists was shown by the outrage upon the convent at Charlestown (Mass.), by acts of incendiarism in Maine, by bloody riots in Philadelphia, and by bloodshed in Kentucky. The kindly disposition manifested toward Rome during the earlier period has never returned.

The Roman Catholic Church, of course, maintained her external appearance of unity, but her inner harmony was marred by many a discord. Sharp conflicts in all parts of the country arose over "trusteeism," that is, the demand of the laity in the Catholic Church to manage the church property. The administrative abilities of the American bishops were put to a sharp test and more than one congregation was put under interdict before the laity could be forced to submit. The issue continued to vex the peace of the church for more than three decades until in 1854 trusteeism was finally eliminated. The harmony of the Roman Church was further menaced by the jealousies of the various orders among the monks and by the antagonisms of the different races and nationalities among the laity.

The Protestant Episcopal Church too incurred the distrust and dislike of other churches. The high church party began to predominate over the low church party, thus strongly emphasizing the distinctive feature of this communion. In 1832 action was taken to exclude from Episcopal pulpits ministers who had not taken Episcopal orders. Then came the Oxford Movement within the church, and accusations of Romanism from without, and the practical isolation of the church from all co-operation with others.

The close federation of the Presbyterians and Congregationalists in the famous "Plan of Union" was now broken. The doctrinal conservatism of the Presbyterians and their difference in polity from the Congregationalists led the Old School majority of the General Assembly in 1837 to abrogate the Plan of Union and to withdraw from co-operation with the Congregationalists in missions and in ministerial education. The Congregationalists, after the dissolution of the Plan of Union with the Presbyterians, divided on the administration of benevolences, and Hartford faced Yale. At the same time questions of orthodoxy and of church polity led the Old School Presbyterians to cut off the New School Presbyterians who constituted four-ninths of the body. Each of these two bodies split again just before the war into North and South.

Both Methodists and Baptists began to assume sharply defined denominational attitudes and to withdraw from the unionistic benevolent societies into their own denominational organizations for benevolence. Then, when the Methodists in the South found that slaveholders could not become bishops, and when the Baptists in the South found that slaveholders would not be employed as missionaries, these two churches also split into North and South.

In 1844 the German Reformed Church also began to rally from the effect of the evangelical movement and to manifest the natural influence of that movement in the renewed energy of its own proper life. Its spirituality was deepened and its Christian activity enlarged. And in the next ten years this church became more conscious than ever before of its denominational character and mission. In this case the stimulus came from the so-called Mercersburg movement and its able leaders, Dr. Nevin and Dr. Schaff. The result was a long, fierce struggle within the church nearly ending in schism, and a bitter quarrel with her ecclesiastical twin-sister, the Dutch Reformed church.

In the Lutheran church, after her disastrous experience with evangelicalism, the revival of denominational consciousness ran parallel to that in other churches although here again somewhat belated. By 1850 the return to historical Lutheranism was well under way. The Lutherans began to withdraw from co-operation with other churches in benevolence. As early as 1841 Heyer had refused to go as a missionary under any but Lutheran auspices and henceforth there were Lutheran missions. In 1845 the Home Missionary Society of the General Synod was organized. Similar Lutheran organizations in other spheres of benevolence followed rapidly.

In matters of doctrine also the day of indifferentism among Lutherans was over. Doctrinal hostility to the Synod of North Carolina and to the newly formed General Synod had led the Henkels to form the Tennessee Synod, and the fires of hostility burned hot during this period. The Joint Synod of Ohio, once favorably inclined toward the Reformed church in that state, in this period reverted strongly to historic Lutheranism, so that for nearly a century it was unable on account of its conservative and confessional standpoint to form a lasting union with any of the larger general bodies of Lutherans. In

1839 there arrived in Missouri a group of Saxon Lutherans imbued with a double portion of the spirit of confessionalism. Their fiery zeal for the whole body of Lutheran doctrine was made even more intense by the ardor of their piety. This union of denominational zeal and religious fervor gave extraordinary power of propagandism, so that the few shiploads of Saxon pilgrims grew into one of the largest of Lutheran bodies, the Missouri Synod, and helped to raise the general standard of confessional loyalty in this country. It was in 1839 also that a body of "Old Lutherans," separatists from the Prussian Union in Germany, came to this country and shortly thereafter formed the Buffalo Synod.

The revival of Lutheran consciousness was partly the result of new vigor imparted to all American Christianity by the religious movement earlier in the century. It was due in part to a renewed interest in the history and doctrines of the Lutheran church, and in part to the immigration of rigid confessionalists from Germany and the Scandinavian lands. But this confessional reaction quite naturally led to internal controversies long continued and acute, and in its conflict with the laxity of the former period it led to further divisions of general bodies. In this respect the history of the Lutheran church runs significantly parallel to that of other denominations and that of American society in general. The era of disruption in the church corresponds to the era of sectionalization in the history of our country.

CHAPTER 16

ORGANIZED BENEVOLENCE

Most of the work of applying Christianity in benevolence at home and spreading it through missions abroad had been done hitherto by great national societies binding Christians of various names. Now, with the recovery of denominational loyalties, the work of the gospel in all its departments and in all lands was seen as the function of the individual church body. One by one the churches withdrew from the interdenominational organizations, which, for the most part, permanently disappeared from American Christianity. The denominations pursued the practical tasks of Christian love by organizing their own separate agencies. Within a few decades these agencies of benevolence were stimulating further competitive spirit among the denominations and their fractions. In the Lutheran church, benevolent and missionary operations developed steadily until at the close of the period they were thoroughly organized and active.

A principal development was in the work of home missions. Before the organization of the General Synod in 1820, the work of caring for scattered members of the Lutheran family proceeded slowly, hampered by the lack of men and of organization. The task devolved upon individual pastors or churches, and later upon separate synods unprepared for the enterprise. Most of the synods, as they came into being, sent out one or two missionaries each year on preaching tours among the vacant pastorates or the spiritually unguided communities in various parts of the country. This work, at great sacrifice on the part of the missionaries, accomplished much good, particularly by calling attention to the need and thus attracting pastors to the pioneer communities. But this unorganized work was desultory and often ineffective.

Even after the organization of the General Synod, with an express purpose of planning for "missionary institutions," the prevailing dis-trust of centralized authority delayed the development of missions for fifteen years. Then in 1835, the "Central Missionary Society of the Evangelical Lutheran Church in the United States" was formed by a convention of Lutheran ministers called by the General Synod. The new society met at the same time as the General Synod but had no official status, since its membership was individual and not representative. It undertook to establish a "system of societies throughout the Church." In 1837 it reported that it had employed six missionaries. Its chief work was that of C. F. Heyer, who explored the Mississippi Valley, traveled thousands of miles to discover fields for at least fifty missionaries, and finally settled in the Pittsburgh area. Other missionaries of the society served in Boston, western Pennsylvania, Ohio, Indiana, and Illinois.

A similar society connected with the Pennsylvania Ministerium worked in harmony with the Central Missionary Society. Ezra Keller, afterwards founder of Wittenberg College, was for a time the missionary of the Ministerium and reported in 1836 that he had traveled three thousand miles through western Virginia and Ohio into Kentucky, Indiana, and Illinois. He laid the foundations for many churches flourishing there today.

The Central Missionary Society, however, failed to receive the support of the synods and its work ceased. The work for the Pennsylvania Ministerium lagged on account of the attention paid to the new enterprise of foreign missions. But in 1845 the sentiment for more adequate organization crystallized in the formation of the "Home Missionary Society of the General Synod" with auxiliaries within the district synods. It had no valid authority to act for the church as a whole, yet for more than twenty years it carried on the general home missionary operations of the General Synod section of the church, receiving and disbursing several thousands of dollars annually and aiding hundreds of missionaries in many different states.

As the institutions at Hartwick and Gettysburg furnished increasing numbers of young ministers able to preach in English and adaptable to the changing conditions of American life, these pushed out into new mission fields. Their expansion of home missionary work during this period resulted in the organization of a number of new synods whose names indicate the successive stages in the expansion of the church and the westward movement of her organization. The Allegheny Synod was organized in 1842 and the Pittsburgh Synod three years later. The East Ohio Synod had been formed in 1836, the Synod of Miami in 1844, the Wittenberg Synod in 1847, and the District Synod of Ohio in 1861. In Indiana the Olive Branch Synod was organized in 1848 and the Northern Indiana Synod in 1855. The Northern Illinois Synod came into being in 1851 and that of Central Illinois in 1862. The Synod of Iowa dates from 1855, the Canada Synod from 1861, the Synod of Kansas from 1868, and the Synod of Nebraska from 1871. In the South, the Southwestern Virginia Synod was formed in 1842, the Texas Synod in 1851, the Mississippi Synod in 1855, the Georgia Synod and the Holston Synod in 1860. Meanwhile the territory of Pennsylvania was further divided and the East Pennsylvania Synod began in 1842, the Central Pennsylvania in 1855, the Susquehanna in 1867. Nearly all of these synods ultimately found their way into the General Synod. The organization of the Pittsburgh Synod in 1845 with its missionary zeal and its apportionment system, and the founding of Wittenberg College and Seminary that same year as a literary and theological center for the newly formed synods in Ohio, gave great impetus to the home missionary efforts of the General Synod.

Meanwhile the feeling grew that the Home Missionary Society should be bound up organically with the life and prestige of the General Synod. This delicate change was begun in 1866 when the constitution of the society was amended to make all the delegates to the General Synod members of the society. It was completed in 1869 when the society transferred all its funds and interests to the General Synod, and the General Synod assumed direct control of its home missions and committed their administration to a board as its representative. Thus was established the important principle that missionary work is the church's own proper business. The board as the agent of the entire church directed the work for the entire church, administered funds received from all parts of the church, and applied them to the entire field as the need and opportunity demanded and without regard to synodical bounds or the measure of synodical contributions.* This method of organized benevolence continued in use throughout the remaining half century of the General Synod's life and it is the practice today in most of the larger bodies of Lutherans in this country.

The development of foreign missions followed similar lines. The Central Missionary Society had as one of its objects "ultimately to co-operate in sending the gospel to the heathen world." The call to definite action on the foreign mission project came through the strong appeals of the celebrated C. F. A. Gutzlaff of China and the indefatigable C. L. E. Rhenius of India. A convention in 1837, held in connection with the meeting of the General Synod, organized "The Foreign Missionary Society of the Evangelical German Churches in the United States." That title was used in the hope of drawing all Germans, Lutheran and Reformed, into the society. The Ministerium of Pennsylvania was represented but the Reformed and Moravians declined to co-operate, so the title was changed from "German" to "Lutheran." The society formed auxiliaries in the various synods and gathered funds to help Rhenius at Palamcotta, India. Rhenius had been laboring under the Church Missionary Society of England, but his strong Lutheran convictions had led to his dismissal from the service of the Anglicans and his subsequent appeal to Lutherans throughout the world. Through the efforts of the Lutheran Foreign Missionary Society in America substantial aid reached his hands.

In 1840 the society decided to send its own missionary to India and appointed C. F. Heyer. He had been interested by the reports of those first Protestant missionaries who had gone out from Halle to India. But when the society decided to transact its business through the American Board of Commissioners, "Father Heyer," as he was called, resigned the appointment, declaring that he did not want to "be dependent on other Christian denominations." The day of interdenominational agencies was indeed passing. Heyer offered himself to the Ministerium of Pennsylvania, which had maintained a separate missionary organization. After some hesitation this body accepted the responsibility, and Heyer sailed for India in October, 1841, the first foreign missionary sent out by the American Lutheran church. He began work at Guntur. Two years later he was joined by Walter Gunn and wife, who had been sent out by the general Foreign Missionary Society.

The work in India made steady progress and new missionaries were sent out from time to time. The Pennsylvania Ministerium co-operated with the society of the General Synod. In 1850 the Rajahmundry field was accepted from the hands of the North German Missionary Society, which was in financial straits. In 1857 Dr. Heyer retired from the field and devoted himself to home missionary work in Minnesota. But in 1869, after the General Council had been formed, Heyer, although seventy-seven years old, returned to India, just in time to organize the Rajahmundry field under the auspices of the General Council and thus prevent its delivery to the Church Missionary Society in England. That same year the General Synod decided to assume direct responsibility for the work of the Foreign Missionary Society both in India and in Liberia, Africa, where a mission had been started by Morris Officer in 1860. A board was appointed to have charge of the work, as had been done in the case of home missions, and so this department of benevolence was finally organized under the direct care of the church.

In 1853 a Church Extension Society was organized in much the same way as the Home Missionary Society and the Foreign Missionary Society. Its purpose was to give strength and permanence to the missions of the church by granting them loans without interest. The aim from the beginning was to raise a fund of $50,000. Only one-fourth of that amount had been secured by 1869. Then the work was committed to a board elected by the General Synod. This opened a new era in the work of church extension and this agency of benevolence was one of the chief means of advance in the General Synod.

In this same period the foundations were laid for the organized eleemosynary work of the church. The founder of the Pittsburgh Synod, W. A. Passavant, inspired by Pastor Fliedner of Kaiserswerth, Germany, took the lead in establishing institutions of mercy. He began in 1849 with a hospital in Pittsburgh, followed by an orphanage at the same place, later transferred to Zelienople and then to Rochester, Pennsylvania. That same year he brought some Lutheran sisters from the Kaiserswerth institutions and thus introduced the Protestant order of deaconesses into this country. Hospitals were founded in Milwaukee, Chicago and Jacksonville, Illinois, and orphanages at Mt. Vernon, N. Y., Germantown, Pa., and Boston, Mass. Altogether Passavant secured more than a million dollars for his Lutheran institutions of mercy.

Further evidence of the growing spirit of benevolence and increasing loyalty to the Lutheran church in this period was the establishment of a number of new educational institutions. A college was started at Gettysburg, Pa., in 1827, to prepare men for the seminary there. Wittenberg College and Seminary were founded in 1845. The South Carolina Synod had begun a seminary at Lexington in 1830 and from this educational beginning came Newberry College in 1856. The Ohio Synod began its seminary at Canton in 1830 but the next year removed to Columbus. There in 1850 a collegiate department was established as Capital University. Roanoke College in Virginia was founded in 1853 and North Carolina College at Mount Pleasant, N. C., in 1858. Meanwhile the westward expansion of home missions led to the establishment of Illinois State University in 1852, and from this came Carthage College in 1870. Difference of opinion within the General Synod led to the founding of the Missionary Institute (now Susquehanna University) at Selinsgrove, Pa., in 1858. Toward the close of this period organic division in the ranks of the General Synod resulted in the establishment of the Philadelphia Theological Seminary in 1864 and of Muhlenberg College in 1867.

A number of church periodicals came on the scene during this period to foster the operations of the church, to furnish light on all manner of religious and theological topics, and to add heat to the controversies of the times. During the preceding period several attempts had been made to establish official or synodical journals. Such were *Das Evangelische Magazin* of the Pennsylvania Ministerium (1811), *The Lutheran Intelligencer* of the Maryland Synod (1826), *The Lutheran Magazine* of the Western Conference of New York (1827), and *Das Evangelische Magazin* of the West Pennsylvania Synod (1829). None of these lasted more than six years. But such was the ecclesiastical zeal during the period now under review that at least five journals beginning at this time have been able to maintain themselves to the present day, or until merged in larger undertakings. The first of these was the *Lutheran Observer* begun in 1831 by Dr. J. G. Morris of Baltimore. Except for a few years in the possession of the Maryland Synod, it was privately owned, and it became the organ of less conservative elements in the General Synod. In 1843 at New Philadelphia, Ohio, Dr. Emanuel Greenwald began the *Lutheran Standard*, which still survives as the official weekly of the American Lutheran Church. Dr. Passavant of Pittsburgh, unable to purchase the *Observer*, in 1848 began publishing the *Missionary* to foster appreciation of historical Lutheranism. This was merged in 1861 with the Philadelphia *Lutheran*, which had been founded in 1856. This paper was the popular English spokesman for conservative Lutheran thought and practice in this period, and for many years carried the scholarly articles of Dr. Charles Porterfield Krauth, who was also its editor for several years. The *Evangelical Review*, begun at Gettysburg in 1849, is the oldest theological magazine of the Lutheran church in this country. After 1872 it was called the *Lutheran Quarterly*, and in 1928 it merged with the *Lutheran Church Review* to become the *Lutheran Church Quarterly* (merged in 1949 with the *Augustana Quarterly* under the name of *Lutheran Quarterly*). For a long time it was the chief source of Lutheran theology for the English-speaking part of the church.

While all of these periodicals reflected the controversial spirit of their times, they nevertheless contributed immensely to the growth of Lutheran loyalty, the fund of Lutheran information, and the progress of the organized benevolence of the church.

In all these lines of benevolence and literary activity additional luster was given to the chronicle of Lutheran achievements in this period by large and aggressive bodies of Lutherans newly arrived from Europe and now favorably located for the most part on the broad expanse of the Mississippi Valley. These also we must consider if we would understand the general course of Lutheran history in this period of internal discord.

CHAPTER 17

IMMIGRATION AND CONFESSIONAL REACTION

From the denominational rivalries and antagonisms of this period a very substantial asset accrued to the kingdom of God. The sharpening of loyalty prepared the churches to meet the sudden rush of immigration, greater than the entire population of the Republic at its birth, that now spread itself over a great domain four times the size of the original colonies.

To transform this alien multitude into American citizenship and gather it into the fellowship of the Christian churches, the utmost zeal on the part of the churches was demanded. Certainly the torpid uniformity of the preceding period would not have availed. Only the spontaneous vigor of a multitude of agencies, each built on church loyalty and invigorated by denominational zeal, each forging its own distinctive weapons, could have accomplished the wonder of American church history, the gathering in of these millions of immigrants.

❧ The great immigration of the period was caused both by the allurements of America and by the hardships of Europe. Inviting the immigrants were a liberal homestead policy, easy naturalization laws, the loud call for labor, the facility of transportation, and the discovery of gold in California. Driving them from Europe were repeated failure of crops, the overpopulation of the farming districts, the destruction of local trades and industries through the new factory system, misgovernment, and the forced military service to great and petty European rulers. In addition, some groups fled religious conditions in the homeland, and some individuals joined friends who were already prospering in America. Conditions promoting immigration to America had peculiar force in Germany, especially after the middle of the century. A little later a strong tide of immigration set in from the Scandinavian countries. The result was an enormous increase in the Lutheran population of America.

German immigration began to increase about 1840, and reached a peak in the decade preceding the Civil War, when nearly a million Germans reached American shores. After the war they continued to come, about 130,000 annually. Many of these German immigrants were Roman Catholics, or swelled the number of the churchless and godless in the new land. But the greater portion of them were Lutherans. The new arrivals imposed an enormous responsibility on the Lutheran church in America and profoundly impressed every aspect of her history. Her numerical strength, her standing among the churches, her influence on the life of the nation, her benevolent and educational activities, her doctrinal position—all were deeply and beneficially changed by the new arrivals in her midst. During the first forty years of the Republic, the communicant membership of the Lutheran church had multiplied threefold, just keeping pace with the increase of population. But during this second forty years, while the population at large was increasing threefold, the membership of the Lutheran church increased more than ninefold, reaching in 1870 a total of about 400,000, and placing the Lutherans fourth among the Protestant churches.

Fortunately for the church, the advance guard of the army of Lutheran immigrants were stoutly loyal to the Lutheran confessions and able to give reasons for their faith. It was equally fortunate that this advance guard planted its outposts in the heart of the Mississippi Valley where the vast majority of the newcomers were to find their homes. The older Lutheran elements, of the Muhlenberg line, had for the most part solved their problems of rationalism and unionism, had developed their synodical organizations, and were prepared to absorb the new arrivals. But of themselves they would never have met the responsibility imposed by the great immigration. The majority of the incoming multitudes were to belong to an entirely different branch of Lutheranism in America, which was destined to help along the confessional reaction that had already begun within the bodies of Muhlenberg descent.

This new accession to the Lutheran church in America came into the country chiefly by way of the Gulf of Mexico and the Mississippi

River. The earliest arrivals settled in Missouri at St. Louis and in Perry County, about 110 miles south of St. Louis, in February, 1839. St. Louis became the gate of entrance for the German immigration and the headquarters for shepherding them into congregations. The first group of newcomers, from Saxony, were in flight from the rationalism of the official church there, and were characterized by intense pietism and strict Lutheran orthodoxy. Their leader was Martin Stephan, a powerful preacher and a man of remarkable personality and great organizing ability. As pastor of St. John's Church in Dresden, feeling himself hampered by his ecclesiastical connections, he decided to gather a company of followers and emigrate. Encouraged by Dr. Benjamin Kurtz, who was in Germany to collect money for the Gettysburg Seminary, he determined to lead his company to America. A glowing description of Missouri which he happened to read fixed his choice on that state as his location.

In Stephan's company there were five other ministers, ten candidates for the ministry, a number of teachers and professional men, merchants, craftsmen, laborers, and farmers—a total of 612 souls. Their spiritual motivation is made clear by the "Emigration Regulations," signed by all before leaving Germany, which might be called their "Mayflower Pact": "All the undersigned acknowledge with sincerity of heart the pure Lutheran faith as contained in the Word of God, the Old and New Testaments, and set forth and confessed in the Symbolical Books of the Lutheran Church. After deliberate and mature counsel, they can, humanly speaking, see no possibility of retaining in their present home this faith pure and undefiled, of confessing it and transmitting it to their posterity. Hence they feel in duty bound to emigrate and to look for a country where this Lutheran faith is not endangered and where they can serve God undisturbed in the way of grace revealed by Him and where they can enjoy fully and without interference or modification the means of grace ordained by God for men unto salvation and can preserve them in their integrity and purity for themselves and for their children. . . . Such a country as they are looking for is the United States of North America; for there, as nowhere else in the world, perfect religious and civil liberty prevails."

Even before the company reached America, however, their leader had fallen into doctrinal error and into immorality. Gradually developing hierarchical tendencies which moved him in the direction of Roman conceptions of the church and the ministry, he assumed the title of bishop, and pledged many of the pilgrims to implicit obedience to him in both spiritual and business affairs. Very shortly after the Saxons arrived in Missouri, Stephan was convicted of "defalcation and gross wickedness," and he was expelled from the colony.

In the disgrace and confusion that followed, the leadership of the Missouri Lutherans fell to the youthful C. F. W. Walther, one of the six pastors of the first group of immigrants. From 1839 to his death in 1887 the history of Missouri Lutheranism is closely identified with the story of Walther's life, and he takes his place with Muhlenberg, Schmucker, and Krauth in the quartet of the most outstanding personalities in the history of the Lutheran church in America.

Walther was born in Saxony in 1811 of a long line of ministers. At the University of Leipzig, he belonged to a little band of students who refused to accept the popular rationalism of the day and who cultivated their spiritual lives by studying the Bible and various books of devotion, among them Luther's works, which he read with eagerness. He became pastor at Braeunsdorf, Saxony, in 1837. Here his evangelical position soon involved him in difficulties with his rationalistic superiors. The oath of his office bound him to the Book of Concord, but the entire liturgy, the hymnbook and the catechism that he was compelled to use were rationalistic. So too were the textbooks in the schools. His conscience was sorely oppressed by the situation. His efforts to introduce Lutheran doctrine and practice met with determined opposition. The young pastor's position was intolerable. Accordingly he had welcomed most heartily the invitation to help establish an ideal church in America.

But in Missouri the exposure and banishment of their leader plunged the colonists into great distress. Some of the pastors, Walther among them, began to doubt their call to the ministry. They had followed a false guide. How could they justify their course before the world and before their own consciences? Some thought they should return to Germany. Many of the colonists felt that it was contrary to God's will that they had come to America. They doubted that they were really Christians or that the true church of Christ existed among them at all. Divisions began to appear among them. The confusion and distress of conscience were indescribable. Furthermore Stephan had squandered the money in the general treasury and poverty stared them in the face.

It was Walther who saved the colonists from complete despair. Having continued his study of Luther and the Lutheran theologians, he was ready, early in 1841, to clarify the issues. By a series of propositions which he successfully maintained in debate he showed that the church consists of an invisible communion of saints, that where the true faith is, there the true church is, irrespective of the continuity of human organization. Consequently, he maintained, these congregations of the colonists must be regarded through their knowledge of the Christian truth as part of the true church of Christ, and as having full authority to call pastors. This not only eased the minds of the colonists but also established the fundamental principles of church organization which characterize the Missouri Synod to this day.

A few weeks after this disputation Walther accepted the call to the congregation in St. Louis, which was to become the mother church of the Missouri Synod and the mainspring of all its activities in missions and benevolence. Here he gained a high reputation as a preacher. But soon his talents were called to educational and executive tasks. In 1844 he began publication of *Der Lutheraner* to defend the church of the Reformation against attack and to expound the doctrines and principles of Lutheranism. Vigorously polemical, the paper purposed "To reveal the false and misleading teachings that are current today, to refute them and warn against them, and especially to unmask those teachings that falsely call themselves Lutheran but under this name spread error, unbelief and fanaticism, and thus arouse against our Church the worst kind of prejudice in the minds of people in other denominations." The paper had also constructive purposes on behalf of confessional Lutheranism. *Der Lutheraner* attracted wide attention to Walther and his work and to the doctrinal positions of the Lutherans in Missouri.

As German immigration continued to increase, steps were taken in 1845 to form a new synod, and two years later, at Chicago, Walther became the first president of the "German Evangelical Lutheran Synod of Missouri, Ohio and other States." This organization, numbering at first only twelve congregations and twenty-two pastors, soon became one of the largest and most vigorous bodies of Lutherans in America. At the time of Walther's death in 1887, the synod numbered about fifteen hundred congregations and nearly a thousand ministers, while *Der Lutheraner* had a circulation of nearly twenty thousand.

The confessional basis of the new synod was stated to be all the symbolical books, as "the pure and uncorrupted explanation and statement of the Divine Word." Parochial schools were established, and every possible safeguard was erected to maintain purity of Lutheran faith and practice. Representation in the synod was by congregations and no synodical resolutions were in force until ratified by the congregations. Inspection of congregations by district presidents was provided for. The constitution and the entire spirit of this influential body came from the mind and heart of its youthful first president.

Meanwhile there came other streams of Lutheran immigrants, like in spirit to the Saxons of Missouri. Some helped to organize the Missouri Synod in 1847 and the Synodical Conference in 1872, but most of them held aloof or separated from the Missourians to organize independent synods. Their history we must now sketch.

In 1817 the King of Prussia began efforts to unite the Lutherans and the Reformed into the "Prussian Union." He succeeded only in reviving differences between the two confessions. And when a royal decree of 1830 abolished the old church books and sought to enforce a uniform liturgy that was neither Lutheran nor Reformed, some of the most orthodox Lutherans separated from the state church. Called "Old Lutherans," they were persecuted in Prussia, and many emigrated to America. The first company came in July, 1839. Their leader was J. A. A. Grabau of Erfurt. They numbered nearly a thousand and settled in and near Buffalo, New York, and Milwaukee, Wisconsin, a few months after the Saxon Lutherans had reached Missouri.

Hopes that some union might be effected between these two groups of orthodox Lutheran colonists ended in December, 1840, when Pastor Grabau sent a pastoral letter to vacant congregations warning them against ministers who had not been properly ordained. Walther detected here the same false views of the ministry and of the church as those whose fatal consequences he had witnessed in Stephan. This and other errors of the Buffalo Lutherans he regarded as thoroughly Romanizing. A long and bitter controversy raged between the two pastors and their followers. In 1855 the Missouri Synod at Walther's suggestion founded the monthly theological journal, *Lehre und Wehre*, which Walther edited and used as his chief medium of discussion. The

113

Missourians succeeded in convincing a considerable number of pastors and congregations among the "Prussian Lutherans" and in 1867 a majority of their pastors joined Missouri. The conflict became caustic. Although the Buffalo Synod, organized in 1845, had begun to train its own pastors in rigid doctrine and discipline, it did not grow very rapidly, and now barely succeeded in holding the descendants of the original colonists. Some of its pastors and congregations joined the Wisconsin Synod.

Another independent body, the "Synod of Iowa and Other States," organized in 1854, was a breach in the ranks of the Missourians. Wilhelm Loehe, pastor at Neuendettelsau, Bavaria, was interested in developing the Lutheran churches in America, and began to prepare men for the ministry here. His graduates entered the service of the Missouri Synod. But Walther and his brethren discovered in the writings of Loehe and in the views of his followers the same errors concerning the church and the ministry that they had so long debated with the Buffalo men. Walther and one of his colleagues went to Germany in 1851, conferred with Loehe, and temporarily averted an open breach.

Grabau also visited Loehe, and in 1853 Loehe gave his consent for his emissaries, Pastors G. M. Grossmann and John Deindoerfer, and twenty of his adherents, to leave the Franconian colonies in Michigan and migrate to Dubuque, Iowa. There in 1854 they organized the Iowa Synod. They feared that the extreme congregationalism of Missouri would overthrow all church order, but they could not agree with the extreme hierarchical position of the Buffalo pastors. The Iowa Synod took a middle position. They protested against the Missourians' "legalistic misuse of the symbols." They adhered firmly to all the symbolical books, but insisted that there are certain "open questions," that is, scriptural doctrines that are not clearly defined and therefore should not prevent fellowship of pulpit and altar among differing Lutherans. The brothers Sigmund and Gottfried Fritschel were early leaders, and the Dubuque Seminary the main source of ministerial supply of the Iowa Synod, whose work soon extended over a very wide territory.

The Missouri Synod from the very beginning established educational institutions, prepared its own pastors, and avoided dependence on European ministry. The modest "institution of instruction and education" that they began in St. Louis in 1839, a few months after their arrival, was a well-equipped college by 1850, with Walther as president and professor of theology. In 1861 the preparatory school was removed to Fort Wayne and in 1874 a practical seminary was organized at Springfield, Illinois. The theological department remained at St. Louis where it has become the largest Protestant seminary in America. In 1850 Walther retired from the presidency of the synod to give all his time to writing and teaching, and the influence of his magnetic personality was felt widely.

By this time the Missouri Synod, representing a more conservative Lutheranism than that of the older bodies of the East, had spanned the country and become the rallying point for the German pastors of new waves of immigration. They came from all parts of Germany, and those from the North soon outnumbered the Saxons. The University of Göttingen was as well represented as Leipzig. Many of the newcomers to the synod were highly educated, many were filled with missionary zeal. As the center of ultraconservative Lutheranism, the synod also attracted a number of older American congregations with their pastors. Its districts increased until they covered the whole country with a thorough organization. It soon occupied all the strategic points in the great Middle West, had strong outposts in the very centers of the older bodies in the East, and was looking toward the Northwest and the Far West.

Walther's successor as president of the synod was F. C. D. Wyneken. Wyneken had studied theology at Göttingen and Halle, traveled widely, and learned the English language. He heard of the spiritual "destitution" of the German-speaking Lutherans in America, and in 1838 came as a missionary. He accepted service for the Missionary Committee of the Pennsylvania Ministerium as a traveling missionary to the Lutherans on the western frontier. After three years of heroic work in Indiana and Michigan, he returned to Germany, and won many friends for his American cause and many missionaries for the field. Wyneken's first knowledge of the Missouri Lutherans came in 1844 with the first issue of *Der Lutheraner*. "Thank God!" he exclaimed, "there are still some Lutherans in America." He severed his connections with the General Synod and entered the Synod of Missouri, where he soon became one of the most eminent leaders. To Wyneken's enthusiasm and zeal the Missouri Synod owed large numbers of its recruits from Lutheran churches of Germany as well as the co-operation of Wilhelm Loehe.

The third master builder of the Missouri Synod was Wilhelm Sihler. Born in Silesia, son of a Prussian military officer, about ten years older than Walther and Wyneken, with a doctorate from the University of Berlin, he first came in contact with pastors of pronounced Lutheran convictions as an instructor at Dresden. He gave up his rationalistic views and, responding to Wyneken's appeals, came to America in 1843. He began preaching at Pomeroy, Ohio. Like Wyneken he learned to know Walther through *Der Lutheraner*, and in 1845 severed his connection with the Ohio Synod and became Wyneken's successor at Fort Wayne. He took part in the conferences leading to the formation of the Missouri Synod and became its first vice-president. Dr. Sihler wielded a vigorous pen, and wrote extensively, for forty years championing confessional Lutheranism. He led in the practical activities of the Missouri Synod, presided over Concordia College at Fort Wayne, and helped to establish there the Practical Seminary which is now at Springfield, Illinois.

Of the conservative Lutherans who came to America and found their way into the older congregations and synods of the East, many ignored Wyneken's and Sihler's example and, remaining where they were, made vigorous contributions to these less conservative bodies. A number of influential Württembergers joined the Pennsylvania Ministerium and helped to deepen the current of confessional loyalty. More of the North Germans went into the New York Ministerium, with a similar result. Others, imbued with a lively Lutheran consciousness, came from Germany and took their places in less conspicuous sections of the General Synod.

Another stream of Lutheran immigration in this period that helped to swell the tide of confessional reaction came from the Scandinavian countries. The great volume of Scandinavian immigration came later, but the beginnings are here.

Norwegians in the late thirties began to settle in northern Illinois, came during the next decade in greater numbers to southern Wisconsin, and in the fifties spread across the Mississippi to northeastern Iowa. These immigrants came not so much for religious reasons as for better material conditions and a more free and independent life. From 1836 to 1842 only a few hundred came each year. Most of them were farmers and sought homes in the Middle West. In 1843 the number of immigrants from Norway rose to 1,600 a year. Because of unfavorable economic conditions in Norway in 1847, the annual number rose to more than 4,000, and so it continued until the outbreak of the Civil War in America.

The spiritual condition of these immigrants reflected the wide variety of religious points of view flourishing in Norway at that time. Alongside of confessionalism, state-church loyalty, and indifference, there were elements of rationalism, pietism, puritanism, anti-clericalism, Quakerism, and Mormonism.

The first Norwegian Lutheran settlement in America was established by eighteen families who came in 1834 to the Fox River Valley, La Salle County, Illinois, about sixty miles southwest of Chicago. Most of these Lutheran settlers were followers of Hans Nielsen Hauge, a determined lay evangelist who incited opposition to the clergy of the Norwegian state church. Hauge's type of evangelism was promoted in acute form in Illinois by Elling Eielsen, who arrived in 1839 after seven years of free-lance lav evangelism all over the Scandinavian countries.

The Norwegian colonists who came to Wisconsin in 1839 and settled at Muskego, twenty miles southwest of Milwaukee, and at Koshkonong, fifty miles farther west, were also low-church Lutherans and followers of Hauge, but they were milder in their attitude and not opposed to the clerical office. After a few years in America they beckoned for ministerial help from Norway. Claus Lauritz Clausen, a young Danish volunteer for missionary work, came in 1843 to Muskego. Early the next year J. W. C. Dietrichson settled at Koshkonong.

By this time there were settlements also in Illinois at Chicago (1836), Leland (1836), Rock Run (1839), Lisbon, Queen Ann, and Long Prairie (about 1841), and in Wisconsin at Beaver Creek (1837), Jefferson Prairie (1838), Rock Prairie (1839) and Hamilton (1841). Most of the settlers in the Fox River settlement had come from Stavanger in Norway where there were many Quakers of the revolutionary type and much animosity against the clergy and office-holding class. In the Wisconsin settlements the immigrants had come from Voss, Numedahl, and Telemarken, where there had been social revolution but where the people had retained their respect for their pastors.

Pastor Dietrichson, one of a family accustomed to leadership, ordained by Bishop Sörensen at Oslo, undertook to organize the Norwegian Lutherans in America along state church lines. He developed a standard form of organization for congregations and a constitution for a proposed synod whose doctrinal basis resembled that of the Missourians. The specifications of doctrine and polity set down by Dietrichson laid the essential foundation of church life among Norwegian Lutherans in America.

But a new synod was not organized at once. It was prevented by resistance to Dietrichson's domineering personality and his exalted ideas of his office, until after his return to Norway in 1850. Then a new leader, Herman Amberg Preus, in 1853 completed the organization of "The Norwegian Evangelical Lutheran Church of America," afterwards changed to "The Synod for the Norwegian Evangelical Lutheran Church in America." It embraced seven pastors and seventeen congregations. Preus was strictly orthodox, and determined to purge out all traces of Hauge's influence and that of the Danish reformer Nikolai Grundtvig. The doctrinal basis was the ecumenical creeds, the Unaltered Augsburg Confession and Luther's Small Catechism. It was specified that ministers must be ordained only after proper examination and call.

The Joint Synod of Ohio invited the new Norwegian body to affiliate, and to establish a professorship in the seminary at Columbus. But the pastors and some of the laymen of the Norwegian Synod, reading Walther's *Lutheraner*, began to question the quality of Ohio's Lutheranism. In an effort to solve the problem of training men for the ministry, the Norwegian Synod sent a commission to visit the seminaries at Buffalo, Columbus, and St. Louis, and, on its report in 1857, unanimously resolved to establish its theological professorship at St. Louis. This was regarded as a temporary arrangement to provide pastors immediately; it would, however, also "bring the Synod into contact with a church-body established on a truly Lutheran foundation." Before the Norwegians established their own seminary in 1876, one hundred and twenty-seven of their pastors had come from the Missouri Synod seminary. Moreover, there was co-operation between the two bodies in missionary work among the Indians, and both had helped to form the Synodical Conference. Any hopes which the

Joint Ohio Synod may have had for leadership in middle western Lutheranism were now shattered.

In the meantime the low-church element of Norwegian Lutherans, centering in the Fox River settlement in Illinois, the Haugeans under the leadership of Elling Eielsen, had effected an organization of their own. Eielsen had gradually overcome his prejudice against what he called "constitutional claptrap," and in 1846 at Jefferson Prairie, Wisconsin, he and his followers formed a loose organization which was called at first "the Evangelical Lutheran Church of North America," later the "Eielsen Synod." This was the oldest synod among Norwegian Lutherans in America.

When, during the next two years, Eielsen stubbornly disregarded the provisions of the constitution, his younger co-workers in 1848 read him out of the synod and themselves looked about for new associations. One of the young leaders, Paul Andersen of Chicago, had received his college education in the Congregationalist school at Beloit, Wisconsin, and had only vague ideas of Lutheran doctrine. His colleague, Ole Andrewson, had been ordained by the liberal Franckean Synod in western New York. Both of these men, like Esbjörn before them and Hasselquist afterwards, received financial aid from the American Home Missionary Society (Congregationalist). For a few years after the break with Eielsen these two men, together with Ole J. Hatlestad, were members of the Franckean Synod. This synod carried on missionary work in Wisconsin, and the Norwegians were attracted by its aggressive opposition to slavery. But the main body of the Franckean Synod was far away, its fellowship limited, and its doctrinal position liberal. So in 1851 the three Norwegian pastors joined with Lars P. Esbjörn, a Swede still liberal in his views, and with their congregations participated in the organization of the Synod of Northern Illinois, a district of the General Synod. Then as the leaven of confessionalism continued its work, they became dissatisfied with the fellowship of the General Synod and in 1860 withdrew from the Synod of Northern Illinois and united with the Scandinavian (Norwegian and Swedish) Evangelical Lutheran Augustana Synod of North America.

Another breach in the thin ranks of the Eielsen Synod came in 1856. With the aid of Peter Andreas Rasmussen, who had just come from Norway as a school teacher, Eielsen called his friends together at Koshkonong in 1850 to reorganize under the Old Constitution of 1846. The body soon came to be called Eielsen's Synod. Rasmussen studied theology for a year under Sihler in the Missouri Synod's seminary at Fort Wayne, and in 1854 was ordained by Eielsen's Synod to be pastor at Lisbon, Illinois. He was an eloquent preacher and a skillful writer. Because of his aversion to any semblance of hierarchical organization, he soon became involved in violent controversy with Preus of the Norwegian Synod on doctrinal questions, particularly concerning the church and the ministry. But in 1856 Eielsen began to suspect Rasmussen himself of high-church tendencies and frankly voiced his suspicions. When Eielsen rejected the proposal of Rasmussen and his friends to impose certain restrictions on lay preaching, the Rasmussen faction, more than half of the little synod, separated from Eielsen. This left only five ordained pastors in the Eielsen Synod, formally named the Evangelical Lutheran Church in America. After six years of groping for wider fellowship, the Rasmussen group of pastors and congregations united with the Norwegian Lutheran Synod, cherishing the hope that Hauge's piety might dwell together peacefully with Norwegian orthodoxy.

Still another division among Eielsen's followers resulted in 1876 from dissatisfaction with the Old Constitution of 1846. It denied church membership to anyone who could not give clear proof of genuine conversion, and it placed the Apostles' Creed and the Augsburg Confession on an equality with the Word of God. A majority of the members in 1876 approved a revision of the Old Constitution on these points and changed the name of the body to "Hauge's Norwegian Evangelical Lutheran Synod in America." Eielsen and a few of his pastors refused to be bound by this action and were dismissed from Hauge's Synod. They retained their organization under the Old Constitution and the old name, and their successors continue to this day as "The Evangelical Lutheran Church, Eielsen Synod," with five pastors, twelve congregations, and 1,350 baptized members. Eielsen continued as president of the synod that bears his name until his death in 1883. But Hauge's Synod was the true successor of the organization formed in 1846, and it continued its separate existence until the great Norwegian Lutheran merger in 1917.

In 1870 the Norwegians who had joined the Synod of Northern Illinois ten years earlier withdrew to form the new Scandinavian

Evangelical Lutheran Augustana Synod of North America with only twenty-four pastors and thirty congregations. But they could not agree on their organization. Should it be a conference, to emphasize the independence of the congregation, or a synodical type of church government with considerable powers of legislation? The group which favored a free association of congregations was led by Professor Weenaas and Pastor C. L. Clausen, who had withdrawn from the Norwegian Synod on the ground that it was "priest-ridden." This group with fourteen pastors organized "The Conference of the Norwegian-Danish Evangelical Lutheran Church in America." The others, nine pastors, led by Pastor O. J. Hatlestad, organized as "The Norwegian-Danish Augustana Synod."

The Norwegian Lutheran Synod with its 74 pastors, its 335 congregations, and its 75,000 members in 1870 was easily the dominant organization among Norwegian Lutherans in this country. As their numbers grew through continued immigration from Norway and through missionary expansion in the Middle West, the Norwegian Lutherans developed new controversies in theology, particularly with the Missouri Lutherans. They also made amazing progress in the unification of their forces. But this belongs to the second generation of Norwegian Lutheranism in America and to a later date.

Swedish immigration during this period, becoming significant in the 1840's, brought to America less variety of faith and practice than the Norwegian. The Swedes kept in closer touch with the Americanized part of the Lutheran church.

The causes of the emigration from Sweden were complex. There was overpopulation in some areas, and restricted availability of land. Industries were crowding out the trade guilds and the free craftsmen. Life was burdened with humiliating class distinctions, limited franchise, and compulsory military service. Public schools and improved education brought impatience with political and social restrictions. The many alluring accounts of America, the land without aristocrats, the land of unlimited opportunity and freedom, had produced a veritable "American fever" at the beginning of the fifth decade.

In the Church of Sweden also there was unrest. The evangelical movements agitating the religious circles of other countries found fertile soil in Sweden. Pietists from Germany, Methodists from England, advocates of "lay activity" from Norway, temperance reformers from America, all combined to foster the sentiment of separatism from the church and emigration from the country. The evangelical ferment led not only to movements for moral reform but also to the wide distribution of Bibles and tracts, active interest in foreign missions, conventicles of lay people for cultivating their spiritual life, and movements for social reform. A minority of the pastors in the state church favored the evangelical movements. The theological faculty at Uppsala was sympathetic with the evangelical view of the church as "the priesthood of believers," but the faculty at Lund held to the hierarchical or new-Lutheran view of the church. The efforts of political and ecclesiastical authorities to stem the tide of the evangelical movements by repressive measures was one of the reasons for the exodus to America in the middle of the nineteenth century.

The beginnings of Lutheran church life among the new Swedish immigrants to mid-America were in Jefferson County in southeastern Iowa, about fifty miles west of Burlington. Here five pious families from Sweden settled in 1845 and called the place New Sweden. The settlement grew, and in January, 1848, the seventeen families organized a Lutheran congregation. As pastor, they pressed into service a devout and fluent young shoemaker, M. F. Hokanson. In succeeding years additional groups of Swedish Lutherans settled in that part of Iowa, and across the Mississippi at Galesburg and still farther northeast at Andover in Henry County, Illinois.

The autumn of 1849 brought the first ordained pastor. He settled first at Andover, but his extensive ministry in all these Swedish settlements earned him the title, "The Prairie Shepherd."

Lars P. Esbjörn had received his theological training at Uppsala. For seventeen years he had served as schoolteacher and pastor in Sweden. During his pastorate at Hille he experienced what he called a spiritual awakening. One result was a deep interest in missions. He also came into close contact with the English Methodist, George Scott, and the American temperance worker, Robert Baird. He felt attracted to America with its "religious freedom and its congregations organized as voluntary associations of believers." He traveled throughout Sweden lecturing on temperance. He was outspoken in his criticism of clergy and professors, and he incurred much personal enmity. Through letters from friends already in America he learned of the great spiritual need among his countrymen there and offered his services to the Swedish Missionary Society, which was more unionistic and less high-church than the newly organized Lund Missionary Society. With about 150 other immigrants, and after many difficulties, he arrived at New Sweden October 24, 1849.

Esbjörn found the Swedish settlements thoroughly discouraged. Cholera and other sickness had taken an awful toll of life. Poverty prevailed everywhere. Many of the people had been lured off by the Methodist brothers Hedström. There was great need for spiritual guidance. In March, 1850, Esbjörn organized a Lutheran congregation with ten charter members. He visited other settlements in Illinois with his ministry of comfort, including Galesburg, Berlin, Rock Island, and Princeton.

Knowing little about Lutherans in other sections, he applied to the American Home Missionary Society (Congregational) and there received salary support. But soon there were other contacts. During the summer of 1850, W. A. Passavant of Pittsburgh and W. M. Reynolds of Capital University at Columbus made a "missionary journey" among the Norwegian and Swedish settlements of "the West." On their return Passavant published in his paper *The Missionary* a ringing appeal for work among the Scandinavian Lutherans. He proposed the printing of information about their needs, missionary chaplains at New York and other seaports to distribute useful tracts among these Lutheran newcomers and furnish them guidance, a Scandinavian professorship to train pastors for them, and the organization of a Scandinavian synod. Passavant forecast quite accurately the position that Scandinavians have attained in the Middle West during the past century.

On Passavant's invitation Esbjörn visited the East in 1851, secured funds for his work, and made the acquaintance of a number of American Lutherans. He also learned of Paul Andersen in Chicago and other Norwegian Lutheran pastors. Soon he was traveling about among the Swedish settlers in Iowa and Illinois, bringing them the gospel and the sacraments and spiritual ministry. He was repelled from the Methodists by the fact that so many of them were slaveholders. He saw also that the aggressive proselytism of Jonas Hedström would destroy the Lutheran church among the Swedish settlers. This threat and the effects he saw of sectarianism and subjectivism on the frontier, clarified and deepened his Lutheran convictions. He was impressed with the fact that there were already eight Lutheran synods in America with about two thousand congregations and that they were moving perceptibly toward confessional Lutheranism. As he had opportunity he discussed with the Norwegian Lutheran pastors Passavant's suggestion for a Scandinavian synod. When the Northern Illinois Synod was organized in 1851, Esbjörn and his congregations at Andover, Galesburg, and Moline became members. For linguistic reasons the Swedish congregations formed their own Mississippi Conference within the synod. Esbjörn took a leading role in the affairs of the synod, and joined with the conservative group of that body in making reservations concerning the confessional statements of the General Synod.

Five years after the organization of the Synod of Northern Illinois it decided to set up a Scandinavian professorship of theology at the Lutheran school in Springfield called the University of Illinois. Esbjörn was unanimously chosen to fill it, and began his teaching in 1858. But at Springfield and throughout the synod tensions developed rapidly, confessional tensions, linguistic tensions, and personal tensions in the faculty and among students. The Scandinavians were proceeding rapidly with the sharpening of their confessional consciousness, and the older faction in the General Synod was pointing up its "American Lutheranism." Suddenly in 1860 Esbjörn and his family quit Springfield for Chicago. At the meeting of the Synod of Northern Illinois that spring, all the Scandinavians withdrew from membership in the synod. The exodus included exactly half of the ministers on the roll and more than half of the lay membership in the congregations.

Meanwhile other church leaders had arisen among the Swedish Lutherans. Chief among these was Tuve Nilsson Hasselquist. Early in his ministry in America, Esbjörn had persuaded the congregation at Galesburg to send a call to this earnest evangelistic preacher at Skäne and he had arrived in America in October, 1852. Like Esbjörn he was a pietist and puritan, an ardent evangelical, and a diligent pastor, willing to endure hardship and opposition for Christ's sake, but unlike Esbjörn he was modest, decisive, learned, a product of Lund, a conservative biblical scholar, and a skillful writer. He was destined to become the foremost leader among these Swedish Lutherans, as preacher and synodical president, as editor, and as college and seminary president.

After Hasselquist's arrival only three more pastors came from Sweden before the Augustana Synod was organized in 1860. These were Erland Carlsson, Jonas Swensson, and O. C. T. Andren. Others were trained in Sweden but ordained in America, among them Eric Norelius, Andrew Andreen, P. A. Cederstam, and Peter Sjoblom. These men and their congregations all joined the Synod of Northern Illinois, where they greatly outnumbered the Norwegians.

When Esbjörn and the other Scandinavians withdrew from the Synod of Northern Illinois because of the conflict with the liberal element of the General Synod, each side had already learned much from the other. The Scandinavians had been introduced to the practical methods and procedures of a synodical type of church polity, and the men of the General Synod had been impressed with the swelling tide of conservative Lutheranism in the Middle West. While the General Synod men, or some of them, continued for a few years their efforts to stem the tide, the Scandinavians proceeded to organize a synod on the American pattern. At Jefferson Prairie, near Clinton, Wisconsin, in June, 1860, a new synod was formed by twenty-seven pastors and thirteen laymen. The laymen represented about 5,000 communing members of 62 congregations, 49 of them Swedish and 13 Norwegian. Most of the Norwegians did not join this synod but looked toward Missouri. The new synod was called The Scandinavian Evangelical Lutheran Augustana Synod of North America. The name was a broad one, but not its theology. The word "Augustana" in the title was intended to make sure of the confessional position of the new body, which was stated to be "the unaltered Augsburg Confession as a short and correct summary of the principal Christian doctrines, understood as developed and explained in the other symbolical books of the Lutheran Church." The constitution, prepared by Esbjörn and Paul Andersen, showed that a long step had been taken in the process of Americanization. Hasselquist was chosen first president of the Augustana Synod and so continued for ten years.

The Augustana Synod at once provided for a stream of trained ministers from American homes. The college and seminary was established at Chicago in September, 1860, with Esbjörn as its head. When, after three years, Esbjörn resigned and returned to Sweden, the institution was removed to Paxton, Illinois, where Dr. Hasselquist became its president. Here, and at Rock Island after 1875, Hasselquist continued as the head of the college and seminary for thirty years. By his teaching, preaching, and writing he became the most influential leader the Augustana Synod has had.

The union of the Swedes and some of the Norwegians in the Augustana Synod continued until 1870. But the laymen and the congregations, both Swedish and Norwegian, did not share the co-operative spirit of their pastors and church leaders. New congregations, as they were formed, followed nationalist lines. The Norwegian element in the new synod soon became conscious of its own problems. They set up the "Norwegian" chair in the seminary at Paxton in 1868 and called August Weenaas, a patriotic and pietistic young scholar from Norway. Next they received the consent of the synod to establish their own school. They also had the problem of relationships with the Norwegian Lutheran Synod and the independent Norwegian Lutheran congregations. So, after ten years of association with the Swedes in the Scandinavian Augustana Synod, the Norwegians withdrew and, with the Danish Lutherans, formed the Conference for the Norwegian-Danish Evangelical Lutheran Church in America. This left the Augustana Synod a purely Swedish organization.

⁕ Another immigration, this time from Finland, began about the middle of the century. The first to come were fishermen from northern Norway who settled in the "copper country" of northern Michigan. The Finnish immigrants were occupied with mining, logging, and farming. The first Finnish Lutheran congregations were organized in 1867 at Hancock and Calumet, Michigan. Among them were a few Swedes and Norwegians, and for many years they had a Norwegian pastor. The first ordained Finnish minister was Alfred E. Backman, who took charge of the congregations at Hancock, Calumet, and Allouez in 1876.

During the next twenty years the Finnish settlements spread to Minnesota, the Dakotas, and even to Oregon. In 1889 four Finnish ministers decided to organize the Finnish congregations into a synod, and in 1890 with their nine congregations held a first convention at Calumet and joined forces as The Finnish Evangelical Lutheran Church of America, or The Suomi (Finnish) Synod. The Rev. J. K. Nikander was the first president.

The Suomi Synod has 102 pastors, 68 of whom are serving its 153 congregations of about 36,000 baptized members. With a strict Lutheran basis, the synod uses the liturgy of the Church of Finland, either in the original or in English. Its polity is congregational, and executive authority derived from the congregations is vested in a consistory of four members who are the officers of the synod. The synod maintains a college and seminary at Hancock, Michigan. It does its foreign mission work in Southwest Africa and China through the Finland Missionary Society, but in 1950 it began its own work in Japan.

The great Lutheran immigrations in the nineteenth century, with their strong infusion of confessional elements into America, stamped the whole Lutheran church here as indelibly evangelical and forever doctrinally conservative.

But the confessional development among Lutherans in America during the middle of the century was not caused entirely by the immigrants. They did not initiate it, they only helped to swell the tide of confessional loyalty that had its source earlier in a renewed study of the church's confessional writings. Loyalty to historical Lutheranism had never disappeared. The deterioration in liturgy and hymnbook that took place between 1786 and 1817 had been concessions to the spirit of the times, recognized and deplored by many pastors and laymen. The 1792 change in the constitution of the mother synod eliminating all confessional tests and avoiding mention of the Augsburg Confession or the other symbolical books was a sign of spiritual torpor on the part of church leaders. But the constitutions of the congregations continued to specify the Unaltered Augsburg Confession as expressing the faith of the people. Even among the leaders there were always some outspoken confessors, some who regularly lifted their voices against the current of rationalism and unionism. Express renunciation of the distinctive doctrines of Lutheranism never had the assent of a majority of the pastors or people. The Augsburg Confession was put into the professorial pledge at the seminary in Gettysburg in 1826 and into the ordination vow which Professor Schmucker wrote into the constitution for district synods of the General Synod in 1829. In 1849 the *Evangelical Review* began publication at Gettysburg to inform English readers, especially pastors, of theological developments and thus counteract the influence of Dr. Kurtz in the *Lutheran Observer*. It was edited by Dr. William M.

Reynolds the first year and after that by Dr. Charles Philip Krauth of the seminary faculty. About the same time Dr. William A. Passavant, a graduate of the seminary, began to publish a weekly, *The Missionary*, in protest against the positions of the *Observer* and in support of traditional Lutheranism.

The Henkel press in Virginia published Lutheran pamphlets in German and English from 1806 on, and finally in 1851, after seven years work, completed an English edition of the Book of Concord. It is a clear indication of the new spirit that was arising in the General Synod that this English book found a ready acceptance in all parts of that body. Many copies were bought in Pennsylvania and Ohio. The professors and students in the seminary and college at Gettysburg studied it. So also did Dr. Reynolds and Dr. Lehmann and their students of Capital University and its Theological Department at Columbus, Ohio. The South eagerly welcomed it. Three years later, when a second edition was called for, its preparation enlisted the help of such men as Charles Philip Krauth at Gettysburg, W. F. Lehmann of Columbus, Ohio, J. G. Morris of Baltimore, and Charles F. Schaeffer of Easton, Pennsylvania.

West of the Alleghenies also there were many evidences of growing confessional loyalty. As early as 1820 the Tennessee Synod, formed in protest against the "un-Lutheran teaching and practice" of the North Carolina Synod, was based doctrinally on "the Holy Bible . . . and the Augsburg Confession of Faith as a pure emanation from the Bible." In 1827 this synod declared in favor of all the symbolical books of the Lutheran church "as a directory in theology." The Ohio Synod, organized through the Henkels in 1818, exerted constant influence in the direction of conservative Lutheranism.

In 1830 the Tennessee and Ohio Synods held special services celebrating the tercentenary of the Augsburg Confession. Two years later they published and distributed thousands of copies of Luther's Catechism, many of them carrying also the Augsburg Confession. At the same time the Ohio Synod undertook to establish its own synodical paper to counteract "the prevailing spirit of the religious papers which either advocate the cause of new measures and fanaticism or vacillate like Lot's wife." When in 1842 the paper began to appear it was called *The Lutheran Standard* and its purpose was stated "to explain and meekly to defend the doctrines and usages" of the Lutheran church "as exhibited in the Augsburg Confession of faith and as believed and practiced by our pious forefathers." In 1836 the synod, asked concerning its attitude toward the symbolical books of the Lutheran church, adopted a resolution stating that "this Synod strictly adheres to the Augsburg Confession and admits no one to membership in its body who shall deny any part thereof, and that all congregations within its synodical boundaries be advised to receive no one as a teacher who does not fully adhere to this Confession."

The dates of these moves are significant. The tide had begun to turn from confessional indifference to confessional loyalty even before the new immigrants from Europe, having organized and overcome the barriers of language, had influenced the older body of Lutherans. The confessional reaction among the "Muhlenberg" Lutherans corresponds in time with the sharpening of denominational consciousness in other Christian groups in America.

The General Synod felt the confessional reaction in all its parts. In Germany, the revolt against the Prussian Union inspired many pens whose products, bristling with Lutheran orthodoxy, were eagerly read by hundreds of American Lutheran ministers either in the original or in translations that appeared on the pages of the *Evangelical Review*. German theology was studied and Lutheran history expounded even outside the Lutheran church, and this reacted profoundly on the English-speaking portion of the Lutheran church in this country. Walther's writings in the *Lutheraner*, widely read and discussed, clearly pointed the way back to historic Lutheranism. Loehe's *Church News from North America* frankly criticized the liberal element in the General Synod and praised the growing party of conservative Lutherans. Everywhere staunch advocates of "old Lutheranism" arose. Of course the movement towards historical Lutheranism encountered some stout resistance, and resulted in all kinds of internal discord, but whenever the issue was clearly joined, the result always favored the Lutheranism of the Augsburg Confession and the other symbolical writings. Conservative principles spread like a contagion, and the rising generation of ministers soon caught it. Men spoke of the period as "the present transition state of the church," and such it was.

An effect of immigration, with the large and sudden increase in Lutheran numbers, was to compel the other churches to recognize the

Lutheran church as one of the most important and by far the most rapidly growing of the Protestant churches in this country. These new Lutherans took their places quietly in the new land, where their genuine spirituality, the solidity of their church life, and the vigor and warmth of their piety, were patent to all. They were untrained in the habits of free churches and humbled both by the circumstances of their emigration from Europe and by their strange surroundings when they arrived. But their training in the equable, systematic, and methodical ways of state churches, and their constant emphasis on thorough religious instruction and indoctrination, insured them against the irregular fervor of that revivalism that periodically burned over their neighbor churches and helped to guarantee their independence and permanence in their adopted land. If they had much to learn of church organization and administration, they also had much to teach American Christianity of methods of theology and usages of worship, and of solidly conservative denominational loyalty.

CHAPTER 18

"AMERICAN LUTHERANISM"

The rising tide of positive confessional Lutheranism met opposition in some of the older bodies of the Muhlenberg descent. The confessional movement found its antithesis in what was called "American Lutheranism." This was a Lutheranism that was strongly modified by the puritan element of American Christianity and was unable to shake off the denominational indifferentism that had prevailed in the youth of the Republic. Failing to see that the conservative type of Lutheranism would restore to the church something of the ardor and earnestness of Muhlenberg and his colaborers, the "American Lutherans" felt that such a strong infusion of historic Lutheranism would tend to divest the church of spirituality and aggressiveness. They proposed a modification of historic Lutheranism, its confessions and its practices, so as to infuse into it the vigor of Presbyterianism and the warmth of Methodism. In short, they sought to adapt Lutheranism to American soil by divesting it of its distinctive traits and making it conform to the average American type of religion.

The advocates of "American Lutheranism" were a small group, always in the minority both in the district synods and in the General Synod, but they were exceedingly active and aggressive and their leaders were among the most influential men in the General Synod. They refused to be silenced by the growing strength of the conservatives.

The real test of strength between these antitheses within the General Synod came about the middle of the century. The conservative wing had been growing steadily, and by 1850 was clearly in the ascendancy, as European observers noted. Besides the powerful conservative influences of the new Lutheran bodies in the West, several factors favored the increase of traditional Lutheranism in the General Synod

The Book of Concord, translated into English by the Henkels of the Tennessee Synod, was widely circulated and studied. Influential men were reading the contemporary literature of Germany, particularly the writings of the rigid Lutheran theologians opposed to the Prussian Union. Schmid's *Dogmatic Theology* was studied and a translation into English was begun. Church papers were founded to feed the appetite for positive Lutheran literature. The *Evangelical Review*, edited after 1850 by Prof. Charles Philip Krauth of the Gettysburg Seminary, was an effective medium for presenting sound Lutheran theology to English readers. The *Lutheran Standard* of Columbus, Ohio, was firmly pleading for fidelity to the confessions. Dr. Passavant's paper, *The Missionary*, carried many convincing theological articles from the pen of Dr. Charles Porterfield Krauth.

The result of these influences was the dominance in the General Synod of the conservative party. In consequence, some of the men who had sustained the General Synod in the twenties as a bulwark of Lutheranism, a defence against unionism and rationalism, now reacted against the position assumed by the majority in that body. They constituted what was called "the left wing of the General Synod."

One of the leading advocates of "American Lutheranism" was Dr. S. S. Schmucker, the head of the Gettysburg Seminary. We have already seen how zealous he was in his early ministry for the Lutheran church and the Augsburg Confession. His enthusiasm for the General Synod in its infancy, his energetic exertions to save that body from dissolution in 1823, his translation of Storr and Flatt's *Biblical Theology*, his many literary labors to make the Lutheran church known to those beyond her bounds, his activities in establishing and directing a theological seminary and a college for the more adequate training of a native American ministry—all these are unmistakable evidences of his loyalty to the Lutheran church and his merit in maintaining her identity in this country in those critical times. The professor's pledge which he prepared for the constitution of the Theological Seminary in 1825 and the model constitution for district synods which he drafted for the General Synod four years later, show that in his confessional position at that time he was more positively Lutheran than most of his contemporaries. For several decades his great influence was exerted on behalf of conservatism.

But there were elements in Dr. Schmucker's disposition and training that made it impossible for him to keep ahead of the confessional advance that came in the forties and fifties. In his father's home he had acquired a distinct pietistic strain. Under Dr. Helmuth's instruction he had imbibed an aversion for sharp theological definitions. At Princeton Seminary, where he studied for two years, his training measurably influenced his theological views, and his associations there, while they stimulated his zeal for his own church, nevertheless produced a broadmindedness and tolerance toward non-Lutherans that clashed with the spirit of denominational exclusiveness prevailing about the middle of the century. In 1838 he issued his "Fraternal Appeal to the American Churches," calling for the reunion of the churches on "the apostolic basis." He was prominently identified in 1846 with the formation of the "Evangelical Alliance," a union of individual Christians to promote religious toleration and to counteract Romanism and infidelity. That same year he helped to send a circular letter to Germany disparaging the Lutheran view of the Lord's Supper and indicating points of similarity between the General Synod and the Prussian Union. More and more his public utterances indicated his dissatisfaction with the general trend of events in the Lutheran church in America and emphasized "the religion of the spirit" as against the "religion of forms." Dr. Schmucker had fallen behind in the progress of conservative Lutheranism and had lost his leadership in the General Synod. Even in his own institutions at Gettysburg more conservative elements began to prevail. His position had not changed from that of twenty-five years before, but he now became a leader of the opposition to the confessional movement. His role alienated many of his former friends and clouded the evening of his days.

Other leading advocates of "American Lutheranism" were Dr. Benjamin Kurtz and Dr. Samuel Sprecher. Dr. Kurtz was the stormy petrel of the movement, a keen debater and vigorous writer. As editor of the *Lutheran Observer* from 1833 to 1861 he exerted a tremendous influence on the English-speaking portion of the church. During these years the pages of that paper brought repeated arraignments of Lutheran positions, particularly the Lutheran confessions. Even the Augsburg Confession was subjected to serious criticism. All liturgical worship was denounced as formalism. Revival methods were zealously advocated, and personal piety was exalted above everything else.

Those who opposed these so-called "new measures" were called "head Christians" and "catechism Christians." Dr. Kurtz was sure that "proscriptive intolerance" lay on the side of what he called the "Old Lutheran System" and to this he opposed the "evangelical" methods of "American Lutheranism."

Dr. Sprecher had been trained by Dr. Schmucker and adopted the theological views of his teacher. A brilliant teacher and more profound thinker than either Schmucker or Kurtz, and president of Wittenberg College for twenty-five years, he exerted a far-reaching influence on behalf of the "new measures" and a modified Lutheranism. The institutions at Springfield, Ohio, were quite pronounced in their advocacy of "American Lutheranism" as they were without any of the conservative influences that counteracted the teaching of Dr. Schmucker at Gettysburg.

These advocates of confessional modification and radical measures had a vigorous following. Their main contention was that the Lutheran church could develop on American soil only by adjusting itself to its environment. By this they meant that the Lutheran church in America must make wide concessions to the revivalistic and puritanic spirit of the surrounding denominations. The party of "American Lutheranism" was strongly repelled by the sharp polemics of the Missouri, Iowa, and Buffalo Synods. Their contact with the anti-religious element among the German immigrants, particularly those who came in the revolutionary year of 1848, persuaded them that a Lutheranism imported from Germany needed to be strongly modified before it could flourish in America. In its emphasis on Americanism and its attitude of concession toward other denominations this movement was a generation late, but in its controversial spirit it was thoroughly up to date. Harsh criticisms were uttered. Unlovely epithets abounded. But the issues at stake were fought through to a conclusion. A real problem was involved. It was the problem of accommodating Lutheranism to the American spirit. It is well for subsequent history that both sides of the controversy were so ably represented before the decision was reached. It gave a degree of finality to the decision.

The growing strength of the "conservatives" increased the activities of the "liberals." The Hartwick Synod was formed from the western conference of the New York Ministerium in 1830. One reason for the break was that the Ministerium did not sufficiently favor revivals. In the doctrinal basis of this synod as set down in 1837, the Augsburg Confession was modified to conform with the teaching of "all Protestant communions." But, even so, the Hartwick Synod was not sufficiently pious and "American" for some of its members, and as early as 1837 four of them separated and organized the Franckean Synod. This new body abandoned the Augsburg Confession entirely and pressed the "new measures" to the extreme. As it occupied the same territory as the Hartwick Synod the result was a number of bitter lawsuits between the two. The Franckean Synod long afterward became the occasion of disruption in the General Synod.

Efforts were also made to turn back the confessional tide in the older synods and in the General Synod. Dr. Kurtz, a member of the Maryland Synod, tried in vain to commit that body to the "new measures." There was much uncertainty about the official position of the General Synod. The confessional basis it recommended to the district synods was "that the fundamental doctrines of the Word of God are taught in a manner substantially correct in the doctrinal articles of the Augsburg Confession." But great liberties were taken with the words "fundamental" and "substantially correct" and "doctrinal." In order, therefore, to give definition to the pledge of the General Synod, Dr. Baugher, a decidedly conservative Lutheran and afterwards president of Gettysburg College, proposed in 1844 that the Maryland Synod prepare an "Abstract of Doctrines and Practices of the Evangelical Lutheran Synod of Maryland." Its avowed purpose was to correct "various and repeated misrepresentations concerning the doctrines and practices of the Lutheran Church in the United States." But Dr. Kurtz got control of the committee appointed to prepare the "abstract," and the synod refused to adopt the report of his committee because it represented a modified or "American Lutheranism" and omitted or repudiated all distinctive Lutheran teachings.

Both Dr. Schmucker and Dr. Sprecher were deeply interested in the Maryland Synod "Abstract." When the following year the issue was submitted to the General Synod, Dr. Schmucker was made chairman of a committee to frame "a clear and concise view of the doctrines and practices of the American Lutheran Church." But the General Synod no longer followed Dr. Schmucker's lead, and the report of his committee, submitted in 1850, closely resembling the Maryland Synod "Abstract," was rejected by the General Synod.

Meanwhile the church in general continued to move in the direction of a stricter confessional basis. In 1853 the Pennsylvania Ministerium applied for readmission to the General Synod, after an absence of thirty years, and was admitted. The old Ministerium had moved far toward a confessional position since 1823 and had recently come to "acknowledge the collective body of symbolical books as the historico-confessional writings of the Evangelical Lutheran Church" though giving special pre-eminence to the Unaltered Augsburg Confession and Luther's Small Catechism. The cordial welcome of the Pennsylvania Ministerium into the General Synod was another proof that the General Synod was making progress toward more advanced confessional ground. The return of the mother synod and the admission at the same time of the Pittsburgh Synod, the Synod of Northern Illinois, and the Synod of Texas gave still greater strength to the conservative element in the General Synod.

The advocates of "American Lutheranism" now made their last stand. Before the General Synod could proceed to amend its constitution and clarify its confessional basis, now subject to many interpretations, a small pamphlet called the "Definite Synodical Platform" appeared anonymously in September, 1855, and was sent to many of the pastors. It was a revision of the Augsburg Confession, and the synods were urged to adopt it as their confessional basis. It found a number of "errors" in the Augsburg Confession, and these it specified as follows: the approval of the mass, private confession and absolution, denial of the divine obligation of the Sabbath, baptismal regeneration, and the real presence of Christ's body and blood in the Lord's Supper. The articles containing these "errors" were to be modified or omitted. The "Definite Platform" claimed, because it did not omit any "fundamental doctrine of Scripture," to be in accord with the General Synod's basis.

The authorship of the "Definite Platform" was not hard to guess. Dr. Schmucker afterwards acknowledged it. The reception accorded the document greatly disappointed its sponsors. Only three small synods in Ohio, influenced by Dr. Sprecher, accepted it temporarily. Everywhere else it was vigorously rejected. Dr. Kurtz stoutly defended it in the *Observer* but to no avail. Everywhere writers and debaters arose to defend the Augustana. Books were written and conferences were held, even among the newer Lutherans of Missouri and Ohio. One after another the district synods of the General Synod expressed unqualified disapproval of the attempt to revise the creed of generic Lutheranism. "American Lutheranism" was doomed. The episode emphasized the conservatism and Lutheran orthodoxy of the General Synod at that time.

When Dr. Kurtz found himself unable to resist the conservative doctrinal tendency of the Maryland Synod, he withdrew from that body in 1857 and with several kindred spirits organized the Melanchthon Synod. The "declaration of faith" for this new synod consisted of the doctrinal standards of the Evangelical Alliance with slight modifications. The name of the new body is significant. Years later Dr. Sprecher, who lived to acknowledge the mistake of "American Lutheranism," said of the "Definite Synodical Platform" that it was "the culmination of Melanchthonianism." Such it was. The organization of another synod in the territory of the Maryland Synod merely on the basis of "elective affinity" was "American Lutheranism's" declaration of ecclesiastical nullification and secession.

The Melanchthon Synod lasted eleven years. At its largest extent it embraced only eleven country pastorates, in central and western Maryland. It was admitted to the General Synod in 1859 but only because Dr. Charles Porterfield Krauth, the leading theologian among the conservatives, in order to maintain the numerical strength of the general body, advocated its admission. The Melanchthon Synod was, however, warned against schism and asked to withdraw its implied charges against the Augsburg Confession. The synod complied. A few years later, however, the General Synod broke ranks over this compromise.

The issue was settled. "American Lutheranism" was definitely defeated. The leading advocates of a modified Lutheranism, or Melanchthonianism, with all their great personal influence, were in a hopeless minority. After the incident of the "Definite Synodical Platform" their influence waned rapidly. It was the registered conviction of the great host of Lutherans in America that Lutheranism can live and flourish in this country without giving away its own spirit or adulterating its own original life and character. The future of the Lutheran church in America was to belong to the conservative type of Lutheranism. It was worth much to have that decided so that the experiment of "American Lutheranism" might never be seriously undertaken again. The Lutheran church in 1860 was in a position, barring disruption and internal controversies, to make steady and rapid progress in the conservation of her faith and the development of her doctrinal resources.

CHAPTER 19

DISRUPTION AND RECONSTRUCTION

The defeat of the "American Lutheranism" movement did not bring peace to the church. The variety of racial, linguistic, doctrinal, and personal elements in the church after the middle of the century furnished abundant material for internal discord. Antagonisms had always been present, but hitherto, tempered by conciliation and mutual toleration. Now the spirit of unrest and intolerance was abroad in the land and that spirit was aggravated by racial misunderstandings and the friction of strong personalities.

In the church, controversy flared on all sides, on all points of doctrine, and with destructive heat. A multitude of issues gave fuel to the fires of discord. Missouri debated with Buffalo the doctrines of the ministry, the church, and the office of the keys, and the ideal relation of church to state, with resulting disruption among the men and congregations of Buffalo. With Loehe and the men of the Iowa Synod, Walther and the Missourians debated the "open questions," the binding character of the confessions, the divine obligation of Sunday, the right to take interest, whether the Pope is the Antichrist, and other points of difference. The most bitter controversy, and the one that led to disruption in the ranks of the Missourians, concerned predestination. It continued into a later period, and later chapters will describe the resulting separation of the Norwegians from the Missouri Synod, further divisions among the Norwegians themselves, the withdrawal of the Joint Synod of Ohio from the Synodical Conference, and the exodus of a number of German pastors from Missouri to join Ohio.

The literature produced by these controversies and breaks was enormous, and the spirit of exclusiveness and faction was fed to a surfeit.

Meanwhile, among the Lutherans of Muhlenberg descent, new synods were formed, not in amity and peace as in the preceding period but in the spirit of secession and protest. In the territory of the New York Ministerium, the formation of the Hartwick Synod in 1830 and the Franckean Synod in 1837, led to vigorous protests from the mother synod and serious conflicts between the two off-spring. In Ohio a number of pastors of the Joint Synod, dissatisfied with its attitude on the language question and other matters, withdrew in 1836 and formed the East Ohio Synod. This was only the beginning of divisions in that state. In the end, all the elements of Muhlenberg descent that had entered into the original Synod of Ohio in 1818 separated and formed other bodies. Angry charges of "intolerance, oppression and inconsistency" were frequently heard.

East of the Susquehanna there was serious dissatisfaction in the ranks of the Ministerium of Pennsylvania, due partly to the exclusive use of German in its sessions, partly to the confessional and liturgical tendency of the Ministerium, and partly to differences of view in regard to the General Synod and her institutions. In 1842 ten pastors, led by Dr. W. M. Reynolds, a professor at Gettysburg College, left the Ministerium and formed the East Pennsylvania Synod. This covered the same territory as the Ministerium and for many years there was much friction between the two bodies.

Farther south also the spirit of schism was active. The Maryland Synod resented the formation of the Melanchthon Synod on her territory in 1857. And in 1860 the Tennessee Synod was seriously weakened by the withdrawal from its ranks of pastors and congregations to form the Holston Synod.

But more serious than any of these divisions was the disruption of the General Synod. In 1860 the General Synod was more of a "general" body than at any other time in its history, embracing almost all the Lutheran groups stemming from Muhlenberg, and many of the more recent immigrants. It numbered 864 of the 1,313 ministers and 164,000 of the 245,000 communicants, a total of about two-thirds of the Lutheran church in this country. Not a few of the church leaders in that day cherished the hope of making the General Synod the center of a single organization embracing all the Lutherans in America. Instead, during the next six years, the General Synod suffered losses by exodus and disruption that deprived it of nearly half of its membership.

The first break in the strength of the General Synod came in 1860 with the exodus of the Swedes and Norwegians from the Synod of Northern Illinois. We have seen that in 1851 a large number of Swedes and a smaller number of Norwegians, under the leadership of Prof. L. P. Esbjörn, helped to form the Synod of Northern Illinois, a district synod of the General Synod, and co-operated in the work of the Illinois State University. As that synod simply affirmed the Augsburg Confession to be "a summary of the fundamental doctrines of the Christian religion substantially correct" the Scandinavians carefully guarded their rights on entering the body. In 1859 they constituted nearly half of the whole synod, and they exerted a measurable influence in favor of historic Lutheranism. But they feared that the General Synod might not remain doctrinally sound, and because of the barrier of language, they were not able to impress their particular views on that body. Disturbed over the admission of the Melanchthon Synod in 1859, they began to contemplate a separate organization. The following spring after personal troubles with other professors at Springfield, Esbjörn suddenly resigned and moved to Chicago, taking the Scandinavian students with him. Shortly after that all the Swedes and Norwegians formally severed their connections with the Synod of Northern Illinois, and in June, 1860, formed the Augustana Synod. The Springfield school was purchased by the Missourians. One result of this secession of the Swedes was a great weakening of the conservative element in that part of the General Synod.

The second rupture in the ranks of the General Synod came in 1862. Intense partisan rancor, the confusion and anxiety due to the war, had delayed the meeting of the general body for a year. When it met in Lancaster in May, 1862, only one delegate was present from south of the Potomac River. Some declaration concerning the great conflict was inevitable. It is indicative of the religious genius of the Lutheran church and her essential conservatism that up to this time she had not allowed the purely economic and moral issue of slavery to split her organization. The Methodists, Baptists, and Presbyterians had all divided on that issue ten or fifteen years before. But at the time of the Lancaster meeting of the General Synod the southern states had seceded and actual war had been going on for twelve months. The district synods, North and South, had all acted in support of their respective governments. The southern synods, expecting that the political separation between the North and South would be permanent, had taken action looking toward withdrawal from the General Synod of the United States and the forming of a General Synod of the Confederate States. The General Synod at Lancaster, therefore, took vigorous action against the South. As the resolutions were framed, the southern pastors and congregations interpreted them to mean that their return to the General Synod would not be desired even after the union of the states was restored.

After the close of the war, Lutherans of the North made overtures to those of the South, suggesting their return to their former organic relationship. But the southern churches determined to continue their own General Synod, which they had begun in May, 1863. They cited the strong resolutions of 1862 and in addition explained that they now had their own peculiar problems requiring that they should maintain their own general organization and institutions and literature. Moreover, serious division among the northern synods now seemed imminent, and they preferred to have no part in that factional strife. They placed themselves on a more positive confessional basis than that of the General Synod of the North and changed their name to comport with the change in political relations. The organization was later called the "United Synod of the South." This secession of the southern Lutherans withdrew from the old General Synod five of its district synods, North Carolina, South Carolina, Virginia, Western Virginia, and Georgia, embracing 146 ministers, 217 congregations, and over 22,000 members. It further diminished the strength of the conservative party in the General Synod.

But the most serious disruption came with the withdrawal of the Ministerium of Pennsylvania and the organization of another general body on the territory of the General Synod. This was a process extending over four years. It began with the meeting of the General Synod at York in 1864, and was completed by the formation of the General Council at Fort Wayne in 1867.

When the Ministerium of Pennsylvania affiliated with the General Synod in 1853 it carefully guarded the terms of its affiliation. The predominance of the German language and German personalities in the Ministerium, and its strong trend toward conservative Lutheran positions, made its members suspicious of the Lutheranism in the more Americanized parts of the church. The action to unite with the General Synod was not taken without a struggle. It was specified in joining the general body that the Ministerium retained all rights to control its internal affairs and that, if the General Synod should ever violate its constitution and require assent to anything conflicting with the "old and long-established faith of the Evangelical Lutheran Church," the delegates of the Ministerium were required to protest and withdraw from the meeting. At the same convention the Ministerium pledged itself to all the symbolical books. It is clear that the old Ministerium had now reached confessional ground more advanced than the rest of the General Synod.

Several incidents that occurred shortly after the Ministerium had joined the General Synod were disquieting to the conservative leaders in the Ministerium. The "Definite Platform" was overwhelmingly rejected, it is true, but the Melanchthon Synod was admitted in spite of the negative vote of the Ministerium's delegates. The conservative element easily predominated in the General Synod, but they were making concessions to the liberal element that the Ministerium regarded as unwarranted. In those days of universal discord the spirit of unity had left the General Synod and it needed only an occasion to precipitate serious conflict between the two elements.

The crisis came at York in 1864. The Franckean Synod applied for admission to the General Synod. Now the Franckean Synod had never accepted the Augsburg Confession. It had its own "declaration of faith," in which the distinctive doctrines of Lutheranism were not contained. Its application was accordingly rejected until it should "give formal expression of its adoption of the Augsburg Confession as received by the General Synod." But the next day, when the delegates of the Franckean Synod explained that in adopting the constitution of the General Synod they thought that they had also adopted its confession of faith, the question was reconsidered. After a long and spirited discussion it was voted, ninety-seven to forty, to admit the Franckean Synod, but with the express "understanding that said synod, at its next meeting, declare in an official manner its adoption of the doctrinal articles of the Augsburg Confession." This action the minority regarded as unconstitutional and dangerous in principle, and they entered a formal protest against it. The delegation of the Pennsylvania Ministerium further presented a paper recalling the reservations under which their body had united with the General Synod in 1853, recording their conviction that the recent action of the General Synod was unconstitutional, and declaring their purpose therefore "to withdraw from the sessions of the General Synod, in order to report to the Synod of Pennsylvania at its approaching convention."

When the delegation from the Ministerium withdrew, the die was cast. The delegation did not regard their act as the withdrawal of the Ministerium itself, and the Ministerium did not so interpret it. But others did so regard it, and events that transpired before the next meeting of the General Synod made the disruption practically complete. After the withdrawal of the Ministerium's delegation from the York convention, the General Synod at the same meeting adopted a resolution denying that there are any errors in the Augsburg Confession. It also provided for an amendment to its constitution fortifying its position as a conservative Lutheran body and clearly defining in that sense the confessional basis to be adopted by synods desiring to unite with the general body. This was done because the majority in the General Synod were anxious to conciliate the Ministerium and to guard against establishing a dangerous precedent by the admission of the Franckean Synod, and because they wanted to express the confessional advance that had been made since 1829. This amendment was submitted to the Ministerium and was ratified by that body along with a large majority of the other district synods. But it was a time of war and not of peace. The passions of men were deeply stirred. The conflict of strong personalities was one obstacle to restoration of peace in the General Synod, another was the establishment of a new seminary.

In February, 1864, Dr. Schmucker had resigned as the head of the Gettysburg Seminary. Many of the conservatives wanted Charles Porterfield Krauth as his successor. By his many publications Dr. Krauth had shown himself to be the most scholarly among the Lutheran theologians in America. By 1864 he had become thoroughly conservative in his confessional position. If the training of the future ministers of the church could have been committed to his hands, the Ministerium might regard that as a sufficient guarantee against radical tendencies. But there were many who wanted a new seminary. The demand for German pastors was greater than Gettysburg could supply.

The project to strengthen the German teaching force at Gettysburg did not seem feasible, and long before the events of 1864 a number of advocates were pleading for the establishment of a theological seminary in Philadelphia, as Muhlenberg had planned. After the break at York and with no prospect of having Dr. Krauth as Dr. Schmucker's successor, the Ministerium of Pennsylvania proceeded in July, 1864, to establish its own seminary in Philadelphia. Dr. Krauth was called to be its professor of systematic theology. Dr. C. F. Schaeffer, the German professor at the Gettysburg Seminary, and Dr. W. J. Mann became the other professors. This event convinced many that the breach in the ranks of the General Synod was now permanent.

A few weeks later Dr. J. A. Brown was elected head of the Gettysburg Seminary. Dr. Brown was well known for his conservative views as an antagonist of Dr. Schmucker and his "American Lutheranism." Dr. Krauth, Sr., the second professor at Gettysburg, was also known to be conservative. Yet relations between the two institutions were at once embittered by the sudden removal of a professor from the old seminary and the withdrawal of many students. The representatives of the Pennsylvania Ministerium who came as usual to attend the meeting of the Gettysburg Board of Directors were told that they had no place there. A literary war flared up between Dr. Brown and Dr. Krauth. Several of the leaders in the General Synod began to indulge in fierce condemnation of the Ministerium and its seminary. The earlier withdrawal of the Ministerium's delegation at York began to be generally interpreted as the secession of the Ministerium itself from the General Synod.

The General Synod met at Fort Wayne on May 17, 1866, in an atmosphere charged with forebodings of serious conflict. The Ministerium of Pennsylvania sent a delegation, but their instructions breathed defiance. Both sides expected rupture. The purely German element in the Ministerium was determined to separate from the General Synod, and it was charged that leaders of the Ministerium, even before that critical meeting of the General Synod, had begun negotiating for a new general body. On the other hand, the men in the left wing of the General Synod were loudly proclaiming their intention to exclude the Ministerium if they could. But each side to the controversy wanted to place on the other the responsibility for schism in the church.

The president of the General Synod at that time was Dr. Sprecher. With others of the left wing he had planned his procedure, and at the opening of the convention at Fort Wayne he rejected the credentials of the delegates from the Ministerium of Pennsylvania. He declared that the Ministerium was in a "state of practical withdrawal from the governing functions of the General Synod," and that the General Synod must first organize its convention by electing officers before it could consider restoring relations with the Ministerium. Attention was called to the reservation of the Ministerium on joining the General Synod in 1853, but Dr. Sprecher replied that it was not recorded in the minutes of the General Synod and therefore could not be recognized by the officers of that body. An appeal was made from this decision, but the synods already received sustained the chair. On this technicality and against the protest of delegates from other synods, the Ministerium's delegation was excluded from the election of officers.

In this election, however, Dr. Brown was made president. One of those conservatives who wished to preserve the unity of the General Synod, he opposed the summary exclusion of the Ministerium, wishing only to annul the condition which the Ministerium had attached to its admission in 1853. This reservation, which claimed the right to secede, was the nub of a three-day debate over the Pennsylvania Synod that now ensued. Finally the delegates of the Ministerium were asked to "waive what might seem to them an irregular organization of this body and acquiesce in the present organization." This they agreed to do, provided the General Synod would acknowledge their constitutional right to be represented before the election of officers and to take part in it. Such acknowledgment the majority of the General Synod refused to make, because they interpreted the withdrawal of the Ministerium delegates in 1864 as "secession" and they did not want to perpetuate the "right to secede" which seemed to be included in the Ministerium's reservation of 1853. Thereupon the delegation of the Ministerium withdrew for the last time. The break was complete, another strong support of conservatism was withdrawn from the General Synod, and for fifty-two years the Ministerium of Pennsylvania had no organic relation with the other synods in the General Synod.

But the principle of a general organization for Lutherans had strongly commended itself in the forty-six years of experience of the

General Synod. Accordingly, after the break at Fort Wayne the hope was widely entertained of building a new general body that would be more thoroughly Lutheran in its spirit and more general in its extent than the old General Synod. The separation of the Pennsylvania Ministerium had been greeted with satisfaction in many quarters. The Ministerium, therefore, when it approved the course of its delegates at Fort Wayne and formally severed its connection with the General Synod, issued a call to all Lutheran synods acknowledging the Unaltered Augsburg Confession to participate in the organization of a new general body "on a truly Lutheran basis." In response to this call a convention was held at Reading, Pennsylvania, in December, 1866. Thirteen synods were represented. The principal business of the convention was the discussion and adoption of a set of theses that Dr. Krauth had prepared on "The fundamental principles of faith and church polity." These theses were unanimously adopted as the basis of the proposed organization. They placed the new body squarely upon the doctrinal basis of the Unaltered Augsburg Confession and the other symbolical books because they are "in perfect harmony of one and the same scriptural faith." As to ecclesiastical polity the new organization allowed the individual synods a wide range of freedom in regulating their own affairs.

The required number of synods having adopted the "fundamental principles," the first regular convention of the "General Council of the Evangelical Lutheran Church of North America" was held at Fort Wayne in November, 1867. Eleven synods participated in the organization: The Ministerium of Pennsylvania, the New York Ministerium, the English Synod of Ohio, the Pittsburgh Synod, the Wisconsin Synod, the English District Synod of Ohio, the Michigan Synod, the Augustana Synod, the Minnesota Synod, the Canada Synod, and the Illinois Synod. The Joint Synod of Ohio and the Iowa Synod sent delegates but did not unite with the council because they could not be satisfied of its thoroughgoing Lutheranism. The Missouri Synod had been represented at the preliminary meeting in Reading, but did not favor the organization of a new general body and declined to unite with it. From the beginning the General Council was four-fifths the size of the depleted General Synod, and after a few years the younger body was the larger.

The General Council at once took up the work of reorganizing the churches on the confessional basis it had adopted. A liturgy and Church Book were prepared. A model constitution for congregations was devised and debated and finally adopted. In all these lines the Pennsylvania Ministerium took the lead. In the benevolent operations of the church few powers had been committed to the general body, and this work continued to be carried on by the individual synods. From the general character of the council and the purpose of its organization it followed that its sessions were largely given to discussions of principles and debates on differences with other Lutheran bodies. For many years these debates absorbed the regular conventions of the body and engaged the literary activity of its teachers. It was somewhat disappointing that no agreement could be reached with the strictly orthodox Lutherans farther west so that the "general" character of the body might be more nearly realized. Moreover, the General Council had to reckon constantly with internal diversities of language, nationality, and training. But in the rapid enlargement of the church that soon took place the General Council fulfilled its primary purpose in maintaining purity of doctrine and developing sound cultus and practice.

The formation of the General Council also disrupted a number of district synods. Those delegates from other synods who sympathized with the Pennsylvania Ministerium in the events at York and Fort Wayne tried to move their respective synods from the General Synod to the new organization. This developed a new phase of internal discord. When the New York Ministerium united with the General Council, seventeen ministers withdrew to form the New York Synod, and as such joined the General Synod. Similarly a minority in the Illinois Synod formed themselves into the Central Illinois Synod and remained in the General Synod. In the Pittsburgh Synod the minority, refusing to abide by the decision of the majority to join the General Council, claimed the name of the original synod, and were recognized by the General Synod as the Pittsburgh Synod. This disruption of synods caused lasting bitterness. As congregations changed their synodical affiliations, pastors were parted from their congregations by their allegiance to one or the other of the general bodies. Often congregations were divided. Expensive and humiliating lawsuits fought for possession of the properties. Scholarly theologians sat for days in the witness stand of secular courts. Wherever the issue was the essential Lutheranism of the General Synod, that synod always won the settlement. But wounds were inflicted that three generations of time have scarcely been able to heal.

This series of disruptions left the General Synod of 1870 a remnant of the large and hopeful body of 1860, its numbers diminished, its institutions weakened, its "general" character impugned. Its most conservative elements were gone but the left wing had been sobered by the events of the decade and the conservative party was still in the ascendancy. The withdrawal of the Pennsylvania Ministerium and other conservative bodies deprived the General Synod of invaluable conservative scholarship and made the further advance of that body in doctrine and cultus a slow and painful process. And for a time at least, the disruption impaired the progress of conservatism in the Lutheran church as a whole.

In summary, the causes of the Lutheran disruptions of this time appear to have been both doctrinal and practical, both basic and accidental.

Between the majority of the General Synod on the one hand and the Pennsylvania Ministerium and its friends on the other, real differences of doctrine had grown up. The Ministerium had made great speed in its confessional advance and now accepted all the symbolical books, as no other synod in the General Synod had done. The predominating influences in the Ministerium were German, and they harbored a strong aversion to the remnant of revivalism and puritanism that still lingered in some parts of the General Synod. The Ministerium was in more direct touch with the Lutheran reaction in Germany and its inspiring literature, made more constant use of Luther's Catechism and German hymns, and received a larger number of the immigrant German pastors. All this deepened the Lutheran convictions of the Ministerium beyond those of the other synods. The correspondence of the leaders of that period and the columns of the church papers make it clear that doctrinal differences were a potent factor in causing the irritation that produced disruption.

Dissenting views of church government further separated the two parties. The Pennsylvania Ministerium, so much older and larger than the other synods, was always jealous of its rights and unwilling to risk identity in merging activities. The Ministerium claimed that the general organization was only a conference with advisory powers, that the definition of doctrine, the founding of seminaries, the preparation of liturgies and hymnbooks, and the benevolent work of the church, was the business of the district synods and not the General Synod. The majority in the General Synod, on the other hand, stood for a centralized authority whose decisions would regulate the doctrinal and practical affairs of the synods. These two conceptions of church polity may be traced through all the events of disruption and reconstruction. As the events of the Civil War increased the centralization of power in the hands of the federal government, so the withdrawal of the Pennsylvania Ministerium strengthened the centralizing theory of government in the General Synod, and some of the most important practical decisions in the history of the General Synod were made in 1869.

This difference of spirit, growing out of a divergence of confessional position and varied conceptions of church government, was further aggravated by such personal differences as those involved in the establishment of the new seminary in 1864, which in turn greatly increased the conflict of personalities. Personalities also were the main factor in producing the tragic event at Fort Wayne in 1866. But party spirit was everywhere at its zenith. Religious verities were sometimes overshadowed by political expedients. The prevailing tone in all spheres was combat and strife. General unity was lacking in the Lutheran church of Muhlenberg development, and at such a time in the history of the nation it was not to be expected that organic union of the church would be preserved.

It was better, no doubt, that each party should go its way in the providence of God until, in times of a different temper, and with the development of doctrine and cultus and the progress of church polity and benevolent operations, scattered members of the household might be brought together in true unity and organic union.

CHAPTER 20

IN CIVIL CONFLICT

While mid-century American society was being colored by immigrations, the immigrants for their part were ceaselessly affected by consciousness of their role as newcomers. A large part of the Lutheran congregations were immigrants, and this fact helped to develop among Lutherans a diversity of social patterns which increased their diversity in doctrine and polity.

In the East the Lutherans had melted into American society. Only in sections of southeastern Pennsylvania, where the Pennsylvania Germans in the congregations of the mother Ministerium of Pennsylvania and her daughter synods continued as a separate sociological phenomenon by virtue of their dialect, diligence, and devotion, were the Lutherans socially or politically distinguishable. Lutherans were charter members of the Republic and full-fledged citizens. They resented the writers and speakers who identified them with the immigrant Lutherans of the West or regarded their church as foreign or imported.

The older synodical bodies of the East reflected the religious and social practices of other American Protestants of the time. The practice of revivalism and protracted meetings was carried over from earlier years and intensified. The "new measures," with or without benefit of catechetical instruction, were vigorously championed by the *Lutheran Observer* and practiced quite widely among Lutherans in this section. With the advent of the public school early in this period, the responsibility for specifically Christian instruction rested entirely on the pastor with his catechetical class and the congregation with its Sunday school. Until the end of this period practically all of the congregations used the teaching and learning helps of the interdenominational American Sunday School Union. Unlike the Lutherans of the eighteenth and early nineteenth centuries, the English-speaking congregations of the mid-nineteenth century felt no need for congregational schools or even for distinctively Lutheran aids to Bible study.

These Lutherans shared in the puritan zeal of other American Christians—their observance of the Lord's Day, their crusades against intemperance, their war on vice and crime, their animosity toward Catholics and infidels, and their development of Christian educational agencies and institutions of higher learning. No measures were taken to prevent Lutheran ministers or church members from joining with other American Protestants in becoming members of secret societies or lodges.

The unofficial societies for Christian benevolence of various kinds increased in number, size, and variety and continued to be the chief arm of the church people in practical Christian programs. Only after the middle of the century did Lutherans in the East begin to withdraw from interdenominational societies and to organize on distinctively Lutheran lines.

But in the West, among the great mass of Lutheran immigrants, the social situation was different. These new Lutherans spoke languages that were strange to most Americans, or at best used heavy accents. Until well after the middle of the century most of them settled in the agricultural regions of the upper Mississippi Valley in relatively isolated groups. Here they repeated the social experiences of Lutherans on earlier frontiers, on the Atlantic seaboard in the eighteenth century and in the Ohio Valley during the first forty years of the Republic. Because the nineteenth-century waves of Lutheran immigration were so much larger than the earlier, and because they swept farther inland to more isolated regions, their people were more inclined to remain outside American society and its standards and traditions. They reflected their German and Scandinavian origins in their social life, their food and habits, their dress, their houses and barns, their methods of agriculture, their implements and utensils, their festivities and games, their customs at baptisms, confirmations, weddings, and funerals. They read books and periodicals in German or the Scandinavian tongues. They celebrated their own holidays. They did not often intermarry with native Americans. They retained their European attitude toward lodges and secret societies and made them an issue in church assemblies. To outsiders, to the Americans among whom they placed their foreign communities, they seemed aloof, strange and cold.

In church life and theology, as we have seen, these immigrants brought with them the "sense of history" acquired in Europe. They helped to precipitate doctrinal issues in what has been called "the crisis in American Lutheran theology," and to stamp Lutherans as the most conservative group, but in some respects the most aggressive, of all American Protestants.

The Lutheran immigrants, who went mostly to the unoccupied lands, investing themselves and their families in the long-range productive industry of agriculture with tenacity and zeal, soon made themselves economic assets to their adopted country. The "stream of foreign paupers" that vexed legislative assemblies did not include Lutherans. They made few contributions to the delinquent and defective classes of society. They were all literate. They raised large families of sturdy children, often, especially among the Scandinavians, families of ten or twelve future farmers, and occasionally sixteen, eighteen, or even more.

These new Lutherans did, however, help swell the count of the "foreigners" who were stirring the rancor of American "nativism." Under the law, immigrants were invested with the franchise while stilll European in character and opinion. Thus newspapers in foreign languages might guide voters in American elections, voters who time and again turned the scales in state elections, and more than once, probably determined the outcome in national elections, including the election of Lincoln.

The Lutheran groups did not purposely constitute themselves a bloc. The circumstances of migration from their homes in Europe, and their location on the frontier, often shaped them into little cultural islands of inbred and almost unalterable attitudes. This was not the result of political planning. Long before these Lutheran immigrants arrived in America, the government had decided against concentrating immigrants according to nationality, and all schemes for such collective projects failed. But concentration of Lutherans in the West and Northwest during the mid-century made them an element to be used and reckoned with in political issues. Thus they were brought under political attack, and this developed in them a degree of public interest greater than that of the Lutherans who were "charter Americans."

About the middle of the century the "native Americans" whipped up the resentment against "foreigners" into angry violence. The people in the churches worshiping God in their native tongues were not distinguished from political revolutionaries meeting to discuss, in foreign languages, their propaganda on behalf of European ideals. The "nativists" lumped all foreigners together, those who were becoming citizens, who were acquiring land, who cultivated the piety and ideals of their former homes in Europe, as well as those who crowded the cities, cultivated their distinctive national traits, and longed to return home with bulging pockets. Both Catholics and Protestants were among those denounced as "patented citizens," and all foreign-born were involved in the turbulence and rioting that for thirty years disgraced so many of our cities.

In vain did the religious journals seek to ward off these political attacks; they were themselves largely foreign. Moreover, the conservative publications of German Lutherans, as might have been expected, dealt only obliquely with political or social issues. The most influential of the many religious periodicals among Scandinavians was *Hemlandet* (The Homeland), founded in 1855 by the long-time leader among the Swedish Lutherans, Dr. T. N. Hasselquist. It discussed political issues frankly, and like the papers published by the Norwegian Lutherans, led its readers into the Republican party. When the Society of United Americans was formed to keep the government in the hands of native Americans, by methods so secret that its members were called "Know Nothings," Hasselquist found himself in a dilemma. He was opposed to slavery, but he felt that the abolitionists represented the American tendency to go to extremes. He believed that the Catholic Church menaced his adopted country, and he disagreed violently with those "irreligious Germans" who propagated radical political ideas and tried to perpetuate on American soil the evils of the "continental Sunday." However, he could not agree with the Know Nothings in hostility to all foreigners irrespective of origin or position. He finally declared against the Know Nothing Party because of his conviction that a secret society was contrary to the Word of God.

The chief issue during this period in the social and political life of the Lutheran people was that of slavery. The intense political agitation spared no section of the country or any segment of the population. It entered the homes of Lutheran people and divided their families. It influenced the work of Lutheran breadwinners. It caused dissension among church leaders and disruption in church assemblies. As the Lutherans on the Atlantic seaboard in the eighteenth century had been baptized into American citizenship with the blood of the Revolutionary battlefields, so now at the middle of the nineteenth century the American Lutherans, including those of the Middle West newly arrived from Europe, were baptized in the blood of an ordeal involving such abstract principles as liberty and union.

For thirty years the ugly clouds of militant sectionalism gathered on the political horizon and then the storm burst in the Civil War. Lutheran people in all parts of the country were swept into the storm. For the most part the Lutheran churches had remained officially silent on political issues, but Lutheran people and individual pastors saw certain moral and religious principles involved, and as Christian citizens could not remain indifferent. In all sections of the nation, North, South, and West, Lutheran people joined in the controversies, and then fought on the fields of battle.

The issues of slavery and secession were complicated, involving history and constitutional law, politics and economics, but they could be made to appear as pure and simple moral questions. The great national democracy, suffused with moral sentiments and religious traditions, brought face to face with a moral issue, or what appeared as a moral issue, was quickly aroused, and then not easily restrained. Politically this was a conflict between principles of nationalism and of sectionalism. It involved technical questions of interpreting the federal constitution, abstract problems of nullification and secession, which the rank and file of people could scarcely understand. But when the conflict turned on slavery, the average church member was interested and felt qualified to participate.

For most Lutheran people the question of slavery was theoretical. The farmers of the North and the West had few contacts with Negroes. Slavery was limited almost entirely to the southern states where Lutherans were few. But, Lutherans everywhere looked upon slavery as a national issue to be decided on ethical and scriptural principles. Lutherans in each section largely accorded with the prevailing local sentiment, opposed to slavery in the North, favoring it in the South, and divided in the West.

In earlier periods Lutheran people had several times expressed themselves against slavery. The Swedish Lutherans on the Delaware in the seventeenth century had prohibited the introduction of slavery while they were in control there. As early as 1688, Lutherans at Germantown, Pennsylvania, took the lead in a protest to the Quakers against the system of Negro slavery. A generation later the pastor of Hebron Lutheran congregation in Virginia purchased slaves to cultivate the church glebe, but other Lutherans opposed his action. The Salzburgers in Georgia succeeded for many years in preventing the introduction of slaves into their community and reproved George Whitefield for his acquiescence in slavery, although they later purchased children from the slave ships in order to bring them up as Christians, and also acquired slaves to help in the work of the settlement at Ebenezer. The pious Salzburgers provided religious training and favorable living conditions for their slaves, and this was the general practice of other Lutheran slaveholders throughout colonial times.

When the colonies became independent, Pennsylvania, where most Lutherans were settled, took the lead, in 1780, in promoting emancipation. In the national period many Lutherans joined The American Colonization Society which was organized in 1816 to settle liberated Negroes in Liberia, thus solving the problem of slavery in this country and at the same time spreading the gospel in Africa. The leaders in the General Synod, as individuals, and the teachers in the seminaries at Gettysburg, Hartwick, Lexington, and Columbus, exerted their influence in favor of the education and Christian training of slaves with a view to their eventual emancipation.

The *Lutheran Observer,* founded in Baltimore in 1831, supported colonization, opposed slavery, but did not favor the methods and purposes of the abolitionists. Editorials rebuked the North for trying to force its ideas of right and wrong on the whole nation, and took the South to task for threatening a violent breach. The paper circulated in all sections of the country and for thirty years succeeded in maintaining a precarious neutrality.

By 1860, when South Carolina seceded from the Union, it was evident that no one could remain neutral on the question of slavery.

The "irrepressible conflict" now at last entered the councils of the Lutheran church.

In the General Synod, as early as 1837, a small group had called for aggressive action against slavery. In western New York the abolitionists had been quite successful in gaining Lutheran followers. There was much radical sentiment in that area against slavery and slaveowners and the Lutheran people, who were not numerous, shared the attitude of the other people. When the Hartwick Synod in western New York declined to pronounce against slavery, four ministers and a group of laymen separated and in 1837 formed the Franckean Synod. One of the very first actions of the new body was a set of resolutions on "American Slavery," declaring "That slavery as it exists in the United States . . . is a sin . . . opposed to the spirit of the Gospel and a violation of the inalienable rights of man . . . that we have abundant cause for deep humiliation before God, that, as a denomination, we are so deeply involved in the Sin of Slavery, and that so many of our ministers practice the crime, and that so many others justify them in this iniquity . . . that we view the traffic in human beings as carried on in this country between the ministers of the Gospel and members of the churches, as revolting to humanity and as repugnant to the laws of Christ."

Repeatedly during succeeding years these ideas were emphasized at the meetings of the Franckean Synod. Because the *Lutheran Observer* tried to be neutral on the slavery issue, the synod began its own organ, *The Lutheran Herald,* which condemned the Colonization Society and undertook active support of the American and Foreign Anti-Slavery Society. In 1841 the synod declared against pulpit and altar fellowship with slaveholders and issued a "Fraternal Appeal" to all Lutheran synods asking them to take action against the sin of slavery. Three years later it expressed its regret that this sin is "countenanced by the greater portion of the Lutheran Churches and Synods in the United States," and the next year it declared that an appeal to the Scriptures to justify the sin of American slavery is blasphemy. In 1847 the synod amended its constitution so as to deny seats in conventions to ministers and laymen who did not oppose slavery. The intensity of the antislavery crusade of the Franckean Synod grew as the nation became more tense. At the middle of the century the body numbered 25 ministers, 50 congregations, and 3,213 communicants. The sentiments expressed by the synod must have been fairly widespread among the Lutheran people of the Muhlenberg development, although few would have expressed themselves in such violent terms and no other ecclesiastical body among Lutherans was willing to deal seriously with the touchy question.

Only twice did the General Synod give notice to the antislavery agitation of the Franckean Synod. The first instance was in 1839, when the General Synod expressed disapprobation of practices that tend to divide the churches and at the same time exhorted all Lutheran churches to beware of the efforts of some men to cause divisions and offences contrary to the spirit of the gospel. The second notice came eighteen years later, when the General Synod rescinded the action taken in 1839 because it was "not in accordance with the spirit of our constitution and not the sentiment of this convention." Two synods in Ohio took action on the slavery question, both small groups which had separated from the Joint Synod of Ohio because of its increasing use of German and its growing confessionalism. The East Ohio Synod with its sixteen ministers and eighty-seven congregations responded to the "Fraternal Appeal" by the Franckean Synod in 1844 by declaring that "this synod regards slavery as an evil, which all Christians should deplore." The Franckean Synod and many other Lutherans drew a distinction between slavery merely as an evil and slavery as downright sin against God. In the one case it is a matter involved in human relationships that calls for social and political reform. In the other case it involves man's relationship with God and concerns the churchman and the theologian. The Wittenberg Synod which counted sixteen ministers and thirty-eight congregations in 1852 pronounced the system of American slavery "a great national evil and an abomination in the sight of God" and resolved to use its influence for the removal of this evil from the nation. The Allegheny Synod in 1844 stated its conviction that the system of American slavery was "a moral, civil, and religious evil . . . dishonorable to God and man." The Synod of Northern Indiana in 1859 denounced slavery (and intemperance) as "crying sins" and decided to "labor and pray for the abolition and destruction of those great evils."

The Pittsburgh Synod, organized in 1845 with congregations in Pennsylvania and Ohio, responded to the protest of the Franckean

Synod by resolving that slavery is "a moral and national evil . . . condemned by the principles of humanity and the word of God." When this synod declined to join the General Synod in 1851, it gave as its main reason that it did not wish to "become implicated in the sin of slavery," and the General Synod admitted delegates who were slaveholders. The next year the Pittsburgh Synod did unite with the General Synod but recorded the safeguard "that we do not change our relations or positions in regard to slavery."

Meanwhile, some of the Lutherans in the South had expressed themselves. They knew slavery from intimate contact and took the practical point of view. Among the few Lutherans who owned slaves there had been much sentiment in favor of gradual emancipation, but all of them resented attempts of men in the North to interfere in local affairs of the South and were hurt by the aspersions of their Lutheran brethren in the North upon their law-abiding character and Christian morality.

The Synod of South Carolina took early and vigorous action. In 1835 it strongly condemned the conduct of the abolitionists and their "incendiary publications" as injurious to morals and religion. The next year, stirred by the statements of "persons in all probability of our own creed, living perhaps in the far distant North," the synod denounced in severe terms such "intermeddling . . . of affected patriots and more than rotten hearted benefactors," and resolved never to enter into a discussion of slavery. This resolution was kept.

The aggressive actions of the Franckean Synod produced further reactions in southern synods. The Synod of Virginia in 1835 declared abolitionism to be a combination of ignorance, fanaticism, and dishonesty, and four years later expressed its decided disapprobation of "the pretensions assumed by the Franckean Synod" and completely rejected "any such arrogant assumption of synodical censorship." When the "Appeal" of the Franckean Synod reached the border Synod of Maryland in 1842, it was tabled because "this synod cannot entertain any subject not immediately connected with our synodical business." Five years later the effort of the Franckean Synod to circulate for signature a protest against slavery received the same treatment in this synod. The Synod of the West had congregations in Ohio, Illinois, Iowa, Kentucky, and Tennessee. Most of their ministers and people had migrated from the East. There was sarcasm in the reply which this synod made to the "Appeal" of the Franckean Synod: "We feel grateful to the Franckean Synod for their well meant attempt to enlighten us on the subject of American Slavery, and that our minds being always open to conviction on any subject, as soon as conviction has done its work, we will act; at the same time recommend to them the propriety of considering well the measures of abolitionists in the present day before they act." In the North Carolina Synod the protest was called "an incendiary document" and ordered returned to its source.

It will be observed that none of these Lutheran synods except the Franckean initiated action concerning slavery or secession and none made extended statements. Such actions as they did take were in response to a definite inquiry from another synod.

As tension mounted and the public faced the threat of war, sentiment crystallized among the several sectors of Lutherans and their statements became sharper and more contentious. Because the *Observer* remained neutral and did not condemn the abolitionists, the ministers in the South began their own church paper, the *Southern Lutheran*. One public exchange of views was particularly significant. The Middle Conference of the Pittsburgh Synod at its meeting in September, 1857, adopted a report setting forth the brutalities of slavery, its sinfulness and demoralizing effects, and calling on Christians everywhere to testify clearly and to labor vigorously against it in the pulpit and at the ballot box. The proceedings of the conference were published as news in Dr. Passavant's weekly paper, *The Missionary*, which circulated also among Lutheran people in the South. The men in the South turned for their response to their most prominent churchman and ablest writer, Dr. John Bachman, who, brought up in New York State, for more than forty years had been pastor in Charleston, South Carolina, and was thoroughly identified with the southern Lutherans. His defense of slavery as an institution and his vindication of slaveholders as a class, from the point of view of the Scriptures and of Christian principles, is one of the best ever written.

Dr. Bachman's courteous but fervent appeal was also a plea against division in the Lutheran church. It referred to the great task confronting the church. "To our Church in the North and Middle States the high mission is entrusted of gathering in the wanderers from the shores of Europe . . . many of them strongly tinctured with rationalism and infidelity . . . Our Church in our Southern Atlantic States has an equally important mission . . . we preach the Gospel of Christ to the bond and the free." The West and Southwest were fields for common evangelistic work for all Lutherans. This was no time for Lutherans to quarrel among themselves or to indulge in needless discussion of inflammatory subjects. This earnest and eloquent document of about 6,000 words was generously published in full, and then Dr. Passavant, a lifelong opponent of slavery, respectfully replied to all of Dr. Bachman's arguments. But the issue could not be decided by the counsels of logic and reason.

When war broke, Lutherans everywhere cast their lot with their neighbors. The synods passed resolutions supporting their respective governments and invoking divine blessing on their armies. The General Synod postponed its meeting for a year in the vain hope of avoiding a break with the synods in the South, but when it met at Lancaster, Pennsylvania, in 1862, no delegates were present from the southern synods. Dr. Passavant was made chairman of an imposing committee to report on the state of the country. The committee presented five ringing resolutions, which were adopted, ascribing the war to the "continuance and spread of domestic slavery in our land," praying to the God of battles that "our beloved land may speedily be delivered from treason and anarchy," endorsing the President's plan for emancipation of the slaves, and declaring it "the deliberate judgment of this Synod, that the rebellion against the constitutional Government of this land, is most wicked in its inception, unjustifiable in its cause, unnatural in its character, inhuman in its prosecution, oppressive in its aims, and destructive in its results to the highest interests of morality and religion." A special committee was also appointed to call on President Lincoln, present him with a copy of the report, and assure him of the support of Lutherans and of their prayers that Divine guidance be vouchsafed to him. At the same time the General Synod read the southern synods out of its fellowship by expressing its "most decided disapprobation of the course of those synods and ministers, heretofore connected with this body, in the open sympathy and active co-operation which they have given to the cause of treason and insurrection."

These sentiments were shared by the great majority of the Lutheran people in America. The people in the pews of the churches were pleased with President Lincoln's response, in which he expressed his sense of complete dependence on God's favor and spoke of the Lutherans in the United States as "the enlightened, influential, and loyal class of my fellow citizens." The *Lutheran Observer* from Baltimore, eager to retain all subscribers and reflecting the divided opinion among the Lutherans in the border state of Maryland, continued its plea for peace in the church, urging that slavery be only gradually abolished and that slaveowners receive "an honest remuneration" for the loss of their property. It gave general approval to the ideas contained in the resolutions of the General Synod. But the editor, Dr. Benjamin Kurtz, said that the endorsement of congressional measures for emancipation was unnecessary, inexpedient, and calculated to do harm. He regretted the "haste and rashness of expression . . . which embitters to desperation and beyond reclaim the advocates of the domestic institution." But it was now too late for the counsels of moderation.

Among the middle western Lutheran Germans, Norwegians, and Swedes who had recently come from Europe there was great concern over slavery and secession. In Missouri, the scene of much agitation and violence, were many German-speaking Lutherans. Devout Saxons had come here, repelled from slaveholding Virginia, and, as they prospered, were joined by Germans less devout and far less Lutheran. Very few of the nineteenth-century immigrants from Europe, German or Scandinavian, went to the southern states, because the newcomers wanted to avoid a society that supported the institution of slavery.

The vast majority of immigrant Germans of all classes opposed slavery and supported the Union. In Missouri the strong German element saved St. Louis from the secessionists and took the initiative in saving the whole state for the Union. Not all of these Germans were Lutherans. Some were Reformed, or Catholic, some were refugees of the 1848 revolutions and had little religious interest. Some were socialistic or communistic.

There was one notable exception to the antislavery attitude and union sympathies of the German Lutherans in Missouri. That was Dr. Walther himself, the distinguished leader of the Missouri Synod, who could not agree with the overwhelming majority of his fellow-believers. His extreme conservatism led him instinctively to support

the status quo. He was repelled by the radical Methodist abolitionists
and by the liberal or godless refugees from the 1848 revolutions in
Germany. Above all, it was his firm conviction that the Scriptures
teach nothing against the institution of slavery and much in favor
of it, for example, the definite command that slaves should be obedient
to their masters.

Dr. Walther was very careful about expressing his views in public
and wrote only a few innocent items on the subject in *Der Lutheraner,*
although he did publish a series of four lengthy articles by his friend
Dr. Sihler of Fort Wayne defending slavery as an institution. The
minutes of the Missouri Synod and the seminary publications record
nothing concerning these views. But in his letters to friends Walther
frankly expressed his disdain for the hypocrisy of "the Republican
rabble" with which the forty-eighters had allied themselves. He
accused the antislavery men of making their voice the voice of God.
He regarded the United States as a federation, somewhat like the old
Holy Roman Empire in Germany, and therefore he placed loyalty to
the state government above loyalty to the Union. But until near the
end of the war he made it a point to keep his political views from
the general public, and always he counseled obedience to the government de facto. This saved him and his seminary from violence, although not from threats.

It was characteristic of the Missouri Synod scholars that even
after the issue had been decided in battle, they continued the
theoretical discussion. Near the end of the war, when the decisive
battles had been fought, Dr. Walther's only colleague on the seminary faculty, Professor Gustav Seyffarth, published in *Der Lutherische
Herold* of New York a series of four articles in which he claimed
that Dr. Walther held that the North had violated God's law in
carrying on the Civil War, that Negro slavery in the United States
was "a divine institution," and that those who did not agree were
neither Lutheran nor Christian. Walther replied with a series of four
weighty articles in *Lehre und Wehre,* the official Missouri Synod
organ, in which he claimed to vindicate his views on secession and
slavery from the point of view of Scripture. The publicity given
these views caused Dr. Walther some embarrassment, split the faculty,
and had repercussions among the Scandinavian Lutherans farther
north.

The Norwegians and Swedes did not allow the barrier of language to dim their native interest in public affairs. The Norwegians arrived in America just as the agitation about slavery was beginning to reach full swing. They had refused to settle in Missouri because that state was by that time known to permit Negro slavery. The whole community of Norwegians had a horror of slavery, looked upon it as a great moral and social evil, and identified themselves solidly with the Republican party.

But in spite of the unanimity among Norwegian Lutherans in opposition to slavery, there were heated disagreements concerning the right of secession and the theological and ethical significance of slavery. The Norwegian students who came from St. Louis gave the impression that the Missouri faculty was secessionist and pro-slavery. Early in 1861 the editor of the Norwegian paper, the *Emigranten*, turned to Professor Laurentius Larsen, the representative of the Norwegians on the St. Louis faculty, and an intimate friend of Dr. Walther, for clarification. His answer concerning secession seemed evasive, and that on slavery seemed too abstract to be relevant but did insist that slavery was not sin. These answers were not satisfactory to everyone.

The issue of slavery caused a division between the clergy and the laymen who would not distinguish between sin and evil and considered the distinction trifling. Nearly all of the pastors, the "university men" from Christiana as well as the younger men trained in St. Louis, agreed with Larsen, but made it clear that they favored the gradual abolishing of slavery as an evil. To the laymen this seemed to indicate an aristocratic attitude and a diluted loyalty to the American Union and to Scandinavian traditions. The laymen found a spokesman in C. L. Clausen, who had served a term in the Iowa legislature, for six years was commissioner of immigration, and in 1860-61 had served as chaplain of the Fifteenth Wisconsin Regiment. Clausen was no match for the "office-holding aristocracy" of the other pastors either in the public prints or in the debates on the floor of the synod. But when the pastors tried to get the support of the theological faculty at Christiana, they were disappointed by the attitude of superiority of the scholars in Norway. The pastors were subjected to attack from all sides, except from Missouri, and at times threatened with violence for their "disloyalty."

The controversy dragged on until 1868, when it became a dead issue, but the years of controversy left marks of horizontal cleavage between clergy and laity. The laymen had insisted, early in the debate, that no further funds or students should be sent to the institution "down south" at St. Louis, and Luther College had opened its doors in October, 1862. Any hopes for organic union between the Missouri and the Norwegian synods were now shattered. Moreover, the controversy helped to deepen the lines of division among the Norwegians, because the pastors of Eielsen's Synod and the Scandinavian Augustana Synod took an even more unequivocal stand against slavery than those of the Norwegian Synod. The discussion had also increased "lay activity" among the Norwegian Lutherans and laid the base for their large degree of participation in public life and their long-continued loyalty to the Republican party in political issues.

The attitude of the Swedish Lutherans was similar to that of the Norwegians. They too had come to America with an endowment of independence and with long traditions of interest in public affairs. They avoided the South and Southwest because of slavery, and after 1856 belonged solidly to the Republican party, which they called "the party of moral ideas." A little later in arriving than the Norwegians and a little slower in plunging into public discussions, they were, however, no less earnest about adopting American principles in community life and they soon made their influence felt.

The first ordained minister among the Swedish Lutherans, Lars P. Esbjörn, was opposed to slavery. His antecedents in Sweden of pietism and moral reform, his contacts in America with Congregationalists and Methodists, his associations with the low-church Norwegians in this country and his constant reading of Passavant's *Missionary*, all helped to deepen his sympathy with the cause of abolition.

In 1855, T. N. Hasselquist began his weekly *Hemlandet*, the first Swedish-American newspaper, which discussed quite frankly the important political questions of the day. From the beginning Hasselquist pictured slavery in terms of the average abolitionist and appealed to the Swedes as "the sons of the Free North" to help throw off the social and economic thralldom of slavery. He stated that his political position was the result of "a firm conviction received partly from the Word of God, confirmed by some knowledge of American history and existing conditions." He denounced the Democratic party as the party of Catholics, corrupt, dishonest and lawless, and supported Lincoln wholeheartedly. The majority of the Swedes in America shared Hasselquist's views. But there is no evidence that political opinion entered into their ecclesiastical counsels or caused divisions among them as it did among other Lutherans.

During the years of actual military hostilities Lutheran people shared fully in the fortunes and misfortunes of their several sections. They marched loyally in the military ranks, shared in the casualties, suffered anxiety, grief, and privation in their homes, and in many places the destruction or confiscation of their property. At the outbreak of the war, Lutherans in America numbered somewhat more than a quarter of a million communicants. Of these about one-third were west of the Appalachian Mountains. About forty thousand were in states that joined the Confederacy. Somewhat less than two-thirds of all Lutherans were in synods adhering to the General Synod. Thus the distribution of Lutheran people among the sections was about the same as that of the nation as a whole.

Lutherans as individuals were active everywhere in the relief organizations that grew out of the war. When the United States Christian Commission was organized in November, 1861, Lutheran congregations made liberal contributions of funds. Lutheran women volunteered and served as nurses. Lutheran ministers served as chaplains. Lutheran laymen, particularly ministerial students, visited camps, hospitals, and battlefields, assisted the chaplains and surgeons, and helped to circulate literature. The General Synod commended the commission, and requested congregations to take regular collections of money, food, and clothing for its work. After the war was over this relief work on the part of Lutheran congregations was extended to their distressed brethren in the South.

Meanwhile, the Lutherans in the South affirmed their support and loyalty to the new government and the new Lutheran General Synod. Lutheran ministers joined in the appeal made by all the Protestant churches in the South in January, 1863, protesting the "horrible" efforts of the North to subjugate the South and appealing to enlightened Christian sentiment everywhere to intercede "against war, against persecution for conscience' sake, against the ravaging of the church of God by fanatical invasion." And the Lutherans in the South bore their share of the economic collapse that attended the end of the war and their share of the humiliation and suffering that came with reconstruction.

Many of the Lutheran congregations in the border states suffered property damage during the war. This was true, for example, of the churches at Winchester, Virginia, at Antietam, Maryland, at the old Hebron church in Madison County, Virginia, and the Ebenezer church that had been built by the Salzburgers in Georgia. In Charleston, South Carolina, soldiers of the North inflicted personal violence on Dr. Bachman, burned his valuable library, and damaged his church, because of his views.

The work of the Lutheran colleges and seminaries, North and South and West, was disrupted or completely suspended and in some cases their property was damaged. At Gettysburg, Dr. S. S. Schmucker, during thirty-five years, had taught nearly five hundred Lutheran ministers that slavery is a moral evil, that slaves should be educated and emancipated, and that slaveowners should be compensated for their loss of property. This he taught by precept and practice and print. During the decisive battle around the seminary buildings, Dr. Schmucker's house was invaded and damaged by the soldiers of the South, and his library partly destroyed. Only his flight from Gettysburg prevented personal violence. The main building of the institution was struck many times and severely damaged. For several months all the seminary buildings were used as hospitals.

In one respect the war was something less than calamity to Lutheran people: it helped to speed the process of Americanization among the immigrants. Through four anxious years their sons fought by the side of other Americans to preserve the Union. This created a sense of belonging, a sentiment of proprietary interest in the new homeland. Their neighbors also regarded them as genuine participants in the salvation of the Republic. The young men who served in the army had their eyes opened to possibilities in America beyond the homesteads of their parents, and this, together with the free-homestead policy of the government, led them to step out boldly into the alluring American world. The war had provided them with a body of heroes of whose American achievements they could be proud. It gave them good reasons to participate with other Americans in national holidays, especially memorial days. It opened their eyes to the prospect that ultimately their distinctive features would disappear and their special culture would become one of the many elements in the American social amalgam.

Moreover, the war greatly improved the economic status of the western farmer. After the panic of 1857 there was little market for the products of the fields, and the grain had piled high in the store-houses. The coming of the war made the prairie acres yield a high return in cash. The end of the war found many a rich Lutheran farmer where before there had been a poor Lutheran immigrant. He gave up his old log cabin for a new frame house. He reached out in various directions to lay hold on the culture of his adopted country. Because these immigrant Lutherans in the West and Northwest were involved in the great civil conflict so soon after their arrival in America, their transition in language and customs to full-fledged membership in American society proceeded more rapidly than that of the German Lutheran immigrants on the Atlantic seaboard in the eighteenth century.

Part V

IN THE DAYS OF BIG BUSINESS

(1870-1910)

Expansion and Enterprise

CHAPTER 21

GENERAL BACKGROUND

Beginning with the year 1870 the United States entered upon a period of phenomenal economic growth. This new economy brought changes that affected every department of human interest. It influenced profoundly the general trend both of politics and religion.

During the forty years following 1870, the country's population increased from forty millions to ninety-three millions. Nearly half of this increase was due to immigration. In constantly swelling numbers Europeans were again invading American shores. From 400,000 in 1870, the annual number of immigrants grew until during the last five years of this period it passed the million mark. The earlier immigrants came largely from central and northern Europe and settled down chiefly to agriculture in the Middle West and the Northwest. This greatly increased the resources and responsibilities of the Lutheran church. But after 1890 the tide began to flow in increasing proportions from southern and eastern Europe. This new type of immigrant, with his illiteracy and low standards of living, helped to increase the crowded conditions of the cities and raised a host of political and religious problems. The large-city population of the nation grew from twenty per cent of the total in 1870 to forty-six per cent in 1910 (with about twenty-one per cent in towns and villages), and the farmers now numbered less than one-third of the total population.

But while the population of the country was increasing two and a half times, the wealth of the nation was being multiplied by ten. Railroads, for instance, with the opening of new territory in the West and development of resources and industry in the whole country, by 1910 operated on a quarter of a million miles of track. They embraced one-seventh of the nation's wealth. More significant than the growth

Consolidation of management

of the railroads was the consolidation of management. By 1904 all the important lines were owned by seven or eight groups of capitalists. This destroyed competition and permitted discrimination in rates. Throughout the period efforts were made to regulate such abuses. But the business was too big for individual states to control. In 1887 the national Congress legislated on the whole matter and created the Interstate Commerce Commission to investigate complaints and punish *ICC* violations. Opinions differ as to the success of this commission in overcoming monopolies and preventing "conspiracies in restraint of trade," but in any case the federal government was forced to recognize the new situation created by "big business" and to assume new powers in the interest of the common good.

The consolidation of capital and management that began in the field of transportation soon spread to other lines of production and commerce. Small individual enterprises gave way to large combinations. Small stores merged into department stores. Small firms grew into corporations. Corporations invented "trusts" of such size that competitors were quickly driven out of business. Irresponsible monopolies were created. Trusts began with the Standard Oil Company, but soon invaded such important commodities as meat, steel, and others. For many years the efforts to control the trusts occupied the public interest and influenced national politics.

Another "big business" was the public service corporation. The growth of cities and the concurrent increase of comfort utilities such as water, electricity, gas, telephone, and street cars, brought huge combinations of capital which monopolized a service of an entire city. These corporations furnished almost unlimited opportunities for corruption, and public graft became an organized business. Occasional outbursts of public indignation, heard also in the church, proved ineffectual to uproot the evil until at the turn of the century they grew into a mighty tide of reform.

Despite the vast increase in national wealth and due to the centralization of this wealth in the hands of the business specialist who was called the capitalist, great multitudes of the people were worse off than their fathers had been, and one-fifth of the nation was in a constant state of poverty. Opportunities to rise out of poverty were greatly diminished. The typical laborer, the factory hand, had practically no chance to become a capitalist. The relations between employer and employee became wholly commercial. Trusts reduced the chances of the laborer to compete in the labor market and women, invading the labor market, helped to reduce wages. There were no more free lands to be had from the public domain.

One effect of these developments was a wave of social unrest. Socialism grew until, in the elections of 1910, it polled nearly a million votes. In his desperation the laboring man took a leaf from the business man's book and began to organize and combine. Already in 1870 forty trades had national organizations. The spirit of enterprise that moved the captain of industry was caught by the artisan and craftsman, and the trust found its counterpart among the laborers in the national "union." The trade unions soon organized into the strong American Federation of Labor, counting millions of members. With capital and labor thoroughly organized, war between the two was inevitable. The weapon most frequently used by labor was the strike, wielded with increasing frequency and success. The disastrous effects of strikes on the public led to a variety of efforts of control, and soon the national government began to devise machinery to lessen strikes and end the labor war.

It will be observed that every aspect of big business verged on politics, and finally involved the national government. A result was the diminishing of sectionalism. The South, no longer distracted by political reconstruction, began to share in the industrial development. Mines and forests were turned to economic advantage, manufactures began, and the old agricultural South was slowly transformed into a new South of diversified industries. The radical social changes that grew out of the nation's marvelous economic growth created a new national consciousness that called for the exercise of new powers of government. The business age had produced the business specialist or millionaire, and the labor specialist or union, and the political specialist or boss. The continued progress of the nation, therefore, demanded the government specialist or reformer. From both of the great parties he came in generous numbers. He overturned many outworn political traditions, and his prophesying of the "new nationalism" answered to the new national consciousness, the new demand for social and industrial freedom, that had evolved since 1870.

States and regions were now no longer the decisive political groupings of the American people, and divisions of power among federal and state units of government were not of primary concern. Instead, the horizontal cleavages separating opposed classes of the people were now the important boundaries of political units and action. The question was how to meet social and industrial problems, no matter whether by state or federal power. In every part of the social fabric there must be control, either state or national, as protection against predatory special interests.

The young reformers' crusade against vested wrong, against special privilege and secret monopoly and corrupt political middlemen, required new weapons of national dimensions. Their new and progressive political machinery included ballot reform, direct primary nominations, provisions against corruption in elections, the recall of officials, direct legislation by initiative and referendum, commission government of cities, and the direct election of United States senators. At the same time a formidable body of new federal laws and agencies dealt with questions that transcended the bounds of states. In these ways the progressive movement in politics moved to curb the tyranny of special privilege and at the same time to take the sting out of organized socialism.

Further strengthening the national government in dealing with nation-sized business, antitrust laws were given a cutting edge and the Interstate Commerce Commission was invested with powers touching a great variety of public interests. Congress also aided states in their warfare against injurious practices of various kinds. The provision of an elastic currency by means of federal reserve banks under federal control increased the national authority. Of special significance was the doctrine of the conservation of national resources, the movement in the direction of federal ownership and control of forest lands, mineral lands, swamp lands, waterways, water-power sites, and so forth. The new nationalism strengthened the bonds among the states and multiplied the powers of the central government, but did not for a moment diminish the functions of the individual states. This is the chief distinction between the nationalism that characterizes this period and the spirit of American nationality of the early years of the Republic.

The age of big business saw the communicant membership of the churches multiply more than twice as rapidly as the general population, from six and one-half millions or eighteen per cent of the population in 1870, to thirty-five millions or forty-three per cent of the population in 1910. This great increase in the relative strength of American Christianity increased the responsibilities of the churches at the same time the growing complexity of American society was confronting them with special problems. The immense stream of immigration that poured into this country during these forty years and the changing character of that immigration raised a score of problems affecting the churches. The Roman Catholic Church received the largest number of the newcomers, but the Lutheran church was a close second. All the churches were obliged to deal with the problems arising out of the congested foreign quarters in the cities, the discouraging condition of "downtown" churches, the abandoned country churches, the multiplication of languages, and the sudden migrations from older to newer states. To solve these extraordinary problems a double spirit of enterprise was needed in American Christianity. This was not lacking; the same spirit of large undertaking that characterized men in the affairs of business moved them also in their religious activities. The churches grew, and prospered as they grew.

The wealth of the nation was reflected in church finances. All over the country old and outgrown church buildings were replaced with large and expensive structures. In every new community, suburban or rural, church buildings were among the first to appear. The refined tastes of cities and towns were manifested in the erection of costly cathedrals and large churches of modern character. Expensive church adornments and elaborate furnishings became the order of the day. Exact business methods were applied. Budgets were devised and the lists of items were often quite formidable. Local activities were multiplied and in general the calls of benevolence were met with liberality. With the increased resources of church members a new spirit of stewardship and enterprise was awakened.

The new machinery that was invented in the sphere of politics had its religious counterpart in the more intensive organization of the churches. The American churches conceived the absorbing purpose of saving the world by transforming society; the fulfilling of that purpose they reduced to a regular business. They invented agencies of the widest variety. It was an age of specialists and the religious specialist came on the scene in many guises. Systematic and businesslike organization was one of the outstanding characteristics of the church. In its completeness and enterprise it resembled in many ways the great commercial projects of the period, and in some cases the volume of its transactions rivaled that of the trusts. The gospel enterprise created committees, societies, leagues, unions, and other organizations innumerable, covering both sexes and every stage of human life, for study, for prayer, for praise, for service, applying to every sort of human need and aimed at every habitation of man. No exigency was overlooked. The churches were filled with a frenzy of big businesslike organizing.

The attitude of denominations toward one another began to change under the influence of new preoccupations. The intolerant sectarianism of the past gave way to the realization that the various types of Christian life represented in the various Christian churches might be different without being necessarily in conflict.

Historical studies contributed to the changed attitudes. Superficially these studies of the past thought and work of the churches might have enhanced sectarianism, but continued further, they created an awareness of the life shared by all.

But earlier confessional laxity and moves for uniformity among denominations in matters of belief or ritual or administration did not reappear; there was simply a longing for toleration, for the laying aside of the ill will and jealousies and hostility that had characterized the middle period of the nineteenth century. The supreme allegiance of the churches to Jesus Christ did not hinder them from remaining true to their separate histories and cultivating their denominational consciousness, as the states could maintain their allegiance to the whole nation while yet cultivating their several sectional interests. Among themselves they divided the territory in which all labored, so as to leave no camping ground for such special privilege as the world, the flesh, and the devil. Yet there was no tendency whatever to surrender distinctive denominational interests.

As a matter of practice this did not mean a trend in the direction of church union, but towards the consolidation of the denominations, each within itself. Many facts illustrate this, such as the Pan-Presbyterian Alliance, the Ecumenical Methodist Conferences, the World-Baptist Congress, and the various efforts of the smaller sects to return to the larger bodies from which they had split off.

For American Christianity in general there was an increase in what is sometimes called churchliness, in some quarters an increase in confessionalism, and in others an increase in particular theories of church polity. Everywhere it meant a decided increase in the enterprise of evangelization, both at home and abroad.

In the Lutheran church in this period, therefore, we find a deepening of church consciousness and an increase in loyalty to historic Lutheranism in doctrine and worship and practice, and at the same time a more tolerant attitude towards all Christians everywhere, a new spirit of enterprise and large undertaking in the proper business of our church, a rapid growth and zealous activity of new general bodies of Lutherans in this country. "American Lutheranism" and internal discord give place to that "Pan-Lutheranism" and mutual understanding that foreshadows an age of larger units.

CHAPTER 22

GROWTH IN NUMBERS AND BENEVOLENCE

The confirmed membership of the Lutheran church in the United States increased from less than half a million in 1870 to nearly two and a quarter millions in 1910. This was the largest relative increase among the large denominations. The number of Lutherans passed the number of Presbyterians, and the Lutheran church advanced from fourth to third place among the Protestant churches in the country. Only the Methodists and the Baptists surpassed her numbers. Much of this increase was due to immigration that not only swelled her numbers and expanded her reach, but also presented a great home missionary challenge and infused the spirit of enterprise into every line of the church's benevolence.

The immigration of Germans, greatly reduced by the Civil War, began to roll in again. From 1866 until 1873 they came at the rate of one hundred and thirty thousand a year. The American panic of 1873 reduced the numbers by about two-thirds until 1880 when another upward bound began; 1882 was the record year with more than a quarter of a million German immigrants. After 1885 the numbers steadily declined, reaching the lowest point in 1898 with seventeen thousand immigrants. This decline was due to Germany's great growth as an industrial nation, her less severe requirements of military duty, the disappearance of free land in America, and the increasing competition in the United States with cheap labor from southern and southeastern Europe. After the beginning of the twentieth century, Germans came at the rate of about twenty thousand annually and directed their course chiefly to the western provinces of Canada.

The three million German immigrants of the period were not uniformly devoted to the church. Many of them were people of culture and education. But they differed from the German immigrants of earlier periods in that they were chiefly interested in gaining economic and commercial advantages. Many of them became prominent in technical and professional vocations. Large numbers of them went to swell the multitude of the churchless. These Germans went to all parts of the country and greatly enlarged the responsibilities of the Lutheran church all over the land. But the largest numbers of them settled on the belt that spreads westward between the Ohio River and the Great Lakes and onward into the neighboring two tiers of trans-Mississippi states. All the large cities received tens of thousands of them, but the zone of densest German settlement lay along the shores of Lakes Ontario, Erie, and Michigan, along the Ohio River and down the Mississippi from St. Paul to St. Louis. The Lutheran bodies in the Middle West were confronted with a tremendous home missionary opportunity and every Lutheran synod in the land felt an unprecedented impulse to missionary activity.

More than a million and three-quarters of Scandinavians also came to America during these years, contributing greatly to the size and spirit of the Lutheran church. Half of them came from Sweden, a third from Norway, and one-sixth from Denmark. Before the Civil War these Northmen averaged fewer than two thousand a year. But the glowing reports they sent back to the fatherland, the alluring terms of the American Homestead Act of 1862, and the revival of business after the war, caused a rapid increase in the number of immigrants from these northern kingdoms until in 1882 it reached the high-water mark of more than one hundred thousand. Toward the end of the century financial stagnation in the United States produced a great decline in the number of immigrants. But the revival of prosperity in the first few years of the new century greatly swelled the number again until in 1903 seventy-seven thousand arrived. After that date the figures diminished rapidly.

That the Scandinavian immigrants came to America to better their economic conditions is indicated by the way their numbers fluctuated with the changes in American business conditions, and by the location of their settlements in the rich, unoccupied farming lands of the upper Mississippi Valley. Minnesota became their chief home, and before the end of the period that state had a Scandinavian population of over a million. Other states that received large numbers of the Northmen were Wisconsin, the Dakotas, Illinois, Michigan, and Iowa. During the later decades, with an increase in the proportion of skilled laborers, especially among the Swedes, some of the eastern cities, such as New York and Brooklyn and the cities of New England, retained a considerable number. But fully three-fourths of them were massed in the fertile agricultural region of the Northwest.

Nearly all of these Swedes, Norwegians, and Danes were potential materials for the Lutheran church in America. But they came in such huge numbers and were so thoroughly massed together in self-sufficient communities on the American frontier that it was not easy for the Lutheran church in America to reach them and assimilate them. Then, too, they were so engrossed in their occupations, and many of them were so glad to be free from the rigors of the state churches in Europe, that they were not zealous in forming church organizations among themselves. It is estimated that only seven per cent of the Danes joined any church, not more than twenty per cent of the Swedes, and somewhat less than thirty per cent of the Norwegians. Nevertheless, the synods that had been formed among the Swedes and Norwegians during the preceding period received large accessions from the new tide of immigration in this period.

After the Swedes and Norwegians withdrew from the Synod of Northern Illinois in 1860, the Scandinavian Lutherans in America developed for the most part independently of the other Lutheran bodies. When ten years later the Scandinavian Augustana Synod separated into the Swedish Augustana and the Norwegian Augustana Synods, the former, now a purely Swedish body, began to respond energetically to the great home mission challenge arising out of the presence of such a large number of their countrymen. In twenty-five years it grew from sixteen thousand members to a hundred thousand, and in the next twenty-five years doubled that number. Meanwhile several educational institutions were established to supplement the work of the schools at Rock Island. Gustavus Adolphus College at St. Peter, Minnesota, dates from 1862, Bethany College at Lindsborg, Kansas, was opened in 1881, and Upsala College at Kenilworth, New Jersey, in 1893. The internal history of the Augustana Synod, as related in the next chapter, clearly shows the effects of its remarkable progress in numbers and benevolence. The synod was not without its inner conflicts, but the growth and activity of the body were exhilarating to its members and it succeeded in unifying the great Swedish constituency of the Lutheran church in America. Its theological thought was steadily directed into conservative channels by Dr. T. N. Hasselquist, who for more than a quarter of a century was president of Augustana College and a teacher in the Theological Seminary there and editor of the *Augustana*, the official organ of the synod.

But the Norwegians were even more successful in gathering their countrymen into the Lutheran church. The Norwegian Lutheran Synod, organized in 1853, with only seventeen congregations, grew rapidly during this period to a membership of more than a hundred and fifty thousand. For several years the Norwegian Synod was a member of the German Synodical Conference. But the largest body of Norwegian Lutherans was formed in 1890, when the strong Anti-Missouri Brotherhood, which had separated from the Norwegian Synod, united with the strong Norwegian-Danish Conference, and the smaller Norwegian Augustana Synod, and organized the United Norwegian Church. This body numbered more than a quarter of a million members before the end of the period. Altogether the various organizations of Norwegian Lutherans in this country counted over half a million members in 1910. Their chief seminary is at St. Paul, Minnesota. Their largest college is St. Olaf College at Northfield, Minnesota, founded in 1874. Luther College at Decorah, Iowa, dates from 1861. Another large institution is Concordia College at Moorhead, Minnesota, which was opened in 1891. Their official organs are the *Lutheraneren,* and in English, *The Lutheran Herald*. The Norwegian Lutherans' patient labor for unity was not to be successful until 1917 with the organization of the Evangelical Lutheran Church.

The Danish immigrants effected two church organizations. The first, begun in 1872, was called the Danish Lutheran Church in America. It claimed to be a branch of the national church of Denmark and received aid from the Danish government, but never numbered more than twenty thousand members. The second organization began in 1884 when many of the Danes in the Norwegian-Danish Conference withdrew. In 1896 they united with those who had separated from the Danish Lutheran Church in America because of its alleged false doctrine and its state-church ideas, and formed the United Danish Lutheran Church in America. This organization is more than twice the size of the older body of Danish Lutherans. The Danes have been much distracted by factional differences on questions of polity and of practice, and have not been so successful as the Swedes and Norwegians in gathering their immigrant countrymen into their churches or even in maintaining their hold on their own sons and daughters. These two groups today are known respectively as the American Norwegian Evangelical Lutheran Church and the United Evangelical Lutheran Danish Church.

Since more than three-fourths of the Scandinavian immigrants did not unite with the Lutheran church, and a very small percentage united with other American churches, the vast majority of them presented a most inviting mission field for the Lutheran church in this country, especially for the Lutheran church of Scandinavian origin. The sturdy personal qualities of the Scandinavians together with their uniform loyalty to historic Lutheranism impelled them under this challenge to a vigorous development of the practical activities of the church. As these Scandinavians constituted nearly one-fourth of all the Lutherans in America, their spirit reacted favorably on the entire church.

Apart from the increase due to the immigration of European Lutherans, much of the growth in the church is accounted for by the natural increase of the Lutheran population in America and by the aggressive missionary spirit that began to pervade all branches of the church. The impulse of big business was strongly felt in the benevolences and the practical affairs of the church. Since the General Synod in 1869 had centralized its chief branches of benevolence in the hands of general boards, the energies and resources of the entire general body were marshaled for rapid development. Other general bodies saw the practical advantages of unifying their benevolent forces and, as rapidly as church polity permitted, they set up new machinery for combining agencies. The result was more effective work in older lines of benevolence as well as the new branches of benevolence that now began to receive cultivation and in the new fields that were opened by missionary agencies.

The General Synod and the General Council vied with each other in sending their home mission agents westward across the Mississippi

Valley and the Rockies and on to the Pacific Coast. One by one the most strategic places were occupied. The only limit to the harvest was the lack of laborers to man the fields. The General Synod moved due westward from Ohio, Indiana, and Illinois. In its line of march, the Kansas Synod organized in 1868, the Nebraska Synod in 1871, the Rocky Mountain Synod in 1891, and the California Synod the same year. The General Synod was especially concerned with the old-American Lutherans who had migrated from the East, but also helped to organize the immigrant Germans. The German Wartburg Synod sprang from the Central Illinois Synod in 1872 and united with the General Synod, and the German Nebraska Synod, organized in 1890, also joined the General Synod.

While this westward expansion, together with the increases in the older synods, more than tripled its membership, the benevolences of the General Synod increased tenfold. The Board of Home Missions, exploring the land and planting the church, in forty years expended more than a million and a half dollars, and established over six hundred new congregations, which themselves contributed more than five million dollars for benevolence. In this work substantial aid was given by the Board of Church Extension, whose assets at the end of the period were approaching a million dollars.

To meet the need of pastors for English-speaking congregations of the western synods, Midland College was founded in 1887 at Atchison, Kansas, and in connection with it the Western Theological Seminary in 1893. Both were later removed to Fremont, Nebraska.

The Germans of the General Synod were the special concern of Dr. J. D. Severinghaus. He brought pastors for them from Germany, especially from Breklum Seminary. In 1883 he established a German Seminary in Chicago, but thirteen years later the Wartburg and the German Nebraska Synods took charge of the work and transferred it to Atchison. The German Nebraska Synod afterwards established its own seminary, the Martin Luther Seminary at Lincoln, Nebraska. The German element in the General Synod founded its own publishing house at Burlington, Iowa, and its own church paper, the *Lutherischer Zionsbote*. But the General Synod became constantly more English and in 1910 only one-tenth of its pastors and congregations used the German language. The care of the Lutherans from Germany devolved largely on other Lutheran bodies.

In the General Council it was the Pittsburgh Synod that carried on home missionary work most extensively. It sent missionaries to Canada, Minnesota, and Texas, and laid the foundation for the synods that were afterwards organized in these parts. The moving spirit in this work was Dr. Passavant. The work was furthered and co-ordinated by the General Council's English and German Mission Boards. The missionary operations were pushed with special zeal in the fertile Lutheran territory of the Northwest, where the General Council made good the loss of the Wisconsin, Minnesota, Illinois, and Michigan Synods, which had joined the Missourians in the Synodical Conference. The General Council in 1871 organized the Indiana Synod (changed to Chicago Synod in 1896) and in 1891 the English Synod of the Northwest, organized to conserve the many English missions that the General Council had established at strategical points in Wisconsin, Minnesota, the Dakotas, Utah, and Washington. In 1891 also a number of German congregations in the Canadian Northwest were united in the Manitoba Synod. With the organization in 1901 of the Pacific Synod formed of the western part of the Synod of the Northwest, the General Council also reached the Pacific Coast. Immediately the work was pushed northward, and the Nova Scotia Synod was formed of part of the Pittsburgh Synod in 1903 while the Central Canada Synod was organized by the General Council Board in 1908.

As these new synods flourished, new schools were established. Thiel College was established in 1870 and finally located at Greenville, Pennsylvania. Wagner College was founded at Rochester, New York, in 1883, and afterwards transferred to Staten Island. Dr. Passavant was instrumental in establishing the Chicago Theological Seminary in 1891, and under Dr. R. F. Weidner's direction it grew to great usefulness, particularly in furnishing ministers for the English congregations of the Northwest. The German Canada Synod and the Central Canada Synod drew their ministers largely from the Kropp Seminary in Germany, but when this course was cut off in 1913, they began their own seminary at Waterloo, Ontario. The Manitoba Synod established its school at Saskatoon in 1913. The Pacific Synod in 1911 founded a theological seminary at Portland, Oregon, but soon removed it to Seattle, Washington. Thus the geographical line of the educational advance also reached the Pacific Coast.

But while the missionary forces of the church were following the westward movement of the population across the continent, they were at the same time helping to solve the problems growing out of the enormous increase of city populations in the East. These problems were met with a high spirit of enterprise by all parts of the Lutheran church, and a variety of methods and agencies. City missions and inner missions came on the scene with their respective boards, committees, and superintendents. The eastern synods grew rapidly. In greater New York City alone, where at the close of the Civil War there were only two English Lutheran churches and twenty-two others, and where in 1870 there were only thirty-four in all, there were in 1910 no less than one hundred and thirty-four Lutheran churches, and in 1918 one hundred and sixty-six. Lutheranism had become a force in the religious life of the nation's metropolis. Similar progress was made in the other large cities of the land. But with all her city increases during this period, the Lutheran church continued to be predominantly rural. Her membership in the country districts did not show the losses of many other denominations, but grew and multiplied, so that in 1910 three-fourths of her members were found in rural communities and towns of less than 25,000 people.

The enterprise of the church in this period is further indicated by her foreign missionary achievements. In 1869 the field among the Telugus in India was divided, the Guntur station being assigned to the General Synod and the Rajahmundry station to the General Council. The two missions maintained cordial relations. The work was well supported by the church both with men and with means. The number of the missionaries increased to thirty. The outstanding names are Unangst, Harpster, and Uhl of the General Synod, and Heyer and Schmidt of the General Council. More than a thousand native workers were employed in Christian work. A hospital and a college were established at Guntur, and the medical and educational work of the mission received wide recognition. In 1910 the native membership on this field was nearly fifty thousand.

The mission established on the west coast of Africa by the General Synod through Morris Officer took an awful toll of the lives of missionaries because of the deadly climate. But reinforcements arrived from time to time and this mission furnished many examples of heroic faith and courage. Dr. David A. Day succeeded in continuing his splendid labors for more than twenty years before the dread African fever carried him off.

In Japan the Lutheran church of America was first represented by the United Synod of the South. In 1892 work was begun in the city of Saga on the island of Kyushu. The mission soon extended its work to other cities on that island. The General Council co-operated in this work and in 1908 also established its own mission in Tokyo. Thus was laid the foundation of a large missionary undertaking in that empire.

The total contributions for foreign missions in the General Synod, the General Council, and the United Synod of the South during the last biennium of this period reached the half million mark.

The foreign missionary activity of the Joint Synod of Ohio and the German Synod of Iowa was carried on through the societies of Germany. The work of the Missouri Synod calls for a separate statement. The Scandinavians responded nobly to the call of the foreign missions. The Augustana Synod co-operated with the General Council in its work in India, and in addition helped the societies of Sweden to carry on a very successful work in China. The Norwegian Lutherans in America also were very active in China, and their different bodies contributed $118,000 to this work in 1915. The Norwegians are likewise laboring extensively in the southern part of Madagascar. Altogether the various bodies of Lutherans in America in 1910 were making an annual expenditure for missions and other benevolences of two and a half millions of dollars, and for local purposes an additional ten millions.

The Lutherans' growth in numbers and the expansion of their benevolences show that the church was alert to every opportunity to help establish the kingdom of God on earth. She was ready to employ all manner of organization, the newest inventions of science, and the most approved methods of business in that completely organized, business age. She quickened all her movements to keep pace with those strenuous times. She accepted the peculiar responsibility devolving upon her to minister the age-old gospel to the new needs of a rapidly growing nation. She no longer apologized for her existence on this continent, nor did she try to tone down her distinguishing characteristics. With a strong appeal to her membership for deeper devotion and more intense loyalty she drew together her forces, conserved her faith and her talent, and quietly proceeded to make her impress on the land of her adoption and to take her place as one of the outstanding forces in American Christianity of the twentieth century. But great as was the advance during the days of big business, this was only a dim prophecy of greater things to come.

CHAPTER 23

THE DEVELOPMENT OF THE AUGUSTANA LUTHERAN CHURCH

It is a stalwart type of Lutheranism that is organized in America under the name of the oldest of Protestant creeds, the basic confession of all Lutherans. The Augustana Lutherans came to America from the land of Lutheran archbishops and cathedrals, of high Lutheran liturgies and firm Lutheran loyalties.

After the colonization project of Gustavus Adolphus and the settlement of the Swedish Lutherans on the Delaware River in 1638, Swedish immigration to America soon ceased. Descendants of the settlers in the neighborhood of Philadelphia and Wilmington had lost all contact with old Sweden and the Lutheran church, and were forgotten among the people of Sweden, when about 1840 the king of Sweden's new liberal policy let his subjects emigrate without permits and heavy fees. Emigration began again from the Lutheran parishes of Sweden, but the formerly Lutheran churches on the Delaware gave it neither impulse nor direction.

These new immigrants came from a different background in Sweden, with different motives, and to a different part of America. Settling on the prairie lands of the upper Mississippi Valley, they came just in time to be baptized as Americans in the fire of civil war and in time to give direction to the main stream of Swedish immigration that followed.

The postwar spirit of expansion and enterprise of American Christians and of Lutherans in particular, was nowhere more evident than among the Swedish Lutherans. The foundations for a solid synodical structure had been wisely laid amid difficulties; immigration provided the superstructure of organization and service. In the decade of the

1850's Swedish and Norwegian immigrants together numbered about 20,000. During the following decade that number was multiplied more than fivefold. Between 1870 and 1880 the number of Swedish immigrants alone was 116,000, and during the next ten years nearly 400,000. In the last decade of the nineteenth century the number was 230,000 and during the first decade of the twentieth century about a quarter of a million.

The Middle West continued to be the destination of the vast majority of these Lutheran immigrants, but as the stream flowed on decade after decade it sent great numbers also to the forests and cities of the Northwest, and during the closing years of the nineteenth century to the cities of the East with their multiplying opportunities in industry and commerce. In the twentieth century they reached to the deep South and the far West, and so to almost every state in the union.

Practically all of these immigrants came from Lutheran parishes in Sweden. Here was abundant personnel for the building of a strong Lutheran church in America. While less than one-fourth of the immigrants found their way into Lutheran congregations in the New World, those who did become church members were a worthy multitude, and the others constituted a perpetual challenge to the missionary agencies of all the Lutheran churches.

The settlers who came before 1860 suffered many of the hardships of frontier life, but they persistently cultivated their faith. At many places the settlers came together regularly each week and selected one of their number to lead the Sunday worship until an ordained pastor could be obtained. Those early days do not present the familiar picture of pastors seeking congregations, but of congregations seeking pastors. Yet the call for pastors met with little response in Sweden, because the authorities, both in church and state, looked upon the emigrants to America as deserters. However, a few pastors in Sweden were impressed by the personal letters they received from America. They saw the great need among their friends and former parishioners now in the New World, and they answered the call. Devoted souls and wise leaders, they laid solid foundations for a strong Lutheran church among the Swedish immigrants. We have already told of the pioneer and patriarch among the early Swedish Lutherans, the "Prairie Shepherd," Lars P. Esbjörn. Not the least of his accomplishments was to induce other pastors in Sweden, men of learning and practical ability, to join him in building the church in America. Such were Hasselquist and Carlsson, Andren and Norelius, who became the pillars of the Augustana Lutheran Church.

The ten years preceding 1860 were decisive for the temper and policy of the future Augustana Lutheran Church. During this period congregations continued to grow in size and number throughout Indiana, Illinois, Iowa, and Minnesota. Hasselquist arrived in 1852 and Carlsson the next year. Hasselquist began his American ministry at Galesburg while Carlsson took charge of Immanuel Church in Chicago. But neither of these talented men limited his influence to his own congregation, each had a part in determining the character of the entire Augustana Synod.

During his pastorate of twenty-two years in Chicago, Carlsson laid down the principles that were afterwards adopted by the congregations of the whole synod. In the constitution which he prepared for his own congregation and for the Swedish churches in Indiana, the basis for membership in the congregation is halfway between the comprehensive character of a state church and the exclusiveness of sectarian congregations. Carlsson adhered to the external forms of the Swedish Church, and in this respect he exerted a profound influence on his brethren. Above all a zealous Christian, he set an example of sane, practical religion that left its traces on the synod with whose early life he was identified. In home mission activity and educational work Carlsson started lines of development that are still continuing.

At the same time that Carlsson was working in Chicago, Hasselquist in Galesburg and other places was impressing on the formative congregations something of his own simple, earnest piety. His preaching had lasting effects on the hungering souls to whom he ministered. Swedish Lutherans still regard him as the ideal of the evangelical pulpit. Through his periodical Hasselquist reached countless others, and long before it became the official organ of the Augustana Synod it brought inspiration and edification to the new Swedish communities throughout the Middle West.

Both of these men encouraged talented and consecrated young men of the congregations to prepare themselves for the gospel ministry and to receive ordination. They themselves undertook the work of teaching these younger men and thus gradually built up a native ministry.

Among the founders of the synod, mention must be made also of O. C. T. Andren. He came from Sweden in 1856 to the congregation at Moline, Illinois. His devout Christian spirit and his effective organization of his congregation influenced the whole church. When the seminary was established, he was sent to Sweden and Norway in 1860 to secure funds and books. After much difficulty, he secured five thousand volumes from the private library of Charles XVI as the nucleus for the seminary library. Special collections were authorized in the churches of the realm, and from these the seminary in America received more than ten thousand dollars. Failing health prevented Andren from returning to America.

Among these early leaders, Eric Norelius had a more varied activity than any other. Coming to America in 1851 at the age of eighteen, he completed his theological education at the Columbus Seminary of the Joint Synod of Ohio, became more strictly confessional than his older colleagues, and made his contributions to Swedish American Lutheranism in the realm of thought rather than in the realm of action. For more than half a century, until his death in 1916, he served the Augustana Synod with distinction as pastor, missionary, professor, editor, and synodical president.

These Swedish Lutheran pastors and their congregations held membership, as we have seen, in the Northern Illinois Synod, one of the districts of the General Synod. Here they had fellowship also with a small number of the Norwegian Lutheran pastors and their congregations. These Scandinavians found certain elements in the spirit of the General Synod quite congenial. They had come from those circles and communities in Sweden and Norway where "lay activity" was cultivated, and they were attracted by the spirit of the men in the General Synod who encouraged the organization of voluntary "societies" for aggressive evangelism and other Christian work like temperance reform, Sabbath observance, spiritual refreshing, and the cultivation of genuine personal piety. They did not agree with the doctrinal position of the General Synod because its subscription to the Augsburg Confession was not unqualified, but the General Synod did not prescribe to its districts in matters of liturgy or doctrine.

However, the Swedish and Norwegian pastors were conscious of their distinctive problems and for that reason in 1855 they organized the United Scandinavian Conference. This was not intended to interfere with their wider fellowship in the Northern Illinois Synod. The conference was a deliberative organization in which the pastors and laymen of both nationalities met to discuss matters of common interest, such as congregational constitutions, care of vacant pastorates, religious instruction, church music, and matters of liturgy. Relations to other Lutheran bodies and the training of ministerial candidates also received much attention. The Scandinavians were sending their ministerial candidates to Illinois State University, an institution of the Northern Illinois Synod, and from 1858 maintained Lars P. Esbjörn as their professor of theology there. But this arrangement grew increasingly unsatisfactory. Moreover, the Scandinavians felt the constant jibes of the more orthodox groups, the Missouri Synod, the Joint Synod of Ohio and the Norwegian Synod, who charged that in joining the Synod of Northern Illinois they were the victims of deception by nativists and Know-Nothings, and that they were guilty of unionism, un-Lutheran theology and Reformed polity.

The Scandinavians had secured changes in the constitution of the Northern Illinois Synod in the direction of more definite subscription to the Augsburg Confession, and they had insisted on binding their professor of theology to the Unaltered Augsburg Confession. But it soon became evident that there was a serious difference between the United Scandinavian Conference and the rest of the Northern Illinois Synod. For various reasons the Scandinavians continued to grow in their Lutheran consciousness, and events in the General Synod increased their distance from it. Open discussion was avoided for several years; the barrier of language contributed to the quiet but increased the tension. The incident of the "Definite Platform" in the General Synod in 1855 was disquieting to the Scandinavians, and finally the reception of the Melanchthon Synod into the General Synod in 1859 made the break inevitable.

When suddenly in the spring of 1860, Esbjörn left Illinois State University with the Scandinavian students, the Scandinavian Conference approved, and issued a call for the organization of a new synod. Thus at Jefferson Prairie (near Clinton), Wisconsin, in June, 1860, the Augustana Synod was born. Hasselquist was the first president. The new synod embraced 3,747 communicant members in thirty-six Swedish congregations, fifteen in Illinois, thirteen in Minnesota, three in Iowa, three in Indiana, one in New York, and one in Pennsylvania. There were twenty-five Swedish pastors. The Norwegians in the synod numbered 1,200 communicant members, thirteen congregations, and eight pastors.

The Augustana Synod has developed through several well-defined periods. The first decade witnessed the steady growth of the synodical idea. The next twenty-five years is characterized by the growing importance of the conferences in the synod. Since 1895 the synod has continued its growth and internal reorganization, and for thirty years has been agitated with problems of centralization and decentralization.

During the synod's first decade the few remaining traces of dependence upon the church in Sweden were wiped out. With the founding and development of the seminary in Paxton, the synod was assured of ministers from Scandinavian homes in America. Turning to the task of home missions, the synod felt itself responsible for the vacant congregations and unorganized fields among the Swedes of America. A missionary committee secured means and commissioned men as rapidly as possible to carry the ministry to Swedish Lutherans in Kansas, in the Lake Superior region of Minnesota, in western Iowa, in New York State, in Massachusetts and Vermont, in Michigan and Nebraska. In this way the geographical borders of the synod were extended by leaps and bounds.

During this same difficult war decade, the Norwegians in the synod began to consider a separate organization. Their relations with the Swedes had always been cordial, in the Northern Illinois Synod and in the conferences that preceded the Scandinavian Augustana Synod, but as the preponderance of Swedes and the Swedish language increased in the synod and in the seminary the Norwegians became restless. Paxton was rather remote from the Norwegian congregations, and the Norwegian professor at the seminary, a young patriot from Norway, agitated for separation. Moreover, some of the Norwegians wanted to use the liturgy of the Church of Norway in their congregations. Then, too, H. A. Preus and other leaders in the Norwegian Synod kept up a running criticism of the doctrinal basis and the practice of the Augustana Synod. The Swedes deplored the separatist spirit of the Norwegians, but when the formal parting came at the convention in 1870 it was entirely peaceful. The strength of the Norwegians at the time of their separation from the Scandinavian Augustana Synod was 24 pastors, 30 congregations and 1,784 communicant members. The Swedes had 46 pastors, 99 congregations and 16,376 communicant members. Thirteen congregations were mixed and were called "Scandinavian." They had a membership of 659.

The withdrawing Norwegians divided into two groups, one the Norwegian Danish Augustana Synod, the other the Conference of the Norwegian Danish Evangelical Lutheran Church in America. The Swedes continued the old organization and until 1894 bore the name "The Swedish Evangelical Lutheran Augustana Synod." Friendly relations continued among the two main branches of Scandinavian Lutheranism in America, but for more than half a century, until pressed by problems of world war, there was no co-operation between them.

At the same time the Swedes lost the Norwegians, they entered a much larger fellowship with a body of Lutherans centering in the East. Present at the organization of the General Council in 1867, Dr. Hasselquist was sufficiently impressed to urge his own synod to join. He believed in centralization and community of effort. He assured the conservative leaders in the East that the Swedish Lutherans had no desire to build up a nationalistic church in this country and would lay aside the Swedish language as soon as possible. But his brethren in the Augustana Synod were cautious, in part perhaps because they had painful memories of a former alliance. They disliked the pulpit fellowship and the lodge membership tolerated among these Lutherans of German descent, and the drinking habits they practiced. But because the General Council was not planned as a strongly centralized organization and functioned largely as an advisory body, and because its district synods retained all of their powers, doubts had largely disappeared by 1870 and union with the General Council was carried out. It was felt that certain tasks of the church could best be undertaken in common with other synods, and a common adherence to the Lutheran confessions was considered sufficient cause for union. Accordingly the Augustana Synod united with the General Council and began a relationship that continued almost half a century.

But there was so much disparity between the Augustana Synod

and the other district synods in the council that in certain parts of the Augustana Synod the demand eventually arose for withdrawal from the council. This was particularly true after 1895 when the problem of language and the difficulties of policy concerning English missions became acute.

When the Augustana Synod joined the General Council in 1870 its ninety-nine Swedish congregations had attained a high degree of solidarity and had developed a clear consciousness of their mission. Then began a new period in the history of the synod. The next twenty-five years were a period of such rapid growth that the synodical organization of the congregations became unwieldy. It made necessary a wide diversification of work among them, and this in turn made necessary a new definition of the relation of the congregations to the synod. This period brought a tremendous number of immigrants from Sweden, and membership lists grew rapidly. The 16,000 members of 1870 were more than doubled in the next five years, and between 1880 and 1890 the membership doubled again. In 1895 the hundred thousand mark was passed and the 99 congregations had grown to 818, served by 400 pastors.

In the face of these conditions the old Mission Committee of the synod gave way to a new agency called the "Central Committee." This, as its name implies, was mainly a clearing house for the missionary work of the conferences. As the synodical agency saw that it could not care for the whole field, conference divisions were recognized and even subdivisions into districts. Each conference became responsible for missionary work in its territory, although its mission board was subordinate to that of the synod. This decentralization not only relieved the Central Committee of an enormous task but also prompted the conferences to the performance of that task. More and more the conferences became the units of work within the synod. Kansas, Nebraska, and New York established their own institutions of learning in this period. Nebraska, Illinois, and Minnesota started hospitals. Iowa, Kansas, New York, and Illinois began orphanages. In general, these were years of intensive labor, and the comparative freedom given the conferences stimulated local endeavor.

By 1880 the synod had so far recognized the work of the conferences as to establish a synodical council of representatives from the conferences to prepare the work of each meeting of the synod and to attend to any matters committed to it by the synod. In 1894 the new constitution of the synod officially approved of the conference organization and thus made permanent what necessity had originated. At the same session it became evident that the synod had now grown to such dimensions as to make impossible universal representation from the congregations. So it was decided that thereafter the conferences should elect representatives to the meeting of synod in proportion to their membership. The conferences practically became district synods. Much of the authority of the president of the synod and many of his duties were transferred to the hands of the conference presidents. The meetings of the synod became general conventions of the conferences. Scholarly E. Norelius lent the weight of his influence to these decentralizing tendencies.

When the synod was first organized it was intended to have one theological seminary and a single college, both for the purpose of preparing men for the ministry. As the territory of the synod expanded and the programs of the conferences enlarged, it was felt that the conferences, either singly or in groups, should establish and maintain their own colleges or academies, not only as feeders for the one seminary but to train men and women for various professions. Bethany College, founded in 1881 at Lindsborg, Kansas, by Pastor Carl Swensson, became a responsibility of the Kansas Conference of the synod and began to offer a variety of courses. Within another decade, to Augustana College and Bethany College were added Gustavus Adolphus College at St. Peter, Minnesota, Luther Academy at Wahoo, Nebraska, Hope Academy at Moorhead, Minnesota, and Emanual Academy at Minneapolis, Upsala College in Brooklyn, New York, and even Martin Luther College in Chicago which was within the same conference as Augustana College. Only the economic depression of the nineties halted the educational decentralization in the Augustana Synod.

The larger powers of the church still remained in the hands of the synod, such as ordination of ministers, ministerial education, ministerial pensions, church extension, deaconess work, publication of literature, and matters pertaining to the liturgy, the hymnal, and the catechism. The synod likewise retained the responsibility of approving congregational constitutions and of furnishing the congregations with religious literature. One important instrument in fostering a degree of solidarity in the synod and cultivating a sense of common interest among the various conferences was the official paper *Augustana* which began in December, 1879, as a merger of a number of unofficial journals. The pension fund was put under synodical control. But of home mission work, the synod had left to it after 1880 only such fields as were beyond the confines of the conferences: the Pacific Coast, Mormon territory, and Idaho, Montana, Alabama, and Florida. All of these fields, except the Pacific Coast, continued to be cared for by the general body. In addition, the synod, as distinct from the conferences, had responsibility for work among Mexican Americans, Negroes, migrants, and the Jews.

As its home mission field decreased, however, the synod became more and more interested in the foreign field. The proposed mission to the American Indians came to naught. But in 1880 the synod undertook to support the work of the General Council among the Telugu peoples in India. From that date to the present the Augustana Synod has contributed much, both in men and means, to this field. In 1899 the mission in Puerto Rico was begun by an Augustana man and claimed missionaries from that synod until in 1903 the mission was assumed by the General Council. Of missionary character also are the Immigrant and Seamen's Missions which date from this period and which were controlled directly by the synod.

The period between 1895 and 1950 was one of continued growth and internal reorganization. The membership has once more doubled itself. The congregations now number about 1,200, the pastors more than 1,000, and the baptized membership more than 500,000. Its thirteen conferences span the continent.

As it grew the synod greatly increased its practical activities. It expanded its own home mission work and helped the weaker conferences in theirs, and further extended its activities in foreign missions. In 1908 the China Mission Society turned over the control of its work to the Augustana Synod. For some years this field had an annual budget of $400,000, but in recent years missionary work among Chinese had been limited to Hong Kong and Formosa. In 1917 work was begun in the field of Tanganyika in East Africa and today more than a hundred missionaries are maintained there. Since 1950 the Augustana Lutheran Church has been sending missionaries to Japan. The work of co-operation with the United Lutheran Church among the Telugus in India has continued.

Inner mission work of the synod was carried on in the metropolitan centers. It ministered not only to Swedish people but to all people in need. There were fifty-four institutions. Among them were twelve children's homes, eleven hospitals, twenty-one old folks' homes, and ten hospices. The deaconess mother house at Omaha, for which the synod assumed responsibility in 1903, had eighty-eight deaconesses. The Lutheran Seaman's Center in New York City serves hundreds of men and expends nearly $50,000 a year. Both in the number and in the quality of its institutions of charity the Augustana Synod, in proportion to its size, led the Lutheran bodies in America and stood among the first of all American Protestant bodies.

Meanwhile the Women's Missionary Society, the Brotherhood, and the Luther League had built up strong nationwide organizations. The synod gathered a Ministerial Pension Fund of nearly five million dollars. The Augustana Book Concern, begun in 1884 and acquired by the synod five years later, made net sales of about a million dollars annually.

The flourishing educational institutions, all except the seminary at Rock Island, were owned by the several conferences. For more than two generations the status of Augustana College was a matter of spirited discussion involving the whole internal polity of the Augustana Synod. The latest decision, made in 1947, assigned the maintenance of the college to the Illinois, Iowa, and Superior Conferences, and left the seminary alone as the educational responsibility of the whole synod.

The rapid development of English language work among the congregations led in 1908 to the formation of the Association of English Churches with duties and powers similar to those of the conferences. The organization grew rapidly at first, because English was rapidly becoming the language of the people in the congregations of the synod. One reason for this was the sharp decline in the number of immigrants from Sweden. Even before the beginning of World War I the number had dropped to less than 10,000 a year. After the war the transition to English was rapid, and few congregations used Swedish exclusively. The change is most clearly seen in the circulation of the official organs, Swedish and English. In 1917 the *Augustana* had a circulation of more than 20,000, the *Lutheran Companion*, less than 7,000. Ten years later the circulation was the same for the one paper as for the other, and in 1952 the Swedish journal had 5,000 subscribers while the English had 57,000. In 1924 it was decided to publish the minutes of the synodical conventions in English only. By 1930 English was the language of the conventions, both of the synod and of the conferences, and the next year the Association of English Churches was dissolved. It had become superfluous. Today none of the congregations uses Swedish exclusively and not many have even an occasional Swedish service.

Significant of the internal reorganization of the synod are its changes in name. Begun in 1860 as the "Scandinavian Evangelical Lutheran Augustana Synod," ten years later after the peaceful separation of the Norwegians, it became the "Swedish Evangelical Lutheran Augustana Synod." After a quarter century of expansion and Americanization, the nationalist part of the name was omitted. The new name, the "Evangelical Lutheran Augustana Synod of North America," expressed not only the American outlook of the body but also its purpose to span the continent. It meant that there was no longer any hope of realizing Hasselquist's dream of a quick fusion of Swedish Lutherans with all other Lutheran elements in America. Nor would Augustana become merely a geographical district of the General Council.

As the Augustana Synod itself assumed the character of a general body with conferences as districts, its relation with the General Council raised serious questions. While there was no important difference in doctrine or ecclesiastical practice, the men of Augustana preferred a stricter moral code. The Swedes favored prohibition, which the German element regarded as puritan legalism. The General Council people rejected the disciplinary methods of the Augustana Synod with reference to secret societies and favored "educational" methods. But the real difficulties grew at first out of the difference in language and later out of differences in organization and home missionary activity. As early as 1904 the Minnesota Conference petitioned for the withdrawal of the synod from the General Council. In 1911 the synod elected its first native-born president, L. A. Johnston. Dr. Johnston was interested in the extension of English home mission work among Swedish people, and he was not very friendly to the General Council. Beginning in 1883 the Home Mission Committee of the General Council had sent missionaries to the territory of the Minnesota Conference of the Augustana Synod. The English-speaking congregations resulting from this work were recruited largely from the Swedish population, but instead of uniting with the Augustana Synod they formed in 1891 the Synod of the Northwest as a district of the General Council. In 1891 the General Council also established a theological seminary in Chicago and invited the Augustana Synod to move its seminary to the same place. The invitation was emphatically declined, the bonds of affiliation with the General Council grew weaker, and threats of secession grew more frequent in the meetings of the Augustana Synod.

When plans were laid in 1917 for merging the General Council with the General Synod and the United Synod of the South, efforts were made to conciliate the Augustana Synod and to enlist its participation in the merger. For example, the fundamental instrument for the proposed merger stated that any "constituent synod" in the new general body might continue its established lines of work if it desired, and it was specified that theological education and ordination are not to be the interests of the proposed general body but are to continue as responsibilities of the constituent synods, either individually or in groups. But it was clear to the men of the Augustana Synod that under the constitution of the United Lutheran Church in America the synods would expressly delegate wide powers of jurisdiction to the general body. The Augustana Synod, therefore, decided that its distinctive needs and problems required that it continue its identity, declined to enter the merger, and withdrew from the General Council. Under the leadership of the genial president of Augustana College and Theological Seminary, Dr. Gustav A. Andreen, and of the diplomatic president of the synod, Dr. Gustaf A. Brandelle, the separation was accomplished peacefully.

The synod thus became an independent body. At the same time it began a new era in its history—one of Lutheran co-operation. The intermediate position of the Swedes gave them exceptional opportunities to further co-operation and conference and organic union among Lutherans.

In 1922 the constitution of the synod was changed to provide more power at the head of the synod: the president was made a full-time officer, his term was extended from two to four years, and he was given more authority. Six years later a budget system was adopted by the synod. A full-time secretary of stewardship was provided for, and a layman was elected to this new position. The annual reports of the president thereafter devoted more space to polity and programs than to preachments and doctrine. Field after field of service was brought to the attention of the conventions. The practice of Christian stewardship was emphasized by laymen. The substantial pension fund was gathered largely by the laymen of the synod. The reports of receipts by the treasurer grew more and more impressive as the needs multiplied and the sense of stewardship grew more keen. Total contributions increased from four and a half million dollars in 1940 to more than fourteen million in 1950; the per capita contribution from $17.50 to $43.30.

In the decades that followed the election of P. O. Bersell as president of the Augustana Synod in 1935, the synod rapidly developed the spirit of enterprise and expansion that characterized the nation at that time. Many changes were made. Synodical headquarters were established in Minneapolis. The boards of the synod were manned with full-time secretaries. The conferences grew from three to thirteen. New agencies were set up, such as Stewardship Education, Finance, Youth Activities, Audio-Visual Service, and Architecture.

Among the 1948 amendments to the constitution is the change in name to "Augustana Lutheran Church," the change from Synodical Council to Executive Council, and the change permitting biennial instead of annual convention. These changes reflect a tendency towards centralization.

In the meantime the synod experienced significant developments in liturgical practice. Through most of its history it manifested a strong attachment to the liturgical patterns set by the mother church in Sweden. When the Norwegians separated from the Augustana Synod in 1870 the Swedes selected a liturgic committee and charged it with the task of creating forms of worship that would meet the needs of an expanding Lutheran church in America. Not much was accomplished until 1898, and then the only result was an English translation of the Swedish service. By 1905 the entire missal, including occasional services and ministerial acts, was available in English. The preference for the Swedish order was so strong, even among the English congregations, that the Common Service in use among the other synods in the General Council after 1890 was not introduced into the Augustana hymnbook until 1924.

The Swedish influence had been apparent also in the vestments. The traditional clerical garb of Sweden (*praestrock*) was in common use until the introduction of the Luther gown in 1924. The most recent action concerning ministerial garb was taken in 1946 when the synod resolved that "Synod calls attention to the praestrock with bands; the black gown with bands or stole; or the cassock, surplice and stole as duly authorized garb for pastors. Synod holds that the black gown with stole is to be preferred."

Greater independence from European influence and closer co-operation with the liturgical development in America was evident in 1936 when the synod established a permanent commission to act for the synod in matters of liturgical practice. After that the Augustana Synod was active in co-operative efforts to create for all Lutherans in America a common liturgy, a common hymnal, and uniform practices in worship.

In general the Christian life within the congregations was a simple and devout character. Since the bitter Waldenstromian controversies in the seventies, concerning the doctrine of the atonement, the synod had been free from doctrinal strife. The later teachers and leaders, such as O. Olsson, S. P. A. Lindahl, P. J. Sward, Carl A. Swensson, and others, continued in the spirit of the earlier fathers.

Although the Augustana Lutheran Church had not succeeded in enrolling all the immigrants from Sweden, it brought together about half a million souls and conserved the best traits that the immigrants brought with them. To a very high degree it succeeded in transplanting into American life those Christian virtues that were the peculiar fruits of four centuries of Christianity in old Sweden. The rapid growth and expansion of the synod, its effective organization, and its high spirit of enterprise in the practical tasks of Christian love, constituted a worthy parallel in the life of the church to the general spirit in the nation at large during this period.

In the next general part of our narrative, the period of larger units among Lutherans, we shall see how the Augustana Lutheran Church took a place of leadership in proposals for complete organic union among the Lutheran bodies in America.

CHAPTER 24

FAITH AND WORKS IN THE LUTHERAN CHURCH—MISSOURI SYNOD

One of the largest and most aggressive synodical units of Lutherans in America is the Missouri Synod. It embraces nearly one-third of all the Lutherans in the land. Organized in 1847, for more than a generation under the dominant influence of the devout and orthodox Dr. Walther, the synod grew very rapidly. Its zeal for the pure Lutheran interpretation of the gospel, its thoroughgoing system of schools and publications, its rapid transition to the English language, its skillful use of mass communication, and its great energies spent in missions and benevolence, have given the Missouri Synod great importance in Lutheranism in this country.

During the century that followed its organization the Missouri Synod multiplied its twelve congregations to more than five thousand, with more than 1,900,000 baptized members. It has congregations in every state of the Union and in six provinces of Canada. This rapid growth and expansion was due largely to the synod's zeal in home missions among the German immigrants during the second half of the nineteenth century. Until 1917 it bore the name The German Evangelical Lutheran Synod of Missouri, Ohio and Other States. At that time the word "German" was omitted, and in 1947 the official name was changed to The Lutheran Church—Missouri Synod.

In its faith the Missouri Synod has stood virtually alone among Lutheran bodies in America. Cultivating strict devotion to the Scriptures and the entire body of the Lutheran confessions, the synod, like the smaller bodies in the Synodical Conference, has the strictest doctrinal basis of all Lutheran groups in America. It reads: "The Synod, and every member of the Synod, accepts without reservation: The

Scriptures of the Old and New Testament as the written Word of God and the only rule and form of faith and practice; and all the Symbolical Books of the Evangelical Lutheran Church as a true and unadulterated statement and exposition of the Word of God." The three ecumenical creeds and all of the writings in the Book of Concord are enumerated by name. One of the chief purposes of the synod is provision of "a united defense against separatistic and sectarian abuses." One of the conditions of holding membership is "renunciation of unionism and syncretism of every description." This renunciation "shall be understood to include also the ungodly lodge system." And the constitution of the synod provides for rigid supervision of the congregations and pastors with reference to these matters by the annual visitation of constituted officers.

The practice of the synod through a whole century has been to insist that its pastors and congregations and church members give strict loyalty to this confessional position and its implications. They must also refuse all church fellowship and all fellowship of worship with those who even tolerate beliefs or practices contrary to this position.

The zeal of the Missouri Synod for the maintenance of pure Lutheran doctrine, which inspired its system of parochial schools and was largely responsible for its wide range of church activities, involved it often in doctrinal controversy with other Lutherans. Before the Civil War, and until about 1870, leaders of Missouri debated with Grabau of the Buffalo Synod the doctrine of the church and the ministerial office. Dr. Walther succeeded in defending his view that the church is essentially invisible, that the ministerial office is simply the spiritual priesthood that belongs to all members and is transferred to an individual by the call of a congregation, and that ordination is wholly a human institution which serves only as a public confirmation of the transfer.

In that period also the Iowa Synod, led chiefly by the Fritschel brothers, broke from the Missourians in 1854 on the issue of the rights of the Lutheran congregation and the significance of ordination, maintaining against the Missourians that the office of the ministry is not simply a transfer of the spiritual priesthood from a congregation to an individual Christian but from the visible church as a whole. Iowa and Missouri differed also in their general attitude toward the confessions of the church. The followers of Loehe in the Iowa Synod maintained that there are certain teachings of the Scriptures that are not clearly defined in the confessions, that on such matters the confessions are not binding, and therefore differences concerning such issues should not be allowed to interfere with church fellowship. This attitude the Missouri Synod condemned as "unionistic poison that drives congregations into the arms of skepticism and infidelity," and Missouri insisted that there can be only one correct interpretation of each doctrine taken from the Scriptures.

These differences in attitude toward the Scriptures and the Lutheran confessions led to further controversies between Missouri and Iowa. For example, Dr. Walther and his colleagues insisted that every genuine Lutheran must hold that the Pope at Rome is the Antichrist in person, because this is taught by prophecy in Scripture, by Luther's interpretation, and by a statement in the Smalcald Articles. The men in the Iowa Synod agreed that the papacy as an institution contains anti-Christian elements. But they could not agree that the pope himself is the last Antichrist referred to in the New Testament; this they held to be mere human conviction, an open question, and not necessary for church fellowship.

Also, there was a difference between Missouri and Iowa concerning Sunday observance. Both agreed that the proper observance of the first day of the week as a Holy Day is good Christian practice with genuine apostolic antecedents. In both groups most writers denied that the observance of the Lord's Day rests upon divine obligation, because it is neither taught in the Scriptures nor to be inferred from the fact that God rested one day in seven. They differed only in their attitude toward those who insisted that the observance of one day in seven is an ordinance of God and binding upon the Christian conscience. Missouri would exclude them from church fellowship, while Iowa would tolerate them.

These and other issues, such as millenialism and the right to charge interest, agitated the Lutherans of the Middle West during the third quarter of the century. In spite of the large measure of doctrinal agreement among them, in spite of their wide divergence from the non-Lutherans all about them, in spite of their common language, their common origin in Europe, and their common experiences on the American frontier, they battled over their differences with conscientious obstinacy, and even after nearly a century of mutual toleration the theological ramparts erected in those days of sectarianism and schism have not been demolished.

But these debates were merely skirmishes. During the period now before us, the last quarter of the nineteenth and the beginning of the twentieth centuries, predestination became the issue of a raging controversy that permanently split the Ohio Synod from the Missouri Synod, alienated from Missouri the main body of Norwegian Lutherans, who until this time had fostered intimate fellowship with Walther and his group, and deepened the breach between Missouri and Iowa. Even the theologians of the older Lutheran bodies in the East, when they expressed themselves on the subject, took issue with the Missourians.

That so many of his former friends and other Lutherans rejected his reasoning and withdrew from his fellowship was a bitter experience for Dr. Walther. For forty years he had cherished the hope of realizing a single Evangelical Lutheran Church of North America, and when the sharp controversy on predestination blasted that hope, he regarded it as a peculiar triumph of Satan. Certainly the long and bitter controversy on predestination did more to split up the Lutheranism of America than all the issues raised in an earlier generation by the ill-fated "American Lutheranism."

To those who would labor for the union of all Lutheran forces in this country it is a matter of special regret that the predestinarian controversy came just at the time it did. The discussions with Buffalo and Iowa and Ohio on other points had about closed. In the three older groups in the East, the General Synod, the General Council, and the United Synod South, conservative influences had gained control. In 1880 a general union of all Lutherans in America might have been expected after a generation of transition in language. But this stubborn theological dispute among the immigrant Lutherans caused divergences of faith and organization that postponed total Lutheran union indefinitely. Yet all parties acted with deep earnestness and good conscience.

How is the position of the Missourians to be understood? Some opponents have charged that Dr. Walther and his colleagues in their teaching on predestination were really setting forth a disguised form of Calvinism. But the matter is not so simple. The Calvinist doctrine of predestination and election is clear and consistent and easy to fit into a system of thought, whereas the Missouri Lutheran doctrine is not concerned with system or logic but rests solely upon pertinent passages of Scripture, of Luther, and of the Lutheran confessions. Consistent Calvinism teaches double predestination, not only the salvation of the elect but also condemnation of the others. Lutherans debated only concerning those who are elect and predestined to salvation.

The question may be reduced to its simplest form. The man who believes in Christ and his atoning merits is saved. In God's plan he is one of the elect, he is predestined to be saved. But shall we say that God's predestination is the cause of his faith and his salvation, or shall we say that his faith is the cause of his predestination? The Missourians took the first of these alternatives and insisted that according to the Scriptures a man cannot believe in Christ unless God causes him to do so; that God elects a man to faith and this faith in the merits of Christ is the effective cause of his salvation. On the other hand, Ohio and Iowa and the Norwegians took the second alternative and insisted that God elects a man to salvation "in view of his faith" in the merits of Christ. Dr. Walther pointed out that the expression "in view of his faith" is not found in the Scriptures or in Luther's writings, but only in the theologians of the seventeenth century, and at best its meaning is uncertain. The opponents of Missouri argued that if one takes Lutheran teachings as a whole and the Scriptures as a whole the teaching is clear that God elects a man to salvation "in view of the faith" he foresees in the man.

There have been several stages in the controversy. The question emerged into open discussion in 1880 when Dr. Walther publicly answered certain people of his synod who had disagreed with him in his rejection of the phrase "in view of his faith." The alarm had been sounded by the Norwegian professor, F. A. Schmidt, who established a monthly magazine, *Altes und Neues* (*Old and New*), to expose Walther's "new" doctrine and to prove his un-Lutheran tendency. At the meeting of the Missouri Synod the next year, Pastor Allwardt and Professor Stellhorn of Ohio opposed Walther, and at its convention that year Ohio protested against "Missouri's heresy" and withdrew from the Synodical Conference which was dominated by the Missouri Synod. In 1882 the Norwegian Synod also abandoned its fellowship with Missouri in the Synodical Conference in order to reach agreement among its own members. In the meantime Iowa had adopted a formal declaration against this new error on the part of Missouri and entered the lists of the opposition. Thus Missouri stood alone and the scene was set for the great debate.

The disputants rarely met one another personally. The discussion was carried on through sets of theses and countertheses, through pamphlets and periodical articles, and through stately volumes. Most of the debate was in German. Dr. Walther filled hundreds of pages of his *Lehre und Wehre*, insisting upon his position as the only scriptural and true Lutheran position. Repeatedly he emphasized that the expression "in view of his faith" does not occur in the Scriptures or in the Lutheran confessions. He pointed to various passages of Scripture that leave man no freedom of choice concerning his salvation but place him in the absolute decree of God. "God did not choose the elect because he knew they would be saved; but because they are chosen they will be saved." When asked why then God did not elect all men to be saved, since he certainly has power to overcome even the most willful resistance, Dr. Walther answered that we cannot ask such questions on the basis of Scripture. "It is incomprehensible now, but we believe it." He pointed to Luther's book *The Bondage of the Will*.

Dr. Walther passed away in 1887 without having forfeited the respect of his opponents, but without having convinced them. The controversy went on.

After 1890 other phases of the discussion came into prominence. There was, for example, the question of harmonizing the many Scripture passages expressing the universal grace of God, such as John 3:16, with the several passages that indicate the special election of a few, such as Acts 13:48. When the opponents of Missouri tried to harmonize these passages by reasoning that God's decree of election for individuals is part and parcel of his universal provision of redemption for all men, the Missourians declared that the two sets of passages are contradictory and must so remain, and that any effort at harmony among them is a form of rationalism.

Ohio and Iowa sought to identify God's decree of predestination for individuals with his general benevolent will for the conversion of men and their preservation in the faith. They regarded the election of individuals as a small circle within the much larger circle of God's unlimited love in Christ. Both Christ's atonement for all men and the application of it to a few men through faith are the result of one and the same divine will. The interpreters for Missouri, on the other hand, insisted that the circle of God's general will and the circle of his special will are outside each other, the result of two different divine decrees that we humans should not try to harmonize. Unless this contrast is maintained there can be no assurance of continuing faith. Unless God is the author of faith and elects the individual by special decree he can have at best only a temporary faith. A really persevering and saving faith is the effect of God's eternal election of the individual and not merely of his general good will.

After the turn of the century the discussion on predestination led to the question whether individual passages of Scripture must not be interpreted in the light of Scripture as a whole. Allwardt and Stellhorn, on behalf of Ohio and Iowa, declared at Milwaukee in 1903 that the Christian doctrines constitute a harmonious whole that can be recognized as such. This organic whole is the highest standard for interpreting Scripture. It is composed of teachings drawn from perfectly clear passages of Scripture and must be applied in the interpretation of passages that are not clear in themselves. This was called "the analogy of faith" in the interpretation of the Bible. Professor August Pieper of the Wisconsin Synod vigorously condemned this idea as another form of rationalism, an accursed effort to harmonize God's special election of individuals with his general election of all mankind to salvation. His brother, Franz Pieper of Missouri, declared that the passages on election are not dark but clear, and any effort to connect passages with one another when the Word of God does not connect them is nothing but modernism.

In the 1920's the controversy turned again to the relation of predestination to man's conversion and the freedom of the will. Missouri stoutly resisted every position that opened the way for even the faintest degree of synergism, i.e. man's co-operation in his own conversion. When the question was asked why some men are saved and some are not, the Missouri theologians answered that it is not because some men are able to cease their resistance to the grace of God and others are unable. They insisted that all men are equally depraved. If any are saved, it is because they are predestined to faith and God breaks down their resistance. The opponents of Missouri, particularly Iowa, tried to answer the question by referring to "a psychological mystery," the distinction between the natural resistance of a man and his willful resistance which even God cannot overcome if man is to continue to be man. But the Missourians declared that the mystery is "a theological mystery." God, they said, can break down any resistance, and the mystery is not in man but in the Godhead himself. They demanded that the distinction between natural and willful resistance be abandoned in discussing the doctrine of conversion. At the same time they insisted, as against Stellhorn and the Fritschels, that there is no such thing as a gradual conversion—it is completely the work of God and always the complete act of a moment.

These in the main are the issues involved in the controversy on predestination. The issues have not yet been resolved. In the last analysis the differences rest upon differing attitudes toward the Lutheran confessions and the interpretation of Scripture. In recent years there have been serious efforts to find some ground of agreement so that there may at least be a larger measure of co-operation among all Lutheran bodies. Several sets of these have been drawn up, as, for example, at Minneapolis in 1925, at Chicago in 1928, and at Milwaukee in 1931. There has been no general agreement on the doctrinal issues involved, but the passing of the decades and the current confrontation of stupendous problems for all Lutherans has led the disputants on predestination and its related problems to something like an armistice. It is certain that toleration on the basis of mutual respect and for purposes of co-operation even in externals is far better than the surrender of conviction or the artificial setting up of ambiguous and compromising declarations.

It is certain also that the faith of the Lutheran Church–Missouri Synod, as set forth in the course of these debates, is definite and steadfast. The sole purpose has been to maintain scriptural positions, to deny to man any part whatsoever in his own salvation or his own conversion, to exalt above all else the grace of God in Jesus Christ, and to give to God alone the glory. At the same time there has been conscientious effort to avoid fellowship with those, even of the same name, who seem to deviate from correct scriptural positions as interpreted by Missouri. Whatever may be argued about the correctness of Missouri's doctrinal and confessional positions, it cannot be denied that her deep convictions and faithful persistence have helped to produce a volume of Christian enterprise that constitutes a fine record for Lutheranism in America.

In its organization, the Lutheran Church—Missouri Synod emphasizes the responsibility of the congregations for the work of the church and the participation of the laymen in the outreach of the gospel. Nowhere among Lutherans is the autonomy of the individual congregation more carefully guarded than in the Missouri Synod. The constitution that was prepared by Walther in 1846 has been revised repeatedly, but it still shows a distinct dread of hierarchy. The synod is the creature of the local congregations which unite for common work. The synod has no judicatory relations with the churches but only advisory relations. It meets in national convention only every three years, and the meeting is called the "Delegate Synod" because only those may vote who have been elected and delegated by the congregations. There are about seven hundred delegates at each convention. No resolution of the synod imposing anything on the individual congregation is of binding force "if it appears to be inexpedient so far as the condition of the congregation is concerned." The convention elects all officers, boards, and commissions to carry on the work of the church. Doctrinal supervision of the synod and all its parts is entrusted by the congregations to a doctrinal committee consisting of the president and the four vice-presidents.

The synod is organized in thirty-four districts. The districts are geographical, except the English District. One of them is in the Argentine, another in Brazil. Each district meets annually, has its own officers, and does the home mission work of its own area. Some districts maintain their own educational institutions and their own church papers. At meetings both of the districts and of the triennial conventions clergy and laity are equally represented, and clerical delegates must be pastors of congregations. At these conventions much time is given to discussion of doctrinal papers, but the educational and missionary work of the church is also considered.

The educational work of the Missouri Synod is planned for the thorough preparation of an orthodox and efficient body of pastors and teachers. Much of the synod's strength comes from its efficient system of schools. It begins with the parochial school and culminates in the theological seminary. In order to bring up their children in the nurture and admonition of the Lord, the Missouri Lutherans maintain Christian day schools in connection with many of their congregations. Their program of full-time elementary education is the largest in American Protestantism. In 1952 there were about 1,250 parish schools in connection with the five thousand congregations. They were taught by about 3,000 men and women, and attended by about 90,000 children. This represents a percentage of total membership comparable to that of Roman Catholic children who attend Roman Catholic parochial schools. These parochial schools are so highly esteemed that they are attended regularly by nearly 6,000 children who do not belong to Missouri Synod congregations. For twenty years, however, the number of parish schools has been diminishing while the number of congregations has been increasing, and the percentage of children in the schools has been steadily declining.

Most of the teachers for these Lutheran parochial schools are prepared by the synod at Concordia Teachers College at River Forest, Illinois, with an enrollment of about 600, and at Concordia Teachers College at Seward, Nebraska, with an enrollment of about 400.

The Sunday schools of the synod enroll about half a million pupils and engage about 50,000 teachers. The vacation Bible schools attract more than 125,000 pupils. More than one fourth of the children in these schools are from non-Lutheran homes.

The Missouri Synod concentrates its theological education in two seminaries, among the largest in the country. The chief seminary is Concordia at St. Louis. It has 23 full-time professors and six instructors, and a student body of over 750. The practical seminary, Concordia at Springfield, Illinois, has eleven full-time professors, two assistants and an enrollment of nearly 400. There is also a small seminary in Brazil, and one each in the Argentine, India, Japan, Mexico, and Formosa.

The synod also maintains thirteen high schools and ten junior colleges. Another educational agency that is also evangelistic in its nature is the celebrated "International Lutheran Hour." This is a radio program with the largest hook-up in the world. It is sponsored by a laymen's organization of more than 50,000 men and is broadcast each week over 1,150 stations in 43 countries.

The synod's Concordia Publishing House in St. Louis is one of the large denominational publishing firms in the United States, with annual business in excess of $3,000,000. Among its notable publications are a German edition of Luther's works in twenty-five handsome volumes and the 852-page *Lutheran Hymnal* of which nearly a million and a half copies have been sold. Concordia publishes the church papers, the schoolbooks, and all the other books needed for the work of the church. Its profits are turned into the synodical treasury for missions and other work.

The periodical publications of the synod and its districts and institutions number almost one hundred. The best known are the *Lutheran Witness* and the *Concordia Theological Monthly*. The *Witness* is biweekly and has a circulation of 330,000. It represents the official doctrinal position of the church body and is under the editorial review of the faculty of Concordia Seminary at St. Louis. The *Theological Monthly* was begun in 1930 by combining the three theological magazines, *Lehre und Wehre*, the *Theological Quarterly*, and the *Homiletisches Magazin*. The *Monthly* is also edited by the seminary faculty in St. Louis. Since 1945 it has appeared entirely in English.

The home mission enterprise receives much attention from the Missouri Synod and its districts. The founders of the synod regarded as a foremost duty the building of Zion in the land of their pilgrimage, and bent their energies to the preparation of men who would go out among their German brethren and gather them into congregations pledged to thoroughgoing Lutheran orthodoxy. The heroic sacrifices and ceaseless toil of these home missionary pioneers account in large measure for the rapid growth of the synod. Most of the home missionary operations today are conducted by the district boards. The general body receives contributions from the congregations in all the districts and uses its funds to supplement the work of such districts as are unable to support all the missionaries they need. More than half of the districts employ field secretaries to direct the missionary work in their respective areas. About two and a half million dollars are spent annually in intensive home missionary evangelism, and during recent years new missions have been founded in the United States and Canada at the rate of two each week. The annual increase in the membership of the Missouri Synod during the past several years has never been less than 70,000; two-thirds of these are adults, the remainder confirmed children of Missouri Synod families. It is interesting also to observe that by actual count the number of accessions to Missouri Synod congregations from the Roman Catholic Church is over three thousand a year, nearly five times the number lost to that church.

The Missouri Synod has thirty full-time pastors among the deaf, more than all other Lutheran bodies and all other Protestant denominations combined. They preach to small groups of deaf throughout the country, holding more than 4,000 services a year. Their thirty organized congregations have more than 8,000 baptized members. Unique in American Protestantism is the Lutheran Institute for the Deaf, a higher educational institution in Detroit employing the latest methods for communication with the deaf. Another school of this kind is located at Long Island, New York.

Missionaries of the synod have been in South India since 1895, in Brazil since 1899, in the Argentine since 1905, and in China since 1915. Since World War II new mission stations have been established in Japan, New Guinea, the Philippine Islands, Guatemala, the Canal Zone, Hawaii, Mexico, and several South American countries. The largest of these fields is that in South India with 409 stations, 33 missionaries, and 23,000 souls. In China until recently there were 24 stations and 26 missionaries; in the Philippines 18 stations and 10 missionaries; in Japan 22 stations and 11 missionaries; in New Guinea 19 stations and 3 missionaries. The synod's foreign missions claim about 110,000 native Christians.

‘ Part of the strength of the Missouri Synod lies in its encouragement of individual initiative on the part of independent associations. A striking example is the Laymen's League with its "Lutheran Hour" on radio, its production of attractive and inspiring Christian films, its gathering of a large fund for ministerial pensions, and its Lutheran hospital for polio and spastic research at Vicksburg, Mississippi. The synod itself produces an impressive program on television called "This is the Life."

Another independent affiliate of the synod is the International Walther League. It provides the major emphasis on youth work, and its program is assisted and endorsed by the synod. It embraces 3,000 Walther League societies with a membership of more than 80,000 young people. The major activities of the youth group include publication of *The Walther League Messenger*, development of parish programs for youth, and support of a sanatorium for tubercular patients at Wheatridge, Colorado. The League formerly published *The Cresset*, a monthly review of literature, the arts, and public affairs, and *The Bible Student*, a study guide. The former is now published by Valparaiso University, the latter by the synod.

Through the Division of Social Welfare (formerly called Associated Lutheran Charities) the congregations of the Missouri Synod maintain 19 hospitals, 10 orphans' homes, 23 child agencies, and 14 old folks' homes. The aggregate service of these institutions provides a ministry of mercy to hundreds of thousands of needy persons each year.

The spirit of stewardship has been increasing steadily. Total contributions to all purposes amount to more than sixty million dollars annually. One tenth of this is for benevolence. The annual budget for the synod itself is more than five millions. The average contribution for each communicant has tripled during the last decade. During one year alone (1950) the property value of the congregations increased by thirty-four million dollars.

Language has been a continuing problem in the synod. Long predominant in its congregations were people of German birth, background, and education. Few of them were intimate with English-speaking people in America. Their evangelism was entirely among German immigrants. What they saw and heard of the "English religion" did not attract them to the English language. They loved Luther's translation of the Bible and the beauty of the German chorale, the fervor of their religious hymns and the deep inwardness of their devotional literature. Moreover, they felt that the German language was an aid in the propagation of the gospel and the advancement of true Christianity. They were afraid that if they gave way to English they would be swept from their high confessional stand. As they set up parochial schools in order to defend their children against the paganism of the public schools, so they resisted the inroads of the English language as the channel of liberalism and rationalism. In the end these fears proved mistaken. The transition to English was, of course, inevitable, but it came by easy stages and in an orderly manner, and so it did not cause a division in the ranks of the synod nor did it make any change in the doctrinal position of the body.

The leaders in the first generation of Missouri's history, Dr.

Walther and Dr. Sihler, opposed the introduction of English in their own congregations but apparently did not much try to influence the synod at large, here again leaving the choice to the congregations. For more than half a century the services were predominantly in German. The first congregation to use English in its services was St. Peter's in Baltimore, in 1850. As other congregations in eastern cities followed this example, they sometimes transferred to the Ohio Synod, in which there had always been a number of English congregations. But when the Ohio Synod finally broke away because of the predestinarian controversy, Missouri took measures to retain her English-speaking congregations.

In 1872 several conservative Lutheran pastors who were accustomed to services in English moved from North Carolina and Tennessee to Missouri. There they contacted the professors of Concordia Seminary and, with Walther's blessing, organized that summer "The English Evangelical Lutheran Conference of Missouri." Professor F. A. Schmidt spoke English and helped foster the new conference, but when he separated from Walther and Missouri on the predestination issue and returned to the Norwegian Synod, the English Conference languished for a number of years. However, in 1886 the congregations in the conference took on new life, started English parochial schools and English missions, and the next year asked to be admitted to the German Missouri Synod as a separate English District. The German synod advised them to organize an independent English synod, and in 1890 with eight congregations and eleven pastors, they gathered in St. Louis and organized "The English Evangelical Lutheran Synod of Missouri and Other States." It was agreed by the German synod that as the districts in their home missionary operations organized English-speaking congregations, these congregations all across the land would not affiliate with their respective districts but with the English Synod of Missouri.

The English synod grew rapidly. As an English-speaking generation grew up, as a new generation of ministers trained for services in English came into the pulpits, and as the need for missionary work in English became more evident, the number of English services multiplied. The English synod soon covered the same territory as the German synod. It had now become perfectly clear that English-speaking people could be soundly Lutheran. From the beginning the

English synod took over as its official organ the *Lutheran Witness* which had been founded by the Cleveland Conference in 1882. Its congregations maintained parochial schools in the English language. By 1893 it had two colleges. It also established its own publication house and began to issue an English hymnbook with the Common Service that had been adopted by the three older Lutheran bodies in the East. English editions of the catechism were published. By 1905 there were three hundred and seventy-six congregations and mission stations that were holding some or all of their services in English.

Then the German synod and the English synod began to negotiate earnestly for amalgamation. The German synod in 1905 dissolved its English Mission Board because the districts had taken up the work of establishing English-speaking congregations. Many of these congregations declined to join the English synod and remained in the districts of the German synod. So rapid was the growth of English services, both in bilingual congregations and in all-English congregations, that in 1911 it was found that there were more English services in the German synod than in the English synod. At that point the merger was completed, and the English synod became a district of the German synod. It had the one specific purpose of promoting English work in the entire synod and of undergirding the all-English congregations in districts still predominantly German. The *Lutheran Witness* became the official English organ of the German synod. The publishing business in English was transferred to the Concordia Publishing House. In the constitutional revision of 1917 the designation "German" was eliminated from the title of the synod. By 1925 only half of the synod still used the German language in any of their services.

The transition in language was retarded somewhat by the fact that so large a part of the synod was rural. Even today more than half of the people in the congregations of the synod live in towns of 2,500 inhabitants or less or in townships of 10,000 or less. This condition is slowly changing, but it does account for the persistence of German, particularly in Canada.

On the other hand, the transition to English was hastened by a series of incidents during World War I. At the outbreak of the war against Germany, the German language was still widely used in families and church services of the Missouri Synod. Many people spoke of it as "the German Lutheran Church." The charges of disloyalty made against these German-speaking citizens were mostly false. Some originated in religious prejudice. Nevertheless a number of instances of violence occurred, and several states passed laws forbidding the use of German in public services. After 1914, therefore, the change which was already well under way proceeded more rapidly. The change in the language preference of the people is most clearly seen in the relative circulation of the English organ, *The Lutheran Witness*, and the German organ, *Der Lutheraner*. In 1910 the *Lutheraner* had three times the subscription list of the *Witness*. In 1925 the two were about equal. In 1950 the English paper had about fifteen times as many as the German paper.

At present all the official business of the synod and of the districts, their convention proceedings, reports and resolutions, are published in English and in most instances only in English. Few congregations now use only German. Less than five per cent of the people in the Missouri Synod commonly speak German, and the number is steadily diminishing. The most "German" part of the synod is in the Canadian provinces west of Ontario, where about one-third of the services are held in German. In the Districts of Northern Illinois and South Wisconsin about one of ten services is in German. The transition to English has been nearly completed, without division or unrest or any change in the faith of the Missouri Synod or her zeal for good works.

The Missouri Synod was federated with three other equally conservative Lutheran synods in The Evangelical Lutheran Synodical Conference of North America. They are the Evangelical Lutheran Joint Synod of Wisconsin and Other States, the Norwegian Synod of the American Evangelical Lutheran Church, and the Slovak Evangelical Lutheran Church of America. The Missouri Synod is four times as large as the other three synods combined.

The Synodical Conference was organized in 1872 after some years of negotiation initiated by the Joint Synod of Ohio. The General Council had been organized in 1866 and had hoped to draw into its fellowship not only the Joint Synod of Ohio but also the Missouri Synod and the other conservative German bodies of the Middle West. But as the General Council came to be regarded as too lax in applying its doctrinal basis, and too unionistic in its position regarding lodges and pulpit and altar fellowship, the midwestern synods, Missouri, Ohio, Wisconsin, Minnesota, and Illinois, organized their own federation with Dr. Walther as the first president.

Ten years later the Ohio Synod withdrew because of Missouri's "new doctrine" of predestination. The Illinois Synod became a district of the Missouri Synod, and the Minnesota Synod federated with the Wisconsin Synod. The Norwegian Synod, containing the main body of the Norwegian Lutherans, was a part of the original organization of the conference, but the outbreak of the predestination controversy brought internal difficulties among the Norwegians and in 1883 that synod withdrew from the conference in the hope of adjusting its difficulties more easily. But in 1918 a small group of Norwegians asserted their agreement with Missouri, separated from the Norwegian Lutheran merger of 1917, formed a new Norwegian Synod, and under this name joined the Synodical Conference. The Slovak Evangelical Lutheran Church, formed at Connellsville, Pennsylvania, in 1902, joined the conference in 1908. The Joint Wisconsin Synod is itself a union formed in 1919 out of four district synods of German Lutherans; some account of this merger will be given in Chapter 29. Compared with the nearly two million members of the Missouri Synod, the Wisconsin Synod has 322,947, the Slovak Church 21,187, and the Norwegian Synod 10,663.

As its name implies, the Synodical Conference is not a merger of synods but only an advisory body. The synods retain their full sovereignty and full control of their educational, charitable, and missionary work. The basis of union in the Synodical Conference is the doctrinal unity of the participating synods. They feel themselves knit together by firm ties of confession and practice. The expressed purpose of the conference is mutual assistance in the strengthening of their faith and confession, and the ultimate union of all truly Lutheran synods in America into one orthodox American Lutheran church. The conference is an uncompromising foe of all forms of unionism and will not maintain fraternal relations with any who tolerate error or practice unionism in any form. It is a staunch opponent of lodges and all who tolerate them. The conference meets biennially and busies itself primarily with the discussion of doctrinal questions.

Two lines of practical work are undertaken together by the synods of the Synodical Conference. One is the flourishing mission among the Negro people of the United States. This work was undertaken at the suggestion of the Norwegian Synod. It began in 1877 at Little Rock, Arkansas, and was soon extended to New Orleans. Congregations were organized and parochial schools established. After fifteen years there were seven missions, four in New Orleans, one in Little Rock, one in Virginia, and one at Springfield, Illinois. Then the conference received an appeal for support from four Lutheran Negro ministers and their five congregations who had formerly belonged to the North Carolina Synod of the United Synod of the South but had withdrawn and organized the "Alpha Synod of the Evangelical Lutheran Church of Freedmen in America," with 180 baptized members. In 1892 the conference sent two graduates of Concordia Seminary as missionaries and so began the extensive work among the Negro people of North Carolina where today the conference has twelve pastors, a Negro theological seminary and junior college, a normal school and a high school.

After the turn of the century the work among the Negroes was extended to most of the southern states and to the leading cities in the North. At mid-century seventy-five pastors were engaged in this work, forty-two of them Negroes, and there was a total of 17,341 baptized members. To prepare workers for service in Negro communities there was not only Immanuel Lutheran College and Seminary at Greensboro, North Carolina (with 119 students) but also the Lutheran Academy and College at Selma, Alabama (with 130 students). The Missionary Board of the Synodical Conference which directed the work among the Negroes in the United States, also administered foreign missions among the Negroes of Nigeria, Africa, with 29 missionaries and about 25,000 native Christians. After about 1950 this work ceased as a separate branch and was merged with the total program of the synods.

The second line of practical work in which the Lutherans of the Synodical Conference co-operate is the Lutheran Deaconess Association with headquarters at Fort Wayne, Indiana. This was organized in 1919 and has a membership of 3,800, a member being either an individual or a society. Under the sponsorship of the Association the deaconesses are trained at Valparaiso University, a Lutheran institution owned and operated by a company of Lutherans within the Synodical Conference. The Association at mid-century had 49 deaconesses in service. The people and congregations of the bodies in the Synodical Conference co-operate also in the management and support of a large number of health and welfare agencies. Among these agencies are 27 hospitals, 25 institutions for the care of children, and 17 homes for the aged.

Christian benevolence has found ample support in this large and conservative synod. The lay membership, stoutly loyal, have shown themselves ready to accept the responsibilities of Christian discipleship, and large resources have been placed at the service of the church and its agencies. Modern methods of publicity and business administration have been applied.

During the past several decades the Missouri Synod has formed co-operative relationships with Lutheran bodies beyond the Synodical Conference in certain specific areas, including spiritual ministry to Lutherans in the armed forces and service to prisoners of war.

Their present less rigid attitude toward Christian fellowship with other Lutherans and other Christians, their rapid growth in numbers and expansion in territory, their contagious enthusiasm for conservative evangelical doctrine, their constant emphasis on thorough educational methods, and their relatively large supply of ministerial candidates, make this Missouri branch of the Lutheran church one of the most vigorous elements in American Christianity.

CHAPTER 25

THE LITURGICAL DEVELOPMENT

In this period the Lutheran church had become conscious of her power, not only of her numbers and her piety and her confessions, but also the power of her worship. But of the many liturgies in use in various parts of the church, not one was a faithful expression of the Lutheran spirit or the rich liturgical heritage of the church. While it was recognized that uniformity in worship is not necessary to the true unity of the church, Lutherans, like other churches of that day, began to realize the desirability of such uniformity. So a search began for a common form of worship that would more completely express the power of the Lutheran heritage in that sphere.

Men began to remind themselves of the wish of the patriarch Muhlenberg that "all the Evangelical Lutheran Congregations in the North American States were united with one another, that all used the same order of service, the same hymnbook, and in good and evil days would show an active sympathy and fraternally correspond with one another."

The resulting liturgical movement, including practically all the English-speaking Lutherans in this country and a very large portion of the German-speaking Lutherans, paralleled the great ventures of capital and other interests in politics and industry. It was a big undertaking, calling for profound research and wisdom, for co-operation and forbearance, but it resulted in a common order of worship and a common hymnology that has met the devotional wants of most of the Lutherans in America. It was the first occasion of official co-operation among the three divisions of the Muhlenberg development and the forerunner of a period of larger harmony and co-operation in the Lutheran church in America.

Until just before 1870 no single Lutheran liturgy in general use was worthy in character, form, or completeness of the Lutheran church and her people. For more than a century individual synods and the General Synod had been laboring with the problem. The adoption of a liturgy was one of the principal tasks that occupied the attention of the first meeting of the Ministerium of Pennsylvania in 1748. The liturgy then adopted, as prepared by Muhlenberg, Brunnholz, and Handschuh, was based on the liturgies that were used in those parts of Germany where Muhlenberg and Brunnholz had lived. Authorities have pronounced that liturgy of 1748 the noblest and purest Lutheran service possessed by the church in America for more than a century— but it was not printed. Copied by the pastors and introduced into their congregations, about forty manuscript copies were in circulation. It came to be materially altered, and was first published by order of the Ministerium in 1786 in a revision that did injury to the pure Lutheran type of the older service. The liturgical taste of the church was suffering a decline. This service was translated into English by Dr. Kunze and published with a collection of English hymns in 1795 as part of his effort to prevent the defection of the English-speaking youth to the Episcopal church. When Reformed and rationalistic influences made themselves felt, a number of independent efforts were made to devise a liturgy that would receive general acceptance. In 1817 the New York Synod published its liturgy in a collection of hymns and prayers. This was mainly the work of Dr. Quitman and shows throughout the marks of his rationalistic hand. The following year the Ministerium of Pennsylvania issued a revised liturgy which shows on every page the effects of the relaxed doctrinal position of that body. The responsive character of the service is almost entirely lost. The observance of the Church Year is not adhered to. It seems probable that the Pennsylvania liturgy was strongly influenced by that of New York.

When the Ministerium of Pennsylvania recovered its Lutheran consciousness, the liturgy of 1818 proved very unsatisfactory, and in 1839 a complete revision was ordered. The new liturgy, largely the work of Dr. C. R. Demme, appeared in 1842 and at first received approval from various synodical bodies. The General Synod published an English translation in 1847. But it did not satisfy men of correct liturgical tastes and was soon found inadequate to the needs of the church. Another effort, the liturgy of 1855, published in English five years later, was a distinct reaction against the "low" uses of the previous period and an improvement over its immediate prede- cessors. `It restored the responses, used many primitive orders, and was scripturally pure; it included all the essential features of a true Lutheran service. But it contained a great deal of superfluous matter and the order of its parts did not accord with good liturgical con- struction. The English translation of 1860 made many changes in the original which showed that the leaven of a purer liturgical principle was at work. This translation prepared the way for the *Church Book* of 1868, published by the Ministerium of Pennsylvania and subse- quently adopted by the entire General Council. Most of this book was a monument to the learning and taste of Dr. B. M. Schmucker. It was based on a thorough scientific study of liturgical and hymnological sources. It wrought a great change in Lutheran worship in this country.

Meanwhile the General Synod had made a number of efforts to devise a liturgy that would satisfy the needs of its congregations and thus introduce some degree of uniformity into their worship. This was one of the purposes of the founding of a General Synod. The "Proposed Plan of Union" adopted in 1819 specified that the "General Synod has the exclusive right with the concurrence of a majority of the particular synods to introduce new books for general use in the public church service as well as to make improvements in the Liturgy," and the constitution provided for the accomplishment of that work, though it specifically disclaimed "the power of *prescribing* uniform ceremonies of religion." But in its early weakness, the General Synod accomplished little along the line of liturgy except the appointment of a committee on the subject. Not until 1832 did the first liturgy of the General Synod appear, the work of Dr. G. A. Lintner of the Hartwick Synod. The original committee had been instructed to "adhere particularly to the New York Hymn Book and the German Liturgy of Pennsylvania as their guides." This instruction was fol- lowed in part. Eleven of the twelve sections in the new liturgy are forms for ministerial acts. The other section, dealing with public worship, provides only a form of confession and prayer to be used at the opening, two forms for general prayers, and one for a benediction. The congregation is given no active part in worship except the sing- ing of hymns.

At its next meeting the General Synod appointed a new committee with instructions to amend and enlarge the liturgy of 1832. In the hope of securing a degree of uniformity throughout the church, the committee watched the liturgical changes of the New York and Pennsylvania Synods. The guiding principle for the General Synod was expressed in a resolution declaring that "uniformity in public worship among us can only be secured by providing for the use of the church a liturgy that by its superior merits shall receive the sanction of the church at large." But the General Synod did not publish another liturgy until 1847. This was a translation, with only a few changes, of the German liturgy that had been prepared by a joint committee of the New York Ministerium, the Pennsylvania Ministerium, and the Ohio Synod. High claims were made for this new liturgy, especially for its scriptural and historical character. It was an improvement over that of 1832 and showed that the liturgical taste of the English-speaking part of the church was also improving. The preface contained many excellent suggestions as to the value and the advantages of a liturgy. But it was by no means a responsive liturgy. The people still stood silent before the minister except in the hymns. It did not commend itself to the church at large.

Almost immediately the General Synod appointed a committee to receive suggestions for the improvement of its liturgy. Many suggestions were made. The committee tried to make the changes and improvements that would meet the wishes expressed in various quarters of the church, but finally gave up in despair because of the great diversities of taste and the many irreconcilable differences of view. But the General Synod refused to leave the matter to the district synods because, as one writer put it, "the conviction is extending itself more and more that our church is liturgical, that such forms ought to constitute a part of our public worship, and that there should be uniformity in their use." So the committee was continued, and in 1855 enlarged to embrace one member from each of the district synods, including the Pennsylvania Ministerium which had now joined the General Synod. The "pocket edition" of the liturgy was published in 1856 and differed from that of 1847 by including the Lord's Prayer and the Apostles' Creed. The liturgical influence of Dr. B. M. Schmucker now began to be felt in the General Synod.

But after the break in 1864 at York, liturgical matters in the General Synod were in a rather chaotic condition for several years. In 1866 Dr. S. S. Schmucker, as head of the Committee on Liturgy, submitted a "Provisional Liturgy" that represented a great advance over previous liturgies in the General Synod. But it was never adopted. Two years later a new committee was appointed and the number of members reduced to three, most active of whom was Dr. J. G. Butler of Washington. The committee submitted a new liturgy to the General Synod in Washington in 1869. This "Washington Service" was adopted with enthusiasm. It depended largely on Dr. Schmucker's "Provisional Liturgy," but added the Gloria Patri after the opening sentences, the Kyrie after the Confession of sin and prayer, and the Gloria in Excelsis after the Apostles' Creed. It was the nearest approach to a historical order of service yet made by the General Synod. But it was only the harbinger of a yet brighter day.

Of some forty different liturgies that had appeared in various quarters of the church during less than a century, the *Church Book* of 1868 prepared by the Pennsylvania Ministerium and adopted by the General Council, and the "Washington Service" of 1869, prepared and adopted by the General Synod, marked the highest tide of liturgical attainment up to that time. But neither was entirely satisfying to its constituents, and the deep longing for uniformity of worship among Lutherans was still unfulfilled.

Yet the many liturgical efforts since Muhlenberg's time had been an educational process for the church. Liturgical scholars had been developed and sound liturgical tastes had been cultivated. It had become clear that, to find general acceptance in the Lutheran church, a liturgy must conserve the treasures of the past and also adapt them to the devotional needs of the present. The time was ripe at last for preparation of a common order of service, a common hymnbook, and a common order of ministerial acts.

Quite appropriately, the initiative came from the United Synod in the South, in confessional position and liturgical practice about midway between the General Synod and the General Council. By a resolution in 1876 the United Synod invited the General Synod and the General Council to co-operate in preparing "one common service for all English-speaking Lutherans in the United States." The General Council resolved to co-operate, "provided the rule which shall decide all questions in its preparation shall be: The common consent of the pure Lutheran liturgies of the sixteenth century, and when there is not an entire agreement among them, the consent of the largest number of those of greatest weight." The General Synod was busy trying to secure a revision of the "Washington Service" that would satisfy its congregations, but in 1883 it received a petition from fifty-five of its pastors asking for an entirely new order of service "more in harmony with historic Lutheran books of worship and enunciating more clearly the doctrines of the church." That same year the General Synod decided with enthusiasm to co-operate in the work on a common service and expressed its agreement with the condition set forth by the General Council.

The three committees appointed by the general bodies were organized in 1885 as a joint committee which adopted several preliminary principles and set to work upon its delicate task. The committee understood that its work was not to collect the private preferences of the members of the committee nor to devise anything new, but to "place on record the undisputed facts as to what constitutes a Lutheran Order of Service." It was agreed that the proposed service should be used only while it served to edification, and no service could be made binding on any congregation. The committee worked under the rule of "the common consent of the pure Lutheran liturgies of the sixteenth century."

The Common Service was completed in 1888, "not without a painful sacrifice of personal views and prejudices on the part of every member of the joint committee." It was adopted at once by all three of the general bodies, and afterwards by the Joint Synod of Ohio and the English Synod of Missouri. It represented a heroic attempt to demonstrate the essential unity of the Lutheran church in America, and no other Lutheran order of service ever had such wide acceptance. It was the high tide of liturgical achievement in the Lutheran church, an undertaking worthy of the times in which it appeared. It was not an invention. It was the "Common Service of the Christian church of all ages," the fruit of a historical growth whose roots go back to the earliest days of the church, whose essential parts were universally recognized by the Reformers, and whose development through the Christian centuries was possible only because it satisfied the devotional wants of the Christian heart and the worshiping congregation. It gave evidence of fervent love for the old faith and placed the church of our day in communion with the devout assemblies of ancient days, enabling her to join her praises with the angelic hosts, and chant her hymns in the courts of glory.

When it appeared, however, that the Common Service resembled the form used by the General Council in its *Church Book* of 1868, it encountered some opposition in the General Synod. Efforts were made to modify the action adopting the Common Service. It was charged that unwarranted changes had been made since the preliminary draft which the General Synod had adopted so spontaneously in 1885. The respective merits of the "Washington Service" and the "Common Service" were the subject of heated discussions. It was decided to publish them both in the General Synod *Hymnal*. A sharp controversy ensued within the General Synod, a controversy that was prolonged by personal and confessional issues. An "Abridged Common Service" was published separately in 1895. However, the General Synod never modified its original acceptance and the controversy served to deepen appreciation of liturgical principles. The Common Service increased in popularity until the "Washington Service" became the exception.

Meanwhile the Joint Committee had prepared a standard English translation of Luther's Catechism and had been authorized to prepare a common book of ministerial acts and a common book of hymns. *The Hymnal* was ready in 1915 and appeared from the press in October, 1917. It was embodied in the *Common Service Book with Hymnal*. In this new book the rubrics of the Common Service were greatly simplified. The musical settings for all the parts of The Service were improved and of course standardized for all three of the bodies. The collection of hymns differed from preceding hymnals in that it was prepared in harmony with the spirit of the liturgy and with the evangelical principle of the Church Year. In the chaste and appropriate selection of hymns, in the high standard of literary merit, and in the adaptation of the music to the text, the common hymnal represented the highest achievement of Lutheran devotion and scholarship yet attained. It received unstinted commendation from competent critics even outside the Lutheran church.

The liturgical practices of the Lutheran churches established in the Mississippi Valley in the nineteenth century ran parallel with those of the churches descended from Muhlenberg.

The Joint Synod of Ohio had earlier co-operated with the eastern synods in preparing and publishing a liturgy. In 1884 it published its own German liturgy, and ten years later, after a few changes, translated it into English. Some further revisions were made in 1902, the German and English were made identical in 1909, and the liturgy of 1884 remained in general use for more than a quarter of a century. After the appearance of the Common Service of 1888 among the Lutheran bodies of the East, many of the Ohio Synod pastors used it, and after the Common Service was revised in 1917 the synod adopted it.

Among the other large Lutheran bodies of the Middle West there was no uniformity of practice until well into the twentieth century. Individual pastors were guided by their antecedents in Europe or in America, or by the facilities available in each congregation. When uniformity among the congregations was desired, the usual practice was to use the liturgies brought along from the European fatherland, to revise and improve those liturgies as revisions and improvements were made in Europe, and then, as the transition was made to the English language, to lean heavily upon the Common Service of 1917.

The Missouri Synod was slow to adopt a liturgy for general use among its congregations. The pastors used either the Saxon Agenda to which they were accustomed in Germany or the agenda which Loehe had prepared for the use of the German congregations in America. A revision of the Saxon liturgy was published in 1856. About twenty years later the Lutheran churches of Germany began to recover from the effects of pietism and rationalism and to restore a pure Lutheran liturgy, and the effects of this were soon felt in the Missouri Synod and the other parts of the Synodical Conference. Moreover, the liturgical development among the Lutheran bodies in the East were reflected in the English Synod of Missouri which in 1906 adopted the Common Service, but with a separate musical setting. In 1917, after the English Synod had become a district of the Missouri Synod, a liturgy much like the Common Service was approved and published by the synod. With some changes and additions a second edition was published in 1921. But the congregational polity of the Missouri Synod does not seek to secure uniformity of liturgical practice among the congregations and this large body of Lutherans has been slow to recover from what its historian has called "our liturgical chaos."

The Augustana Synod in its early history used the liturgy that had been introduced into the Church of Sweden in 1811. The service was greatly altered and simplified by most of the pastors. When the Church of Sweden improved its liturgy in 1894, the Augustana Synod issued a completely new agenda based on the Swedish revision. When an English translation was adopted in 1905 it followed the further developments in Sweden which were in the direction of the historic Lutheran service prepared by the Swedish reformer Olavus Petri in 1531. In 1924, when the Augustana Synod issued its *Service Book and Hymnal*, the Common Service was included as an alternate form, and it soon came into wide use among the congregations of the synod.

Among the Norwegian Lutherans in America there has been even wider variety of liturgical practice than among the other large Lutheran bodies. This was due to their native individualism and to their variety of organization. But the general trend among them runs parallel with that of the nineteenth-century Germans and Swedes. The liturgy of the state church of Norway, recovering from the depressing liturgical effects of rationalism, returned in 1920 to the Lutheran forms of the Reformation period, and many of the Norwegian pastors and congregations in America followed. As the transition to the English language was completed, liturgical scholars among the Norwegians in America led their people to an appreciation and use of the Common Service.

The greatest achievement of Lutherans in the area of liturgy and hymnody came at the middle of the twentieth century. This was the *Service Book and Hymnal* of 1957 (see Chapter 43).

CHAPTER 26

CONFESSIONAL CONSERVATION

Less tangible but none the less real and important than the development along the lines of benevolence and liturgy during this period was the progress of the church along doctrinal lines. It was a necessary preliminary to the period of larger harmony and union that was to follow.

The General Synod advanced to a much clearer definition of its doctrinal basis. In deference to the New York Ministerium and the Pennsylvania Ministerium, its 1820 constitution had made no mention whatever of the Augsburg Confession. But in 1825 the professor for the theological seminary the General Synod was organizing was pledged to the Augsburg Confession and Luther's Catechisms as "a summary and correct exhibition of the fundamental doctrines of God's Word." In 1829 the model constitution that was recommended to the district synods required the candidates for ordination to declare their belief "that the fundamental doctrines of the Word of God are taught in a manner substantially correct in the doctrinal articles of the Augsburg Confession." This indefinite statement led to confusion and difficulties. So in 1864 the General Synod resolved that all of the doctrines taught in the Augsburg Confession are fundamental doctrines of God's Word and that the manner in which they are taught in the Augsburg Confession is entirely correct. In 1866 an amendment to the constitution of the General Synod changed the doctrinal basis of the body to make it receive "The Word of God as contained in the canonical Scriptures of the Old and New Testaments as the only infallible rule of faith and practice, and the Augsburg Confession as a correct exhibition of the fundamental doctrines of the Divine Word and of the faith of our Church founded upon that Word." Some interpreted the amendment to mean that certain subjects treated in the Augsburg Confession are not *fundamental* truths of the Bible and that on these points the Confession was not binding. The conservative party in the synod was in a clear majority and felt the need for a clearer definition of confessional basis, but the bitterness caused by the founding of the General Council produced strained relations between the parties in the General Synod and retarded the development of confessional Lutheranism. The controversy over the Common Service also helped to prevent an impartial consideration of the confessional question. But the conservatives gained steadily in influence. The annual Holman lecture on the Augsburg Confession at the Gettysbury Seminary led to a better understanding of that instrument. The publication of the English translation of Schmid's *Dogmatics* enabled the pastors to acquaint themselves with a conservative statement of Lutheran doctrines. The growing conservatism of her theological schools and the influences of other Lutheran bodies, among other factors, contributed to the conservation of the faith in General Synod circles.

By 1895 the smoke of battle had cleared away sufficiently to permit the passing of a resolution that "This convention of the General Synod expresses its entire satisfaction with the present form of doctrinal basis and confessional subscription, which is the Word of God, as the infallible rule of faith and practice, and the Unaltered Augsburg Confession as throughout in perfect consistence with it—nothing more, nothing less." This committed the General Synod definitely to the entire Augsburg Confession. And here for the first time the Unaltered Augsburg Confession was mentioned. This is the term that was used by all other Lutheran bodies to specify the first edition of the Confession in contrast to later editions which were changed in important parts. It was the first edition that all parties had always had in mind, but now it was clearly specified. Another effort at clearer definition was made in a resolution of 1901: "We hold that to make any distinction between fundamental and so-called non-fundamental doctrines in the Augsburg Confession is contrary to the basis of the General Synod as set forth in our formula of confessional subscription."

But in spite of these resolutions the General Council and other Lutheran bodies persisted in questioning the sound Lutheranism of the General Synod. These criticisms were based on the fact that the resolutions of 1895 and 1901 were not incorporated in the constitution, that no mention was made of the other confessional writings of the Lutheran church besides the Augsburg Confession, and that the constitutional amendment of 1866 spoke of "the Word of God as *contained* in the canonical Scriptures," the very expression used by negative critics to discredit large portions of the Bible. To silence these criticisms and repudiate the charges growing out of them the General Synod in 1909 adopted a long series of statements repeating and explaining the previous declarations, maintaining its adherence to the proposition that "the Bible *is* the Word of God," disavowing any real change in its confessional basis since 1866, but adding its appreciation of the other Lutheran confessions "as a most valuable body of Lutheran belief, explaining and unfolding the doctrines of the Augsburg Confession."

Then, in order further to clarify the confessional atmosphere, another important step was taken. The General Synod's Committee on Common Service was charged with the duty of gathering these various doctrinal statements into concise form and preparing them to be embodied in the constitution of the General Synod as a restatement of its doctrinal position. This was done. Two new articles were inserted in the constitution. The article "on doctrinal basis" said that the General Synod holds "the canonical Scriptures of the Old and New Testaments as the Word of God" and "the Unaltered Augsburg Confession as a correct exhibition of the faith and doctrine of our Church as founded upon that Word." A separate article on "secondary symbols" said that the General Synod recognizes the other confessions in the Book of Concord as "expositions of Lutheran doctrine of great historical and interpretive value." This constitutional amendment was unanimously approved by the district synods. It was the culmination of a splendid forward movement in the confessional conservation of the General Synod, a movement that extended over a period of forty years and placed that body on an unequivocal Lutheran basis.

The General Council never changed "the fundamental principles of faith" that it had adopted when it was organized. The doctrinal position assumed in those principles was the distinguishing mark of the General Council throughout the fifty years of its life. It asserted that the Unaltered Augsburg Confession is by "pre-eminence" the Confession of the Lutheran faith, being "throughout in conformity with the pure truth of which God's Word is the only rule," that the other confessions in the Book of Concord are in perfect harmony with the Augsburg Confession, and that the confessions in order to be a bond of union must be understood in the same sense by those who subscribe to them. Thus the confessional basis of the General Council was very clear and very definite from the beginning, and no party within the body ever called it into question. As a doctrinal position it might have furnished the basis for a union of all the more conservative Lutheran bodies in America.

But the General Council was not static. It had to make its way forward to the solution of big problems. It was soon found that even among Lutherans of the strictest orthodoxy there were wide differences of opinion concerning the doctrinal teachings of the confessions. The variety of interpretation cropped out particularly in several matters of practice. The result was that the Missouri Synod refused to join the Council and most of the other western synods withdrew after the organization was formed, the Joint Synod of Ohio, the German Iowa Synod, and then the Wisconsin, Minnesota, Illinois and Michigan Synods. Throughout this period the General Council labored toward the solution of serious questions concerning the practical implications of the confessions.

At the very first convention of the General Council the Joint Synod of Ohio, supported by the German Iowa Synod, asked for a declaration on four subjects afterward noted as the "four points." The first was the question concerning chiliasm. Some theologians then in the council had taught that the advent of Christ would be premillennial. This matter was settled when the Council in 1868 repudiated "Jewish opinions" and everything else condemned in the seventeenth article of the Augsburg Confession.

But the rest of the "four points" were not so easily settled. One of them concerned secret societies. It was charged that in congregations belonging to synods in the General Council there were many members of secret societies which in their worship denied Christ, imposed oaths contrary to God's Word, and interfered with supreme loyalty to the church. Ohio and Iowa demanded immediate and drastic discipline of such members. But the majority in the General Council preferred gradual education to summary discipline. In 1868 the Council declared un-Christian those that fall under the description in the complaint, warned its members and ministers against all fellowship with such societies, and threatened prompt discipline against those who persisted in their "connection with infidel and immoral associations." This statement and the subsequent practice of the General Council were too mild to please the Lutherans of Ohio and Iowa, and for years they debated the subject with the General Council.

The other two of the "four points" that occupied so much attention of the General Council concerned the exchange of pulpits with ministers who were not Lutheran and the admission of non-Lutherans to the Lutheran communion altar. There were differences of opinion within the General Council and the agitation extended over many years. In the synods of the East it had been customary for Lutheran preachers to preach occasionally in the pulpits of other evangelical denominations and occasionally to invite or admit ministers of other denominations to preach in their pulpits. To this practice the representatives of some of the western synods objected on the ground that it meant indifference to error. In all sections of the General Council, particularly among the Germans and Scandinavians, were some who objected to the "general invitation" to the holy communion on various grounds, especially on the ground that it undermined church authority and church discipline and proclaimed the indifference of the pastor and the congregation to the view of the Lord's Supper held by the communicant.

Several official deliverances were necessary before these questions of pulpit and altar fellowship were settled. In the course of the agitation several of the western synods withdrew from the Council. Of those that remained the New York Ministerium was especially zealous in demanding stricter regulations. The final action of the council on these points is known as "the Galesburg Rule," from the place where the body was meeting when the action was taken in 1875. Three years before at Akron, Ohio, a statement of the president of the Council was made the official action of the body as follows: "1. The rule is: Lutheran pulpits are for Lutheran ministers only; Lutheran altars are for Lutheran communicants only. 2. The exceptions to the rule belong to the sphere of privilege and not of right. 3. The determination of the exceptions is to be made in consonance with these principles by the conscientious judgment of pastors, as the cases arise." This simply meant that no one was to be admitted either to the pulpit or the altar unless the church, or its officers acting for it, were satisfied as to his fitness and preparation. It stated what was generally understood to be the practice in the churches of the General Council. But at Galesburg the first sentence of the Akron statement was reaffirmed and a clause inserted to make it read "The rule, which accords with the Word of God and with the confessions of our Church, is," etc. Then a long controversy broke out over the meaning of terms and over the question whether the clause inserted at Galesburg did not dispense with the second and third articles admitting exceptions. Session after session and year after year was occupied by the discussion. The strict constructionists denied the possibility of exceptions, interpreted "Lutheran" very exclusively, and understood "rule" in a legislative sense. But the author of the Akron Declaration defined the word "rule" to be "not governmental but educational." The Council had long before declared that the persons to be excluded from the Lutheran altar are the "fundamental errorists," that is, "those who wilfully, wickedly, and persistently desert, in whole or in part, the Christian faith." And in 1889 it was finally decided that the entire Akron Declaration was still in force. This meant that exceptions to the rule were permissible and it left the whole matter largely to the discretion of the individual pastors.

These were some of the major difficulties with which the General Council had to deal in establishing unity among those who had originally adopted "the fundamental principles of faith and polity." The difficulties related to the practical application of the principles. The discussions were often prolonged and the issues confused by differences of nationality and language, and for years they proved a serious hindrance to the development and growth of the body. But in nearly every case they were carried through to complete clarity and thus solved some of the most pressing problems confronting the Lutheran church in America.

Now the man who gave the fullest and deepest utterances on all these questions was Charles Porterfield Krauth. His was the most profound insight and his voice and pen spoke always with the highest degree of authority. Dr. Krauth had been trained in the college and seminary at Gettysburg, where his father was president and professor. He had preached five years in Baltimore, eight years at Martinsburg and Winchester, Virginia, and four years in Pittsburgh. In 1859 he came to Philadelphia as pastor of St. Mark's, but two years later he resigned the pastorate to become editor-in-chief of the *Lutheran and Missionary*. His own theological views underwent a development whose stages are easy to follow. That development was completed in 1865 shortly after he became professor of systematic theology in the new seminary in Philadelphia. His theological position and his great personal talents pre-eminently fitted him to take the chief part in reviving conservative Lutheranism and placing it on a secure basis among the English-speaking Lutherans in America. His incisive and exhaustive articles in the *Lutheran and Missionary* made him easily the most brilliant religious pamphleteer among that generation of Americans. His thorough scholarship was widely recognized outside of the Lutheran church. He was professor of philosophy at the University of Pennsylvania from 1868 to his death in 1883, and several of his books were in philosophy.

Dr. Krauth took a prominent part in the formation of the General Council. It was he who wrote the "fundamental principles of faith and polity" that established the basic character of the body. He composed the model constitution for congregations that was adopted in 1880. He co-operated actively in producing the *Church Book*. From 1870 to 1880, that critical period in the history of the General Council, he was its president. The Akron Declaration in 1872 and the one hundred and five theses on altar and pulpit fellowship in 1877 were his composition. His most important published work was *The Conservative Reformation and Its Theology* of 1872. This was largely a series of articles that had appeared before, but because of its profound learning, exhaustive research, and brilliant style it is widely recognized to this day as the most complete statement in English of the position of the Lutheran church in America. As professor of systematic theology in the Philadelphia Seminary he molded the views of most of the ministers in the Council. In short, the personality, scholarship, and theology of Charles Porterfield Krauth, more than that of any other man, determined the character of the General Council throughout its history.

In addition to the discussions on the "four points" the language question figured prominently in the development of the General Council. Germans, English, Swedes, all had strong representation in the body. At the urging of the Swedes English replaced German as the official language of the Council, but the controversy on the subject extended over many years. It was finally agreed on all sides that it is just as possible to hold the Lutheran faith and to observe Lutheran usages in the English language as the German.

Toward the end of this period the General Council began to interpret its "fundamental principles of church polity" in such a way as to permit a greater centralization of the practical work of the council. The home mission work especially, it was seen, could best be carried on through a central agency. Then the policy of unification gradually came to be applied to other lines of benevolence, as in the General Synod. This was largely due to the influence of Dr. T. E. Schmauk, the president of the General Council during the last fifteen years of its existence. Through his energy, scholarship, and broad statesmanship, he exerted a more varied influence on the life of the church than any other leader since Muhlenberg. He knew how to fuse the diverse elements within the Council. He magnified the importance of the general organization over which he presided, and by his skillful administration gathered steadily more power into the hands of the General Council and increasingly brought its boards, committees, and voluntary agencies under the direct control of the general body. This process of centralization was greatly retarded, however, by the special claims of the large Swedish Augustana Synod aided by the General Council guarantee of the internal independence of its constituent district synods. Thus not administrative control, but conservative doctrinal guidance, remained the chief function of the General Council.

In the South also the Lutherans reached a more definite confessional basis during this period. The General Synod of the South, organized in 1863 by delegates of the Synods of Virginia, Southwest Virginia, North Carolina, South Carolina and Georgia, stated in its doctrinal basis that the "Apostles' Creed, the Nicene Creed, and the Augsburg Confession contain the fundamental doctrines of the Sacred Scriptures" which "*are* the Word of God," but allowed a difference of interpretation of several articles of the Augsburg Confession. In the revised constitution of 1868 no mention is made of a difference of interpretation of the Augsburg Confession; and the candidate for ordination is required to pledge fidelity to "the Word of God and to the *Confessions* of our Lutheran Church founded thereon." In 1872 the General Synod of the South declared that "It has placed itself unequivocally upon the Ecumenical Creeds and the Augsburg Confession in its true, native and original sense." Further progress in appreciation of the confessions is shown by its declaration in 1880 acknowledging "the symbols adopted subsequently to the Augsburg Confession . . . as in accord with and an unfolding of the teachings of the Unaltered Augsburg Confession."

By 1886 the Tennessee Synod, always highly conservative since its organization in 1820, was willing to unite with the synods of the General Synod South and with the Holston Synod to form the "United Synod in the South." The constitution of the new body planted it squarely upon the symbolical books "as true and Scriptural developments of the doctrines taught in the Augsburg Confession, and in the perfect harmony of one and the same pure Scriptural faith." In accordance with this doctrinal basis the theological seminary was reestablished in 1892 at Newberry, later removed to Charleston, and finally located at Columbia. For years the United Synod was obliged to discuss the troublesome questions of secret societies and pulpit and altar fellowship. But the church in the South was averse to controversy and declined to legislate on these subjects. It was finally agreed to leave the questions undecided and to recognize that difference of opinion exists, though sentiment constantly gravitated towards the stricter practice.

As to the general bodies of Lutherans centering in the Middle West, we cannot properly speak of an advance in loyalty to the Lutheran confessions. Among the Missouri, Ohio, Iowa, and the Norwegian Lutherans, supra-confessional ground was taken from the beginning, and held. There was no progress either in doctrinal positions or in their interpretation. A number of serious controversies on doctrinal and practical matters served only to define more clearly the differences among the general bodies. In confessional positions there were no changes and in doctrinal development little progress.

It is interesting to observe, therefore, that the progress of every Lutheran body in this country has been marked by an increasing appreciation of the confessions of the church. It was no accident that the culmination of the confessional development in the older parts of the church took place in the age of big business, at the very same time when the church was making unprecedented strides in numerical increase, in geographical expansion, in benevolent operation, and in liturgical achievement. The same spirit of enterprise and large undertaking that charged the atmosphere of society in general and characterized the life of American Christianity as a whole and manifested itself in other lines of activity among Lutherans, naturally made itself felt also in the sphere of doctrine and brought most of the general bodies of Lutherans into such close approach to one another in their attitude towards the confessions that it foreshadowed an era of still larger undertakings among them.

Part VI

IN AN AGE OF LARGER UNITS
(1910-1950)

The National and International View

CHAPTER 27

GENERAL BACKGROUND

In the second decade of the twentieth century, both church and state caught the thrill of a lofty idealism and then almost immediately felt a chilling reaction from it. A new political situation, in effect, a world-wide revolution, called up new alignments, new political machinery, and larger combinations both national and international of political and cultural forces. Likewise a new spiritual atmosphere, highly charged with possibilities, spread over the earth and called the Christian church to unimagined opportunities demanding larger units of organization.

The United States emerged as the most powerful and politically most important nation of the world. Before the close of the nineteenth century the government had begun feeling its way in international politics, had adopted a more aggressive foreign policy and had made the nation's influence felt throughout Latin America. The Spanish War left the United States in possession of Porto Rico, Hawaii and the Philippines, with a protectorate over Cuba. Shortly afterward the American government took the lead in establishing the "open-door" policy in China that preserved the integrity of that country, and thenceforth American diplomacy was a powerful factor in the Far East. Repeatedly the United States took a hand in South American affairs to prevent European powers from seizing territory. The federal government built the Panama Canal. The United States participated creditably in the Hague conferences on international arbitration. And finally America took the decisive part in two great world wars. The government of the United States, a mere rope of sand when it was founded a century and a quarter before, was now a world power of the very first rank.

Forced to realize that the progressive arts and sciences of civilization had drawn the whole world together into one neighborhood, the people of America renounced for a time their vaunted isolation and became citizens of the world. A flood of international organizations covered practically every sphere of human activity—religious, social, educational, industrial, political. In the foreground was the international political organization. The great war of 1914-1918 had clearly indicated the solidarity of the human race and convinced thoughtful persons in every nation that there are wide areas of common interest among all the peoples of the earth. It proved the need for a body of international law that would be as binding on the nations as civil law is binding on individuals, lest another war mean the death of civilization. At the Paris peace conference the United States insisted upon formation of an international organization that would secure permanent peace, and for a time the world's hopes seemed to rest in the united states of the world, the League of Nations.

The new internationalism in politics was paralleled by a new inter-denominationalism in religion. The wartime situation made new and extraordinary demands upon the churches that could not be met by the denominations acting separately. Even before the war broke out there were a number of movements among the Christian churches of America looking toward federation or administrative union. The Young Men's Christian Association and the Young Women's Christian Association were old organizations that had no official relations with the denominations. But now a number of new organizations were born that sought to secure co-operation among the official churches, though only to limited purposes. The Foreign Mission Conference of North America, established in 1893, was an officially representative body chosen by the foreign mission boards of the denominations and reporting to those boards. The Home Missions Council, organized in 1908, was similarly related to the home missionary agencies of the churches. The Council of Women for Home Missions, dating from 1908, and the Federation of Women's Boards of Foreign Missions, dating from 1916, were associations of representatives from the corresponding women's boards of the denominations. The Council of Church Boards of Education was formed in 1911 and united the educational agencies of the churches. And the Sunday School Council of Evangelical Denominations, established in 1910, afterwards called the International Council of Religious Education, consisted of the officially appointed representatives of the Sunday school agencies of the churches. All of these organizations helped to create a new spirit of common counsel and co-operation among the churches, and all of them were increased in zeal and scope by the demands of the war.

The earliest effort to go beyond such administrative joint actions and to federate the denominations themselves was the organization in 1908 of the Federal Council of the Churches of Christ in America. Its purpose—not union but federation—was to encourage mutual counsel concerning the spiritual life and the religious activities of the churches and to secure co-operation in all matters affecting the moral and social condition of the people. Thirty denominations officially ratified the plan. The Federal Council at once began to serve as a clearinghouse for denominational and interdenominational activities, co-ordinating existing denominational agencies and establishing new ones to carry out tasks which could not be accomplished by separate denominational agencies.

At the outbreak of the war the churches perceived their tremendous responsibilities and appointed the necessary commissions, sometimes by a considerable stretch of denominational authority. But it was soon found that they had set themselves nearly identical forms of service with startling similarity of spirit and method, and that some of these responsibilities were too great for individual denominations to assume. Guided by the example of unity among the nations at war, as well as that of parties, classes and economic interests, the Christian churches could not refuse to join with one another. Moreover, much of their wartime work involved the churches with the government, which could not deal with them separately.

In this emergency the Federal Council of Churches, representing the evangelical churches of the United States, organized its General Wartime Commission as an information clearinghouse, a co-ordinating agency, and an instrument for joint expression and administration. Interdenominationalism had never before gone so far.

Another group of American Christians in 1918 organized an administrative union of denominations called the Inter-Church World Movement which sought to unite practically all of the official agencies of the churches. But the World Movement was precipitate and lacked definition, and hopes placed in it were soon dispelled by the change of spirit that came over society after the war.

Another movement to promote understanding and co-operation among all Christian churches, fostered by Archbishop Söderblom, Lutheran primate of Sweden, was called the Universal Christian Council on Life and Work. International as well as interdenominational, its conferences met at Stockholm in 1925 and at Oxford in 1937 with representatives from practically all Christian churches except the Roman Catholic.

Meanwhile several efforts were made to go beyond federation or administrative union and to achieve organic union. The World Conference on Faith and Order initiated by the Protestant Episcopal Church in 1910 sought to unite all Christendom through ecumenical conferences and the gradual growth of common understanding. Conferences at Lausanne, Switzerland, in 1927, and Edinburgh in 1937, faced up frankly to the problems involved in organic union, and one result was to show what great distances separate some Christian communions from others.

Organic union was again fostered by a series of conferences held in Philadelphia beginning in 1918 at the invitation of the Presbyterian church. Aiming at the eventual union of the churches by gradual merger of their missionary and benevolent agencies, this movement had little success.

For all these efforts, organic union of the Christian churches of the world, or even of the United States, proved as impossible of realization as a supergovernment to which the nations would yield their individual sovereignties.

The third decade of the century witnessed a sharp reaction against both internationalism in politics and interdenominationalism in religion. Unified efforts that had been secured during the war by social or political pressure, or by the stirring of deep passions, vanished completely when the pressure lifted and the passions subsided. Only a few months of peace showed that what had seemed to be unity of churches or states was largely superficial, unreal, or temporary.

Moreover, inequities of the peace, between nations and races and classes, produced a rising tide of nationalism, racial patriotism, and economic disturbance. The United States rejected the internationalism of the League of Nations and gradually withdrew from entangling alliances in Europe. Differences and ill will were soon manifest among the victorious nations, and there was a sharp reassertion everywhere of national prejudices, ambitions, and fears.

In the wake of this political fragmentation came devastating economic depression. The maladjustment of international relationships had disturbed credit among the nations and paralyzed foreign trade. Overinflation within the creditor nations bore fruit in a prolonged period of enforced deflation.

The condition of social, political, and economic life now called for new organization. If the world was not to drift back toward the rampant sectionalism and the conscientious sectarianism of the middle of the nineteenth century, some organizational arrangement was needed among the nations and among the churches and among the classes that would enable each group to retain its independence and initiative while delegating power in matters of common interest to a central organization. Such federation rests upon representation and co-operation, avoids the contrasting dangers of centralization and sectionalism, and seeks to express both liberty and unity in human relationships. This federalism has come to be the dominant spirit among the churches of America and, to a lesser extent, among the churches of the world.

Self-determination was felt among the churches as well as the nations. Artificially formed unions, so persistently attempted during the decade preceding the war, came to nothing, or were crowded into the background by more absorbing interests. The denominations found that they had their own internal problems as serious as those of the nation. But in the face of the world's appalling needs, and the impending world chaos, genuine unity of spirit was more important than either formal union of organizations or denominational separateness.

In the Lutheran church the tendency toward consolidation into larger units appeared earlier than in the other churches. But almost all of the Christian churches of America began to reach out and cultivate co-operative movements among American Protestants. Administrative unions across denominational lines increased. The Federal Council of Churches was changed in structure in 1932 to provide for service in new areas of the practical Christian task that had been disclosed by the world war. At the same time the council was made more responsive to the wishes and needs of its participating member churches.

Organization in 1923 of the Lutheran World Convention set the pace among Protestants for other "ecumenical denominations." Contacts multiplied across national boundaries and across denominational lines. The two Christian movements that sought to be ecumenical, the Universal Christian Council on Life and Work and the World Conference on Faith and Order, prepared to merge and form a World Council of Churches.

Before this could be accomplished, however, the international political situation burst into World War II. This great conflict, 1939-1945, and its aftermath brought changes that were more general and more profound than those recorded in any other equal space of time. Again the cry for self-determination rang out among all races and nations around the globe. Again the churches everywhere were deeply involved. Political revolutions and vast shifts in population suddenly presented the churches with gigantic problems. Movements that are directly hostile to Christianity as a system of thought gathered great strength during and after the war. The whole missionary movement of modern times was forced to make radical changes. In many areas Christian forces were confronted with political power that was both absolute and hostile. The appalling needs of many millions of human beings called for Christian action on an unprecedented scale.

In their splendid efforts to maintain their Christian witness and to answer the calls that came to them during and after World War II, the churches advanced in several directions. More effective agencies were organized to spread the gospel around the globe. The International Missionary Council, begun in 1921, became a federation of twenty-six regional and national societies that entered into co-operative planning for world-wide evangelism. The new churches that were born of the modern missionary enterprise took their places as autonomous members in the great family of Christian churches. These "younger churches" help to account for a wider distribution of Christianity since World War II. Indeed, it became quite clear that the Christian faith had taken deep root far beyond Europe and the West and was about to put forth new shoots of vigorous growth.

Christian leaders were stimulated by the war to efforts on behalf of peace among the nations. Many of them undertook the task of creating a better economic, social, political, and international order through the application of Christian principles. Organizations like the Church Peace Union and the World Alliance for International Friendship Through Religion were then succeeded by the Stockholm and Oxford conferences on Life and Work. These were serious efforts to obtain a united voice of the Christian churches in behalf of a better society. They created a sense of common interest among Christians, even across the lines of battle. They kept conscience and hope alive and led the churches to show more power of resistance against ruthless dictators than any other group of society.

The vitality of the Christian faith also kept alive the dream of an international government that would guarantee permanent peace. The League of Nations did not endure, but the courage and idealism of Christian men in various governments brought forth the United Nations as another comprehensive attempt to insure peace and justice on a world-wide scale. Here the voice of the Christian churches is heard constantly in behalf of humanity and enlightenment, in favor of peace and justice on all levels, and in defense of elemental human rights of all kinds. Here the victims of disaster and oppression and exploitation have a court of appeal, the displaced person, the refugee, and the other victims of war's desolations and mass migrations. In these and other ways the churches have exerted their influence in behalf of individual rights, religious and intellectual liberty, political self-government, and economic opportunity. In the turbulent era that followed the two world wars, the Christian churches manifested rapid gains not only in numbers and geographic spread, but even more in their vigorous labors for the safety and happiness of the human race.

The organization of the World Council of Churches which had been proposed in 1937 and 1938 but was interrupted by the outbreak of World War II, was carried to completion in 1948. Even during the war the "Provisional Committee of the World Council of Churches in Process of Formation" accomplished a vast amount in furthering the purposes of Life and Work and Faith and Order. As finally organized in 1948, the World Council of Churches was the most complete expression of the ecumenical idea that had yet been attained. It was for the Christian churches a global expression of federalism. Through its constitution it safeguarded the integrity of the individual church and confession and at the same time it provided the platform and implements for co-operation through representatives. It specifically disclaimed any purpose of organic union. On this basis it rallied to its program the major portion of Protestantism. It is therefore the most striking religious event in this age of larger units.

All of these developments furnish the framework within which to interpret the history of the Lutheran churches of America during the years 1910-1950. The mergers within the Lutheran family set the pace for a whole series of similar events in other denominational families. The formation of the Lutheran World Federation parallels the outreach of other American churches into the field of international organization. The great achievement by the National Lutheran Council, not only for the solution of social problems in America but also for the elemental needs of the suffering human race itself, proves that Lutherans share fully in the new social dynamic that two world wars have infused into American Christianity in general. In these and other ways Lutherans reflected the general spirit of the twentieth century. They prepared to accept their responsibility as a vital element in American Christianity and they moved out to take their proper place in the international scene.

Such was the general temper of Lutheranism in America as history moved into the second half of the twentieth century. This will be clear if we now turn to a narrative of details.

CHAPTER 28

THE EVANGELICAL LUTHERAN CHURCH

The first definite expression of the growing solidarity among Lutherans during this period was the union in 1917 of the three larger bodies of Norwegian Lutherans in America. Their organization, embracing nearly ninety-two per cent of the Lutherans of Norwegian nationality in America, is known today as The Evangelical Lutheran Church.

From the beginning of their history in this country about 1850, as we have seen, the Norwegians were divided by questions of doctrine and church practice. But with regard to the great issue of preserving the Lutheran faith as they had inherited it from their fathers, they were all animated by the same spirit. Their desire for freedom in the management of church affairs was combined with a conservatism in doctrine which has its roots in the national character and which has given their church in this country its dignity and strength.

This essential unity in evangelical faith together with the common ties of race and language early suggested organic union among the different groups of Norwegian Lutherans in America. But many years passed before the various factions could be brought together on a common platform. During the period of internal discord in American society and in the American churches, divisions increased among the Norwegian Lutherans. In 1872, they had about 150 pastors, 600 congregations and 110,000 members. They were divided among no less than five separate Norwegian Lutheran synods or organizations in 1876, and one more was added in 1887.

The oldest of these six bodies was Hauge's Synod, organized in 1846 by Elling Eielsen, a follower of Hans Nielsen Hauge, Norway's great evangelist-reformer. This group always insisted on definite marks of Christian experience, on positive and courageous evangelism, and on vigorous development of lay leadership. Its first name was "The Evangelical Lutheran Church in America," but it was commonly known as the Eielsen Synod. Thirty years later some of the provisions of the constitution were revised, the body was reorganized and the official name was changed to "Hauge's Norwegian Evangelical Lutheran Synod in America." A minority group led by the original founder, and still insisting upon positive proof of conversion for admission to church membership, separated from the main group and organized "The Evangelical Lutheran Church of America (Eielsen Synod)."

A third, and the largest of the Norwegian Lutheran groups in 1876, was the Synod for the Norwegian Evangelical Lutheran Church in America, usually called simply the Norwegian Synod. Formed in 1851 and reorganized in 1853, it was sponsored by a group of men whose names became highly respected among all Norwegians, such as Clausen, Dietrichson, Preus, Stub, Brandt, and Ottesen. These men, with the exception of Clausen, came from the upper classes in Norway, were trained in the university, and were ordained by the state church. In America they stood for a strict interpretation of doctrine and adherence to the ritual and church practices of Norway so far as frontier conditions permitted. They denied the right of laymen to conduct evangelistic meetings, and they had no dealings with the followers of Hauge. They co-operated with the Missouri Synod in the support of the seminary in St. Louis and sent their theological students to Missouri for their training. In 1872 the Norwegian Synod joined with the Germans of the Missouri and Wisconsin Synods in forming the Synodical Conference.

Two other bodies of Norwegian Lutherans were the Norwegians who separated from the Swedes in the Scandinavian Evangelical Lutheran Augustana Synod in 1870 and themselves divided into the Conference of the Norwegian-Danish Evangelical Lutheran Church in America and The Norwegian-Danish Augustana Synod. The fourteen pastors who organized the Conference insisted upon extreme congregationalism with nothing more than a free association of the congregations in the larger body, while the nine pastors who organized the Synod prepared a closer approach to the American or synodical type of organization. The use of the word Danish in the titles of these bodies was the expression more of hope than reality, for the Norwegian-Danish Conference had only eleven pastors of Danish birth and the Norwegian-Danish Augustana Synod had none. As a rule these bodies were called simply "the Conference" and the Norwegian Augustana Synod.

Thousands of Norwegian immigrants, pastors and lay people, who came to the Midwest in the last quarter of the nineteenth century were attracted by the middle position of the conference. It avoided the rigid orthodoxy of the Norwegian Synod, the emotional pietism of the Hauge-Eielsen groups, and the "Americanizing" tendencies of the Norwegian Augustana Synod. In spite of attacks from all directions, in Norwegian, German, and English, the conference grew rapidly. And then it promptly developed acute internal problems. The trouble was partly a clash of personalities, but largely problems of polity and church practice. The "new school," as it was called, insisted upon applying everywhere the free congregational principle, while the "old school" proposed that the congregations unite organically. The new school gained the ascendancy, largely through the coming of two brilliant theological teachers from Norway, Sven Oftedal and Georg Sverdrup.

More serious was the doctrinal division in the ranks of the older and more powerful Norwegian Synod. The controversy on predestination, as we have observed, not only led the Norwegian Synod in 1883 to sever its fellowship with the Missourians in the Synodical Conference, but also split the ranks of the synod itself. Many pastors of the synod agreed with Professor Schmidt in his debate with Dr. Walther on election, and others were impatient with the rigid orthodoxy and exclusiveness of Missouri. But separation from the Synodical Conference did not bring peace in the Norwegian Synod. The group following Professor Schmidt did not differ greatly in their theology from the rest of the synod, but in 1887, with about one-third of the synod, they withdrew and formed the Anti-Missourian Brotherhood. They soon numbered more than 100 pastors and professors, with 268 congregations.

Meanwhile the rate of immigration from Norway increased. By 1890 there were about 325,000 Norwegians of the first generation and an equal number of the second and third generations scattered through every state, and Canada. Most settled in Minnesota, Wisconsin, Illinois, Iowa, and the Dakotas. Of the six ecclesiastical groups preparing to minister to this multitude of Lutheran immigrants in the tongue and teaching of the church in their homeland, the largest was the Norwegian Synod with 187 pastors and 516 congregations. Next in size was "the Conference" with 115 pastors and 379 congregations, then the Anti-Missourian Brotherhood with about 100 pastors and 268 congregations, Hauge's Synod with 65 pastors and 185 congregations, the Norwegian Augustana Synod with 28 pastors and 41 congregations, and the Eielsen Synod with 8 pastors and an indefinite number of preaching points. In many communities on the frontier that were almost entirely Norwegian and Lutheran, two or more of these different Norwegian Lutheran bodies were represented, if only with small congregations.

But the era of larger units brought a new spirit among the Norwegians. The possibilities of union had become clear in a series of conferences, reaching across synodical boundaries, which, after 1880, occurred at least annually. At first "free" conferences, in which the participating individuals were without official standing, after 1883 they were "joint" conferences and the participants were chosen by their several bodies. Some of the leaders saw that elements of all the larger bodies were much alike, both in doctrine and practice, but most of the old Norwegian Synod, under the strict influence of men trained in Missouri's Concordia Seminary, could not be expected to join in a merger with the other bodies that had participated in the long series of conferences looking to that end. But separation of the Anti-Missourian element from the Norwegian Synod led to positive steps toward organic union.

The initiative came from P. A. Rasmussen. This devout and active pioneer, who had left the Eielsen fellowship and in 1862 led a small group of pastors and congregations into the Norwegian Synod, was a leader of the Anti-Missourians. He influenced his fellows to invite "the Conference," the Norwegian Augustana Synod, and Hauge's Synod to a joint meeting for the discussion of union. At a meeting in 1888 doctrinal agreement was reached, articles of union adopted, and a constitution for a united body agreed upon. The representatives of Hauge's Synod finally decided to continue their separate organization, but the representatives of the other three groups submitted the proposed constitution and articles of union to their respective congregations and synodical conventions and they were properly adopted.

In 1890 the three bodies met in Minneapolis, concluded their separate existence, then met together to form "The United Norwegian Lutheran Church of America."

The "United Church" was now easily the largest organization among Norwegian Lutherans with 260 pastors, about 830 congregations, and some 152,000 members. This was more than half of all the Norwegian Lutherans who had been gathered into congregations in America, about one-fourth of the entire Norwegian population of the first and second generations.

The new body set to work at once to prepare further union among the Norwegians to face the challenge of continuing immigration. The church was divided into nineteen geographical circuits and a pastor was designated for each one as a visitor. Two union committees were appointed, one to deal with the Norwegian Synod and one with Hauge's Synod. A home mission committee was appointed and a superintendent called to organize and oversee the work among the Norwegian diaspora. Vigorous resolutions were adopted against the liquor traffic and the "insulting efforts" of other Protestant bodies to make proselytes among Norwegian Lutherans.

But the new body was not a year old before difficulties arose over the Augsburg Seminary in Minneapolis. In 1869 the Norwegians in the "Augustana College Seminary" at Paxton, Illinois, had separated from the Swedes and established their own institution at Marshall, Wisconsin. When, next year, the Norwegians of the Scandinavian Augustana Synod withdrew to form the Danish-Norwegian Conference and the Norwegian Augustana Synod, the synod got the property at Marshall. The conference in 1872 took its students and its professor and set up Augsburg Seminary in Minneapolis. As the conference grew its seminary was strengthened. It was to become the headquarters of "the new school," the wing that developed under the leadership of two recently arrived professors, Sven Oftedal and Georg Sverdrup. These men, coming to America in 1873 and 1874 respectively, were soon the recognized leaders of the church. As such they minimized the value of doctrinal discussion and sought to avoid spiritual strangulation by keeping the congregations free from a dominating church body. They tried to promote healthy growth of vital piety, and they regarded lay activity as a gift of grace and one of the signs of true spiritual life. With these ends in view they developed at Augsburg Seminary a highly integrated program of training in piety and evangelism that extended from the preparatory department through the college and included the seminary. This program was consistently maintained until the merger of 1890.

When St. Olaf College at Northfield, Minnesota, which had been the unofficial school for the Anti-Missourian Brotherhood, was made the college of the new United Church, seminary President Sverdrup and Professor Oftedal opposed transfer of the seminary to control of the same body. They contended that a divinity school must embrace the total training of a minister from preparatory school through theological seminary, else he would be "secular" and "humanist" and not fitted to serve a free congregation. The ensuing controversy became very bitter, and led to examination of principles for church-related educational institutions, to all manner of personal charges, to parliamentary battles, legal maneuvers and court trials, and even to special acts of the Minnesota legislature. The strife continued year after year and schism became inevitable.

The "Friends of Augsburg" organized in 1893, held regular meetings, and in 1897 withdrew from the United Church, with the seminary, and formed the Lutheran Free Church. In spite of subsequent mergers among other Norwegian Lutherans the Free Church has maintained its separate existence. Convinced that no church can have a higher unity than a congregation, the Free Church is very simply organized. The annual conference is made up of pastors and congregation members who are able to attend, and it determines what activities shall be recommended to the congregations. There is a committee on organization, a superintendent of home missions, and a board of directors for Augsburg Seminary and College. The various branches of church work are not carried on by the church body but by the boards, which are separately incorporated and whose members are nominated by the annual conference. Everywhere the central emphasis is upon the responsibility and autonomy of the congregation and upon bringing souls to a personal experience of salvation so as to make the Lutheran confession a vital reality in the experience of every individual and in the fellowship within the congregation. Professor Georg Sverdrup was president of Augsburg Seminary and the outstanding figure in this church from 1876 to 1907. His son, Dr. Georg

Sverdrup, was president of the institution, and a leader in the church, from 1911 to 1937. Since 1930 the church has been under the vigorous and constructive leadership of President T. O. Burntvedt. During the past decade the congregations in the Lutheran Free Church have increased about twenty per cent, and now number 354 with about 60,000 souls and 237 pastors.

The controversy over Augsburg Seminary and the resulting schism shook the United Church and seriously retarded its activities and growth for a decade. But the missionary program and the ideal of church union were never lost from sight. With Augsburg Seminary lost, the United Church proceeded with other arrangements for the training of its missionaries and pastors. Unified by its travail, the United Church adopted St. Olaf as its college and set up its theological seminary in St. Paul. The United Church caught up the fine spirit of enterprise that was then current in American Christianity and began a vigorous program of missionary expansion, education, and philanthropy.

The Norwegian Synod and Hauge's Synod, although remaining outside the United Church at the time of the merger in 1890, had kept the door open to further negotiations. In a number of conferences of the three bodies before 1900, the Norwegian Synod was uncompromising in its insistence upon minute doctrinal definitions, and Hauge's Synod refused to yield any of the privileges of the laity in the ministries of the church. The United Church looked upon itself as the mediator between the "high-church" orthodox tendency in the former and the "low-church" pietistic tendency in the latter. The differences among the three bodies seemed insurmountable and for several years the conferences ceased. Then in 1905 Hauge's Synod took the initiative and proposed that union be once more discussed and if possible all Norwegian Lutherans in America be organically united. Before the sincere efforts at mutual understanding, the barriers to union that had seemed insurmountable began to crumble. Within a year agreement was reached concerning lay ministries in the church. The agreement recognized lay activity as a gift of grace to be used by the congregation, but confined the functions of the office of the ministry, except in emergency, to those properly called. The new accord set forth the necessity for definite regulation of lay activity and made it clear that such regulation is secured by emphasizing the call and supervision of the church rather than the ordination of the minister.

Doctrinal questions of conversion and election were more difficult. The Norwegian Synod took much the same positions as the Missouri Synod, and was opposed by the United Church and Hauge's Synod. The controversy reflected not only differences in theological position and historical background, but also clashes of strong personalities in the Missourian element of the Norwegian Synod and the Anti-Missourian element in the United Church. Thus did Walther's "new doctrine" on predestination, as the "definite synodical platform" of midwestern Lutherans, continue to retard Lutheran union.

At conferences in 1907 and 1908, first steps were taken toward doctrinal agreement. It was agreed that God initiates the call to repentance and salvation and that he bestows the power to accept. The agreement said that man can refuse to heed the call and so resist the Holy Spirit. God is responsible for man's acceptance of grace, but man is responsible for his rejection of grace.

Understanding was furthered by lay societies in whose fellowship laymen and clergymen crossed boundaries of synods and of doctrines. There were literary clubs, welfare groups, singing societies, temperance societies, sports associations, lodges, and societies reflecting patriotic devotion to communities in Norway. As union was delayed, much resulting lay pressure was brought to bear upon the doctrinal disputants.

During the summer of 1911 new committees on union negotiations were appointed by the United Church and the Norwegian Synod. New men, largely parish pastors, took the places of the veteran contenders and began more rapidly to approach common ground. In 1912 the joint committee unanimously agreed upon a statement concerning the doctrine of election. It declared that there are two ways of interpreting the teaching of the Formula of Concord on this doctrine, and that neither contradicts any doctrine revealed in the Word of God. This seemed to settle the doctrinal differences, but many problems of organization remained to be solved before actual amalgamation could take place.

In 1914 a joint committee was appointed to define the conditions of union, and another to prepare a constitution for organic merger. In two years a full doctrinal basis had been agreed upon and arrangements completed for the practical co-ordination of the funds, institutions, missions, and publicity organs of the three bodies. Much leeway was given to liturgical practices, and it was specified that the churches would cultivate lay activity and not regard prayer meetings and revivals as fanatical. The three seminaries were to be consolidated in St. Paul. Both Luther College and St. Olaf were to be maintained by the merged body. Arrangements were made for the maintenance of other educational institutions of the three synods, and the merger or the co-ordination of their work in missions, publication, and philanthropy.

So, in 1917 the three bodies celebrated the quadricentennial of the Reformation by holding their final conventions as separate bodies and then meeting together and organizing "The Norwegian Lutheran Church of America."

This new organization was an eloquent witness to the growing solidarity among Lutherans, and its merger convention in St. Paul was the scene of great enthusiasm. With 2,362 delegates, the impressive ceremonies on June 9 and 10 of that quadricentennial year are regarded as the greatest church demonstration ever held by Norwegians anywhere in the world.

In 1946, when the Norwegian language had been almost entirely replaced by English in the services of worship, and with many of its membership not of Norwegian ancestry, the name of the body was changed to "The Evangelical Lutheran Church."

This united body in 1952 embraced 1,671 ministers, 2,667 congregations, and 907,124 baptized members. The regular annual benevolence budget was three million dollars. One-fourth of this was devoted to foreign missions in South Africa, Madagascar, China, Japan, and Colombia, South America. Almost an equal amount was invested in home missions, and a new congregation was established every eighteen days. The church maintained a publishing concern which carried on an annual business well in excess of two million dollars. The official English weekly, *Lutheran Herald*, had a circulation of about 66,500 and the official Norwegian weekly, *Lutheraneren*, about 3,500.

In addition to the original seminary at St. Paul and two colleges,

Luther and St. Olaf, the church maintained a small seminary at Saskatoon in Canada, and three other colleges, Concordia in Moorhead, Minnesota; Augustana in Sioux Falls, South Dakota; and Pacific Lutheran in Parkland, Washington.

The Department of Charities maintained forty institutions of mercy; ten children's homes, twenty old people's homes, two hospitals, one hospice, one mission for the deaf and blind, four homes for girls, and two day nurseries. There were two deaconess institutions, one in Chicago and one in Brooklyn, with a total of twenty-three deaconesses.

The church met in general convention every two years. The first president was H. G. Stub, who had been president of the Norwegian Synod before the union. Dr. Stub was succeeded as president in 1931 by J. A. Aasgaard, and he in 1954 by Fredrik A. Schiotz. The church's nine districts in the United States and one in Canada met in those years when no general convention was held.

Doctrinally the Evangelical Lutheran Church rested on unconditional consent to the canonical books of the Holy Scripture as the infallible Word of God and to the confessions of the Lutheran church. The three bodies uniting in the merger of 1917 promised one another not to have church fellowship with church bodies that do not share the Lutheran faith and confessions. But the Evangelical Lutheran Church was desirous of fostering Lutheran solidarity and co-operated with other Lutheran bodies in this country.

The notable success of the unification movement among the Norwegians was due in part to the fundamental unity of their faith, in part to their patience in pursuit of union, and in part to the splendid assistance rendered by their laymen. The Norwegians in this country are intense Lutherans and loyal Americans, and as their relations with other racial elements were multiplied, it was found that closer union was possible with the other Lutherans of America. Thus the consummation of the merger in 1917 can be regarded as a step in the process of consolidation that brings the Lutherans of America into ever larger units.

Alongside the Evangelical Lutheran Church, with the same spiritual and national ancestry and much the same location, were the four smaller bodies that constitute the remaining eight per cent of Norwegian Lutherans in America. The Lutheran Free Church with 60,000 members included six per cent of all Norwegian Lutherans, three-fourths of those who were not in the Evangelical Lutheran Church. It participated briefly in the negotiations that led to the merger of 1917 but soon decided to continue its separate existence and to cultivate its distinctive polity and piety.

The Norwegian Synod of the American Evangelical Lutheran Church was formed in 1918 by thirteen members of the old Norwegian Synod who inclined so strongly toward Dr. Walther's teaching on election and predestination that they could not accept the doctrinal "settlement" that preceded the merger of 1917. They felt that the terms of the agreement made it possible to credit natural man with the ability to accept the grace of God as well as to reject it. Assured of support from the Synodical Conference, these few pastors refused to join in the merger and sought to perpetuate the old Norwegian Synod. Finding this impossible, they met in 1918 and organized a new "Norwegian Synod," known as "The Little Synod" or "The Minority Synod." It became a member of the Synodical Conference in 1920. Operating a college and seminary at Mankato, Minnesota, it also uses the educational institutions of the Missouri and Wisconsin Synods, and in many places throughout the country its members have joined one or the other of those synods. The synod now numbers about 60 pastors, 64 congregations, and about 10,000 members, or about one per cent of the Norwegian Lutherans in America.

The third of the small Norwegian Lutheran groups outside the Evangelical Lutheran Church is the Eielsen Synod, with three pastors, nine congregations, and about 1,350 baptized members, or a little more than one-tenth of one per cent of the Norwegian Lutherans.

The last of the separate groups is called the Church of the Lutheran Brethren in America. This body was begun at Milwaukee in 1900 by eight Norwegian pastors and five congregations who desired stricter discipline and purer life than they found in the United Church. They had felt the effects of the revival that swept through the Norwegian settlements during the 1890's, and they desired to emphasize a conscious experience of conversion, a godly life, nonliturgical forms of worship, lay activity, and missionary work. This body maintains a theological seminary at Fergus Falls, Minnesota, and it has its old folks' home. It is especially active in foreign missions, in West Africa, China, and Japan. The Church of the Lutheran Brethren is growing and numbers 97 pastors, 58 congregations, and 5,061 members, or about four-tenths of one per cent of the Norwegian Lutherans who have been gathered into churches.

With the passing of the years, the great merger of diverse Norwegian Lutherans in 1917 appears most remarkable for the fact that it suffered no break in ranks. The heritage of European pietism with its subjective tendencies, the heritage of the Norwegian state church formalism with its objective emphases, and the heritage of German Lutheran orthodoxy with its strict refinement of doctrinal details—all these divergent elements developed in The Norwegian Lutheran Church of America a common testimony, a common church life, and a common out-thrust into American society and even to the ends of the earth. How can this be?

One can scarcely avoid the conclusion that the crucible in which these elements were fused was Norwegian nationalism, as found in its American outposts. All the people of the union had been using the same Norwegian hymnody, and the real theology of the people in the pews is always found in the hymns they sing. All of them had been using the same Norwegian version and the same Norwegian explanation of Luther's Small Catechism. The influence of social and cultural associations of lay people and pastors across synodical lines has already been noted. The arguments for union frequently included the nationalistic appeal. There can be little doubt that the bond of a common nationality operated powerfully to restrain the opposing extremes of subjective pietism and objective orthodoxism and thus made possible the enduring fusion of The Norwegian Lutheran Church of America. Although this bond was relaxed during the following generation, the church body which it helped to create held together. Its people have entered fully into American life; they use English Lutheran hymns and new explanations of Luther's Catechism, and co-operate with Lutherans of other national origin and even with non-Lutherans. Intermarriage has had effect, and a great many people not of Norwegian ancestry have come into the church. The change of name removed the nationalist suggestion. Yet, even more firmly than ever, the union persisted. The explanation is found in the sincerity of purpose and devoutness of spirit that was generated by the leaders and caught up by the people in the congregations.

The affairs of Norwegian Lutheranism in America during the first half of the twentieth century were directed by men who were sympathetic with devout personal Christianity, with well-regulated church organization, and with clear definitions of Lutheran doctrine, and who had also lifted their sights to the wider horizons. They saw the dangers implicit in the "social gospel" that infected so many American churches, and they saw the need for Christianizing American society with the full gospel of redemption. They saw the universal implications in the Lutheran understanding of the gospel, and they realized the possibilities of a united witness for Christ in American society and in the whole world. That is why the church body which they brought into being during the first quarter of the century and nurtured into sturdy dynamic life during the second quarter, this new creation in piety and polity and theology, persisted as one of the outstanding units in American Christianity until 1960, when it merged with three other Lutheran bodies to constitute the new American Lutheran Church (see Chapter 39).

CHAPTER 29

GERMAN MERGERS IN THE NORTHWEST

There was other evidence of growing Lutheran solidarity in this period. Among the Germans in the Northwest, on much the same territory as that of the Evangelical Lutheran Church, a merger in 1919 formed the Evangelical Lutheran Joint Synod of Wisconsin and Other States. This synod was sixth in size among the separate Lutheran organizations, exceeded by the United Lutheran Church, the Missouri Synod, the Evangelical Lutheran Church, the American Lutheran Church, and the Augustana Lutheran Church. On many counts, this synod was the most conservative of them all. Its antecedents will help to make clear its present position. We must see how each of its several parts came into existence.

The largest of these was the Wisconsin Synod, dating from 1850, which had helped to organize the General Council in 1867 and had withdrawn in 1871. This synod was based on a German immigration, paralleling that of the Norwegians, that began coming into Wisconsin, Michigan, and Minnesota in the thirties from various sections of Germany, chiefly from the north. Unlike the Germans who located about that time in Missouri, Iowa, and Buffalo, these were people for the most part who came because of dissatisfaction with political conditions in Germany rather than with religious motives. The greatest influx came in the restless years between 1840 and 1854 and again between 1881 and 1884. Many of these refugees refused to identify themselves with any church in America. Many were Catholics. Mormonism, communism, and rationalism made serious inroads among them. Nevertheless they were a fertile field for home missionary effort for Lutherans of Germany and of America.

The first congregation among these new German settlers was

organized in 1833 near Ann Arbor, Michigan, where Frederick Schmid and a number of pastors from the missionary seminary at Basel, Switzerland, labored among them. But the largest settlements were located in the southern and eastern parts of Wisconsin, where the earliest congregations were those at Watertown and Kilbourne Road, near Milwaukee, led by John Weinmann.

The founder of the synod was John Muehlhaeuser. After study at the mission training schools at Basel and Barmen, he had been sent to America as the first emissary of the Langenberg Society, an evangelical association in the Rhineland within the Prussian Union which had been organized for the special purpose of sending pastors to the Protestant German settlers of North America. Muehlhaeuser was ordained by the New York Ministerium in 1837 and located at Rochester. In 1846 he visited the German settlements in Wisconsin as a colporteur for the American Tract Society, and two years later returned to become pastor of Grace Lutheran Church in Milwaukee. He also traveled widely among the German settlers in the state, organizing them into congregations.

Seeing the need for wider organization of the congregations and their pastors, Muehlhaeuser enlisted the help of Weinmann and Wilhelm Wrede, another Langenberg missionary, in laying plans for a synod. The organization was completed at Granville, near Milwaukee, in May, 1850. It was called the First Evangelical Lutheran Synod of Wisconsin. At its organization meeting it enrolled five pastors and eighteen congregations. The first constitution, modeled after that of the New York Ministerium, provided for the licensing of preachers, and characterized the confessional position of the synod simply as Evangelical Lutheran. Muehlhaeuser maintained friendly relations with the Ministeriums of New York and Pennsylvania, and received some financial aid from them, as well as from Germany. But the work of extending the synod and organizing new congregations was carried on largely by missionaries from Germany, the Langenberg Mission Society and the Barmen Training School, and later from the Berlin Association for Emigrant Germans.

But these Prussian societies did not long continue to support the pastors and missions in Wisconsin. Like the young synodical organizations among the Norwegian and Swedish Lutherans in the Midwest at that time, the German Lutherans in Wisconsin soon began to feel the impulses of more conservative Lutheran positions, thus gradually loosening their bonds with the Protestant union groups in Germany. This change came about largely through the influence of new leaders from Germany. John Bading, who had studied with Ludwig Harms at Hermannsburg, came to Wisconsin in 1853 and was active in raising the doctrinal standard of the synod. Edward F. Mohldehnke came in 1861 as field secretary of the synod's missions, and Adolf Hoenecke came the next year. Both taught in the synod's seminary that was established at Watertown in 1863, and both moved steadily in the direction of Lutheran orthodoxy. In 1863 the synod changed its doctrinal position from an indefinite and conciliatory attitude to a definite statement: "This body acknowledges the entire canonical writings of the Old and New Testaments as the sole standard of faith, and also the Symbolical Books as the proper interpretation of the Word of God." The synod demanded uncompromising congregational discipline on this basis. Before the end of the decade it withdrew from the newly organized General Council because the Council's Lutheranism was not satisfactory. In 1869 Augustus Frederick Ernst began his distinguished career of more than half a century at the seminary training the ministers of the Wisconsin Synod and her associate synods in the strictest interpretation of Lutheran positions both in faith and in practice.

Another body that became part of the Joint Synod of Wisconsin and Other States was the Michigan Synod. Most of the German immigrants in Michigan were Württembergers who came in the same stream that brought the North Germans to Wisconsin in the thirties and forties. Pastor Frederick Schmid founded twenty congregations before 1840, when he and two other pastors started the Missionary Synod of the West. By 1845 they had three missionaries among the Chippewa Indians. Some of the pastors sent over by Pastor Wilhelm Loehe at Neuendettelsau joined in this work, but quickly became dissatisfied with the laxity of practice in the Missionary Synod, withdrew, and went to Iowa. Schmid and his colleagues joined the Ohio Synod, and the Missionary Synod of the West was dissolved.

No new synod was formed in Michigan until 1860, when Schmid succeeded in bringing together eight ministers, most of them emissaries of the Basel Missionary Society, and delegates from three congregations, to form what they called the Michigan Synod. The doctrinal basis written into the constitution showed a decided move toward the right since 1840 and would have satisfied Loehe and his men. The new synodical group was active along missionary lines, and grew steadily. In 1867 it took part in the organization of the General Council, but after Michigan's representative, Stephen Klingmann, had protested unavailingly year after year against the council's lax interpretation of the Galesburg rule about closed altars and pulpits, and against the mild attitude of the eastern Lutherans towards lodges, the synod formally withdrew from the General Council in 1888. It built its own seminary at Saginaw under the presidency of Christopher L. Eberhardt and trained a ministry of strict Lutheran faith and practice. The synod planned in 1892 to join the Synodical Conference, but when it developed that such a step would involve the abandoning of its seminary at Saginaw the plan was not carried through at that time.

The third element that entered into the formation of the Joint Synod of Wisconsin and Other States was the Minnesota Synod. The state of Minnesota with its great natural beauty and its many material resources proved attractive to the German immigrants of the mid-nineteenth century. The German Lutherans in that state came somewhat later than their fellow countrymen in Michigan and Wisconsin, but their synod was organized in the same year as the Michigan Synod. Seeing the need of spiritual care for the German Lutheran settlers in Minnesota, but lacking men, the Synod of Wisconsin called the attention of the eastern synods to this promising field. Dr. Passavant of the Pittsburgh Synod was much interested. He visited the settlers in 1856 and through *The Missionary* enlisted interest and funds.

In 1857 Carl Friedrich Heyer was sent to organize them into congregations and to encourage the beginning of Lutheran services in English. Heyer, coming from Germany, had served as a home missionary in Pennsylvania, Maryland, and neighboring states, and had opened the General Synod's Lutheran mission at Guntur, India. In Minnesota he took charge of Trinity Church in St. Paul, organized the year before by Frederick Wier of the Buffalo Synod. In 1860 Heyer joined with five other pastors to organize the Synod of Minnesota. The Swedish pastors in the state had decided to maintain their synodical fellowship with Swedish Lutherans in other states, and a few German pastors continued their allegiance to Missouri. "Father Heyer" was the president and spiritual leader of the new group. In 1864 it joined the General Synod, whose doctrinal basis it shared. But new men coming into the Synod of Minnesota were part of the movement toward a stricter doctrinal position, and in 1867 when the General Council was organized Passavant and Heyer had no difficulty in leading the Minnesota Synod into the new general body. That same year John Henry Sicker became pastor of Trinity Church in St. Paul. A native of Schweinfurth in Bavaria, he had received his theological training at the Gettysburg Seminary, and in 1861 had been ordained by the Wisconsin Synod. Becoming president of the Minnesotans, Sicker turned the synod to stricter Lutheran standards and more conservative practices. Delegates were exchanged with the Wisconsin Synod and the two bodies shared in publication of the official *Gemeindeblatt* and in the work of the Watertown Seminary. Thus the Minnesota Synod was free of dependence for its ministerial supply upon The Pilgrim Mission at St. Chrishona, near Basel, whose atmosphere had become "unionistic." In 1884 it established its own theological college, Dr. Martin Luther Seminary, at New Ulm, Minnesota. At conventions of the General Council President Sicker was unable to secure assurances of pure Lutheran doctrine and strict Lutheran practice, and in 1871 the Minnesota Synod withdrew from the General Council and the next year joined with the Missouri Synod and others in organizing the Synodical Conference.

These three synods, the Wisconsin (1850), the Michigan (1860), and the Minnesota (1860), had common antecedents, a common language, and common interests. What is more, they had reached common positions in doctrine and practice. Before the end of the century it became clearly desirable that all three of the synods should co-operate along certain lines, particularly in education. Wisconsin and Minnesota had participated in organizing the Synodical Conference in 1872, and later the Michigan Synod was induced to join. In 1892 the three synods entered into a federation, the Joint Synod of Wisconsin, Minnesota, Michigan, and Other States, sometimes known as the General Synod of Wisconsin, or the Synod of the Northwest, which was part of the larger federation, the Synodical Conference. The joint synod was not a merger; the synods continued their independence, merely co-ordinating their home missionary activities and using jointly their several educational institutions.

For several years there was a division in the ranks of the Michigan Synod concerning the seminary at Saginaw. Weak, and with no courses in English, by the terms of the federation in 1892 the seminary was to be discontinued as such and to become a preparatory school for the college in Watertown. This plan met with serious objection on the part of twelve of the oldest and strongest congregations and their ministers. Ten friends of Saginaw seminary withdrew from the Michigan Synod and joined the Michigan District of the Joint Synod of Ohio. But in 1906 the breach was healed; those who had seceded returned, the seminary became a preparatory school, and the synod went forward in peaceful and healthful development.

During the twenty years following the federation of 1892 the aggregate size of the three synods was doubled. One of the mission fields of the Wisconsin Synod had become its Nebraska Conference and later its Nebraska District. In 1904, to avoid administrative difficulties, the Nebraska group organized independently as the Synod of Nebraska. There were now four distinct synods in the federation of 1892 which was now called the Joint Synod of Wisconsin, Minnesota, Michigan, and Nebraska. About three-fifths of the pastors and people were in Wisconsin.

In the new century the federated bodies witnessed the unification among Lutherans of Norwegian heritage and those of the Muhlenberg development, and felt a similar impulse. They had a fellowship of about three hundred pastors and about 125,000 members. In 1919, the four synods gave up their loose federation and formed an organic union as The Evangelical Lutheran Joint Synod of Wisconsin and Other States. After several decades it came to be called the Wisconsin Evangelical Lutheran Synod. The whole field was redistricted into eight conferences. The districts met annually, the joint synod biennially. The joint synod now has 801 ministers, 840 congregations, and 350,000 baptized members. Many of the congregations use some German, but English is rapidly displacing it. The merged body was affiliated with the Missouri Synod in the Synodical Conference until 1961.

The synod maintains a theological seminary at Thiensville, Wisconsin, a home for the aged at Belle Plaine, Minnesota, with a staff of eight, a publishing house at Milwaukee, and 221 home mission stations in several states of central and northwestern United States, with 155 workers. Some of the work of the synod was carried on through the Synodical Conference as deaconess work, foreign missions, hospitals, work among Negroes, and child care.

When in 1960 the ranks of the Wisconsin Synod were disrupted by a question of Lutheran orthodoxy, thirty-two of its more conservative congregations withdrew, and in 1961 joined with one congregation from the former Evangelical Lutheran Church and one from the Missouri Synod to form a new body called the Church of the Lutheran Confession. The new church objected to the fact that the Wisconsin Synod remained in the Lutheran Synodical Conference of North America although the Missouri Synod, by far the largest body in that conference, was engaging in such "objectionable doctrinal practices" as co-operating in some of the projects of the National Lutheran Council. The Church of the Lutheran Confession maintains the Immanuel Lutheran high school, college, and seminary in Mankato, Minnesota. It has sixty-nine ordained ministers, fifty-four congregations, and about eight thousand members. Later in that year, 1961, the Wisconsin Synod itself became dissatisfied and severed its fellowship with the Synodical Conference.

The merger of the German synods in the Northwest in 1919 helps to compact the forces of Lutheranism in America. The new body with its flourishing educational institutions, many missionary activities, strict Lutheran orthodoxy, and devout congregational life constitutes a potent factor for the progress of the kingdom of God. Like the mergers of the Norwegian Lutherans and the Muhlenberg Lutherans which preceded it and the merger in the American Lutheran Church in 1930, the Wisconsin Synod bears witness to the growing solidarity among the smaller groups in this period of larger units.

CHAPTER 30

THE UNITED LUTHERAN CHURCH
IN AMERICA

A most significant event in the development of larger church units was the organization in 1918 of The United Lutheran Church in America. It was formed by a merger of the General Synod, the General Council, and the United Synod of the South. After fifty years apart, the organic union of these three bodies took place with a suddenness that startled many observers. But as a matter of fact the times were fully ripe for this realization of Muhlenberg's ideal. In doctrine and liturgy, benevolence and polity, as we have seen, the three bodies of Muhlenberg descent had attained fundamental unity within themselves, and a series of events extending over more than forty years had led to a complete understanding of one another.

One of the first steps toward the reapproach of the three eastern Lutheran bodies was taken less than a decade after their separation. In 1873 the General Synod proposed an interchange of delegates. The General Council proposed instead an informal colloquium of representative men from the different bodies to determine what the Lutheran faith really is. Finally in 1877 an unofficial "Free Lutheran Diet" was called by Dr. J. G. Morris of the General Synod and Dr. J. A. Seiss of the General Council for all Lutherans, clerical and lay, without regard to synodical connections. The proceedings of the diet, and of another the following year, cast much light on living questions in the Lutheran church.

Shortly afterward the three general bodies began successful co-operation in the work of liturgical reform. In the preparation of the Common Service, the Common Hymnal and a common book of

Ministerial Acts, many leading personalities of the different bodies came to understand one another and to respect one another's sincerity and loyalty, and learned to labor together in a common cause. This work, extending over a period of years up to the very time of the merger, helped pave the way for union.

As relations among the three bodies became increasingly harmonious, they began in 1895 to exchange fraternal visitors, and in 1898 officially sponsored the First General Conference of Lutherans in America with the express purpose "to prepare the way for a better understanding and a more harmonious co-operation among the Lutherans" in the participating bodies. Similar conferences were held in 1902 and 1904. The meetings attracted much attention and called together representative men from all three parts of the church. The papers and discussions dealt with practical as well as doctrinal questions, with special emphasis on the common heritage of Lutherans.

Reminders of this common heritage also during the celebration in 1883 of the four hundredth anniversary of Luther's birth had been a factor promoting unity among Lutherans. Many Lutherans awoke for the first time to a real understanding of the distinctive features of Lutheranism. The celebration assembled Lutherans of each locality without regard to synodical bounds and inspired much literature affecting all Lutherans, including English publication of two biographies of Luther.

Among a number of books also cultivating a sense of oneness among the Lutherans in America was Wolf's popular history, *Lutherans in America*. Jacob's history of the Lutheran church in this country helped to develop the historical perspective. Still later Neve's brief history of the Lutheran church helped men to understand the issues at stake among the different bodies by depicting the sources of our various Lutheran synodical organizations. A book on *The Distinctive Doctrines and Usages of the Evangelical Lutheran Church* contained a chapter by a representative of each general body, frankly indicating the differences in point of view and at the same time revealing the fundamental unity among the three eastern bodies. The *Lutheran Manual* by Dr. J. B. Remensnyder, and the several Lutheran "handbooks" and "almanacs," by including all bodies in the enumeration of Lutheran strength and assets in this country, influenced Lutherans to think of themselves as members of the Lutheran church rather than of a particular synod.

In the meantime the General Synod, General Council, and the United Synod of the South had begun to co-operate in practical work, such as that of their foreign missionary agencies. For a time the Lutherans of the South supported a missionary in the General Synod's mission at Guntur in India. Later the General Council and the United Synod co-operated in mission work in Japan. The Foreign Mission Boards of the General Synod and the General Council sometimes exchanged missionaries and services in connection with the missions in Guntur and Rajahmundry, so enhancing the fraternal attitude. In the home mission field, increasing efforts were made to prevent friction between the General Synod and the General Council. The latter appointed a Committee on Arbitration in 1895 and a Commission on Practical Co-operation a few years later. These were consolidated in 1909 as the Home Mission Arbitration Commission, which, working with a similar commission of the General Synod, reduced friction in the home mission enterprises. Thus in foreign and home missionary fields the interests of the church as a whole were put above the interests of the separate organizations.

Also laying the groundwork for eventual merger were agencies that brought together representatives of the different bodies in face to face fraternity. One of these was the Luther Society of New York City. Originated in the Luther Jubilee of 1883, this was an association of laymen, without regard to synodical affiliation, which annually celebrated Reformation Day and met for a banquet in the winter. Another such organization was the Lutheran Social Union of Philadelphia which for many years has brought the ministers and laymen of the different bodies together socially. Other cities had similar associations. The Young People's Lutheran Association, which in 1893 changed its name to "The Luther League," spread over all the general bodies and trained the rising generations of church members in Lutheran unity. Other such organizations were the pan-Lutheran missionary conferences among students, the conference of Lutheran educators, the conference of Lutheran editors, the Lutheran Brotherhood, the Laymen's Missionary Movement, the Lutheran Historical

Society, the Lutheran ministerial unions in various centers, and the Women's Missionary Society.

Through the years, also, internal doctrinal, liturgical, and practical problems of the several bodies had been solved in ways that brought them closer. By the second decade of the twentieth century relationships among the bodies were so cordial that Lutheran unity was taken for granted and organic union became a subject of discussion wherever representatives of the different bodies gathered. Only an extraordinary occasion was needed to bring about an actual merger of the three bodies.

The precipitating occasion was the 1917 Quadri-Centennial of the Reformation. As early as 1909 the General Council had invited the General Synod, the United Synod and other Lutheran bodies in the United States, to co-operate in a worthy celebration. The three eastern bodies appointed committees which in 1914 organized as the "Joint Committee on the Celebration of the Quadri-Centennial of the Reformation." The joint committee opened offices in Philadelphia with an executive secretary, and there the first formal step was taken toward organic union.

At a meeting on April 18, 1917, several lay members of the joint committee presented a resolution asking the committee to arrange a general meeting of Lutherans to formulate plans for the unification of the Lutheran church in America. After all-day discussion, in which the laymen pressed for immediate and organic union, the following resolution was adopted with near unanimity: "Believing that the time has come for the more complete organization of the Lutheran Church in this country, we propose that the General Synod, the General Council and the United Synod of the South, together with all other bodies one with us in our Lutheran faith, be united as soon as possible in one general organization to be known as The United Lutheran Church in America." The presidents of the three general bodies responded as asked, and appointed a committee to prepare a constitution for the new organization for submission to the general bodies at their meetings that same year.

The United States was now involved in World War I, and events moved rapidly. In June, 1917, a few weeks after the committee had completed its draft, the proposed constitution was ratified by the General Synod. The General Council adopted it at a meeting in October and the United Synod of the South in November. The instrument was then submitted to the forty-six district synods composing the three general bodies and promptly ratified by every one except the Augustana Synod, which, because of its distinctive problems and needs, and in a friendly spirit, withdrew from the General Council.

The three bodies now appointed a joint Ways and Means Committee to prepare the foundation and set up the practical machinery for the operation of the new church. Beginning on November 11, 1918, the day of the armistice in Europe, each general body held an adjourned meeting in New York City, completed its business as a separate organization, and then, November 14-16, joined in the general meeting that constituted the first convention of The United Lutheran Church in America. As the first president of the new organization the convention elected F. H. Knubel, of New York City, a member of the New York Synod of the General Synod, and president of the National Lutheran Commission for Soldiers' and Sailors' Welfare. The first secretary was M. G. G. Scherer, a member of the South Carolina Synod and president of the United Synod of the South. The first treasurer was E. Clarence Miller, of Philadelphia, a member of a congregation of the Pennsylvania Ministerium and of the General Council.

The United Lutheran Church aroused the greatest enthusiasm among its constituents and became immediately one of the most potent forces in American Christianity. The new body embraced 45 district synods covering all parts of the United States and Canada and aggregating almost 800,000 confirmed members, with about 2,800 ministers and nearly 4,000 churches. It soon outnumbered the Missouri Synod in baptized membership, and through the forty-five years of its life was the largest Lutheran body in America.

The objects of the new organization were stated to be the extension of the pure teaching of the gospel, the strengthening of the church in the unity of the true faith, the outward expression of the spiritual unity of Lutheran congregations, and the co-ordination and direction of the energies of the church in training ministers, in prosecuting missionary work, in regulating the externals of worship, and in publishing literature.

For its doctrinal basis the United Lutheran Church received the canonical Scriptures as the inspired Word of God and the only infallible rule of faith and practice, the three general creeds as important testimonies drawn from the Holy Scriptures, the Unaltered Augsburg Confession as a correct exhibition of the faith and doctrine of the Lutheran church and the generic creed of Lutheranism, and the other symbolical books as in harmony with one and the same pure scriptural faith. The preamble of the constitution invited all Evangelical Lutheran congregations and synods in America who agree with this doctrinal basis to unite with the United Lutheran Church on the terms of its constitution. Thus the door was left open for further denominational consolidation.

The liturgy and hymnody recommended by the new body were those of *The Common Service Book with Hymnal* and the common book of *Ministerial Acts* which were completed by a joint committee of the three bodies shortly before the merger.

Concerning the polity of the United Lutheran Church it may be observed that larger powers were conferred on the general organization than in any other body of Lutherans in this country. A specific and fundamental principle of the organization was that the congregations are the primary bodies through which power committed by Christ to the church is normally exercised. But by the provisions of the constitution and bylaws wide jurisdiction was expressly delegated by the synods to the United Lutheran Church. Legislative powers were vested in the biennial convention of the delegates from the constituent synods, and were absolute in such matters as the external relations of synods, conferences, or boards, with general organizations or movements. The convention of delegates also had absolute power in matters affecting the United Lutheran Church as a whole, in inter-synodical affairs, in protecting the doctrinal basis, and in publishing books of devotion and instruction. Its judicial authority was the Court of Adjudication and Interpretation, which interpreted laws and principles and decided disputed questions of doctrine and practice.

The executive functions of the United Lutheran Church were vested in the officers of the general body, the Executive Board, and eight other boards, all elected by the conventions of delegates, and in a dozen or more standing commissions and committees appointed for special purposes. It was here that the greatest concentration of power was effected. The president and secretary were salaried officials devoting their entire time to the duties of their offices. They were ex-officio members of the Executive Board. Wide jurisdiction was committed to the Executive Board, which was required to carry out the resolutions of the United Lutheran Church; to fill vacancies not otherwise provided for; to receive reports from the other boards, regulate their propaganda for funds and review and co-ordinate their work; to present a budget and propose apportionments to the conventions; and to represent the United Lutheran Church and attend to its business during the interim between conventions. Actions of the conventions over the years authorized the Executive Board to initiate action where it seemed desirable, to be responsible for the work of all the other boards and agencies of the church, and to supervise certain aspects of the life of the several synods.

The constitution of the United Lutheran Church specified that if any district synod should desire to continue its established lines of work for reasons satisfactory to the general body, such privilege may be granted, but in practice the work of the church was done through the general boards as representatives of the church at large rather than through the individual synods or their agencies.

The form of organization of the United Lutheran Church, strong, compact, involving the surrender of many cherished rights and the legal transfer of millions of dollars in property, gave notice from the beginning that the merger of the three general bodies was intended to be thoroughgoing, effective, and permanent. It was more organic and irrevocable than a federation. Taking the organization as a whole its spirit and structure resembled the spirit and structure of the United Synod of the South more nearly than either of the other general bodies uniting in it. The satisfaction with the union was due to the previous fact of genuine unity. The United Lutheran Church in America was the logical consummation of the events of half a century.

Of course the early years of the United Lutheran Church were a period of adjustment. Relationships among constituent synods and with external organizations remained to be defined. Duties of the several boards and committees had to be determined and correlated. A satisfactory financial plan had to be evolved. Model constitutions had to be set up both for congregations and for constituent synods. All the practical bearings of the constitution and bylaws of the new body had to be worked out.

A great step in defining the policies of The United Lutheran Church in America was taken at its second convention in Washington, D. C., in 1920. The Executive Board submitted a comprehensive statement outlining fundamental principles concerning inner organization of the church and its external relations. Adopted with slight amendments, the statement is known as the "Washington Declaration of Principles." It lays down policies on language usage, on relations with other Lutheran bodies, on co-operation among Protestants in general, and, by implication, on pulpit and altar fellowship and secret societies.

The Washington Declaration not only created solidarity within the church but was also an important factor in preparing the way for the ultimate solution of problems that still confronted the church. It defined the Lutheran idea of Christian unity and explained how such unity should express itself. It explained the relation of the several churches to the one apostolic church. The United Lutheran Church declared that she recognized no doctrinal grounds against complete co-operation and organic union with all bodies that call themselves Evangelical Lutheran and subscribe the confessions that have always been the standards of Evangelical Lutheran doctrine. The organic union of all Protestant churches was declared to be a matter of expediency and not of principle, and, until a more complete unity of confession was attained, The United Lutheran Church in America declared itself bound in duty and in conscience to maintain its separate identity as a witness to the truth which it knew. At the same time the declaration expressed an "earnest desire to co-operate with other church bodies in all such works as can be regarded as works of serving love through which the faith of Christians finds expression," and it set forth in detail the conditions for such co-operation. The declaration also warned all pastors and congregations against organizations and societies that may be regarded as injurious to the Christian faith. The declaration of 1920 was an effective guide for the policy of the United Lutheran Church in its external relations.

The United Lutheran Church grew steadily in numbers and achievement, and in harmony and Lutheran consciousness as well. Its five home missionary boards and committees were consolidated into the Board of American Missions. A fund of four million dollars was collected for ministerial pensions and relief. Its 2,800 ministers had increased by 1962 to more than 5,100, and its 800,000 confirmed members to more than 1,700,000. Its baptized membership passed the two-and-a-half million mark.

In the meantime the processes of unification went steadily forward, partly cause, partly effect of the general readjustment of synodical boundaries. Formation of the United Lutheran Church had joined synods which not only varied in practice, but even overlapped in territory. While all forty-five synods were placed on the same doctrinal basis, committed to the same general practices, and brought to conduct their general benevolent and missionary operations through the same general boards, it was soon clear that the United Lutheran Church would not be truly united until synodical sections were drawn into more compact units in their respective territories. The constituent synods, as the component parts of the United Lutheran Church, were charged with the administration of affairs on their territory, and no unifying power of general bodies is nearly so effective as the bonds of union in the educational, missionary, and benevolent institutions within a given territory. Overlapping synods, therefore, began negotiating the readjustment of boundaries. Coupled with this adjustment was a movement in the direction of larger units. The merging of constituent synods was only the organic completion of the merger creating the United Lutheran Church.

The first merger of synods took place within a year after the organization of the United Lutheran Church. It came in the Pittsburgh district, which had been a great battleground among Lutherans in 1867. The original synod, organized in 1845 by eight clergymen and six laymen, had grown vigorously, and at the time of its split in 1867 included 67 pastors and 136 churches. Between adherents of the General Synod and those of the General Council there was much bitter feeling, but the missionary spirit of the old synods was maintained in both divisions, and Lutheranism flourished in the Pittsburgh territory. On November 18, 1919, the two divisions reunited their 244 pastors, 318 churches, and 64,582 confirmed members under the original name, Pittsburgh Synod, to preserve historical continuity. It was in 1953 the fourth largest synod in the United Lutheran Church.

In 1920 two mergers of constituent synods occurred on the same day. One of these was in Illinois, where the congregations belonging to the United Lutheran Church were separated into four district synods. Three of these had belonged to the General Synod—the Northern Illinois Synod (organized 1851), the Central Illinois Synod (1862), and the Southern Illinois Synod (1901). The other, the Chicago Synod (organized 1896), which had belonged to the General Council, was only partly in the state. On June 10, 1920, practically all of the Illinois congregations of these synods joined to form the Illinois Synod. It counted 115 pastors and 126 congregations with a confirmed membership of 24,000.

Another merger completed on June 10, 1920, was that of the Michigan Synod, formed by the congregations of the Northern Indiana Synod of the former General Synod (organized 1855) and portions of the Chicago Synod (1871) lying in Michigan. This merger crossed state lines because it was felt that the congregations in Michigan would not be strong enough to take advantage of their home missionary opportunities. So the entire Synod of Northern Indiana was incorporated in the Michigan Synod, with the understanding that when there were 25 pastorates in Michigan these Indiana congregations would unite with the Indiana Synod. The new synod numbered 50 pastors and 87 congregations with about 12,000 confirmed members.

Two weeks later the Indiana Synod was formed by a merger of the Olive Branch Synod with a portion of the Chicago Synod. The Olive Branch Synod, organized in 1848, had belonged to the General Synod. On June 24, 1920, its 45 congregations with 7,500 members, one-third of them in Kentucky and Tennessee, and the rest in Indiana, united with 25 congregations and 2,500 members of the Chicago Synod to form the Indiana Synod. It lies south of Logansport, Walton, and Portland, Indiana, and at its organization stretched southward to the southern boundary of Tennessee. It had eleven congregations in Louisville and Jefferson County, Kentucky, and one other congregation in southern Kentucky, and six congregations in Tennessee. The rest of its congregations were in Indiana. In 1934 the congregations located in Indiana but belonging to Michigan Synod were transferred to the Indiana Synod. The new synod had a rapid growth, particularly in southern Indiana.

On November 3, 1920, the Ohio Synod was formed of Ohio congregations of the United Lutheran Church which had been divided among four synods, about equal in size. Three of these had belonged to the General Synod—the East Ohio Synod (dating from 1836), the Miami Synod (1844), and the Wittenberg Synod (1847). The District Synod of Ohio (1857) had belonged to the General Council and had congregations scattered over the entire state. The Ohio Synod of the United Lutheran Church, fifth largest synod in the general body, counted at the time of its formation about 200 pastors and about 300 congregations with more than 53,000 confirmed members.

Early in 1921 the Lutherans in North Carolina formed the United Evangelical Lutheran Synod of North Carolina. For a hundred years they had been divided into two synods. The North Carolina Synod was organized in 1803, but in 1820 the Tennessee Synod was formed out of its ranks by men who stood for a distinctive Lutheran faith and practice. In 1886 both synods united with others in the United Synod of the South, but continued their separate existence on the same territory. The North Carolina Synod gradually came to a strict confessional basis and practically the same conception of Lutheran practice as that of the Tennessee Synod. Thus the synods moved toward the merger completed on March 2, 1921, which brought together 113 pastors, 200 congregations and 27,000 confirmed members.

A second merger of synods that had previously belonged to the United Synod of the South was effected on March 17, 1922, with the creation of the Lutheran Synod of Virginia. Its components were the Virginia Synod (1829) with 35 pastors and members of about 7,000, the Southwestern Virginia Synod (1842) with 22 pastors and a membership of 5,000, and the Holston Synod (1860) of the eastern part of Tennessee with 11 pastors and over 2,000 members. The three bodies brought similar interests not only geographical but also in education and missions to the new Lutheran Synod of Virginia.

The next year two synods in north-central Pennsylvania, the Central Pennsylvania Synod and the Susquehanna Synod, were merged. Both had formerly belonged to the General Synod. The Central Pennsylvania Synod was formed in 1855 in territory of the West Pennsylvania Synod. The Susquehanna Synod was formed in 1867 of a conference of the East Pennsylvania Synod. On September 5, 1923, they united to form the Susquehanna Synod of Central Pennsylvania with 80 pastors, 167 congregations, and 45,541 members. Its name was changed in 1932 to the Susquehanna Synod, and six years later it lost its identity in a larger merger.

In Canada also the tendency to larger units was manifest. The original Canada Synod, organized in 1861 as a result of the missionary work of the Pittsburgh Synod, was one of the synods that withdrew from the General Synod in 1867 to form the General Council. It was largely German in its constituency and drew most of its pastors from the Kropp Seminary in Germany. On much the same territory the Synod of Central Canada was organized in 1908 as a result of the English missionary activity of the General Council, and its constituency was mostly English-speaking. These two synods of the General Council supported the college and seminary at Waterloo, Ontario. Both joined the United Lutheran Church in 1918. As the barriers of language began to disappear, they decided to merge, and formed the new Synod of Canada on June 12, 1925. At the time of the merger the Canada Synod numbered 48 pastors, 75 congregations, and 21,799 members, while the Synod of Central Canada numbered 18 pastors, 17 congregations, and 3,123 members. The name of the united body is the Synod of Canada.

Another merger among constituent synods of The United Lutheran Church in 1929 produced the third largest synod in that body. The three synods in the merger embraced all the forces of the United Lutheran Church in the state of New York, in New England, and in northern New Jersey. The oldest was the New York Ministerium, dating back to 1786, which included the more German and more conservative elements of Lutheranism in the state. The New York and New England Synod had been organized in 1902 largely on the issues of introducing the English language and prosecuting missionary work. The third was the New York Synod, organized in 1908 of the Hartwick Synod (1830), the Franckean Synod (1837), and the New York and New Jersey Synod (1872). The first two belonged to the former General Council, the third to the former General Synod. The union took place at Albany, June 5, 1929. At the time of the merger the Ministerium of New York embraced 173 pastors, 147 congregations and 97,846 members. The New York and New England Synod numbered 111 pastors, 93 congregations, and 56,485 members. The New York Synod embraced 201 pastors, 162 congregations, and 59,345 members. Overlapping interests in this merger called for many adjustments in congregational organizations and in educational and missionary activities, but a compact organization was achieved.

The significant merger which created the Central Pennsylvania Synod on June 8, 1938, united four smaller synods, with common interests, located between the Pennsylvania Ministerium on the east and the Pittsburgh Synod on the west. This union was not the result of overlapping territories but of common interests on the part of the smaller synods and the encouraging example of much larger synodical units on both sides. The merging bodies were the Synod of West Pennsylvania (1825), the East Pennsylvania Synod (1842), the Allegheny Synod (1842), and the Susquehanna Synod (1924). With common responsibility in educational institutions, home missionary programs, deaconess work, and in the National Lutheran Home for the Aged in Washington, these synods also had distinctive methods in benevolence and distinctive church practices which they sought to conserve. Nearly equal in size to the Ministerium of Pennsylvania, the new body embraced more than 600 congregations, nearly 500 ministers, and about 300,000 baptized members. With a staff of full-time officers the synod has been carrying on an active campaign of evangelism and stewardship in its congregations, a vigorous policy of home missionary expansion, and generous support of its educational institutions.

The formation of the Central Pennsylvania Synod led directly to the problem of overlapping territory with the Ministerium of Pennsylvania. Through the former East Pennsylvania Synod, the new body included congregations located in almost every part of the Ministerium from Harrisburg to Trenton, New Jersey. This situation was part of the heritage of the split in the General Synod in the midnineteenth century. After the organization of the United Lutheran Church in 1918 the problem that had persisted for a hundred years called for solution, and became acute with the formation of the new Central Pennsylvania Synod in 1938. Negotiations for adjustment of boundaries proved so difficult that only after fifteen years was a north-south line of division drawn between the two synods. Then 196 congregations on either side of the line were encouraged to transfer their synodical connection to a new body, and by the summer of 1954 this was accomplished.

The ranks of the United Lutheran Church were increased slightly in 1942 by the admission of an independent synod of Scandinavian origin. The Icelandic Synod, consisting mostly of rural congregations in western Canada and northwestern United States, was organized in 1885, ten years after the earliest Icelandic settlement in America. The first Icelandic missionaries were Paul Thorlackson and Jon Bjarnason. For twenty-three years Bjarnason was president of the synod, and during this period the synod developed all the instruments and agents of a continuing church body except educational institutions. The congregations were organized but they lacked ministers. The synod used some of the schools of the Norwegian Lutheran church. In its missionary work it was affiliated with the General Council and later with the United Lutheran Church, where friendly relations developed. At the convention of the United Lutheran Church in 1942, the 15 pastors and 49 congregations of the Icelandic Synod with their 7,000 baptized members became a constituent synod of the United Lutheran Church.

It should be noted also that in 1937 the name of the German Synod of Nebraska was changed to the Synod in the Midwest, and in 1947 that of the Manitoba Synod was changed to the Synod of Western Canada. Further, in 1954 the Kansas, Nebraska, and Midwest Synods merged into the Synod of the Central States, thus reducing the number of constituent synods.

In the meantime five new synods were organized within the United Lutheran Church. The year after its formation, its Immigrants' Mission Board asked the church to sanction the organization of a Slovak Lutheran Synod that might embrace the Czechoslovakian ministers and congregations of western Pennsylvania and other states. Accordingly at Braddock, Pennsylvania, on June 10, 1919, the Slovak Evangelical Lutheran Zion Synod was organized. Its 19 pastors had increased by 1953 to 42, its 32 congregations to 48, and its membership to about 21,000.

Another new synod was created in Florida. The influx of Lutherans from other states during the land boom of the early twenties presented a strong home missionary appeal there. On January 15, 1929, at Jacksonville, the Florida Conference of the Georgia Synod reconstituted itself as the Florida Synod and was accepted as a constituent synod of the United Lutheran Church the next year. Its 13 pastors, 13 congregations, and about 1,900 baptized members multiplied more than threefold in 25 years.

Twenty-five congregations in Kentucky and Tennessee belonging to the Indiana Synod and the Ohio Synod organized in 1934 under the direction of the Executive Board of the United Lutheran Church as the Kentucky-Tennessee Synod. In about 20 years its 20 ministers increased to 32, and its 3,700 baptized members to 10,500.

The movement to trim synods to state or other geographical lines brought forth another new synod in 1950. For years the Lutherans of New Jersey had considered the desirability of organizing all the divergent Lutheran elements of that state into a separate synod. In 1949 approval of a proposed new synod was secured from the three synods whose congregations were involved, and the Executive Board of the church approved a proposed constitution. In 1950, 70 congregations were dismissed from the Synod of New York and New England, 39 from the Ministerium of Pennsylvania, and 19 from the Central Pennsylvania Synod. These 128 congregations and their pastors then united to form the Evangelical Lutheran Synod of New Jersey. The baptized membership of the new synod was more than 73,000.

A new member in the United Lutheran Church in 1952 was the Caribbean Evangelical Lutheran Synod. It is a mission synod, a product of the Board of American Missions of the United Lutheran Church. Some of its congregations are very old but none is entirely self-supporting. There are nineteen congregations with fourteen pastors. Five congregations with more than 2,000 baptized members are in the Virgin Islands, a constituency dating from the Danish colony of nearly three centuries ago. They use the English language. Fourteen congregations and more than 4,000 baptized members are in Puerto Rico. They came from a Roman Catholic background during the past half-century, and use Spanish. For some time there has been a conference of Lutherans in the Virgin Islands and one in Puerto Rico, and through these organizations the Board of American Missions has been assisting the congregations, helping them to develop a program of stewardship and to cultivate their Lutheran faith under adverse conditions. During recent years the congregations have begun to yield their own candidates for the ministry. The organization of these congregations and conferences into a synod can be expected to hasten the development of self-government and self-support and to help consolidate Lutheranism in the West Indies.

There are Lutherans also in Hawaii and Alaska. The California Synod of the United Lutheran Church has four congregations in

Hawaii with a total of nearly 700 members, and for this reason, among others, changed its name in 1954 to the Synod of the Pacific Southwest. The Pacific Synod has two congregations in Alaska (Juneau and Sitka) with about 400 members. There is also a Missouri Synod congregation in Hawaii with about 250 members, and there are two in Alaska with about 200 members. In Alaska there are also eight congregations of the Evangelical Lutheran Church with about 1,300 members. The Christians in Alaska belong chiefly to the Presbyterian, Episcopal, and Roman Catholic churches. As the means of transportation improve, the Lutheran churches of the United States and Canada plan to reach out more aggressively to their constituency in the Caribbean region, to Hawaii, and to Alaska.

While these five new constituent synods were being added to the United Lutheran Church, mergers reduced synod affiliations from the original forty-five to thirty-two in 1962. The church expanded and at the same time solidified. A similar process of expanding activities and merging organizations took place in the boards of benevolence and the general committees of the church.

In addition to responsibility for each of thirty-four constituent synods, the United Lutheran Church had special obligation toward several "younger churches," the products of her foreign missionary program. At the request of its Board of Foreign Missions in 1926 the United Lutheran Church decided to recognize the newly organized "Lutheran Church in the Andhra Country in India" and to enroll it as an "associate synod" of the United Lutheran Church with seat and voice in the conventions of the church. As the autonomy of the younger churches on the mission fields grew with the rising spirit of nationalism, the courtesy of associated relationship with the church in America was extended in turn to the Lutheran Church in Japan (1927), the Lutheran Church in British Guiana (1943), the Lutheran Church in Argentina (1948), and the Lutheran Church in Liberia (1948). In 1950 the convention of the United Lutheran Church changed its constitution to designate these associated bodies as "affiliated churches," and the Board of Foreign Missions tried to secure the attendance of nationals from these churches as fraternal delegates at the church conventions. But only official delegates of the constituent synods were entitled to vote in the conventions.

The thirty-two synods and five affiliated churches of the United

Lutheran Church in 1962 listed more than 5,100 ministers, about 200 of them living beyond the United States and Canada. There were more than 7,100 congregations, about one-third of them in foreign lands, and some 2,800,000 members of whom more than a quarter of a million are in the affiliated foreign churches.

The higher educational program was conducted through 12 theological seminaries with nearly 800 students and through 14 colleges with more than 10,000 students.

The problem of language has taken care of itself. Only sixteen congregations in the entire United Lutheran Church in 1955 used German exclusively in their services of worship; thirteen of these were in the Synod of Western Canada, two in New York, and one in Canada. Two hundred and forty-five congregations used some German as well as English in their services, more than one-third of them in Western Canada. The German monthly published under the auspices of the church, the *Kirchliches Monatsblatt*, had a current circulation of about 3,000.

In its home missions work the United Lutheran Church had responsibility for 735 congregations with a total of nearly 200,000 members. Abroad the church extended support to the United Evangelical Lutheran Church in Argentina (nine missionaries), to the Evangelical Lutheran Church in British Guiana (five missionaries); to the United Lutheran Mission in China (formerly at Tsingtao in Shantung); to the Andhra Evangelical Lutheran Church in India (56 missionaries); to the Evangelical Lutheran Church in Liberia (36 missionaries), and since 1953 to a new field in Malaya (6 missionaries). The total number of baptized members on these fields in 1962 was over 300,000. The total number of foreign missionaries was about 100.

The social and inner mission work of the church in 1953 was carried on through 31 institutions for the care of children, with 4,468 children; 36 homes for the aged, with 1,710 guests; 32 inner mission societies and special agencies that served 216,735 persons and spent over 2 million dollars; 28 chaplaincy services in institutions; 4 congregations for the deaf; 6 immigrant services; 14 hospitals in America and 10 on mission fields; 10 settlement houses; 4 welfare camps; 4 hospices; 2 deaconess mother houses and training schools with 157 deaconesses and 34 students.

The publication interests of the church were concentrated in the

United Lutheran Publication House in Philadelphia. Besides new books, the Publication House published an extensive literature for the Board of Parish Education, and the official weekly called *The Lutheran*. Altogether the church and its synods, agencies, and auxiliaries published 60 church papers with a total circulation of more than 650,000.

The church's Committee on Evangelism directed an extended work among the congregations in the effort to stimulate church members to a fuller use of the means of grace, to reclaim indifferent members, and to wage an aggressive campaign for souls outside of Christ. The Brotherhood of the church organized the men of the individual congregations and cultivated their loyalty to the program of the church both in the congregation and in the church at large. The Laymen's Movement for Stewardship sought to cultivate in all the members of the church a sense of stewardship with reference to time, influence, life, and possessions, to promote the annual every-member canvass in all the congregations, and to support needy students for the ministry. The Luther League of America was the young people's society of the church, with nearly 1,300 societies and about 30,000 members of various ages.

The United Lutheran Church in America was a member of the National Lutheran Council and of the Lutheran World Federation. It participated in the Stockholm Conference on Life and Work in 1925, and in the Lausanne Conference on Faith and Order in 1927 and the Edinburgh Conference on Faith and Order in 1937, and it cooperated actively in the formation of the World Council of Churches in 1948. It was a member of the National Council of the Churches of Christ in the United States of America. It sought to bear witness to the Lutheran understanding of the gospel and its implications wherever there was reason to believe that this testimony would receive a respectful hearing.

CHAPTER 31

THE AMERICAN LUTHERAN CHURCH (1930)

The urge toward Lutheran solidarity produced in 1930 another organic union called The American Lutheran Church. Three groups of Lutherans who had dwelt side by side for three-quarters of a century in close relationship but with separate organization were the Joint Synod of Ohio, the Iowa Synod, and the Buffalo Synod. Their doctrinal and practical differences had gradually been resolved and they had many practical interests and problems in common. For encouragement in their efforts to unite they had the example of mergers among the Norwegians in 1917, among the Germans in the Northwest in 1918, and among the Lutherans of Muhlenberg descent in 1918. The times were propitious. The union of the three bodies was completed in August, 1930.

For more than a decade this union had been preparing. In 1918 the Joint Synod of Ohio and the Iowa Synod had established pulpit and altar Fellowship between them. These two bodies had much the same constituency. In a sense, it will be recalled, the beginnings of the Joint Synod of Ohio go back to 1818 when the Ohio Synod was organized from the Ohio Conference of the Ministerium of Pennsylvania. In the 1840's German immigrants to Ohio changed the constituency of that synod, and the descendants of the Muhlenberg line, now largely anglicized, separated to form other synods which joined the General Synod and the General Council, were later incorporated in the United Lutheran Church, and merged in 1920 into the present Synod of Ohio.

The older Ohio organization, with its changed constituency, altered its doctrinal basis in 1847 to include not only Luther's Small Catechism and the Augsburg Confession, as heretofore, but all the confessions of the Book of Concord as "the pure and unadulterated explanation and exposition of the Word of God." In 1850 it founded Capital University at Columbus, and the seminary, then twenty years old, became its theological department. As the Evangelical Joint Synod of Ohio and Other States it expanded beyond Ohio and western Pennsylvania into sections of Indiana and Michigan, and after 1881 into the Northwest and Canada. With Missouri and other synods it organized the Synodical Conference in 1872, but ten years later withdrew because its theologians could not agree with the Missouri Synod's "new doctrine" on predestination. By 1930 the synod had congregations in 29 states and five provinces of Canada, a total of 1,134 congregations, 814 pastors, and over 250,000 baptized members.

The second party to the 1930 merger was the Evangelical Lutheran Synod of Iowa, known as the German Iowa Synod, also largely a product of German immigration in the fourth and fifth decades of the nineteenth century. The German settlers on the plains of the Middle West presented a home missionary problem to other Lutherans. Dr. Wyneken of the Missouri Synod enlisted the interest of Wilhelm Loehe in Neuendettelsau in Bavaria, and Loehe poured a stream of devoted pastors into the field. Most of them affiliated with the Missouri Synod, but after Loehe's breach with the Missourians on doctrinal grounds some of his men left and organized the independent Iowa Synod. This synod expanded into twenty-one states, chiefly Texas, Wisconsin, Illinois, Nebraska, Ohio, and the Dakotas. It developed educational institutions and missionary operations at home and abroad. In 1930 it listed 1,046 congregations, 610 pastors, and 217,000 baptized members. Some of the German pastors in the Texas Synod claimed that their synod was not an organic part of the Iowa Synod but only co-operating with it and that the merger of 1930 was a four-way one.

The Iowa Synod insisted on "open questions," that is, problems not definitely settled by scriptural authority on which there may be a certain amount of speculation within the limits set by the Bible and the confessions. It was related in spirit and constituency to the Joint Synod of Ohio.

The first steps toward union were taken by districts of the Iowa Synod. The eastern district meeting in June, 1919, asked the Executive Board of the Iowa Synod to approach the Ohio Synod on the matter, and other districts and conferences took similar action later in the year.

At synod meetings in August, 1920, a joint committee of the two bodies was appointed to confer on the questions at issue. On the recommendation of this committee, the two synods in 1922 appointed a larger committee representing the various interests of each body to consider detailed plans for a merger and to draw up a definite policy for future action. This committee in 1924 agreed to recommend organic union. The Joint Synod at once referred the recommendation to its eleven districts and all approved. An informal vote of the nine districts of the Iowa Synod disclosed that a great majority of its pastors and laymen favored the union.

At this point in the negotiations the Lutheran Synod of Buffalo entered the scene. Also a product of German immigration, when it was organized in 1845 it was called "The Synod of the Lutheran Church, which Emigrated from Prussia," but because of the location of its headquarters and its theological seminary, its name was changed in 1886 to the Lutheran Synod of Buffalo. It spread to Wisconsin, Michigan, Ohio, Illinois, and Ontario, but barely held its own in numbers, and in 1930 listed 53 congregations, 44 pastors, and about 11,000 baptized members. In 1925 it expressed its desire to become a part of the proposed new body.

A joint commission of members of the three synods was instructed to prepare a constitution and bylaws. The Iowa Synod in 1926 formally expressed its willingness to enter the organic union. But the wording of the confessional paragraph in the proposed constitution caused a delay of two years. Ohio pressed for a strict literalism in the statement on inerrancy of the Scripture against some Iowa opposition. After long discussion the Iowa Synod adopted the constitution, with the stricter statement. The Buffalo Synod had agreed at once.

The formal adoption of the constitution and the ratification of the merger took place at Toledo, Ohio, August 11, 1930. The new body took the name, The American Lutheran Church. The convention elected as president C. C. Hein, of Columbus, Ohio, who had been president of the Joint Synod of Ohio. For first vice-president the choice fell on K. A. Hoessel, of Milwaukee, Wisconsin, who had been president of the Buffalo Synod. The secretary chosen was E. J. Braulick, of Seguin, Texas, a member of the Iowa Synod. The various boards, committees, and agencies of the three synods were instructed to merge their operations as quickly as possible and to operate as agencies of The American Lutheran Church. The new body officially began existence on January 1, 1931.

The Joint Synod of Ohio contributed more than 55 per cent of the constituent elements of the new body, the Iowa Synod about 41 per cent and the Buffalo Synod less than three per cent.

The American Lutheran Church in 1953 was the fourth largest general Lutheran body in this country. It comprised 1,890 pastors, 2,017 congregations, and more than 790,000 baptized members. Its assets totaled more than $100,000,000, and its total contribution to benevolence each year was more than $5,000,000. The general body met biennially. It was divided into districts which met annually. Nine of these districts was organized in 1930, the Wisconsin, Michigan, Ohio, Eastern, Minnesota, Dakota, Central (i.e. Nebraska), Iowa, and Illinois. Four more were organized the following year, the California, Texas, Northwestern, and Canada. The names of the districts indicate the extent and distribution of the new church body.

The American Lutheran Church made extraordinary progress in compacting its forces, expanding its program, enlarging its borders and developing its sense of stewardship. Born into economic depression, burdened with the accumulated debts of the merging bodies, the newly formed church was under heavy strain. But in two decades its baptized membership increased 50 per cent, its contributions for benevolence increased from less than one million to more than five millions, and its total congregational expenditures from $4,500,000 to $21,000,000. Of special significance was the development of lay participation and lay leadership in the programs of church advance and missionary expansion.

The general work of the church was assigned to nine official boards whose members are elected at the biennial conventions: the Board of Trustees, the Board of American Missions, the Board of Foreign Missions, the Board for Christian Social Action, the Board of Parish Education, the Board of Higher Education, the Youth Board, the Board of Publication, and the Board of Pensions.

The young people's organizations of the three merging bodies were consolidated in the Luther League of the American Lutheran Church. The women's missionary organizations combined to form the Women's Missionary Federation of the American Lutheran Church. There were 151 home missionaries serving 226 mission stations in 26 states and four provinces of Canada. Much of this work was done in Texas and Mexico.

The foreign missionary work of the church was carried on in two fields. In South India there were 20 ordained missionaries and about 12,000 baptized members, and in New Guinea (Madang and Finschhafen) 48 ordained, 45 lay missionaries, and 110,000 baptized members.

In 1942 the Brotherhood of The American Lutheran Church was organized to stimulate lay participation in the whole program of the church. It numbered nearly 30,000 men, and in addition to its primary object it promoted significant contacts of Lutheran laymen with one another across synodical boundaries.

The Board of Education supervised three colleges, one university and two seminaries. The seminaries were at Columbus, Ohio (Capital University, with 145 students), and Dubuque, Iowa (Wartburg Seminary, with 132 students). The two English weeklies were merged into the *Lutheran Standard*, with a circulation of 86,500, and the two German weeklies into the biweekly *Kirchenblatt*, with circulation of 4,500. These figures speak for the status of the two languages in this church. The church used the *American Lutheran Hymnal*, published in 1930, embodying the Common Service.

The American Lutheran Church declared against the "separatism" of the Missouri Lutherans because they "refuse to recognize certain other synods as Lutherans, unless these others accept their method of presenting biblical truth as the only method permissible in the Lutheran Church, and . . . carry this spirit so far that they will not even pray with these others." At the same time it declared against the "unionism" of the Lutherans in the United Lutheran Church because they "fail to apply the Galesburg Rule: 'Lutheran pulpits for Lutheran pastors only and Lutheran altars for Lutheran communicants only' and continue to tolerate pastors who are affiliated with Masonic lodges and permit pastors and congregations to engage in unscriptural practices." But the American Lutheran Church co-operated heartily in the work of the National Lutheran Council, the American Lutheran Conference, the Lutheran World Convention, and the World Council of Churches. It was also an active participant in plans for further Lutheran union (see Chapter 36). In 1960 it merged with the Evangelical Lutheran Church to form a much larger body also called The American Lutheran Church (see Chapter 39).

CHAPTER 32

THE NATIONAL LUTHERAN COUNCIL

After the formation of the Norwegian Lutheran Church and The United Lutheran Church in America, the next logical step in denominational consolidation was the formation of a unit embracing both of these and still other Lutheran bodies. Such was the National Lutheran Council, an outgrowth of the wartime National Lutheran Commission for Soldiers' and Sailors' Welfare.

The National Lutheran Commission had been organized in October, 1917, as an emergency organization to meet the necessity which the churches felt of ministering to their men in armed service. The initiative in this ministry came from a group of Lutheran laymen, belonging to various general bodies, who were concerned with the religious and moral well-being of the soldiers in camp and battle. Their plan was received with such enthusiasm that in a short time 60,000 men were enrolled in support. But the projected ministry was so vast and complex that it required the united effort and the official endorsement of the church bodies; so representatives appointed by seven Lutheran churches organized the formal Commission and set to work at once on a program of service. They were soon joined by six other church bodies and the Synodical Conference agreed to co-ordination of effort. This agency, born of the emergencies of war, was the first organization to include virtually all Lutherans of America.

The Commission employed 150 camp pastors, helped to appoint and equip 89 army chaplains and 11 navy chaplains, sent commissioners to France to confer with the French Lutheran church and to assist chaplains and service men, maintained four service houses in eastern cities and 26 other service centers, labored among interned aliens, ministered to the sick and dying in about 60 hospitals, vindicated the loyalty of the Lutheran church in this country, and rendered a great variety of special services to individuals and families.

The laymen continued to be active in the Commission, but in November, 1917, also founded their own organization, the Lutheran Brotherhood of America. The Brotherhood carried on a vigorous program of erecting and equipping buildings to facilitate the work of the Commission. After the war it continued with a program of developing lay leadership and fostering intersynodical relationships.

The various Lutheran church bodies, except those in the Synodical Conference, co-operated with the utmost harmony in the work of the Commission. When the Commission asked for $750,000 to do its work, they responded with $1,360,000. Organized solely for soldiers' and sailors' welfare, the Commission could not use its funds for any other purpose. But as the only general Lutheran organization, and one with a fine balance in its treasury, it received many requests for services lying outside its proper sphere of action. The war created an urgent need for missionary work in the growing industrial centers, especially in the munition plants and ship-building centers. The Lutheran churches in Europe would obviously need physical and moral aid in reconstruction. Many matters of common interest invited common action by the Lutheran organizations. The Norwegian Lutherans had united, the union of Muhlenberg Lutheranism was assured, and the success of the Commission suggested the benefits of practical co-operation.

The presidents and other representatives of the general bodies that had co-operated in the National Lutheran Commission met on July 17, 1918, and appointed a committee to plan for the creation of a national council of Lutherans. But the situation seemed to demand immediate action, even before the general bodies could meet and ratify the plans. So, on September 6, 1918, representatives appointed by the presidents of the general bodies, in the ratio of one representative for every 150,000 communicant members or fraction thereof, met in Chicago and formally organized the National Lutheran Council. Its officers were: President, H. G. Stub, president of the Norwegian Lutheran Church; Vice-President, John L. Zimmerman, of the United Lutheran Church; Secretary, Lauritz Larsen, of the Norwegian Lutheran Church; Treasurer, E. F. Eilert, of the United Lutheran Church.

The objects of the new organizations were stated as follows: 1. To speak for the Lutheran church and give publicity to its utterances on all matters which require an expression of the common conviction and sentiment of the church. 2. To be the representative of the Lutheran church in America in its attitude toward, or relation to, organized bodies outside of itself, including national and state governments. 3. To bring to the attention of the participating bodies all such matters as require common utterance or action. 4. To further the work of recognized agencies of the church that deal with problems arising out of war or other emergencies; to co-ordinate, harmonize, and unify their activities; and to create new agencies to meet circumstances which require common action. 5. To co-ordinate the activities of the church and its agencies for the solution of new problems which affect the religious life and consciousness of the people, e.g., social, economic, and educational conditions. 6. To foster true Christian loyalty to the state; and to labor for the maintenance of a right relation between church and state as distinct, divine institutions. 7. To promote the gathering and publication of true and uniform statistical information concerning the Lutheran church in America. An eighth item was afterwards added: To undertake additional work with the specific consent of the participating bodies. The Council expressly disclaimed the right to interfere with the inner life of its participating bodies or in any way to prejudice their confessional basis.

Each body co-operating in the execution of the program of the Council was entitled to one representative for every 100,000 confirmed members or one-third fraction thereof. The church bodies that officially ratified the organization of the National Lutheran Council were the United Lutheran Church, the Norwegian Lutheran Church, the Augustana Synod, the Joint Synod of Ohio, the Iowa Synod, the United Danish Church, the Lutheran Free Church, the Danish Lutheran Church, the Icelandic Synod, and the Buffalo Synod. But in 1920 the Iowa Synod withdrew because it feared that the Council was about to interfere in the internal affairs of the participating bodies. In 1925, disappointed because the Council's postwar international program relegated its domestic program to a secondary position, the Buffalo Synod and the Danish Lutheran Church also withdrew. But upon its creation in 1930 the American Lutheran Church, including the Buffalo Synod, joined the Council, and in 1937 the Danish Lutheran Church returned. This restored the Council to its original constituency, about two-thirds of the Lutherans in the United States and Canada. The Icelandic Synod's joining the United Lutheran Church in 1942 ended its separate representation in the Council, but that same year the Suomi (Finnish) Synod joined. Other participating bodies changed their names: the Norwegian Lutheran Church to the Evangelical Lutheran Church, the Augustana Synod to the Augustana Lutheran Church, the United Danish Lutheran Church to the United Evangelical Lutheran Church, and the Danish Lutheran Church to the American Evangelical Lutheran Church. But the constituency of the National Lutheran Council remained virtually the same through thirty-five years of its existence, while its program of activities multiplied many times. Only the Missouri Synod and the other bodies of the Synodical Conference did not use it as their agency of co-operation.

During its first thirty-five years the Council passed through three distinct phases of its life. The first twelve years was a period of clarification of program. Born of emergencies, the Council gradually defined its methods. It became clear during the twenties that the Council was to be no more or less than an agency of the participating bodies, and in no sense a super-church. It also disclosed an ample field for such an agency.

From about 1930 to the entry of the United States into World War II, the Council's domestic program expanded and responsibilities eased abroad. During these years the Council won the complete confidence of the bodies whose agency it was, and made Lutheranism a potent element in American Christianity.

Since 1942 the Council has been lifted from the status of an emergency organization to the level of a permanent agency built into the structure of the participating bodies. Its work on other continents helped fashion a body of world Lutheranism. The Council abandoned the "code of regulations" under which it had operated since its organization and adopted a formal constitution and bylaws, carefully defining its relationships and functions and procedures, and clearly analyzing its work in divisions, departments, commissions, and bureaus. At the same time it adopted a long-range program of action, acquired its own permanent headquarters, and continued to enlarge its staff and expand its activity.

The administrative work of the Council was originally placed in the hands of an executive secretary. This office was abolished in December, 1920, and the duties of administration were committed to the president, an office to which Lauritz Larsen, formerly executive secretary, was chosen. After Dr. Larsen's death in 1926, an executive director was provided to supervise and direct the various activities of the Council. The executive director from 1926 to 1930 was John A. Morehead. Then for eighteen years the office was held by Ralph H. Long. Since 1948 the executive director has been Paul C. Empie.

The National Lutheran Council at its founding set up headquarters in New York City, where the Lutheran Commission for Soldiers' and Sailors' Welfare had placed its office and experienced personnel at the service of the new agency. An office was immediately opened also in Washington with the secretary of the Council in charge, whose duty was to keep in continual touch with the various government agencies and express the churches' united front in securing rights of Lutherans and countering the war and postwar misunderstandings of the church.

Immediately facing the Council at the time of its organization were the great needs for home mission work in various wartime industrial communities. The Council assumed the task until the home mission boards could undertake it. This suggested some action to prevent the duplication and overlapping of home mission efforts by various Lutheran bodies, and so the Council brought together representatives of the mission boards to co-ordinate their work and avoid future misunderstandings. A little later, in March, 1919, the Council was instrumental in bringing together a group of theologians representing the bodies belonging to the Council to discuss questions of doctrine and practice which had hitherto been an obstacle to closer co-operation in various lines. The result of this general conference was complete agreement on all fundamental questions under consideration and a declaration that the way is open for complete co-operation among these bodies.

Meanwhile it had become evident that the Lutheran churches should have some central agency of publicity. For this purpose the National Lutheran Council secured the Lutheran Bureau of New York City, an organization that had grown out of the celebration of the Quadri-Centennial in 1917. Its purpose was to gather information of every kind concerning the Lutheran church at home and abroad, in the past and in the present, and to distribute this information as widely as possible through the public press and by other means. It maintained a reference library and information bureau, a clipping bureau, and a complete news service agency. Its modern publicity methods served all parts of the Lutheran church in America and Europe.

The Council also organized a department of statistics to gather and publish uniform statistical information concerning the Lutheran church in America. G. L. Kieffer was the official statistician. Under the direction of an editorial committee headed by the executive director of the Council, Dr. Kieffer and Dr. O. M. Norlie prepared and published the *Lutheran World Almanac and Annual Encyclopedia*, eight volumes of invaluable historical and statistical information. The department of statistics also gathered a reference library and prepared to supply information to any inquirer on any subject pertaining to Lutherans and Lutheranism.

In February, 1919, the Council appointed five commissioners to go to Europe to ascertain reconstruction needs. At the same time an appeal was made to the churches for $500,000 for European relief and reconstruction. The appeal brought more than $600,000, but the commissioners reported much greater needs than had been surmised. In October, 1919, a special appeal was made for clothing, especially for Poland and the Baltic provinces. In response, about 800 tons of clothing were received and distributed and, in addition, $250,000 for transportation and medical and other supplies. One of the commissioners, J. A. Morehead, returned to Europe in February, 1920, to administer the relief work as the standing representative of the Council in its European work. By September, 1921, the Council had distributed more than $1,250,000 worth of gifts of money and food among the sufferers in seventeen European countries, in addition to clothing worth twice that amount. The main beneficiaries of this relief work were Lutherans in Germany, Poland, and France.

After the winter of 1921-22 the Council gave special attention to the four million Lutherans in Russia, its commissioners working in close co-operation with the American Relief Administration. When the worst famine conditions had eased, relief funds were used to rescue Lutheran pastors and churches and to support a new Lutheran seminary in Leningrad. The total expenditures of the Council on account of European relief during the first decade of its life reached the imposing figure of nearly $8,000,000. All this was done on sound principles of charity with a business system that insured the utmost economy and efficiency.

Organized at the request of the Council in January, 1920, the Lutheran Foreign Missions Conference of America took up the cause of the world-wide distress of Lutheran missions. It then asked that the National Council include in its campaign budget for 1920 the sum of $300,000 for the support of these missions. As a result, more than $200,000 was paid toward the support of Lutheran foreign missions in China, Japan, India, and Africa. Additional funds gathered and distributed for this emergency work in foreign missions brought the total in 1930 to $701,274.

The briefest summary of the activities of the National Lutheran Council during its first decade makes it clear that Lutherans from different backgrounds and organized in various groups had found definite fields of united service, had presented a common front before the national government and in the consciousness of the American public, and were now prepared for friendly co-operation on a larger scale.

In the second period of its life, the decade of the thirties, the Council was faced with a difficult situation. Contributions diminished in all lines of benevolence. Although the Lutherans of America were appreciative of the informational and publicity services of the Council, the participating bodies were slow to assign to the Council any of their regular functions in missions or education or welfare. It was widely supposed that the Lutheran churches of Europe were recovering, and needed no further help from America in meeting their own needs or resuming their foreign missions. Moreover, in 1930 the American Lutheran Conference was organized by the five largest bodies of the National Lutheran Council, excluding the United Lutheran Church, and this threatened to split the Council and jeopardized its continuation. In 1933 the Council's operating budget was pared to about $23,000, less than half of the budget for 1926.

The Council was saved by its Executive Director, Dr. Ralph H. Long. Convinced of the Council's worth, he planned a wise and effective program and promoted it with such enthusiasm that it earned the respect and regained the support of the participating bodies. In a few years the Council became the world's most vigorous manifestation of interchurch co-operation among Lutherans.

First the Council made an investigation of Lutheran finances and on the basis of its findings launched an educational campaign for stewardship in co-operation with synodical committees. Then through a series of conferences an enlightened program for aggressive action was formulated. In the deepest trough of the economic depression, the Council began a continuing study of prevailing social problems. A Committee on Social Trends prepared studies on a variety of social topics to arouse in Lutherans a sense of social responsibility and to provide significant guidance. In 1939 the Council organized a department of welfare to co-ordinate the inner mission, charitable, and social welfare work of nearly 300 agencies within and among the participating bodies.

Through a mandate from the Federal Council's General Committee on Army and Navy Chaplains, the National Lutheran Council was charged with responsibility for recruiting chaplains, processing applications, and maintaining contacts between the chaplains and their churches. As a result, before 1939 the number of Lutheran chaplains in the armed services began to approach the Lutheran quota. The Council also began to select the Lutheran preachers for "The Church of the Air," a series of religious broadcasts by the Columbia Broadcasting Company. In 1929 the Council took the lead in stimulating the celebration of the four-hundredth anniversary of Luther's Catechism, and in 1930 the four-hundredth anniversary of the Augsburg Confession. The Council also voiced the opposition of Lutherans to the appointment of a personal representative of the president of the United States to the Vatican. Through the generosity of the Federation of Lutheran Brotherhoods, it published the bimonthly magazine of news and information called *The National Lutheran* and distributed it free to pastors of the participating bodies. In 1937 the expansion of the publicity program required the appointment of a full-time publicity secretary to make the American public better aware of their neighbors in the Lutheran churches, their numbers, their evangelical positions, and their role in American life.

Separation of the work of the Lutheran World Convention from that of the Council had been attempted in 1930, when Dr. Morehead left the Council's secretaryship to give full time to presidency of the

Convention. But the Council continued to be the agent of the Convention in gathering funds for Lutheran World Service, and increasing demands were made upon the Council and its executive director. Then too, currency regulations cut off the parent European missionary societies from their fields, and the National Lutheran Council was again obliged to assume their support. Large numbers of Lutheran refugees, fleeing from Europe to Canada, the United States, and other countries, made further demands upon the resources of the Council. Thus, although confidence in the Council's indispensability had been re-established and a broad domestic program developed, its "emergency work" had begun once more to assume major importance.

A third period in the life of the Council dates from the adoption of a constitution in 1945. For twenty-seven years the Council had operated under a "code of regulations," but the volume and range of its work reached such large scale as to require a more formal and more detailed instrument of government. The adoption of a constitution approved by all the participating bodies was in effect a reorganization of the Council. The new instrument registered changes of function in the Council and changes in the attitudes of the participating bodies. It incorporated into the permanent program of the Council some of the activities that had begun on an emergency basis, and it opened avenues for expansion of the Council's program.

In the annual meetings of the Council, under the new constitution, the thirty-two councilors from the participating bodies receive reports and recommendations from the several divisions, bureaus, and commissions, and then determine the policies and budgets that are to be submitted to the participating bodies for ratification. The Council's work is administered by a staff of more than four hundred persons around the globe, but all operations are integrated and cleared through the headquarters of the Council in New York City.

The Council's Division of American Missions co-ordinates and helps the home missionary agencies of the participating bodies, discovers and surveys areas in which they may carry on missionary work without overlapping. For this purpose it supervises eight regional home mission committees, conducts frequent co-operative home mission institutes, and carries forward a continuous program of study, research, and exchange of information. This makes possible intelligent planning in the organizing or relocating of urban churches, in strengthening rural churches, and in ministering to people in the new communities that spring up suddenly around new industries. In the one year, 1950, the regional committees of the Council assigned 200 fields to the several church bodies for study and 154 new fields for mission work where there would be no duplication or overlapping with older congregations. In 1951 a total of 95 such fields were assigned for new congregations, and in addition, 23 fields were cleared for relocation of congregations already in existence.

In the rapid shifts of population in the United States and Canada, surveys show, Lutherans move as much as the average population. Thirty million people moved in 1952; about 400,000 of them were members of National Lutheran Council churches. One-fourth of these moved across state lines. Year after year this threatens the membership of the Lutheran churches. In trailer camps with as many as 1,600 trailers, in new housing developments all over the nation, in boom towns with as many as 120,000 people, in barracks areas with their congested population, in distant states and cities, the agents of the Council search out these mobile or displaced Lutherans to provide them with the ministry of the gospel. The Division of American Missions has planned improvements in the transfer of members among the congregations, and has had published an all-Lutheran geographical directory of congregations to help pastors direct their members who move to new neighborhoods.

The Division of American Missions also conducts surveys among racial groups such as Jewish people, Negroes, and Indians, guides the participating bodies in their responsibilities among the special groups. The Department for Christian Approach to the Jewish People has engaged a staff of sixteen persons. Nine fields in Negro communities have been turned over to participating bodies, and fourteen other such fields have been under the supervision of the nineteen members of the division's staff dealing with this work. This line of work has slowly brought tangible results.

The rural church also became the object of solicitude on the part of the National Lutheran Council. About one-half of the congregations in the National Lutheran Council bodies are located in the open country or in towns of less than a thousand people. New rural leadership is being recruited, church programs for rural communities are being developed, and the increasing strength of the Lutheran church in rural America is manifested in benevolence and in ministerial candidates.

The Council's Division of Public Relations which grew out of the original department of publicity, research and statistics, interprets the faith and program of the Lutheran church to the people in a great variety of ways. The Division holds public relations workshops among Lutheran students, sponsors regional seminars on the church and national life, furnishes Lutheran speakers for broadcasts of the "Church of the Air," and provides information for Lutherans and others who are engaged professionally in some branch of public relations. It makes arrangements for Lutheran visitors from foreign countries and has charge of the American end of personnel exchange with Lutheran churches and institutions abroad. Its department of research and statistics compiles annual statistics of all Lutheran bodies in America, issues a biennial *Statistical Handbook*, and prepared the all-Lutheran directory of congregations used by the Division of American Missions. During a recent period of eleven months, it issued 140 news releases containing 519 news stories and 29 feature articles. It is responsible for the monthly *National Lutheran* and for publicizing the regular conventions of the participating bodies. The Division of Public Relations is responsible also for the Washington office of the Council, and its secretary there renders a multitude of special services to Lutheran groups and individuals in relation to government departments and agencies.

The third main area of the Council's work as listed in the constitution of 1945 is the Division of Welfare. This is an expansion of the department organized in 1939. Its stated purpose is to co-operate with the welfare agencies of the participating bodies in setting up standards for social service and training workers, in making surveys and extending services to special groups who are in need, and in promoting a unified welfare program for regular and emergency service. Particularly notable was its work in the resettlement of refugees. Some of the achievements of this division are recounted in Chapter 34 of this volume.

The Council's fourth division is for College and University Work, begun in 1946 to conserve the faith, develop the loyalty, and cultivate the spiritual life of Lutheran students both in Lutheran and non-Lutheran educational institutions. The national staff includes an executive secretary, an educational secretary, a program secretary, three regional secretaries, and a regional assistant. The division employs 52 full-time workers, of whom 15 are campus pastors, and nearly 400 part-time workers. Its ministry reaches more than 150,000 Lutheran students in one-third of the 1,800 colleges and universities in the United States and Canada. Lutheran student centers have been established on 29 college campuses at a capital investment of nearly two million dollars. The division varies its program to meet the changing trends in student enrollment and student interest. The campus program consists of services of worship and preaching, personal counseling, fellowship through recreation, directed Christian service on the campus and in local congregations, personal Christian witness in daily student life, and organized study of the Bible, the history and confessions of the church, and the principles of the Christian life. Everywhere the students who are to be the future leaders in American life are faced with the claims of Christ upon them, kept in touch with their church, and asked to consider full-time Christian service.

A survey of credit courses in religion at public institutions of higher learning has shown that in 1953 Lutherans were teaching such courses at 13 state colleges and universities, and would be acceptable at 35 others. Plans were therefore made to establish Lutheran chairs of religion at non-Lutheran schools. In the meantime the division provides noncredit courses in biblical and religious subjects to large enrollments at all of its major centers. The division issues its own promotional materials and many of its textbooks. As rapidly as funds and personnel have become available, the Division of College and University Work has moved to integrate the Lutheran students' total academic experience with a vital Christian faith.

A new Division of Co-operation in Latin America was set up in 1951 after investigations had revealed that 750,000 people in South America belong to the Lutheran tradition but that about one-third of them are without the ministry of the church. Other multitudes there are complete strangers to the Word and sacraments. In the conservation and evangelization program begun or planned, the section on interchurch aid assists the Lutheran theological seminary at Sao Leopoldo, Brazil, undergirds the finances of some of the Lutheran pastors, and helps some Lutheran congregations build churches. The section on ministry to diaspora groups participates in the program of the Lutheran World Federation, gathering into congregations the scattered Lutherans of German, Scandinavian, or other European background and helping them establish themselves in the local culture. The program of the section on evangelization in Spanish is the provision of literature and the training of men for missionary work among the Spanish-speaking natives of South and Central America, an evangelism in which some of the participating bodies have had experience.

This work in Latin America in 1956 became a part of the Council's new wide-ranging Division of Lutheran World Federation Affairs, which embraces all services to Lutherans beyond the Western hemisphere.

Under the constitution of 1945 a Bureau of Service to Military Personnel took over the work of the Armed Forces Services Commission organized by the Council in February, 1940. With its annual budget of half a million dollars the commission had developed a program of aid to Lutheran chaplains, special services to enlisted men through communities adjacent to training camps, and a ministry to selectees through pastors and congregations. Before the end of the war the Council had processed and approved 560 chaplains from the churches participating in the Council, and about 240 from other Lutheran bodies. The number of Lutheran chaplains in the armed forces was brought up to the full Lutheran quota. In 1944, the peak year, the commission had 50 full-time service centers and 37 part-time parish centers, with 81 pastors at work in these centers, and with hundreds of local clergymen assisting in communities where full-time centers could not be established. Attendance at these centers during the year was more than 3,500,000. An *Army and Navy Service Book* was prepared and 400,000 copies distributed. Twice as many service prayer books were distributed, and more than 10,000,000 devotional tracts. These materials were widely used by other Protestants in the national services. Certainly thousands of service men and women were conserved for the church and brought personally into the Christian fellowship.

With the coming of peace and the complete reorganization of the National Lutheran Council in 1945, this emergency commission was succeeded by the permanent Bureau of Service to Military Personnel. The main responsibilities of the bureau are, first, to procure and maintain chaplains in all branches of the armed forces, regular, officers' reserve corps, and the national guard. For this purpose it maintains contacts with the national chiefs of chaplains, keeps church bodies informed on changes in policies or regulations affecting chaplains, seeks to maintain the Lutheran quota of chaplains in the several branches, serves as the clearing agency for church endorsement of chaplains, and renders assistance to chaplains through personal visits, through conferences and spiritual retreats, through the publication of religious literature, and in other ways. The number of chaplains from National Lutheran Council bodies in 1953 was 546 and from the Missouri Synod 210, a total of 756, of whom 303 were on active duty.

The Bureau of Service to Military Personnel also continues services to large numbers of Lutheran men in training camps and the fighting forces. More than fifty service centers and parish centers were in operation in 1953, and more than one hundred "contact pastors" have served in communities where service centers are not practical. Special effort is made to maintain vital contact of the men and women with their home congregations, and in the vicinity of encampments and training centers special assistance is provided for local congregations in ministering to the Lutheran personnel of the camps.

A third activity of the bureau is the publication of literature to assist pastors in their special ministry to members in uniform. One booklet contains a brief order for public confession and the service, including the Holy Communion, together with hymns and devotional meditations. About 80,000 copies of the monthly paper, *A Mighty Fortress*, are sent by congregations to their men and women away from home. About 750,000 copies of other religious tracts and pamphlets are distributed annually.

The National Lutheran Council in its first decade spent more than $700,000 for emergency work in foreign missions. In World War II the Council gave emergency financial assistance to German, Danish, Norwegian and Finnish missionaries and mission fields principally in Africa, New Guinea, India, China, and Palestine. Gifts from 1939 to 1947 exceeded $2,500,000. After the war the Danish and Norwegian societies assumed the support of their fields. The closing of China reduced the possibilities of assistance there, but the reduction was more than absorbed by a five-year reconstruction plan for the 600,000 Lutherans of the Batak Church in Indonesia.

With this background of emergency action, in 1948 the Council set up a Commission on Younger Churches and Orphaned Missions with a longe-range program. Generally called CYCOM, the commission was made the agent of the Council to co-operate with younger churches in need of aid, to study the needs of the orphaned mission fields, to supply them with at least a minimum of personnel and funds, and to plan for their return as soon as possible, entirely or in part, to the care of their parent churches or missionary societies. But inflation, postwar political involvements that limited the sending of funds and missionaries from the German societies, and the upsurge of nationalism, made return to the old order difficult. Furthermore, the Council could not evade the opportunities for expansion. So through CYCOM the National Lutheran Council churches joined hands with other churches in the Lutheran World Federation in a program of support and expansion in Tanganyika, Ethiopia, South Africa, Madagascar, Japan, India, Israel, Jordan, New Guinea, and Formosa. During its first five years the new commission expended nearly $3,500,000 in these fields. Its parent council in thirteen years spent a total of $11,000,000 on this account; in 1953 alone this part of its budget was nearly a million dollars. This work has provided a pattern for the Lutheran World Federation to set up departments of world-wide co-operation among Lutherans. Since 1954 this branch of the Council's work has been administered through the Department of World Missions of the Lutheran World Federation.

A function of the National Lutheran Council is representation of American Lutherans in the Lutheran World Federation. All participating bodies of the Council are also member churches of the Federation, and in 1947 the constitution of the Council was amended to specify that the Council itself shall be the United States National Committee of the Federation, and shall act among American Lutherans on behalf of the Federation. Its chief responsibility is to carry out purposes of the Federation as stated in its constitution: "To develop a united Lutheran approach to responsibilities in missions and education," and "To support Lutheran groups in need of spiritual or material aid."

The first of these purposes the Council achieves partly through its Commission on Younger Churches and Orphaned Missions and by participation in the Federation's Department of World Missions, and partly through its participation in the Federation's Department of

Theology. The second it achieves through a huge program of European reconstruction and inter-church aid, which have involved the Council since its first days. At the close of World War II, a permanent office was set up in Geneva with Dr. S. C. Michelfelder as the agent of the Council to inform the American churches concerning the needs of the distressed churches in Europe and to administer relief and reconstruction. On all sides were confusion and distress. Transportation and communication were severely limited. But, slowly and painfully, needs were ascertained, channels cleared, contacts made, and the outposts manned. By the summer of 1946 the stream of funds and relief supplies in huge quantities began to flow to Europe.

The first emphasis was placed on material relief, quick large-scale provision of food, clothing, and medicine to keep body and soul together. Then came restoration of institutions of mercy, the distribution of Christian literature, and measures to recruit pastors for the depleted ranks. Shelter and spiritual assistance were provided for thousands of displaced and homeless, guidance for uprooted youth, and aid for oppressed minorities.

By 1950 the program was emphasizing long-range plans for the reconstruction of church buildings, the support of church bodies, and the moral and spiritual rehabilitation of the people. More than $3,000,000 were spent for repairs to damaged churches and the erection of new ones. Several times that amount went to the feeding and clothing of children, the care of the aged and the sick, the salaries of impoverished pastors, the needs of penniless students, the publishing of Bibles, catechisms, theological and other books, and devotional materials. From the arctic regions of Norway to the scattered Lutherans in Italy, from the desolation among Lutherans in Poland and the confusion in Hungary and Jugoslavia to the hopeless minority in France and the needy communities in the Netherlands, there were only a few countries in all Europe that did not see one or more of the agents of the National Lutheran Council of America extending the hand of love in the name of Christ and building bridges of understanding and co-operation on the solid ground of charity, brotherly affection, and a common faith.

The National Lutheran Council employed a staff of about 400 persons in its many programs, and other hundreds gave part of their time and energy as volunteers. The Council received and disbursed about

$4,500,000 a year. About one-fifth of this amount was received through the regular budgets of the participating bodies and was applied only to the regular domestic program of the Council. The balance was secured through special annual appeals called, since 1941, Lutheran World Action. As both opportunities and needs increased, the goals of Lutheran World Action grew from half a million in 1941 to ten millions for the 1946-1947 biennium. From 1941 to 1953, nearly thirty-seven million dollars were raised for Lutheran World Action among the ten thousand local congregations in the participating bodies of the Council. These funds were applied in the fields of American missions, public relations, social welfare, student work, service to military personnel and hospitalized veterans, Latin American missions, aid to foreign missions cut off from parent societies in Europe, resettlement of displaced persons and refugees, and inter-church aid and material relief abroad. During that same period more than $25,000,000 in food, clothing, medicine, and other supplies were shipped to twenty-four countries by Lutheran World Relief, the material aid agency of the Council. Altogether, over a period of thirty-five years, the Council's two-thirds of the Lutherans of America by 1954 contributed to its world relief work a total of more than $70,000,000 in cash and goods. The work in their own programs of the participating bodies was of course in addition to this.

An unscheduled by-product of the National Lutheran Council, resulting from its fellowship of leading personalities across synodical boundaries, has been the formation of a number of new general Lutheran organizations and new life in older ones. Such are the Lutheran Deaconess Conference (1896), the National Lutheran Education Conference (1910), the National Lutheran Editors' Association (1913), the Lutheran Publishing House Managers' Association (1914), the American Lutheran Statistical Association (1917), the Lutheran Foreign Missions Conference of America (1919), the National Lutheran Inner Mission Conference (1922), the Lutheran Student Association of America (1922), the Lutheran Welfare Conference in America (1922), the American Federation of Lutheran Brotherhoods (1927), the American Lutheran Home Missions Council (1931), the National Lutheran Nurses Guild (1940), the Conference of Lutheran Theological Professors (1942), the Association of Lutheran Seminarians

(1946), and the Lutheran Hospital Association (1948), and about 30 others.

This summary account makes it clear that the National Lutheran Council did not attempt the functions of a super-synod, nor did it interfere in any degree with the independence of its participating bodies. It did seek to co-ordinate their efforts, and to serve as the agency through which they can work together at tasks for which no one of them alone would be adequate. It also served as a medium of acquaintance among Lutherans, enabling two-thirds of the Lutheran church in this country to discover the extent of Lutheran unity.

Another co-operative group of Lutherans in America, comparable to the National Lutheran Council, but smaller, is the Canadian Lutheran Council, organized December 4, 1952, with headquarters at Winnipeg. Its constituency is the Canadian churches of all National Lutheran Council bodies except the Suomi Synod and the American Evangelical Lutheran Church. During World War II the Canadians formed their own branch of Lutheran World Relief and resettled several thousand displaced persons and more than 3,500 ethnic German refugees. A Canadian Lutheran Commission for War Services was organized to certify Lutheran pastors to the dominion government for appointment as chaplains in the armed forces, disbanded after the war, and in 1951 reactivated to meet the call for the appointment of more chaplains. As requirements of Lutheran action increased, this commission was supplanted in 1952 by the Canadian Lutheran Council. The Council represents 130,000 Canadian members of participating bodies of the National Lutheran Council. Another 65,000 Lutherans in Canada belong to the Missouri Synod, a division of members similar to that in the United States. The congregations, more than a thousand in number, are largely rural, and average only about 200 baptized members. The Lutherans of Canada are scattered over a wide area and have a varied cultural background, but in confessional position their differences are not great, not even between groups in and outside the Council. Many of them hope some day to have their own Canadian Lutheran Church. One of the purposes stated in the constitution of the Canadian Council and approved by all the parent bodies is "to further the interests and work of the Lutheran churches in Canada . . . by promoting free sectional conferences with a view to the achievement of complete Lutheran unity."

CHAPTER 33

THE AMERICAN LUTHERAN CONFERENCE AND INDEPENDENT BODIES

The National Lutheran Council had been in operation only six years when several of the participating bodies took steps in the direction of still closer co-operation. They even began to speak of organic merger among themselves. In 1924 the Joint Synod of Ohio agreed to organic union with Iowa and Buffalo, and at the same time conferred with the Evangelical Lutheran Church concerning closer relationship. All of these bodies in 1925 adopted the "Minneapolis theses" (see Chapter 36) as common ground on which to build closer affiliation. Three years later pulpit and altar fellowship was established between the Evangelical Lutheran Church and the Joint Synod of Ohio. Then, as the Joint Synod of Ohio, the Iowa Synod, and the Buffalo Synod moved toward union, forming the American Lutheran Church, the conferences on closer co-operation were extended among the midwestern bodies to include the Augustana Lutheran Church and the smaller Lutheran Free Church and United Evangelical (Danish) Lutheran Church. Each body decided to admit to its pulpits and altars the pastors and communicants of the other bodies.

Events proceeded rapidly in 1929 and 1930. When it was found that the Minneapolis theses of 1925 could be accepted by all the conferring bodies, their presidents drafted a constitution and bylaws which were promptly ratified by each synod and then published as the official basis for a proposed new organization to be known as The American Lutheran Conference. The organization was effected at Minneapolis in October, 1930, two months after the formation of the American Lutheran Church. The organizing convention was held amid great enthusiasm. The officers elected were: President, Otto

Mees, president of Capital University at Columbus, Ohio, and a member of the American Lutheran Church; Vice-Presidents, T. F. Gullixson (Evangelical), J. P. Nielsen (United Evangelical), and O. H. Sletten (Free Church); Secretary, P. O. Bersell (Augustana).

The American Lutheran Conference united for co-operative purposes the Evangelical Lutheran Church, the American Lutheran Church, the Augustana Lutheran Church, the United Evangelical Lutheran Church, and the Lutheran Free Church, all the participating bodies of the National Lutheran Council except the United Lutheran Church. They embraced about one-half of the communing membership of the Council.

The distinctive mission of the American Lutheran Conference is not easy to find. The secretary of the Conference once said that the new movement was originally "conceived as largely a defensive alliance, created for the purpose of protecting its members against possible aggression by the United Lutheran Church and the Synodical Conference." There were differences between the Conference and the other main bodies of Lutherans, but these were differences not of kind but of degree.

Perhaps the qualities of the Conference are best revealed in the many interests the church bodies uniting in the American Lutheran Conference had in common. Their common doctrinal interests and their harmony in the fundamental concepts of the Lutheran faith were indicated by their common acceptance of the Minneapolis theses. In their attitude toward the confessional writings of the Lutheran church all were less free and historical in their approach than the United Lutheran Church, and less dogmatic and hyperconfessional than Missouri and the Synodical Conference. Moreover, their geographical situation grouped them together. All were planted and nurtured in the Upper Mississippi Valley, between the Appalachian Mountains and the Rockies, and the distinctive culture of that section, a combination of tradition, individualism and progress, characterized these church bodies and differentiated them from the United Lutheran Church. Furthermore, they were predominantly rural. While only thirty per cent of the United Lutheran Church membership were in population centers of 2,500 or less, and forty-two per cent of that of the Synodical Conference, the American Lutheran Conference was fifty-six per cent rural. Finally, the Lutherans of the Conference had been a part of American culture for a much shorter time than those in the United Lutheran Church, and in this respect were closer to those in the Synodical Conference.

In their synodical organization and general church polity they were not so strictly congregational as the Missouri Synod, nor yet so willing to accept centralized authority as the United Lutheran Church. In the variety of their liturgical practice they were more like the synods of the Synodical Conference. They had preserved more of the pietistic heritage of the original Scandinavian immigrants than most of the synods in the United Lutheran Church. In their attitude toward other Protestants they were more exclusive and aloof than the United Lutheran Church, but less narrow and inflexible than the Synodical Conference.

Although, at least in theory, the American Lutheran Conference constituted a stronger bond of fellowship than the National Lutheran Council, it was a federation and not an organic union. Yet it was more than an agent of its members. It was a medium for co-operation and for the cultivation of fraternal relations among Lutheran church bodies who felt themselves at one in faith and practice, and who had formally declared pulpit and altar fellowship with one another.

The objects of the American Lutheran Conference, as stated in its constitution, were twofold: "Mutual counsel concerning the faith, life, and work of the Church, and co-operation in matters of common interest and responsibility." The fields of co-operation were specified as follows: allocation of work in home mission fields, elementary and higher Christian education, inner mission work (Christian social service), student service in state schools and universities, foreign missions, the publication of Christian literature, periodic exchange of theological professors, and such other interests as from time to time may call for consideration. The Executive Committee appointed a commission on each of these spheres of co-operation. These commissions brought to the meetings of the Conference concrete proposals for action by the participating bodies.

Not all of the fields suggested by the constitution were entered by the Conference. The major practical activities of the Conference were its annual inter-Lutheran seminars and its Lutheran preaching missions, conducted in many cities throughout the land, its joint appeals on behalf of the colleges and seminaries within these Lutheran bodies, and its inspirational mass gatherings of youth in metropolitan centers. The Conference in 1936 began publishing its *Journal of the American Lutheran Conference,* after 1944 called *The Lutheran Outlook.*

The bodies participating in the Conference retained their independence of organization and action. They continued their work in the program of the National Lutheran Council. The Conference had only such powers as were specifically delegated to it by the participating or "constituent" bodies. Otherwise its province was limited to counsel and advice in matters of common interest and those in which its advice might be sought.

The functions of the American Lutheran Conference at first seemed to overlap those of the National Lutheran Council. The Conference had purposely included in its membership all of the bodies participating in the National Lutheran Council except the United Lutheran Church, and for a short time the program of the Council lagged until its life hung by a thread. But it was clear, particularly with the approach of war, that Lutherans in America should expand rather than contract the range of their co-operative efforts, and after a period of clarification the program of the National Lutheran Council gathered new momentum. The bodies in the American Lutheran Conference co-operated heartily with the United Lutheran Church in the work of the Council, and within the Conference gave themselves almost exclusively to efforts at organic union among themselves.

During the two decades following the organization of the American Lutheran Conference, many of its objectives were absorbed by the rapidly expanding program of the National Lutheran Council. Moreover, among the member bodies of the Conference a strong movement developed for organic union to take the place of loose federation (see Chapter 36). These developments made the continuance of the Conference unnecessary, and in November, 1954, it held its final meeting and dissolved.

The American Lutheran Conference was the last of the three main groups, including the Synodical Conference and the United Lutheran Church, into which nearly all the Lutherans in America had been gathered. The United Lutheran Church differed from the others in being a compact organic union, while others were both federations, partly advisory and partly co-operative. Each comprised about one-third of the strength of Lutheranism in this country.

There are a few other Lutherans in America. The small independent body of Norwegian origin called the Eielsen Synod with five pastors and 1,350 members, has not joined either of the Conferences or co-operated in the Council, nor has the Church of the Lutheran Brethren in America with its eight pastors and five congregations.

Mention of two other independent bodies of that time makes the record complete. Both are of Finnish origin. When the Suomi (Finnish) Synod was organized in 1890 (page 126), part of the congregation in Calumet, Michigan, declined to join the organization because it feared that the autonomy of the individual congregation would be hampered as it was in the state church in Finland. The dissenting group formed a new congregation and called itself the Finnish National Church. Other congregations joined the separatist group and in 1900 the Finnish National Lutheran Church was organized as a new general body. It has 66 small congregations with an aggregate baptized membership of nearly 8,000, served by 28 ministers. In polity and doctrine the body inclines toward the Missouri Synod. Its growth has been hampered by the lack of educational institutions and pastors. It has also been distracted by doctrinal controversies echoing the controversies in Finland itself. When the other Lutheran bodies in America began to eliminate nationalist names from their titles, this Finnish group changed its name to National Evangelical Lutheran Church. In 1963 it merged with the Missouri Synod.

Another independent organization of Finnish Lutherans until recently bore the official title, The Finnish Apostolic Lutheran Church of America, but is sometimes called the Church of Laestadius. Many of the Finnish Lutheran immigrants who came to America between 1865 and 1880 were followers of Laestadius, the great reformer of the mid-nineteenth century who emphasized lay preaching and the possession of the Holy Spirit. The Laestadians accept in general the confessions of the Lutheran church, but they insist upon evidence of regeneration and they stress the practical importance of absolution from sin. They hold that the forgiveness of sins comes only by placing of hands on the head of the truly penitent during the proclamation of absolution. This insistence led to the exclusion of the Laestadians from the fellowship of the other Finnish Lutherans in America. Organized in 1873 the church is strictly congregational and it has no synod or conference or educational institutions. It carries on extensive evangelistic activity and home missionary work. Apostolic simplicity prevails in home and congregational life. The church buildings are without organs or steeples or any effort at external beauty. It has an estimated 22 ministers, 59 congregations, and 8,000 baptized members. Many Lutherans of this persuasion, about 40 congregations, refuse to join any general body. In 1962 the name of this group was changed to the Apostolic Lutheran Church of America.

CHAPTER 34

THE SOCIAL MINISTRY
OF LUTHERANS

During the early decades of the twentieth century, several events combined to impress the Christian churches in America with their responsibility to society. A phenomenal economic growth presented problems for the churches as well as for government. The increase in immigration and its changing character produced conditions that called loudly for reform. Pacing the extension and consolidation of business were powerful combinations of industrial workers; class struggles involved the happiness and the morality of vast multitudes of the American people. A tide of moral earnestness and reform swept American political life and new political machinery was invented to protect the rights of the common man.

The churches reflected the new spirit, the growing complexity of society, the problems and energies of the nation. Efforts at evangelism and revival were redoubled. Social evils, one by one, were labeled and attacked. The churches cultivated the spirit of Christian stewardship, individual responsibility for the investment of money and time and talent, and corporate responsibility to society in general. Organizations multiplied, both within the churches and among the churches, to apply the gospel to every phase of human culture with the enthusiasm of a great business enterprise. These were the decades of the "social gospel."

Lutherans were not among the first to capture the new spirit and organize for the social gospel. Their individual prophets might advocate the group application of Christian principles, but as churches they remained true to their conservative genius. Their official actions waited for assurance of scriptural warrant, while many other churches organized and swept into action. But when the social needs of Americans and of all people could hardly be any longer ignored, then the Lutherans of America did finally discover the human race and move forward to an acceptance of their responsibility to society. Even then they rejected the "social gospel" which taught that a man can be saved by a change in his social environment, and preferred to speak of "the social implications of the gospel." But today the Lutherans of America can point to a record of service, of human rehabilitation and social change, that speaks eloquently of the social dynamic that is inherent in the evangelical interpretation of the Scriptures.

Long before the era of the social gospel, Lutheranism had great individual prophets of the humanitarian application of the gospel. The founder and organizer of Lutheranism in America, Henry Melchior Muhlenberg, reflected the practical humanitarian interest of his pietistic background in Germany. The pietists taught that the Christian life must go beyond formal confession of Christ and must bring forth deeds of goodness and institutions of charity. Muhlenberg was definitely set upon benevolent activities for the church. He planted that idea in the congregations he organized and the men he trained for the ministry. Of course, the social problems that he faced in the eighteenth century might seem small compared with those confronting his church in the twentieth century.

One of the social ills of Muhlenberg's time was the defrauding and barbarous treatment of immigrants. To remedy this evil the German Benevolent Society of Pennsylvania was organized in the schoolhouse of Muhlenberg's congregation, St. Michael's in Philadelphia, and regularly held its meetings there. The patriarch vigorously opposed the drinking customs of his people and frequently preached and wrote against all use of alcoholic beverages. He also used the pulpit to oppose dueling. War he regarded as God's chastisement of human sin. He sympathized with slaves and appealed for kind treatment of them, but he did not oppose the institution of slavery. He planned and pled for an orphans' home and a home for the aged. His greatest achievements in the improvement of the social status of Lutherans was the establishment of schools among them. But problems of politics and economics were strictly avoided in Muhlenberg's pulpit, and only his most intimate friends knew his views on these subjects. When his sons left the pulpit and entered military and political life, the eminence that they attained did not dissipate his feeling that they had descended to a lower vocation.

In the next generation, Samuel Simon Schmucker, the founder of the educational institutions at Gettysburg, shared the pietistic spirit. Like Muhlenberg he often pointed to Luther's emphasis upon a Christian's duty to his neighbor. He wrote eloquently on the influence of Christianity in producing social change, in mitigating the horrors of war, in raising the status of women in society, in abolishing slavery, in improving conditions among the poor, and in promoting various enterprises of benevolence. He wrote: "The triumph of the Gospel will everywhere be accompanied by its legitimate train of benevolent and meliorating influences on the civil and social institutions of the world; and war itself, the prolific mother of all evil, will retire before the progress of the Prince of peace."

Schmucker went much further than Muhlenberg in his hopes for the kingdom of God on earth. He recognized more clearly the sources of the evils of his day, and made more strenuous efforts to change the social conditions that were responsible. He wrote against the institution of slavery, outspokenly advocated legal abolition, helped to organize emancipation societies, and labored earnestly for the improvement of social conditions among freedmen. An ardent advocate of temperance, and even of legal prohibition, he was one of the earliest organizers of temperance societies in this country. He stoutly maintained the divine obligation of the Lord's Day and gave of his time and energy to agitate for the proper observance of the "Christian Sabbath." The orphan claimed his active interest.

As to the methods for securing betterment, Schmucker agreed with Muhlenberg that ordained ministers should not use their ministerial office or their pulpits to engage in political agitation or to secure social reform. But he held that as a private citizen every Christian is in duty bound to use his talents and experience in the service of the general welfare of society. Schmucker did not hesitate to advocate legislative measures to abolish evils or improve social conditions. Repeatedly he called to the attention of the lawmakers that the application of Christian principles of conduct, for example, the observance of one day out of seven for rest, tends to reduce crime and promotes the physical and moral welfare of the people. He was also active in promoting Sunday schools, distributing Bibles, issuing tracts, and otherwise uplifting the underprivileged classes in society. He was one of the earliest advocates of public schools for Pennsylvania. Legislation and education, Schmucker held, are the interest of every Christian in his relation to society.

For nearly forty years Schmucker was the chief influence in the education of ministers of the Lutheran pulpits of America. His zeal for a Christian society and the social betterment of all classes was reflected from hundreds of pulpits, by actions of district synods, and by many enactments of the General Synod. But nowhere then was there careful analysis of the underlying causes of social evils, nor any long-range effort to overcome those causes.

One of Schmucker's seminary students, William Alfred Passavant, sent out to distribute Bibles in neglected areas, became interested in the underprivileged people in the mountains near Gettysburg and undertook measures to improve their physical as well as spiritual conditions. Later during his ministry in Baltimore and Pittsburgh, he was active not only in missionary and literary work but also in all kinds of charitable work. In 1849 he equipped a small hospital in Pittsburgh and cared for sick soldiers discharged from the Mexican War. He began an orphanage. He made the acquaintance of Theodore Fliedner, the German founder of the Protestant order of deaconesses, and through him helped introduce deaconesses into American churches. In 1855 Passavant resigned his pastorate in Pittsburgh in order to give himself entirely to organizing institutions of mercy and to missionary work among Lutheran immigrants.

Passavant made no progress beyond his predecessors in analyzing the causes of social ills. The role of good Samaritan was the highest expression of practical Christian impulses of that day. But before his death near the end of the century Passavant realized the need for a more scientific analysis of social situations and a more systematic attack upon the fundamental causes of social evils.

A real prophet of social Christianity after the Civil War was Dr. J. H. W. Stuckenberg. An immigrant in early childhood, and an eye-witness of the evils of slavery and drunkenness, he immersed himself in the practical problems of American society. He prepared for the ministry at Wittenberg College and studied for a number of years at Halle and other German universities. In Pittsburgh he served a congregation whose members were mostly laborers. He taught at Wittenberg for seven years. In 1880 his *Christian Sociology* recorded the results of a systematic investigation of the social implications of the New Testament. He took the position that the church must supplement the preaching of the gospel and the founding of charitable institutions with the building of a Christian society in which the ethical and social teachings of the New Testament are systematically applied to human relationships. Without proposing changes in Lutheran theology, he insisted that Lutherans apply their evangelical theology to the solution of social problems.

Stuckenberg and his friend Dr. Passavant together might have led the Lutherans of America in their day to a position of priority in the social application of the Christian gospel. But they went different ways, Passavant to institutions of relief, Stuckenberg to theory. During the next fourteen years in Berlin, Stuckenberg lost touch with the church in America, and his studies led him to new positions. In *The Social Problem*, published in 1897 during widespread labor unrest, he virtually abandoned the Christian grounds for social action and discussed labor problems almost entirely in terms of sociology and economics. Returning to America, he kept aloof from church groups, and counted entirely on the influence of his pen. His major publication was a work of two volumes, *Sociology: The Science of Human Society*, published soon after his death in 1903. This learned, comprehensive work is highly important in the history of sociology as a science, but the scientific overshadows the religious interest. The author was still consciously Lutheran, but his emphasis had shifted from Scripture and theology to science and philosophy. His tendency was the identification of civic righteousness with the righteousness of God.

In the meantime a number of Lutheran writers, and even some synods, were giving attention to individual social evils. In 1868 the convention of the General Synod had expressed itself against intemperance and called for legislation to support a moral reform of drinking habits. In 1880 the Augustana Lutheran Church declared it the duty of the Christian voter "to cast his vote against the manufacture and sale, as a beverage, of all intoxicating drinks," and in 1889 this group vigorously supported prohibition amendments for Pennsylvania and Nebraska. Early in the nineties the United Norwegian Church and the Hauge Norwegian Synod approved all Christian and legal efforts for prohibition and called on every church member to oppose "the godless and ruinous traffic" in liquor. Soon there were resolutions from these bodies on Sabbath reform and actions extending charity to immigrants.

From the pulpits of other denominations came calls for the regeneration of society. But the general position of Lutherans at this time was that the work of the church is to regenerate human souls one by one, and that social reform must begin with individuals, not groups. The program to save men by changing their environment was held to be nothing more than golden-rule ethics which forfeits the spiritual worth of the individual. Lutherans were taught to recognize the need for social improvement, and they were encouraged to co-operate with organizations outside the church in improving social conditions, but the main emphasis of the church continued to be placed on man's sin in his relation to God, the need for regeneration of the individual soul, the relief of physical distress, the activities of the inner missions, and institutions of mercy.

Before the end of the century, occasional writers in Lutheran periodicals called attention to social conditions that were causing sickness and poverty, producing orphans and cripples, and seriously endangering Christian morality. They called on the church and its members to become active in social reform, to be mindful of "the solidarity of the human race." In 1891 the General Synod sent a resolution to the President and Senate of the United States protesting against American debauchery of African natives with slavery and drunkenness. The district synods usually limited their social interest to the evils of intemperance. But the readers of the Lutheran press gradually had their social vision lifted to include prison reform, gambling, slums, and divorce.

Not until well into the twentieth century did Lutheran churchmen and official bodies have anything to say about the industrial and economic situation that produced the major social problems of the time. The obstacles that earlier prevented Lutherans from seeing social needs were partly theological and partly historical. Their emphasis in human relations was upon the regeneration of the individual soul. Sin and evil referred to theology, and there was no social ethics. Their reliance was mainly upon institutions of mercy and human repair. Moreover, to the many rural Lutherans, industrial problems seemed very remote. Among the clergy the problems of labor and economics seemed too political and divisive. In some Lutheran bodies also the barrier of language had delayed active participation in the American social situation.

Lutherans did not generally accept the technology-born doctrine of progress. They held to their doctrine of human depravity. The Federal Council of Churches was organized in 1908 with a resounding "social creed of the churches" and a far-flung program of "social service," and political reformers were generally supported by the churches. But Lutherans for the most part held aloof.

After a decade, a change of emphasis was noted. The advocates of the social gospel began to turn from the ideal of a kingdom of God on earth as outlined by the sociologist to a reliance on the social teachings of Jesus as set forth by the student of Scripture. To Lutherans it was a welcome change. Lutheran periodicals in English began to participate more fully in the discussions of the social implications of the gospel and the principles of the New Testament as the light to guide society to righteousness. Many Lutheran ministers began to inform themselves concerning the social movements of the day and preached special sermons when flagrant evils were brought to public attention.

Among the official Lutheran bodies, only the Pittsburgh Synod, the synod of Passavant and Stuckenberg on the scene of great industrial operations, showed any signs of social concern. Citing statements of the Federal Council, this synod in 1914 protested against labor conditions in industry and social conditions in general. Some of the other synods adopted occasional resolutions on select evils, such as gambling, drunkenness, breaking the Sabbath, divorce, atrocities in the Congo, lynching, and the white slave traffic. But repeatedly the Pittsburgh Synod returned to the need of general Christian social reform. In 1913 it appointed a standing committee on "The Church and Social Service." Responding to challenges from Pittsburgh the General Synod affirmed its interest in existing social conditions but stated its conviction that the church can make its best contribution to the solution of social problems by holding itself strictly to its "churchly" duty of preaching the gospel, winning individual members of society to salvation, and using their consecrated lives in service for

Christ's kingdom. The same sentiment was repeated and emphasized at the meeting of the General Synod in 1915.

With the approach of formation of the United Lutheran Church, in the interest of harmony, churchmen, writers and synods within the General Synod curbed their zeal for social action and stinted their co-operation in general Christian enterprise. The General Council and the United Synod in the South had not as yet felt the impact of the social gospel as had large sections of the General Synod, and they were repelled by the liberalism that then characterized the Federal Council. These bodies had been content to express their social interest by importing from Germany the institution of "inner missions," which included such benevolent activities as homes for orphans and the aged, hospitals and deaconess houses, work with seamen and immigrants, and missions among prisoners and in blighted areas of large cities. These activities, emphasizing Christian evangelism and the responsibility of the congregations, were the main expression of social interest for most Lutheran groups before the 1930's.

The organization of the National Lutheran Council in 1918 gave the Lutherans of America a new sense of strength and responsibility. At the same time they became aware of great social need among Lutherans which called for large-scale emergency measures. This opened a new period in the history of social action among Lutherans.

An express purpose of the Council was "to co-ordinate the activities of the church and its agencies for the solution of new problems which affect the religious life and consciousness of the people, e.g. social, economic, and education conditions." This became an increasing purpose of the Council through the years. The Council's service to wartime industrial communities and program of rehabilitation and reconstruction in Europe had as a by-product the arousing among Lutheran clergymen and laymen of an intelligent interest in the social causes of human misery.

After the Stockholm Conference on Life and Work in 1925, standing committees were appointed in several American Lutheran bodies to report on problems of "social and moral welfare." Some of these agencies made incisive studies of the duty of the Christian churches in relation to social ills. They spelled out the diseases of society and pointed to the moral evils that caused them. They called on their churches to condemn these evils in the spirit of the prophets of the Old Testament and to apply the remedies in the spirit of Christ and the Apostles. They not only condemned such evils as gambling, racketeering, exploitation, bribery, sexual laxity, and class and race prejudice, but pointed to the inequities of the economic system and declared it a basic duty of the church to help remedy the causes of these conditions. They called on organized Christian groups to influence legislation to produce economic and social justice. These reports and the actions of the Lutheran bodies endorsing them received wide publicity. Printed in religious publications and made subjects of comment in Lutheran pulpits, they registered a decided change in the attitude of Lutherans toward their Christian responsibility for the temporal as well as eternal welfare of the human race.

In 1933 the National Lutheran Council set up a Committee on Social Trends, which, with competent assistance, studied the relation of church and state, moving pictures, the use of leisure, family and divorce, crime and lawlessness, gambling, the Sunday question, economic and social security, and the effects of communism. These topics were studied in relation to the teachings of Christ and the life of the church, and a collection was made of all pronouncements of Lutheran bodies on these subjects.

The committee also made a comprehensive survey of the inner mission agencies of all the Lutheran churches in America, as a result of which the National Lutheran Council in 1938 established a Department of Welfare as a clearing-house and co-ordinating agency. Its purpose was to mobilize Lutheran welfare agencies in all the participating bodies, to co-ordinate their work, and to relate their programs of service to those of the local community, the state and the nation. The department undertook Lutheran representation of welfare work before general and governmental agencies. It established standards for social service among Lutherans and promoted the training of workers for Lutheran agencies. It planned the co-ordination of Lutheran efforts to meet common human needs in time of general disaster. Finally, the department from time to time opened up new fields of social service with recommendations for such work as disaster relief and aid to certain racial groups.

Under its 1945 constitution the National Lutheran Council's Department of Welfare became a division, and one of the four major areas of co-operation among the participating bodies. The Committee on Social Trends became the study department of this division. The division now recruits qualified staff workers for all Lutheran agencies and for community services as well. It maintains a consultation and survey service to help Lutheran welfare agencies readjust their programs and methods to meet changing social conditions. The inner mission societies and agencies were brought into official relation with the church, and the division now began to serve more than 350 Lutheran health and welfare agencies and institutions. It assists the Lutheran Hospital Association, organized in 1948, and National Lutheran Nurses Guild, organized in 1940 to represent 14,500 Lutheran nurses. It trains and directs the work of chaplains in 172 veterans' hospitals and elsewhere. It has helped to raise and maintain standards of service to the aging. Through the division, the National Lutheran Council after World War II resettled more than 36,000 refugees at a cost of about $6,000,000. The division maintains services to children and families, to those who are chronically ill, to neglected rural areas and minority groups. It participates in the program of the Lutheran World Federation's Department of World Service. In all this social activity the Division of Welfare emphasizes preventive measures as well as remedial services, and presents social welfare as a part of the Christian mission of the church.

Meanwhile all Lutheran bodies were variously responding to similar impulses and organizing for social work. The United Lutheran Church merged its Committee on Moral and Social Welfare, its Inner Mission Board, and its Committee on Evangelism, to form its Board of Social Missions. The American Lutheran Church changed its Board of Charities into a Board of Christian Social Action. The Augustana Lutheran Church set up a Commission on Social Missions and later added a Committee on Moral and Social Problems. The Evangelical Lutheran Church set up a Board of Charities, as did the American Evangelical Lutheran Church. The congregations of the Missouri Synod organized the Associated Lutheran Charities. All these agencies except the last lean heavily on the National Lutheran Council's Division of Welfare for placement consultation, for coordination of programs, for recruiting, for public relations and fundraising, for surveys and standards, and for other technical services.

Since World War II, Lutheran social activities and pronouncements have entered new areas that would have seemed unapproachable a generation earlier. Lutherans have concerned themselves with Christian citizenship, international affairs, diplomatic representation, the United Nations, Christian interracial principles, tariff and international trade, alcohol, the conservation of food, federal relief to famine sufferers, social security for old age, universal military training, the atomic and hydrogen bombs. The influence of church groups is now regularly exerted upon lawmaking bodies.

Affirming the unity of all spheres of life and refusing to separate religious life from economics and politics, Lutheran theologians and church leaders in America set forth the fulness of the gospel, as Luther taught it and as Lutherans understand it, in every aspect of modern life.

Among all the Lutheran bodies in America in 1963 there were more than 450 welfare agencies and institutions, employing about 16,000 workers, with annual operating expenses of more than $110,000,000, and property worth about $40,000,000. Periodical meetings at national, regional, and state levels bring together National Lutheran Council groups in the Lutheran Welfare Conference in America, an affiliate of the Division of Welfare. The Conference is constituted of about 250 organizations for Christian welfare and social work and about 500 individuals interested in such work. In recent years regional meetings of the Social Welfare Conference have been held simultaneously with regional meetings of the Associated Lutheran Charities of the Missouri Synod, and since 1953 there have been joint sessions of the two national groups.

At mid-century Lutherans were prepared to bear corporate witness to the power of the gospel as a leaven in social life. To the multitudes who are caught in the hard social conditions imposed by the industrial, economic, and political situation of our time, such witness through social action may prove to be more convincing than organic union or any other testimony that Lutherans might present. Certainly it has no less scriptural warrant.

CHAPTER 35

THE LUTHERAN WORLD FEDERATION

With the many international contacts that came after 1910 it was to be expected that the Lutherans of America would establish relationships with the many other Lutherans of the world. Widening horizons suggested ecumenical movements among Lutherans.

Lutheran congregations began to unite into synods as early as 1748. Lutheran synods began to unite into general bodies in 1820. General bodies of Lutherans began to merge into larger units in 1917. Linking these larger units were federations and co-operative agencies. The next step in this historical process was to be Lutheran international organization. This has been achieved, and Lutherans in America have played a large part in its development.

American Lutherans became world-conscious through the work of the National Lutheran Council during and after the World War of 1914-1918. Having felt little of the ravages of war, they were moved to undertake a ministry of mercy among the millions of suffering Lutherans in Europe. American commissioners administering reconstruction and relief funds in some eighteen countries made many personal acquaintances which ripened into fellowship. This experience suggested to some of them that it might be well to form a world federation of Lutheran churches for mutual encouragement and support. Dr. John A. Morehead so proposed in 1919 in the report of the European commissioners to the National Lutheran Council. The idea commended itself as a practical one, with great possibilities for the kingdom of God, and the Council appointed a committee to draft tentative plans for world association and to enter into negotiations with the Lutherans of Europe through the chairman of the European commission.

In Europe for fifty years the General Evangelical Lutheran Conference had been made up chiefly of representative men from the German Lutheran state churches. Men from the free churches joined the conference near the end of the nineteenth century. Meeting at intervals of several years, it gave its time to doctrinal and theoretical discussion. During the first quarter of the twentieth century, men from Sweden, Denmark, Norway, and occasionally other countries met with the conference. Sometimes the General Council in America was represented.

Also in Germany there was the smaller Lutheran League (*Lutherischer Bund*) organized in 1907 by the stricter Lutherans who withdrew from the General Conference because it admitted to full membership those "Union Lutherans" who remained in the Prussian Union.

In the Scandinavian lands there was much Lutheran intercourse across boundaries. From the middle of the nineteenth century their deaconess motherhouses, foreign missions, Lutheran students, Lutheran bishops, and ministers' associations had met in regular and stated conferences. It was easy to reach the Lutherans of the north as a group through the General Lutheran Conference centering in Germany.

To the General Conference and the Lutheran League, the National Lutheran Council in America sent its suggestion for a world convention of Lutherans. They approved. The general bodies in America acted favorably in 1920, and the General Conference and the National Lutheran Council named a joint committee. The representatives of the League, by choice, held a purely advisory relation to the committee.

The Americans on the committee drafted convention plans and the Europeans approved them with modifications. Eisenach in Germany was agreed upon as the place of meeting and August, 1923, as the time. Invitations were issued jointly by the National Lutheran Council and the General Lutheran Conference.

When the roll of the first Lutheran World Convention was called on August 19, 151 delegates responded. The number was kept small to permit personal contacts and thus provide for the free exchange of information and ideas. Delegates came from twenty-two nations: United States, Canada, France, Denmark, Sweden, Norway, Holland, Finland, Estonia, Latvia, Poland, Germany, Czechoslovakia, Jugoslavia, Roumania, Russia, Hungary, Austria, India, China, Australia, and

South Africa. Spain was also represented in the personal greetings of Theodore Fliedner. From America there were seventeen official delegates of all general bodies except Missouri. Thousands of visitors attended. Bishop Ihmels of Saxony presided. Such topics as the plans and progress of international relief, the ecumenical character of Lutheranism, what Lutherans can contribute to Christian unity, and others, were discussed. A dramatic feature of the six days was a celebration at the Wartburg Castle with a public act of confession in the courtyard, the united recital of the Creed, and the rendition of Luther's battle hymn in a great variety of tongues.

So strongly was Lutheran unity felt that a continuation of the World Convention was decided upon, and a permanent organization set up. This doctrinal statement was adopted: "The Lutheran World Convention acknowledges the Holy Scriptures of the Old and New Testaments as the only source and infallible norm of all church doctrine and practice, and sees in the Confessions of the Lutheran Church, especially in the Unaltered Augsburg Confession and Luther's Small Catechism, a pure exposition of the Word of God." Some of the delegates from America were active in drawing up the affirmation of faith and in laying plans for the continuation of the body.

The permanent organization provided for two committees, a large one whose purpose was contact with the Lutheran populations in the various countries, and an executive committee of two members each from America, Scandinavia, and Germany. The executive committee was charged with preparations for the next assembly of the World Convention and with such tasks as the harmonizing of Lutheran relief and reconstruction work, the care of migrating Lutheran groups, provision for emergency co-operation in foreign missions, unity of utterance and action among Lutherans when grave reasons require, exchange of visitors, and the collection and dissemination of significant church news and statistics. With Dr. Morehead as chairman, the executive committee met annually in various European centers to deal, first, with problems of relief, particularly for the Lutherans in Russia. Also plans were laid for a world-wide celebration of the four-hundredth anniversary of Luther's Catechism in 1929 and the four-hundredth anniversary of the Augsburg Confession in 1930.

A second world convention met in Copenhagen, June 26 to July 4, 1929, with 149 delegates from 43 churches, 30 of them from nine

American Lutheran churches. Dr. Morehead presided. The program provided more widely ranging discussion and greater consideration of practical issues than had the Eisenach meeting. The political and economic situation of the world at that time emphasized a host of social issues, and the discussions at Copenhagen reflected the interest of Lutherans in those issues. The doctrinal statement adopted at Eisenach in 1923 was repeated. One day's sessions, incidentally, were held in Lund, Sweden.

The executive committee reported its deputation work among Lutheran minorities, its work of relief among weak, distressed and endangered Lutheran churches totaling over $133,000, its regular publication in English and German of a News Exchange Bulletin, its publication in English, German, and Danish of a handbook of world Lutheranism entitled *The Lutheran Churches of the World* and the success of its efforts to make the convention at Copenhagen more representative and official than the previous one.

At Copenhagen the Lutheran World Convention decided to continue as a free assembly without binding power, with an organization as simple as possible, and with complete autonomy of all co-operating churches. The church bodies were asked to appoint their own committees to further the cause of world Lutheranism within their own bounds. The executive committee was charged with responsibilities relating to Lutheran unity, works of mercy, social problems, publicity, foreign missions, and the exchange of students, professors, and literature. Dr. Morehead was again chosen to head the committee, now as president of the Lutheran World Convention. To accept the office he resigned his post as executive director of the National Lutheran Council in America.

The executive committee continued to devote much care to weak and suffering Lutheran churches throughout the earth, particularly in Soviet Russia. About $75,000 a year was spent for this purpose, including the maintenance of the Lutheran seminary in Leningrad. But additional problems were now presented by world-wide economic depression, the trials of the Lutheran minorities in the states bordering on Russia, the turn of the tide of European immigration to South America, the appeals of the host of Lutheran refugees from Russia gathered at Harbin in Manchuria and the necessity of transporting them to South America, and other special conditions. A vast field for international Lutheran endeavor was opened before the World Convention movement, and our narrative of the work of the National Lutheran Council has indicated what a large part the Lutheran people in America had in that international program.

The third meeting of the Lutheran World Convention was held in Paris, October 13 to 20, 1935. This gathering was in effect an executive session, a "working convention." The 90 delegates came from 21 countries, 15 of them from American Lutheran churches. Representation was limited to the church heads and a few of their advisers, and the program was confined to consideration of the most pressing practical problems: inner missions and human welfare, jeopardized foreign missions, the training of the church's youth, the threatening political crisis, and the oppressed Lutheran minorities. The president of the United Lutheran Church in America, Dr. F. H. Knubel, a member of the executive committee, presented plans for reorganization of the Convention. The purpose of the Lutheran World Convention was now declared to be "to bring the Lutheran Churches and organizations of the world into an enduring relationship with one another in order to promote oneness of faith and confession and to ward off antagonistic and hostile influences." It was decided that the Convention should meet every five years, and that there should be a full-time executive secretary working under the direction of the executive committee. It was also decided to enlarge the executive committee from six members to twelve, thus increasing the number of Americans on the Committee to four. The Committee chose Bishop A. Marahrens of Germany as president, Dr. F. H. Knubel, vice-president, Dr. Hanns Lilje, executive secretary, and Dr. Morehead, honorary president for life.

The Paris convention declared emphatically that the church must help to bring about a better social order, and that the Lutheran church must make its influence felt on society through a sympathetic understanding of the social ills of our age, by witnessing fearlessly to the divinely ordained principles of social justice, by training Christians for the various branches of civic servce, and by establishing a sound social order in its own midst.

After the Paris meeting of 1935 the executive committee of the Lutheran World Convention planned to hold the next general meeting in Philadelphia in 1940. Three commissions were appointed to prepare studies of three topics under the general theme, "The Lutheran Church of Today." To the German commission was assigned the subtopic, "The Church, Word and Sacrament"; to the Scandinavian, "The Church and the Churches"; to the American, "The Church and the World." Six American Lutheran scholars had prepared voluminous reports on the church of today in its various relations, domestic, political, economic, cultural and educational, and the American committee on arrangements was rounding out its practical plans for the first convention of world Lutheranism on American soil, when in September, 1939, the heavy political clouds suddenly burst into World War II. The meeting of the Lutheran World Convention was indefinitely postponed, and even the meetings of the executive committee could not be resumed until 1946.

During the war years the actual work of the Lutheran World Convention rested on the American members of the executive committee and the eight other Lutherans in America who constituted "The American Section of the Lutheran World Convention," while the National Lutheran Council served as their agent in gathering and administering funds for missions, refugees, European relief, and ministry to prisoners of war. In July, 1945, Dr. S. C. Michelfelder was sent to Geneva to organize and direct the ministrations of Americans through Lutheran World Action to the suffering Lutherans in Europe.

At a meeting in Sweden in July, 1946, Archbishop Eidem was chosen president of the executive committee and Dr. Michelfelder recording secretary. The next convention of world Lutheranism was planned for the summer of 1947. Political and economic conditions in Europe at that time made it unfeasible to send delegates to America. So at Lund, Sweden, the fourth assembly of the Lutheran World Convention met from June 30 to July 6, 1947, bringing together 174 official representatives of the Lutheran churches in 23 nations. For the first time since the war, men from former enemy countries faced each other as brethren and in their common faith felt the bonds of concord and understanding. From America came 44 official delegates, representing all the general bodies of the National Lutheran Council. The Missouri Synod sent visitors. Fifty-five German theologians and church leaders were present.

Most of the assembly's time was taken by the three sections to which the delegates had been assigned for the discussion of the general topic: "The Lutheran Church in the World Today." Section I dealt with theological topics under the subtitle, "The Church Confessing the Truth in a Confused World." The section stated afresh the Lutheran position on the Word, the sacraments, and the church. Section II applied itself to a discussion of evangelism, stewardship, missions, reconstruction, and interchurch aid, under the sub-topic, "The Church Performing her Mission in a Devastated World." Section III, dealing with "The Church Facing the Problems in a Troubled World," prepared a report on practical aspects of common efforts for man's freedom, such as racial and political tensions, refugees and displaced persons, and international understanding and reconciliation.

With reference to the theological discussions at Lund the observation of a competent neutral observer is relevant here: "To be noted was the more activistic trend that marked this conference in comparison with earlier Lutheran world conventions. Undoubtedly the stronger influence now wielded by the American and the Scandinavian contingent is indicated by this fact . . . It is not to be denied that the Germans, as hitherto, are more well-grounded theologians than the Americans, who interest themselves in the practical rather than the theoretical. Theologically the Scandinavians stand closer to the Germans."

The most important action at Lund was the adoption of a constitution. For twenty-three years the Lutheran World Convention had functioned without a constitution, guided simply by a few paragraphs adopted at Eisenach in 1923. Before the Lund assembly, a small committee of Americans appointed by the president of the Convention prepared the draft of a constitution which proposed to fashion an organization of world Lutheranism with clear purposes and well-defined functions. A change of name was proposed, from Lutheran World Convention to Lutheran World Federation, to indicate greater compactness and efficiency, to suggest permanence, to make possible wider areas of co-operation, and to insure the official participation of churches without sacrifice of their sovereignty or autonomy. The Lund assembly formally adopted the constitution, and this marked a turning-point in the history of world Lutheranism. The constitution provided the Lutheran forces of the world with more systematic and more durable integration than they had ever known before.

The assembly of the Federation now meets every five or six years and the executive committee every year. There is a national committee in each country. Provision is made for the appointment of special departments and commissions to discharge designated functions in the Federation program. The executive committee was enlarged in 1947 from twelve to sixteen members in order to include representatives of minority churches and the younger churches.

Much of the leadership in the Lund Assembly fell upon Lutherans from America. The entire committee on constitution, and the chairmen of the committees on credentials, on resolutions, and on messages were Americans. The American members of the executive committee were called on to preside over most of the business sessions of the assembly. Of the three sections into which the assembly divided itself for the purpose of discussing reports, the first and second had Americans as chairmen. The preliminary report of Section II on "The Church Performing her Mission in a Devastated World" had been prepared by a committee of Lutherans in America. Lutheran delegates from America were active in the discussions in the sections, in the drafting of the reports for the sections, and in conducting the devotions of the assembly.

American Lutherans were also asked to accept responsibilities for the permanent organization of the Federation and its continuing work. The permanent committee on membership was constituted of Americans. Of the four delegates from America who were elected to the executive committee, one was chosen first vice-president of the Federation and one treasurer of the committee. Of the fifteen international special commissions appointed for particular lines of service, five had Americans as chairmen: World Missions, Stewardship, Student Work, Publications, and Publicity; three others had Americans as vice-chairmen: Evangelism, Inner Missions, and International Affairs. And finally, the office of executive secretary was assigned to Dr. Michelfelder.

After the Lund assembly, the American section secured action by the eight member churches in the United States and Canada authorizing the National Lutheran Council to act as the United States National Committee for the Lutheran World Federation. The constitution of the Council was amended accordingly. The Council is charged with all matters in America related to the work of the

Federation, and for this purpose has a separate Division of Lutheran World Affairs. Not the least of the Council's services has been to make the people in the Lutheran churches of America aware of the Federation and interested in its work.

The second assembly of the Federation at Hannover, Germany, July 25 to August 3, 1952, was attended by 1,150 Americans. Forty-nine were delegates, 40 alternates, and about 100 official visitors. Among unofficial visitors comprising the others from America were 20 guests from the Missouri Synod. The number of delegates from all member churches was 203, the number of alternates about the same, and the number of official visitors, more than four times as large. More than 1,500 Lutheran youth, 279 of them from America, thronged a simultaneous youth convention of their own, concluding with an enthusiastic rally of 25,000 young people. In addition, tens of thousands of visitors from European countries attended the popular evening meetings and mass rallies of the assembly. The climax came at a concluding act of worship in which 65,000 Lutherans from all around the globe joined in song and creed and other testimony. The Lutherans of the whole world were lifted to a new height of solidarity and fellowship.

The central theme of the Hannover assembly was "The Living Word in a Responsible Church." Preliminary reports on six subtopics had been prepared in advance, some in Europe, some in America. Two of the six study sections into which the delegates to the assembly were divided had Americans as chairmen: Section II, "World Missions," and Section IV, "Evangelism and Stewardship." An American helped to draft the report of Section I, "Theology." Another was co-chairman of Section III, "Inner Missions." Lutherans from America were active participants also in the other two sections: Section V, "Students and Youth," and Section VI, "Women of the Church."

Further evidence of the leading role of Americans among the world's Lutherans was their addresses to the assembly, and the chairing of four of the six plenary sessions by American members of the executive committee. Other positions of leadership assigned to American delegates were the chairmanship of the credentials committee, the nominations committee, the business committee, and the staff of recording secretaries.

To make room for more laymen, the Hannover assembly enlarged the executive committee of the Federation from sixteen to twenty.

This gave five members of the central body to each of the major sections of world Lutheranism, Germany, Scandinavia, and America, and five to the younger and minority Lutheran churches as a group. This assembly also took definite steps to publish a Lutheran World Encyclopedia. The structure of the Federation also was improved by the assembly at Hannover. Three "departments" were set up in order to classify and channel the variety of practical tasks that had piled up in the program of world Lutheranism in the course of the years. The Department of Theology was given a threefold aim: to promote co-operative study among Lutherans across international boundaries on such theological themes as may be assigned to it by the Federation assembly or its executive committee; to stimulate and co-ordinate the exchange of personnel, professors, pastors, students, and laymen; and to facilitate the translation and publication of important theological and church literature. The work of this department is expected to discharge the Federation's constitutional function "to cultivate unity of faith and confession among the Lutheran churches of the world." It is intended to qualify Lutherans to confer helpfully with other denominations and to participate constructively in such ecumenical organizations as the World Council of Churches.

The Department of Lutheran World Service was charged with responsibility to survey and list the special needs of Lutheran groups, to plan for the supply of those needs through the co-operation of all the member churches of the Federation, and to alert the entire Federation immediately concerning critical emergency needs that may arise anywhere in the world. This department co-ordinates on an international level all projects of interchurch aid, service to refugees, and other emergency work. It is designed to carry out the Federation's constitutional commission "to develop a united Lutheran approach to the responsibilities in missions and education, and to support Lutheran groups in need of spiritual or material aid." This department is headed by an American Lutheran and will apply the program of Lutheran World Action to all the members of the Federation.

The Department of World Missions was set up to carry responsibility for orphaned missions, to enlarge the areas of co-operation among the mission boards and societies of the sending churches, and to promote contacts and co-operation among the younger churches. This new department is an extension of the National Lutheran Council's

Commission on Younger Churches and Orphaned Missions, and the Council's commission has transferred its entire program and assets to this department of the Federation.

An organizational pattern for the continuing administration of each field of interest has been established. Through the quinquennial assembly, composed of delegates who are the direct representatives of the member churches, the broad policies of the Federation are determined and the executives chosen. Through the national committees the program of the Federation and its agencies is channeled to the individual member churches in all the countries and the needs of the churches are conveyed to the Federation and its executives. Through the international commissions, specialized knowledge and professional skill are applied to long-range studies in various areas of interest to all. And through the newly organized departments the many and varied tasks of the Federation are assembled and grouped for practical execution by a qualified staff of directors and assistants. The new form of the Federation and the new degree of solidarity manifested at Hannover in 1952 were a long step forward toward the goal of world-wide Lutheran faith and fellowship.

The Lutherans of the world were closer to unified intelligence and the consciousness of solidarity than they had ever been in the four centuries of their history. They had lifted their eyes above the limitations of language and nation and ecclesiastical organization. In the conscious efforts toward this end the Lutherans of America had a leading part, and this reacted in a most wholesome manner upon their relations among themselves.

CHAPTER 36

RECENT MOVES TOWARD
LUTHERAN UNION

The organizational history of the Lutheran churches in America since colonial times is a narrative of combinations—of individuals or families into congregations, of congregations into synods or districts, and of synods into general bodies. General bodies have joined in conferences or co-operative groups, and moved toward organic merger. This process has never been facile. Often it has taken the form of contact and rebound, of thesis and antithesis. But the perspective of the generations reveals creative power in the spirited debates of the Lutherans, and their groups have always tended toward better understanding, closer approach, and even synthesis and merger. Lutheran units have diminished in number and increased in size. Gradually Lutherans have prepared for a strong common program of action on behalf of the kingdom of God on earth.

The process of unification has been accelerated in the mid-century. After the formation of the Evangelical Lutheran Church in 1917 and the United Lutheran Church in 1918, and particularly after the organization of the American Lutheran Church and then the American Lutheran Conference in 1930, Lutheran bodies have been looking eagerly beyond their boundaries for new possibilities of larger units. In every major body there is a committee or commission charged with developing inter-Lutheran relationships. Contacts have been multiplied on all levels, and in geographic, administrative, and educational programs. Programs of co-operation have been undertaken among different Lutheran bodies, in cities, counties, and states. The National Lutheran Council has provided a wide program of common action by two-thirds of the Lutherans in America and in a few limited areas has achieved co-ordination with the remaining large Lutheran body, the Missouri Synod.

In these years the discovery of large areas of common faith has dulled the edge of theological animosities, and repeated contacts with Lutherans of other countries and with Christians of other churches has deepened the sense of common interest among American Lutherans. The persistent hostility of the nineteenth century has already given way to armistice and the success of these limited mergers has encouraged efforts at still more inclusive mergers.

When The United Lutheran Church in America was organized in 1918, at a single stroke it had reunited into a strongly centralized organic union one-third of all the Lutherans in America. Not satisfied with this achievement in Lutheran solidarity, the new body in the preamble of its constitution signified its desire to move in the direction of more general union. It stated: "recognizing our duty as the people of God to make the inner unity which we have with one another manifest in the common confession, defense and maintenance of our faith, and . . . conscious of our need of mutual assistance and encouragement, and relying upon the promise of the divine Word that He who hath begun this work will perfect it until the day of Christ Jesus, (we) hereby unite, and now invite and until such end be attained continue to invite all Evangelical Lutheran congregations and synods in America, one with us in the faith, to unite with us, upon the terms of this constitution, in one general organization." This stated no definite terms for a new organization, but invited negotiations that might lead to a united Lutheran church of America.

In its Washington Declaration two years later the United Lutheran Church referred thus to the relation of Lutheran church bodies to one another: "In the case of those Church Bodies calling themselves Evangelical Lutheran and subscribing the Confessions which have always been regarded as the standards of Evangelical Lutheran doctrine, the United Lutheran Church in America recognizes no doctrinal reasons against complete co-operation and organic union with such bodies." This principle of union on the sole basis of the Lutheran confessions continued to be fundamental with the United Lutheran Church but that did not prevent the United Lutherans from joining in conversations and conferences concerning certain details of doctrine and practice. For that purpose the United Lutheran Church in 1928 appointed a Commission on Lutheran Church Unity with instructions to work for "the promotion of Lutheran unification in America."

The first contact made by this commission was with a similar commission of the Augustana Synod. It will be recalled that the Augustana Synod, formerly a member of the General Council which became part of the United Lutheran Church in 1918, and largely middle western, had been deterred chiefly by language barriers from much part in the doctrinal controversies that disturbed the other Lutheran bodies of the Middle West in the second half of the nineteenth century. There were already many ties of friendship between the two bodies when their commissions met early in 1930 and decided to extend their co-operation and to explore organic union between them. But a few months later an Augustana Synod convention voted to join in organizing the American Lutheran Conference, in which the United Lutheran Church had no part. Nevertheless its Committee on Church Unity was instructed to "concern itself in the main with methods of closer co-operation of the Augustana Synod and the United Lutheran Church."

The American Lutheran Conference regarded itself as occupying a mediating position between the United Lutheran Church on the left and the Missouri Synod on the right. The major doctrinal issue of the long and furious controversies waged by the Missouri Synod against a number of other synods was that of election and predestination. It could not be resolved because of different attitudes toward the confessions and the interpretation of Scripture. The other Lutheran churches, facing enormous practical tasks following World War I, gradually developed a further degree of toleration and mutual respect, but Missouri would not yield her fundamental doctrinal position which, as we have seen (Chapter 24), other Lutherans called new and heretical. When the three Norwegian Lutheran bodies adopted the Madison Agreement in 1912 preparatory to their merger in 1917, the Synodical Conference promptly voiced its disagreement, charging that the document is inconsistent because one part of it teaches that faith is the cause of our election to salvation while another part teaches that faith is the result of our election. When efforts to prevent the Norwegian merger failed, Missouri said the union of the Evangelical Lutheran Church was based "on common blood rather than a common Christian faith," and rejected fellowship unless the basic agreement of union was revised "to bring it into harmony with the Lutheran Confessions." The watchmen of Missouri continued to deplore the Evangelical Lutheran Church's continuing on its clerical roll ministers who teach millenarianism, or who, accepting the social gospel, labor for a more Christian social order, or who hold "modern" views of the inspiration of the Bible. They protested that the Evangelical Lutheran Church did not expel from its fellowship laymen and clergymen who belong to lodges, and that it tolerated ministers who make themselves guilty of "unionism" by participating in worship services with non-Lutheran ministers. All these errors of doctrine and practice would have to be corrected before Missouri could consider union with the Norwegian body.

Representative writers and speakers of the Missouri Synod were also very critical at the founding of the United Lutheran Church. They did not object to its confessional basis, but found numerous errors of doctrine on the part of many of its prominent pastors and theology teachers. Questioning the title word "United," they pointed to variations among the constituent synods in doctrine and in practice. They objected to the lack of uniformity in the theological instruction of candidates for the ministry. They pointed out that the writers on theological subjects did not agree with Dr. Walther's new teaching on predestination. They branded many writers and teachers in the United Lutheran Church as "modernists" and "liberalists" because they did not accept the verbal theory of inspiration. They were particularly disturbed because the constitution of the United Lutheran Church left to the constituent synods the discipline of ministers for heresy, for lodgery, and for "unionism," evils that the Missourians found rampant in the United Lutheran Church.

Missouri Synod spokesmen charged the United Lutheran Church with indifference to doctrinal refinements, and wrote: "Factions characterize the U.L.C., and lines of cleavage run horizontally, vertically, and diagonally through the entire body. To look upon the merger (the U.L.C.) therefore as a rallying-point for Lutheran union is simply to ignore facts so evident and so easily ascertained that ignorance on this point is hardly to be excused."

Thus there was clearly no present likelihood of merger between the Missouri Synod and the United Lutheran Church in America. Yet the Missouri Synod said officially that one of its purposes in forming the Synodical Conference was "the uniting of all Lutheran synods of America into one orthodox American Lutheran church," and the United Lutheran Church said officially that it "recognizes no doctrinal reasons against complete co-operation and organic union with such bodies." The Spirit of God working through the historical process would require a full generation to consummate such a union.

In the Augustana Lutheran Church, too, the Missouri Synod found errors of doctrine and aberrations in practice. The Augustana Lutheran Church had officially disapproved Dr. Walther's doctrine on predestination and had approved the teaching that God predestines to salvation those concerning whom He foreknows that they will believe in Christ. Many Augustana Lutherans refused to subscribe to the theory of verbal inspiration, some taught millenialism, it was charged, and some held to the theory of evolution. As to practice, the spokesmen of the Missouri Synod objected to the participation of Augustana ministers and people in union services of worship, to the lowering of the bars against secret societies, to their favorable attitude toward prohibition, to their fellowship with such modernists as the Swedish Lutheran Archbishop Söderblom, and to the friendliness they showed to Lutheran representatives of European state-churchism. Missouri called for conferences to settle these matters before beginning discussions concerning organic union with the Augustana Lutheran Church.

When the American Lutheran Church was formed in 1930 of the former Joint Synod of Ohio, Iowa Synod, and Buffalo Synod, its constitution was subject to careful scrutiny by the theologians of the Missouri Synod. For more than fifty years Missouri had been in process of theological controversy with those bodies without reaching agreement. The men of Missouri were glad to see in the constitution of the American Lutheran Church the paragraphs against unionistic practices and against secret societies. But their joy was tempered by the fact that the constitution of the new body was somewhat indefinite concerning the doctrine of verbal inspiration and the absolute inerrancy of Scripture. Missouri could not be sure the American Lutheran Church intended to make the inerrancy and authority of the Bible apply to its historical and scientific statements as well as to matters of "faith and life." There did seem to be a slight concession to the Missouri doctrine on election, because the American Lutheran

Church did not say that man had any "sense of responsibility" in accepting God's grace but only in rejecting it. But in view of the fact that leaders in the Joint Synod of Ohio had only recently branded Walther's teaching on predestination as "the new-Missouri calvinistic heresy," the men of the Synodical Conference decided to suspend judgment about the possibility of fellowship with the new body until it should become clear what company the new body would keep. In the meantime they admitted, "In its temper and spirit, its public testimony, its preaching, its attitude towards social political questions, the American Lutheran Church is more closely related to the Synodical Conference than the other Lutheran synods."

Then the American Lutheran Conference placed the American Lutheran Church in fellowship with the Augustana Lutherans and the Norwegians, frankly taking a position about midway between Missouri and the United Lutheran Church. Organized with the express purpose of occupying the middle place between extremes, it cherished the hope of mediating between the "right wing" and the "left wing" of American Lutheranism. But both the Missouri Synod and the United Lutheran Church reacted negatively.

The Missouri Synod leaders found objectionable features in the Minneapolis Theses, the doctrinal basis of the American Lutheran Conference. They were gratified with the "Lutheran ring" of the declarations on the Scriptures and the confessions. But, they felt, the paragraph on election should have been more explicit so as to exclude any other view than Dr. Walther's. They found the language on church fellowship vague in one phrase, so that it seemed to leave a loop-hole for those who would fellowship with non-Lutherans or unorthodox Lutherans. Also, the statement against lodges was declared ambiguous, so that it could be interpreted to mean that there are some secret societies that are not actually anti-Christian. Then too, there was no statement at all on such controverted subjects as the church and the office of the ministry.

But the chief Missourian objection to the American Lutheran Conference was that it brought together incompatible elements. The Germans and the Scandinavians held opposing views on millenarianism, on prohibition, on parochial schools. The Scandinavians were not so strict with reference to "secretism" as the Germans. They were friendlier towards bodies whose Lutheranism Missouri regarded as diluted. Among the Scandinavians also there was at least one body that officially repudiated verbal inspiration and many individuals in the other bodies that did so. So Missouri charged. Unless the bases of the federation were revised to remove these objectionable features, the Missouri Synod and its associates in the Synodical Conference could not fellowship with the Conference or any of its member bodies.

The United Lutheran Church maintained a discreet silence when the American Lutheran Conference was organized. The National Lutheran Council continued to be a channel of fellowship and co-operation between the United Lutheran Church and the bodies in the American Lutheran Conference, but for several years after 1930, as we have seen, its program faltered. But it soon became clear that the American Lutheran Conference had not intended to disrupt the National Lutheran Council or to weaken its program, but rather to strengthen the Council and perhaps to develop it into a federation of the participating bodies, or even into organic merger. Normal relations were soon restored between the United Lutheran Church and the bodies in the American Lutheran Conference. One concrete evidence of the purpose of the Conference was its turning over to the Council of its well-developed program of student service, thus merging it with that of the United Lutheran Church. Thereafter the Conference devoted its major efforts to the improvement of relations among all the Lutheran bodies in America.

After 1930 there were three chief moves toward Lutheran union, one from the United Lutheran Church, one from the Missouri Synod, and one, the most promising of all, from a group of church bodies in the American Lutheran Conference.

Shortly after the formation of the American Lutheran Conference, lay circles in several Lutheran church bodies, particularly sections of the United Lutheran Church and the American Lutheran Church, began deploring continued division of Lutheranism in America. At the convention of the United Lutheran Church at Savannah in 1934, eight synods appealed for steps to hasten organic union of the Lutheran forces of America. Special mention was made of union with the American Lutheran Conference or specifically the American Lutheran Church. The convention of the United Lutheran Church then adopted the "Savannah Declaration," which led to a definite move toward Lutheran union. This reaffirmed adherence of the church to the Scriptures as the only standard of faith and practice, and its subscription to the historic confessions of the Lutheran church. It also expressed its determination to "set up no other standards or tests of Lutheranism apart from them or alongside of them." Significant was the statement in the Declaration: "We believe that these confessions are to be interpreted in their historical context, not as a law or a system of theology, but (quoting the *Formula of Concord*) 'as a witness and declaration of faith as to how the Holy Scriptures were understood and explained in matters of controversy within the Church of God by those who then lived'." The practical conclusion was that since all Lutheran bodies in America subscribe to these same confessions, "we already possess a firm basis on which to unite in one Lutheran Church in America and there is no doctrinal reason why such a union should not come to pass."

The president of the United Lutheran Church was instructed to communicate this declaration to the other Lutheran church bodies, to invite them to confer with a view to closer relationships, and to appoint a special commission, with some lay members, to conduct discussions that might result from this invitation. The Commission on Lutheran Unity was dismissed. The larger new commission, half lay and half clergy, was significantly called the Special Commission on Relationships to American Lutheran Church Bodies.

The invitation to the various Lutheran church bodies was promptly declined by two of the bodies belonging to the Synodical Conference, the Wisconsin Synod and the Norwegian Synod. They disapproved of the Savannah Declaration and insisted that the situation requires "an exhaustive study of the doctrinal differences that have arisen among Lutherans." The Missouri Synod, however, accepted the invitation. Commissions of the two bodies held two meetings together and, in spite of the instructions to the United Lutheran Church's commission, they engaged in doctrinal discussions. They found large areas of agreement, but at the second meeting they encountered a point of serious difference concerning the definition of inspiration. The commission of the United Lutheran Church could not accept Missouri's theory of verbal inspiration and the statement that the Scriptures are the infallible truth in all their words, even in those "which treat of historical, geographical, and other secular matters." The representatives of the United Lutheran Church said: "We find the words quoted not in accordance with our Lutheran Confessions nor with the Scriptures themselves." No further meetings of the two commissions were held, but, as we have seen, several minor areas of co-operation between the United Lutheran Church and the Missouri Synod were negotiated through the National Lutheran Council.

The American Lutheran Church also accepted the invitation of the United Lutheran Church, and sent commissioners to discuss bases of fellowship and organic union. Several meetings of the two commissions were held. The commission of the United Lutheran Church proposed organic union of the Lutheran church bodies in America on the basis of the Lutheran confessions, but the commission of the American Lutheran Church proposed only to seek pulpit and altar fellowship between the two bodies, and suggested the discussion of three items: secret societies, pulpit and altar fellowship with non-Lutherans, and the inspiration of the Bible. No fault was found with the official utterances of the United Lutheran Church on these matters but questions were raised about the practices of its pastors and people. There was much difficulty with the question concerning the mode of inspiration of the Scriptures. But after working together for more than four years, the two commissions were able to agree upon statements covering all three of the points. Because these statements were adopted by the joint commission at a meeting in Pittsburgh, they are known as the "Pittsburgh Articles of Agreement."

The Pittsburgh Articles were submitted to the United Lutheran Church and the American Lutheran Church at their conventions in 1940. Both churches adopted the Articles, but both with serious misgivings. The American Lutheran Church regarded the statement about inspiration as the acceptance of verbal inspiration by the United Lutheran Church, and its watchmen announced that it would be their policy to wait and see whether the United Lutheran Church would exercise discipline over its members, particularly its ministers, in the matter of lodges and of pulpit and altar fellowship. In the United Lutheran Church there was serious opposition to all the Pittsburgh Articles, especially to the statement concerning the Scriptures. It was argued that the statements are vague throughout, and that on the matter of inspiration they are completely ambiguous and contrary to the clear and careful statement of the Word of God adopted by the United Lutheran Church at its convention in Baltimore in 1938. During the discussion in the convention three of the United Lutheran Church's commissioners recorded their dissent from the Pittsburgh Articles, and seventy-one other delegates presented a signed protest against the action adopting the Articles. They claimed that the Baltimore statement had definitely declined to commit the church to any particular theory of inspiration but that the Pittsburgh Articles do present "an exclusive view of the mode of inspiration."

Thus the adoption of the Pittsburgh Articles of Agreement did not bring organic union or even a declaration of pulpit and altar fellowship between the American and the United Lutheran Churches. The American Lutheran Church was impressed with the fact that such a large and influential group in the United Lutheran Church was in disagreement with the Articles, and they suggested more meetings of the two commissions. The United Lutheran Church replied that it regarded further doctrinal statements as neither necessary nor promising, declared its readiness for full fellowship immediately with the other Lutheran bodies, but refused to impose tests of Lutheranism in addition to the Scriptures or beyond the confessions, and suggested that all Lutherans now lay emphasis upon larger measures of co-operation in the practical work of the church. Subsequent communications between the two bodies were uniformly friendly but achieved no progress towards union. The United Lutheran Church insisted upon the confessions as a sufficient guarantee of true Lutheranism and an adequate basis for merger, while the American Lutheran Church insisted upon further discussion of doctrine and practice for the purpose of "formulating our Church's teaching in the light of current developments and needs."

In the meantime a move for Lutheran union had come from Missouri. The Missouri Synod had once hoped to convert the Joint Synod of Ohio and the Iowa Synod and the Buffalo Synod to the theology of Dr. Walther and thus bring them into the Synodical Conference. In 1925 representatives of these bodies, and of the Wisconsin Synod, had agreed upon a set of articles of union called the Chicago Theses covering all the points at issue among those bodies for seventy years. But when this remarkable document was presented to the synods themselves in 1929, the merger of three of them was imminent, and all of the synods rejected the Chicago Theses.

After the 1930 merger forming the American Lutheran Church,

the Missouri Synod continued to seek doctrinal agreement with a view to pulpit and altar fellowship. In 1932 its "Brief Statement of the Doctrinal Position of the Missouri Synod" stated in about 8,000 words its understanding of the main items in the Christian faith with emphasis upon election, conversion, the church, and verbal inspiration of the Scriptures. The American Lutheran Church appointed a Committee on Fellowship to confer with Missouri's Committee on Lutheran Church Union. After six meetings, the former committee in 1938 accepted the Brief Statement but set forth its own understanding of certain touchy items in a "Declaration of the American Lutheran Church Representatives."

The Missouri Synod at its triennial convention in St. Louis in 1938 accepted the Brief Statement and the Declaration as "the doctrinal basis for future church-fellowship" but listed four "non-fundamental doctrines" in the Declaration concerning which it hoped that *full* agreement would soon be reached. Missouri promised to seek the consent of its sister synods in the Synodical Conference to its fellowship with the American Lutheran Church, and it requested the American Lutheran Church to qualify itself for fellowship by securing the consent of its own sister synods in the American Lutheran Conference.

At this point serious difficulties befell the negotiations. In the Missouri Synod a storm of protest arose against the St. Louis resolutions, as passing over far-reaching differences of doctrine between the Brief Statement and the Declaration. For several years efforts were made to reconcile the two documents. "A Doctrinal Affirmation" was branded by Missouri as "not definite and precise enough to preclude the possibility of misunderstanding." Then a set of changes were proposed under the title "Clarifications." But the opposition only increased. The other synods of the Synodical Conference emphatically declined to concur in the St. Louis resolutions, and attacked the Missouri Synod for negotiating for union with the American Lutheran Church. Moreover, many Missouri Synod Lutherans were dismayed to think that the American Lutheran Church could in the meantime agree with the United Lutheran Church on lodges, pulpit and altar fellowship, and the inspiration of the Scriptures, as the adoption of the Pittsburgh Agreement seemed to imply. The 1947 convention of the Missouri Synod rescinded its 1938 resolutions and declared itself unready for fellowship with the American Lutheran Church because of "the manifest lack of doctrinal unity . . . the difference in conviction regarding the degree of doctrinal unity required for fellowship . . . and the continued membership of the American Lutheran Church in the American Lutheran Conference."

Meanwhile in the American Lutheran Church many critics claimed to find nothing new in the Brief Statement, but only a refinement of certain teachings that were "new" in Dr. Walther's time and which the Iowa and Ohio Synods had resisted for more than seventy years. They refused even to study seriously the Doctrinal Affirmation and its Clarifications. And the other bodies in the American Lutheran Conference firmly refused to be convinced that the Brief Statement, even "in the light of the Declaration," is compatible with the Minneapolis Theses which constituted the doctrinal basis of the Conference.

This seemed to end the prospect of union of the Missouri Synod and the American Lutheran Church. The Missouri Synod turned to her sister synods in the Synodical Conference to seek a procedure for future negotiations that might be agreeable to all, but these efforts failed. The American Lutheran Church turned to her sister synods with better success. But both the Missouri Synod and the American Lutheran Church expressed the hope of continuing their doctrinal conferences, perhaps in company with other Lutheran bodies. It is significant that the Missouri Synod at this time changed the name of its Committee on Lutheran Union and called it thereafter the Committee on Doctrinal Unity.

A third major effort toward Lutheran union began within the American Lutheran Conference in 1948. At its centennial convention that year, the Augustana Lutheran Church proposed organic union of all the bodies participating in the National Lutheran Council, suggesting that federation might be a necessary intermediate step. On invitation, five of the other seven bodies in the Council, all except the Suomi Synod and the American Evangelical Lutheran Church, sent delegates in January, 1949, to the organization of a Committee of Thirty-four on Lutheran Unity, representing about ninety-nine per cent of the Lutherans in the Council. A subcommittee was appointed at once to prepare a structural plan for "closer organizational affiliation." There some regarded immediate organic union as desirable and possible, others felt that only a federation was then possible, and still others were not convinced either that union was possible or that federation was desirable.

This last point of view is explained by the fact that in September, 1949, the president of the United Evangelical (formerly the United Danish) Lutheran Church had called together delegations from his church (about 50,000), the Evangelical Lutheran Church (900,000) and the American Lutheran Church (800,000) to consider immediate organic union, the resulting plan for which was approved by the three bodies at their conventions in 1950.

When, therefore, all the bodies in the National Lutheran Council at their meetings in 1950 faced the questions presented by the Committee of Thirty-four on Lutheran Unity, the Augustana Church, the American Evangelical Lutheran Church, and the United Lutheran Church favored organic union of all the bodies, or federation, if necessary as an intermediate step. The Lutheran Free Church and the Finnish Suomi Synod were opposed to merger but in favor of federation. The Evangelical Lutheran Church was opposed to both. The American Lutheran Church disapproved merger of the National Lutheran Council bodies but, with the United Evangelical Lutheran Church, approved merger of the bodies in the American Lutheran Conference, with the understanding, however, that negotiations for such a merger must not interfere with the plans already made for uniting three of those bodies.

The Augustana Lutheran Church continued to press for inclusion of all of the bodies participating in the National Lutheran Council. The three bodies planning immediate merger among themselves invited the Augustana Church and the Lutheran Free Church to participate in plans for merging all the bodies in the American Lutheran Conference, with the understanding that such planning for a larger merger would not delay the merger already prepared by the three bodies. Tentatively, and with some misgivings, the Augustana Church accepted the invitation.

In discussions within the "Joint Union Committee of the American Lutheran Conference," the men of Augustana were dissatisfied with the limited range of the proposed fellowship and with the attitude of exclusiveness toward other Christian movements. Like the United Lutheran Church, the Augustana Lutheran Church had been participating constructively and fruitfully in such general Christian movements as the National Council of the Churches of Christ in the United States of America and the World Council of Churches, and both of these Lutheran bodies were reluctant to forego this opportunity for Lutheran witness.

Moreover, one of the items in the plan set up for the tripartite merger was a lengthy document entitled "United Testimony on Faith and Life," detailing the Lutheran position on certain Christian doctrines and on certain church practices. It seemed to safeguard the proposed new body against the so-called errors of Missouri, explained and supplemented the Minneapolis Theses, and provided a doctrinal basis for the proposed merged church. For the Augustana Lutheran Church, adherence to the historic confessions of the Lutheran church was sufficient for Lutheran unity, and no additional doctrinal statements were needed. It therefore had some misgivings about the United Testimony. At its convention in 1952 the Augustana Church expressed unwillingness "to continue in unity discussions which are not open to all Lutheran general bodies and which do not include the consideration of the subject of ecumenical relations." But for purposes of participating in the negotiations for union the church declared itself in substantial agreement with the United Testimony, with the understanding however that if that document should be considered in any discussions of broader Lutheran unity it would be further studied and refined.

A union of three bodies within the American Lutheran Conference, namely, the American Lutheran, the Evangelical Lutheran, and the United Evangelical Lutheran churches, and perhaps also the Lutheran Free Church, now seemed to be moving steadily toward its consummation, and would presumably not affect the program of the National Lutheran Council, in which they had all continued an active role.

Meanwhile two other events gave some promise of possible bearing on Lutheran union in the future.

During its 1948 convention the American Lutheran Church sent a telegram to the United Lutheran Church, also in convention at that time, expressing its readiness to receive suggestions from the United Lutheran Church concerning methods for closer affiliation with any and all Lutheran bodies and possible approaches to fuller unity. The reply repeated the essence of the position consistently held by the United Lutheran Church through twenty years of negotiations for Lutheran unity:

"In the conviction that this is God's day for Lutheran Union in America, in glad response to many voices that are being raised among Lutherans in America proposing constructive action toward that goal, and in order to present to a troubled world a more nearly united front for Christ in the proclamation of His Gospel, The United Lutheran Church in America hereby declares to all the bodies now constituting the National Lutheran Council its desire to merge with all or any of them in organic union, and hereby instructs its Special Commission on Relations to American Lutheran Church Bodies to meet with similarly empowered commissions of these bodies to confer upon and negotiate organic union or steps leading thereto, and authorizes its commission to participate in drafting a constitution and devising such organizational procedures as may seem wise in effecting such union, this commission to report its findings to The United Lutheran Church in America for consideration and final action."

The American Lutheran Church recorded its appreciation for this "generous offer" but repeated its conviction that negotiations for organic union must begin with discussion of doctrine and practice. At the same time the American Lutheran Church expressed its gratitude for the cordial relations between the two bodies and declared its purpose to increase the areas of understanding and co-operation between them.

At that same convention in 1948, after plans for fellowship with the Missouri Synod had failed, and while the negotiations for closer approach among all the bodies in the National Lutheran Council were just beginning, the American Lutheran Church authorized its Committee on Fellowship to continue doctrinal discussions with the Missouri Synod's Committee on Doctrinal Unity. By the end of 1949 the two committees, after five joint meetings, approved and presented to their respective bodies "The Common Confession."

The American Lutheran Church adopted the statement in 1950 and expressed its gratification with agreement on doctrines so long in controversy. At the Missouri Synod convention in 1950 there was much objection to the Common Confession, chiefly on the ground that it was too brief and too indefinite and that it did not set forth the distinctive position of the Missouri Synod on such subjects as verbal inspiration, election, conversion, church fellowship, and others. The synod accepted the Common Confession, but not as sufficient for pulpit and altar fellowship between the two bodies, and called for supplementary statements. It also laid plans to determine whether the practice of all the Lutheran congregations in the two bodies would conform with the Common Confession in matters like lodgery and unionism. And the synod decided to seek the approval of the other synods in the Synodical Conference, and requested the American Lutheran Church to do the same with the other bodies in the American Lutheran Conference.

From this narrative of recent moves for Lutheran union it is possible to record several definite trends at mid-century. First, there was a tendency to narrow the area of discussion. The laymen, heard with increasing volume, did not follow the complicated theological reasoning of their ecclesiastical leaders. They saw mainly practical issues. Many pastors, too, found the bitterness of the doctrinal controversies of the nineteenth century incomprehensible. In many quarters there was a willingness to endorse any "agreement" among the theologians, so long as it remained in the field of mere "theory."

In all Lutheran bodies, growing numbers of laymen and pastors were clamoring for "union now," without waiting for further doctrinal agreements, statements, declarations, clarifications, testimonies, or theses.

Moreover, certain doctrinal differences on which long and earnest debate had brought no real agreement were now being simply ignored. Distinction had been made between fundamental and nonfundamental points, and between doctrines of Scripture and theological deductions from such doctrines. The differences in these deductions were removed from dispute. Even on the extreme right wing of American Lutheranism there was no longer a disposition to insist upon complete agreement in all doctrinal matters, even in minor details, or to permit "one and only one interpretation in the church lest she prove disloyal to the Word of God."

The variety in cultural background of American Lutherans was being recognized as an important element in their variety of faith and practice. The study of Lutheran history in America had promoted understanding across the lines of language, nationality, and cultural outlook. There was increasing reference in discussions of Lutheran relationships to the "distinctive genius" of the several branches and bodies. It had proved rewarding to look at Lutheran varieties in America from the point of view of differences in origin and location and historical experience.

The several Lutheran churches in America have not separated from one another. They were planted in isolation, and grew up separately. If they would coalesce at some point in history, this would not be a "reunion of the church," but the result of creative processes of history producing something new. The golden age is in the future, not in the past—we can afford to be patient with the processes of history.

Some Lutherans whose ancestors founded the nation and passed through all the changes of theological climate in three centuries of American culture, including the early anti-confessional decades, are unjustly charged with the so-called aberrations of their ecclesiastical forebears. Their tolerance toward some American practices which Europeans dislike may not be ascribed simply to perversity or a lack of Lutheran loyalty. Among the nineteenth-century immigrants, it is pointed out, "It was not always easy for the German theologian with his desire for exact formulation point by point to understand the freedom which characterized some of the practices of the Norwegians, the Swedes, and the Danes, and there were times when Scandinavians found it difficult to appreciate the practices of some descendants of German ancestors in matters of conduct and life."

This reference to variety of genius, this difference in historical and cultural background, was sometimes charted in great detail. It was made the basis for many pleas for toleration among Lutherans in the midst of their differences. It was argued that the American nation reaches its greatest strength only if each section and each national strain contributes its distinctive genius to the common whole. By analogy Lutheranism can make its greatest contribution to American Christianity not in terms of the least common denominator among the Lutheran bodies but only as each branch of Lutherans contributes in terms of its own genius, its own cultural treasures, and its own historical background. This line of reasoning that Lutheran union must ultimately come not by concession and subtraction but by conviction and addition met some dissenters in every Lutheran body at mid-century, but it kept gaining and it helped to promote patience with the Spirit of God in the historical process.

Enlarging the areas of Lutheran co-operation as an intermediate step toward union proved fruitful in the mergers already accomplished. Co-operation in the work of the kingdom of God is not so serious in its involvements, not so irrevocable, as organic union.

Many who worked together in the National Lutheran Council learned mutual love and trust, and came to expect that ultimate Lutheran union will come after the Council has become the agency of all the Lutheran bodies in America, has been developed into a federation, and has grown into organic union.

Perhaps the harmony of discordant Lutheran forces in America will finally be found, not in the depths of theological discussion and doctrine, or in rarified wishful thinking, or in impulsive action, but in the slow creative grind of the workaday world, the pressure of un-Christian surroundings, and co-operative participation in the kingdom of God on the good solid earth.

The achievements of Lutherans in many practical tasks of the kingdom of God have impressed their neighbor Christians with the social dynamic that lies in the evangelical interpretation of the Word of God. As Lutherans in America gather their forces for a yet more effective witness, they need not yield their sense of history. But they may well enlarge their historical perspective and catch the thrill of a long view into the future of the whole inhabited world. That they are in process of doing this will be clear if we look now at the place they have taken in the modern ecumenical movement.

CHAPTER 37

LUTHERANS IN THE MODERN ECUMENICAL MOVEMENT

The modern ecumenical movement has three dimensions. One is missionary expansion, another is the Christian leavening of society, and the third is church union or Christian unity.

In all three of these elements the Lutheran people of America are vitally concerned. Lutheran leaders in America have sometimes doubted the wisdom of co-operating in the modern ecumenical movement. This has resulted from one-sided emphasis by some Christian leaders, expecially in America, on church union. But as Lutherans have broadened their contacts to the global level, their experiences with the ecumenical movement have been more reassuring.

Two elements in ecumenicity, as they affect Lutherans, have already been presented. American Lutherans have participated in the expansion of Christianity through home and foreign missions, through the National Lutheran Council and its Commission on the Younger Churches and Orphaned Missions, and in the Lutheran World Federation's Department of World Missions. This work has been completely co-ordinated with an ecumenical agency, the International Missionary Council, formed in 1921 as an outgrowth of a World Missionary Conference held in Edinburgh in 1910 with a few Lutherans from America in attendance. The membership of the council consists of various regional and national organizations representing missionary societies and churches. In 1944 sixteen of the twenty-six societies or councils which constituted the International Missionary Council were "National Christian Councils" in so-called missionary or non-Christian lands. This was therefore another general area of contact between Lutherans and other Christians. The "younger churches" of the mission fields, Lutheran and non-Lutheran, were obliged to determine and define their degree of co-operation and unity with one another. This involved their relations with their parent societies or boards, many of which were in America. In most cases the younger Lutheran churches joined their respective National Christian Councils and there bore witness to their distinctive understanding of the gospel. Recent pronouncements of the International Missionary Council, with their clear note on the absoluteness of the Christian religion, the emphasis on the living church of Christ and its indestructibility, the call for a return to the Bible, and the accent upon the centrality of Christ's person have left no doubt about the direction of Christian thinking among the missionary forces of the churches. This trend of thought encouraged Lutheran churches, younger and older, to broaden the areas of their co-operation with the agencies of other churches and to co-ordinate their missionary work with the operations of the International Missionary Council, as they have poured their millions into the maintenance and growth of the missionary orphans of war.

The interest of the Lutheran churches of America in the vertical dimension of ecumenicity—the permeating of all life and culture with Christian motive—has been described as it occurs in the several Lutheran church bodies. It is concretely expressed also in several of the divisions of the National Lutheran Council, particularly in the Division of Welfare with its varied programs to study social trends, to promote Lutheran welfare agencies and institutions, to provide trained workers for social service in congregations and communities, and to represent human well-being before governmental agencies and others. In the Lutheran World Federation the effort to infuse the leaven of Christian love into every part of the social order is expressed through its commissions on education, inner missions, interchurch aid, and international affairs, and especially through the later Department of World Service.

The effort to make a Christian impact upon society brought Lutherans into organized church-to-church contact with the modern ecumenical movement in the Universal Christian Conference on Life and Work. This move was suggested in 1920 by the Lutheran primate of Sweden, Archbishop Nathan Söderblom, who as early as November, 1914—several months after the outbreak of World War I—had made public appeals across battle lines and among different churches for a program of "Peace and Christian Fellowship." In 1925 Archbishop Söderblom and the Lutheran churches of Sweden became hosts to the first Life and Work Conference at Stockholm. Lutherans of America were represented by ten official delegates from the Augustana Lutheran Church, the United Lutheran Church, and the Lutheran Free Church. Other Lutheran churches of the world helped non-Lutheran churches to make up the total of more than 500 delegates. There were representatives of the Lutheran church in Austria, the Lutheran church in Czechoslovakia, the Church of Denmark, the Church of Estonia, the Church of Finland, the Church of Latvia, the Church of Lithuania, the Church of Norway, the Lutheran church in Poland, the Church of Sweden, the Lutheran church in Jugoslavia, and the Tamil Lutheran church in India.

The Lutheran delegates at Stockholm differed concerning the role of the Christian church in the improvement of society, the delegates from Germany being more conservative and cautious than those from America. But concerning ecumenicity and ecclesiastical relationships involved in the co-operative work of the churches in modern society, the Lutherans stood together.

Bishop J. A. Eklund of Sweden, speaking on Christian fellowship in Life and Work, said "The problem of uniting religious movements is not an easy one . . . Above all, we are convinced that there is no more dangerous enemy to Christian unity than the sort of spiritual compulsion which forces similarity through authority and which would solve the problem by commanding uniformity . . . I firmly hold that the only truly Christian way towards unity is that which permits both individuals and churches to keep their individuality and which respects it."

The voice of the Lutheran Church of Denmark came through Bishop O. Ammundsen: "Our tradition is Lutheran . . . but we do not forget the lesson brought to us from the West. We have seen that according to the intention of our great Reformer the Gospel will also give us the strongest impulses to action . . . This has been obscured in the popular Lutheran tradition . . . So I for my part have become a better Lutheran through Anglo-Saxon influence."

One of the Lutheran delegates from America, President G. A. Brandelle of the Augustana Church, called for a definite statement of faith "so that all may know whether we intend to go to heaven on our own plan or on that set forth by the Lord Jesus Himself . . . An agreement of this sort would naturally cause us as denominations to trust each other more fully in the future than we have in the past. There has been more theological bickering among us than was necessary . . . If we can agree in the main on what has just been said, one would think the time ripe for a united and honest attempt at lifting social, industrial and international matters to a higher plane."

It will be observed from these characteristic utterances that Lutherans stood ready to co-operate with other Christians in the practical tasks of the kingdom of God, but that they had no thought of yielding their identity or of diluting their convictions. They came to Stockholm as official representatives of their respective Lutheran churches, associated freely with their fellow Christians of other names, participated heartily in the discussions on Christian co-operation, and on occasion spoke out frankly. To American Lutherans it was encouraging to see with what respect the Lutheran viewpoint was heard in this ecumenical gathering. The influence of Stockholm was felt at the Lutheran World Convention at Copenhagen in 1929. An American delegate delivered an address on "The Lutheran Conception of the Relation between Christianity and the World," and a Norwegian bishop spoke on "The Lutheran Church and the Social Crisis."

The Executive Committee of the Lutheran World Convention, meeting in America in 1936, issued a lengthy statement on "Lutherans and Ecumenical Movements" in which Lutherans everywhere are admonished to approach the question of their relationship to general Christian movements in the spirit of catholicity and without hostility or prejudice but with the utmost fidelity to the revealed Word of God. But during this period there was little or no further reference to interchurch relationships either in the Continuation Committee of Life and Work or in the groups making research on Christian social problems. This was due partly to the clearer definition of the sphere of Life and Work, and partly to the fact that another "ecumenical" movement had begun with the express purpose of dealing with the matter of church union, the movement on Faith and Order.

When the second conference on Life and Work was held at Oxford in July, 1937, there were only about one-fourth as many Lutheran delegates as had been present at Stockholm. This was due partly to the specialized character of the agenda and partly to the belief that the leaders and most of the participants in the conference would not be chosen by the churches, but co-opted by the established leaders. From America only the Augustana Lutheran Church sent official delegates. Individual members of other American Lutheran churches were present and helped in the sections and committees of the conference, but they did not represent their churches. The Oxford meeting did, however, mark an advance over Stockholm in the concreteness and the relevance of its discussions of Christian responsibility for the social order of mankind.

Meanwhile, in America the National Lutheran Council was carrying on a program called "Co-operative Services." In some areas of work it had been found that duplication could be avoided and some types of work best developed through interdenominational co-operative agencies. For example, when at one time the occupying powers in Germany agreed to finance transportation for a student exchange program bringing Lutheran students from Europe to Lutheran schools in America, the American Lutherans authorized the National Council to represent them for this purpose in the World Council of Churches then in process of formation. Also through the Council large funds were contributed to Church World Service, the World YMCA, and other interdenominational agencies that extended relief in areas where Lutherans were among those needing help. Similar funds went to strengthen the World Council's programs of interchurch aid and service to refugees, which were at all times integrated with those of the National Lutheran Council and the Lutheran World Federation. Lutheran World Relief, an agency separately incorporated as the National Lutheran Council's operating arm for physical relief, held membership in such interdenominational and general organizations as the American Council of Voluntary Agencies for Foreign Service, American Relief for Korea, and the Council of Relief Agencies Licensed for Operation in Germany. In addition, all participating bodies of the National Lutheran Council, both individually and through the Council, generously supported the interdenominational American Bible Society. The cost of this varied support of interdenominational projects in some years was more than $200,000.

These were some of the "co-operative services" through which the Lutheran churches in America have co-operated in the second aspect of the ecumenical movement.

The third dimension of ecumenicity deals primarily with the relations of the Christian churches among themselves. It is the tendency to consolidate. It seeks to bring about unity of all Christians, or even to establish full organic union of all churches into one visible church. In many quarters this aspect of ecumenicity has received disproportionate emphasis. In so far as it has to do with the fellowship of American Lutherans with Lutherans around the globe, it has been seen in American participation in the Lutheran World Convention and the Lutheran World Federation.

But a history of the Lutheran churches in America would not be complete, and Lutherans could not understand their place in the historical perspective or in the Christian world of today, without consideration of American Lutheran contacts with non-Lutherans of the world in movements for Christian unity.

That story goes beyond American or Lutheran church history, and involves fragments of official records, bits and pieces from many sources not easily accessible, and even the personal experiences of the author.

The first World Conference on Faith and Order, initiated by the Protestant Episcopal communion in North America and held at Lausanne in 1927 with more than four hundred delegates present, included about seventy Lutherans representing sixteen Lutheran churches of twelve countries. From America there were official representatives of the United Lutheran Church, the Norwegian Lutheran Church, and the Lutheran Free Church. Lutherans were not so prominent at Lausanne as they had been at Stockholm two years earlier, but Professor Werner Elert of Erlangen, delivering the opening address on "The Call to Unity," made clear the Lutheran insistence that unity in the truth must be the first step and the absolute prerequisite for any kind of union. A meeting of all the Lutheran delegates called by Archbishop Söderblom prepared a statement to the conference, which read in part: "As Evangelical Lutherans we feel it to be our sacred duty to labor for the unity of the church in faith and hope, and, especially in this day of dire need, in serving love to mankind. Of course, according to our confessions it is not necessary to the unity of the church that human traditions, rites or ceremonies should be everywhere alike, but this unity consists in agreement concerning the doctrine of the Gospel and the administration of the sacraments."

The statement of the Lutherans at Lausanne also suggested that the several reports of the conference be sent to all the churches represented for their more careful and leisurely study, with the request that the several churches report their findings to the Continuation Committee of the conference. This procedure was adopted, and the idea proved to be an important one for the entire subsequent process of ecumenical action.

The reports of the conference, referred to the 110 churches that had participated in the Lausanne Conference, dealt with The Gospel, The Nature of the Church, The Church's Confession, The Ministry, The Sacraments, The Call to Unity, and, most weighty of all, The Unity of Christendom and the Relation Thereto of Existing Churches. The reactions of the churches to these reports were later published in a volume called *Convictions*. Those of the Lutheran churches explain later Lutheran actions in the forming of the World Council of Churches, for they indicated that the Lutherans of America were at one with the Lutherans of Europe and at variance with their Protestant neighbors in America in this matter of Christian unity and church union.

In a very discerning response, Professor Fernand Menegoz of Strasbourg, on behalf of the Lutheran Church of Alsace and Lorraine, said of the Lausanne Conference: "The insufficiency of the American conception of the origin of divisions was realized. In endlessly repeating that these divisions are, all of them, the result of 'sin,' one digresses from the facts of history and moves imperceptibly toward the Roman conception of the origin of 'separation' and toward the Roman idea of the remedy. At any rate, Lutherans and Calvinists could not at any price allow the Conference to make it appear that the liberating and saving Reformation of the sixteenth century was due to an act of sin . . . So there became increasingly apparent a very brotherly but very strong movement of protest against the exaggerations of the American thesis . . . It was recognized that there are differences which are necessary and legitimate, since members of the universal church possess different 'charismata,' destined to fulfil themselves in the common service of Christ. It was no longer possible rigorously to maintain the old method which sought to establish a 'uniformity' of the churches in matters of doctrine and constitution."

This protest against the labeling of the Protestant denominations as "sin," particularly by non-Lutherans of America, is supplemented by one of the comments of the Lutheran churches in Germany: "With regard to the essence and aim of the movement toward Christian unity, we would make it clear that the expression 'a reunited church' may give rise to misunderstandings which we must repudiate as tending to error. From the standpoint of the German Evangelical churches we regard the task of bringing the churches closer to each other and, as far as possible, into unity, as a new task committed by God in this age to those particular churches which history has brought into being."

The Lutheran bishops and theologians of Norway recorded their reactions to Lausanne in clear and concise statements of the distinctive Lutheran position on each topic. As to the relations of Lutheran churches to other churches they said: "The Evangelical Lutheran church has from the beginning definitely maintained that the one true Catholic church is not bound to any particular form of organized church communion...It appears to us that the report dwells rather much on the idea that the church's unity must be built on a certain uniformity in church order. On the other hand we are glad to notice those expressions that affirm that the differing types of church constitution in principle must be acknowledged as equally valid, and that it must be the aim of all to contribute with gladness to the common life of the whole church."

The Lutheran churchmen in Sweden also asked for a clearer differentiation between the church as an inner spiritual fellowship and as an outward organized community. They added: "The church developed into three chief forms: Orthodox, Roman, and Evangelic Catholic, with their different varieties, and this we do not believe to be against the will of God but in accordance with His plan, because it was necessary that Christianity should reveal its boundless riches in different forms . . . The doctrine of the necessity of the Apostolic succession lacks biblical foundation and . . . nothing that lacks a clear biblical warrant should be made a condition for unity."

The American Lutherans' reactions to the Lausanne utterances coincided closely with those of their brethren in Europe. With the "American thesis," as Professor Menegoz called the idea that denominations are "sin," these Lutherans had no sympathy. They remarked: "We believe that much damage is done to the cause of Christian unity by that undiscerning spirit which sees in the present divided condition of the Church the one cause of the slow coming of the Kingdom of God on earth. There are other causes which are perhaps more potent and would work with little less power, if not with more, against a monstrous ecclesiastical organization seething with internal divisions."

They also pled for more appreciation of the confessional heritages: "Due regard must also be given to that which the church has attained in the way of doctrinal development and confessional statement since the formulation of the ancient creeds, or may attain in the future . . . We believe that the movement for union should proceed along lines which recognize ecclesiastical order, and we deprecate any impatience which would force the issue without regard to the development of the church as a whole."

The American Lutherans also pressed for a clearer understanding of the difference between unity and union, and they urged a continued and intensive study of the topics touched upon at Lausanne.

Meanwhile, the studies which the Lutherans had suggested at Lausanne were well under way, and their results were presented to the second World Conference on Faith and Order at Edinburgh in August, 1937. There, as at Lausanne, the 344 delegates officially represented their 123 churches. Lutherans sent 49 representatives from 17 churches. From America, the United Lutheran Church and the Augustana Lutheran Church sent six delegates. Lutherans had participated constructively in the study commissions, and at Edinburgh itself were active in all the sections.

The topics at Edinburgh were of profound interest to all Lutherans: the Grace of Our Lord Jesus Christ, the Church of Christ and the Word of God, the Ministry and the Sacraments, and the Church's Unity in Life and Worship. The work of co-operative thinking proceeded much more satisfactorily than it had at Lausanne and the results of the conference as embodied in the reports of the plenary sessions, were more acceptable to Lutherans than those of any previous ecumenical conference.

Two items in the reports of the sections at Edinburgh are of special relevance here. One is found in the report of Section IV which dealt with The Church's Unity in Life and Worship. The statement is made: "Some of the churches represented in the Conference hold that Scripture is not only the supreme but the sole standard and source of Christian faith; they reject any suggestion of the equivalence of Scripture and tradition and any implication that the ancient creeds contain a sufficient interpretation of the Scriptural faith. Some of these churches regard certain later confessions as possessing an importance and authority at least equal to that of the ancient creeds."

This was the voice of the Lutherans, of whom there were twelve in that section of 131, still insisting on the recognition of the confessional principle in any plan for Christian unity.

The report of Section I under the chairmanship of the Lutheran Archbishop of Finland dealt with The Grace of Our Lord Jesus Christ. In the course of the discussion Professor Anders Nygren of Sweden, afterwards president of the Lutheran World Federation, said: "I wish to say a brief word as a Lutheran . . . As a rule I am very suspicious of formulae devised to express unity. They are usually compromises, merely concealing disagreements which still persist. They are therefore dangerous and a hindrance to deeper spiritual unity . . . We Lutherans are very sensitive where right belief is concerned . . . We may not sacrifice anything of the truth clearly seen just in order more easily to achieve unity with other churches. At the same time it is equally important that other churches should not surrender anything of the truth they have clearly seen. That would be treachery, and it would take its revenge." This plea for mutual respect among all confessional groups helped to make the position of Lutherans clear.

The Edinburgh Conference also considered the recommendations of the Committee of Thirty-five, a group which in the Conference on Life and Work at Oxford a month earlier had asked that Life and Work be united with Faith and Order to form a World Council of Churches. With reservations intended to safeguard the churchly character of the proposed organization, Edinburgh approved, and chose a committee of seven to co-operate with a similar committee that had been appointed at Oxford to bring the World Council into being. The resulting Provisional Committee of the World Council of Churches, included seven Lutherans of twenty-eight primary and alternate members. Its activities between Edinburgh in 1937 and Amsterdam in 1948 throw light on the relations between Lutheran churches and other churches, and the involvements of Americans in those relations.

In the work within the Provisional Committee for the World

Council of Churches during the ten formative years preceding the organization of the Council, we see as a result of the principles that Lutherans had expressed so consistently at Stockholm and Oxford, at Lausanne and Edinburgh, the fairly general acceptance of the confessional principle in the relations of Lutherans with other churches.

One step toward this development of such great importance to American Lutherans was taken a few days after the close of the Edinburgh Conference. In August, 1937, the Executive Committee of the Lutheran World Federation (then called Convention) met in Amsterdam. This meeting recognized at once the issue of Lutheran church relationships involved in the proposed World Council. The preliminary sketch of a constitution presented to Oxford and Edinburgh had suggested a Central Committee of sixty members chosen not from the several churches but from the various countries. The Lutheran Executive at Amsterdam reacted to this: "We express our conviction that representation in the proposed General Assembly, the proposed Central Committee, and the proposed Committees and Commissions, should be ecclesiastical and confessional and not territorial." The Lutheran members in the Provisional Committee were asked to insist upon this principle.

The discussions at the Oxford and Edinburgh Conferences had made clear that the churches must be associated with the planning at every stage, and therefore the Committee called a large representative group of church leaders to meet at Utrecht in May, 1938, to prepare a provisional constitution for the proposed World Council. Meanwhile voices were raised on behalf of confessional representation to the proposed World Council, in the American Section of the Joint Executive Committee of Faith and Order and Life and Work. Such voices met with little favor and much opposition, because they ran counter to "the American thesis" that denominations are "sin."

The American Lutherans who went to Utrecht to help fashion a constitution for the World Council of Churches were Dr. F. H. Knubel, president of the United Lutheran Church, and Dr. Ralph H. Long, executive director of the National Lutheran Council. They pled for the strictly churchly character of the proposed council and all its parts. The plea was not granted, but neither was it wholly ignored. The proposed constitution adopted by the majority at

Utrecht allocated the seats both in the Assembly and in the General Committee of the World Council chiefly by territorial regions. Only the Orthodox churches were recognized as a separate church group. But this arrangement was "provisional," not final. The representatives of the Lutheran churches in Europe seemed satisfied with the provision that "world confessional organizations" might designate a certain number of persons to represent "minority churches" in the Assembly and on the Central Committee. So the door was not closed upon the confessions, and at least this minimum of concession to the desires of the Lutheran churches could be welcomed by the Executive Committee of the Lutheran World Federation at its meeting in 1938. The Executive Committee also noted with satisfaction that the confession of the Lord Jesus Christ as God and Saviour was adopted as the basis of the proposed World Council.

Inactive during the war years 1939 to 1945, the Provisional Committee went into action immediately upon the end of the war. The American Lutherans began then also to agitate for a change in the "provisional constitution" to the principle of confessional representation, because they wanted to participate with other Christian churches in the ecumenical movement if they could do so without violating their confession or sacrificing their distinctive understanding of the gospel. The Executive Board of The United Lutheran Church in America called a meeting in September, 1945, of official representatives of all Lutheran churches in America "for the purpose of achieving a common understanding with reference to the World Council of Churches." Nine church bodies sent representatives; this number was unprecedented in American Lutheran history. Although there was much difference of opinion, the meeting decided that the Lutheran churches which had accepted the invitation to join the World Council would unite in pressing the Provisional Committee to amend the provisional constitution "so as to provide for Lutheran representation in both the Assembly and the Central Committee on a confessional basis." The Executive Committee of the Lutheran World Federation was asked to assist in this matter.

At the next meeting of the Provisional Committee, held in Geneva, February, 1946, the plea of the Lutheran churches in America was presented in writing and in person by the Lutheran member from America. The proposal was received with polite coolness, largely because of a feeling that it represented the wishes of only a few Americans. It was pointed out that churches had accepted the invitation to join on the basis of the constitution as it then stood, which could therefore be changed only by the first Assembly of the World Council itself. The proposal was referred to the Committee on Arrangements for the First Assembly, to which the American Lutheran member of the Provisional Committee was named.

When the Executive Committee of the Lutheran World Federation met in Sweden in July, 1946, for its first gathering since 1938, documents were presented to show that not only the Lutheran churches in America, but also those of the Scandinavian lands, Finland, the Netherlands, France, Austria, Poland, Hungary, and Czechoslovakia, and a number of official representatives of the Lutheran churches in Germany were united in desiring confessional representation in the World Council.

When, therefore, the Committee on Arrangements for the First Assembly met in England in August, 1946, the American Lutheran member of that committee, in arguing for confessional representation as against purely regional representation, could speak for the largest group of churches that would participate in organizing the World Council. For the World Council of Churches to become as it professed to be, a "fellowship of Churches," and not merely an ecclesiastical league of nations, it must be constituted directly, not indirectly, of the churches which accepted membership. Moreover, the American member urged, confessional representation would enable the World Council to do more effectively what its constitution proposes—mobilize the churches of Christ for concrete prophetic word and deed before the world. The way to a united Christian testimony, it was pointed out, is in greater danger from political sectionalism than from ecclesiastical sectarianism.

To many of the committee members the perpetuating of confessional groups was a threat to "the ecumenical ideal," and they opposed it fervently. But finally it was agreed to ask the Provisional Committee to suggest to the First Assembly of the World Council a change in the constitution eliminating the portion which allocated seats territorially, and substituting: "Seats in the Assembly shall be allocated to the member churches by the Central Committee, due regard being given to such factors as numerical size, adequate confessional representation, and adequate geographical distribution. Suggestions for readjustment in the allocation of seats may be made to the Central Committee by member churches or by groups of member churches, confessional, regional or national, and these readjustments shall become effective if approved by the Central Committee and the member churches concerned." The same principle of representation was also approved for the powerful Central Committee. The Provisional Committee approved this amendment for recommendation to the First Assembly of the World Council scheduled for 1948.

During the summer of 1947 the Lutheran churches of the world sent representatives to Lund, Sweden, and organized the Lutheran World Federation out of the looser Lutheran World Convention. One of the purposes expressed in the constitution of the Federation is "to foster Lutheran participation in ecumenical movements." The General Secretary of the Provisional Committee, Dr. W. A. Visser 't Hooft, indicated his acceptance of confessional representation in the World Council in his greetings to the Lutheran Assembly which began: "The World Council is deeply aware of the fact that the ecumenical task can only be performed if the main confessional federations and alliances perform their task of bringing the churches of their confessional family together in close fellowship and so prepare the way for the even greater and more difficult task of establishing the wider ecumenical Christian brotherhood. We express, therefore, the wish that the Lund Conference may lead both to a fastening of the ties among the Lutheran churches of the world and to a strengthening of the bonds between the Lutheran churches and those of other communities which find their expression in the World Council of Churches."

Officers of the new Federation, and other Lutheran spokesmen, actively pressed the issue during the succeeding twelve months before the first Assembly of the World Council. They were challenged by some writers on behalf of ecumenicity who insisted that a variety of Christian churches is contrary to the will of God, that "divisions" among Christians are necessarily competitive, and therefore "scandalous," and that the ideal must be a return to pre-Reformation union.

Some Lutherans, on the other hand, suspected that in joining with other churches in a World Council the Lutheran churches were involving themselves in embarrassing ecclesiastical compromise, because, it was claimed, the hidden intent of the leaders in the prospective Council was to become a superchurch. With this in mind the president of the Augustana Lutheran Church in America requested from the Provisional Committee "a clear statement of the honest intention and purpose and proposed scope and activity of this organization." The committee's response was reassuring. It said: "The World Council of Churches, composed of churches which acknowledge Jesus Christ as God and Saviour, owes its existence to the desire of its member churches to express their unity in Him. The Council seeks to promote this unity among its members and to serve them as an organ whereby they may bear witness together to their common faith and co-operate in matters requiring united action. The Council does not aim, however, to usurp the functions which belong to its constituent members, nor in any way to control or legislate for these bodies. Moreover, while earnestly seeking the co-operation and unity of all the churches that accept its basis, the Council disavows any thought of becoming a single unified church structure dominated by a centralized administrative authority.

"The Christian unity for which the Council stands is of a different order. It strives after a unity in which Christians and Christian churches, joyously aware of their oneness, shall in times of need give help and comfort to one another, and at all times inspire and exhort one another to live worthily of their common membership in the Body of Christ."

Encouraged by these developments, five of the Lutheran churches in America sent delegates to the First Assembly of the World Council which met at Amsterdam in 1948. These were the American Lutheran Church, the American Evangelical Lutheran Church, the Augustana Lutheran Church, the United Lutheran Church, and the United Evangelical Lutheran Church. Their 27 delegates, alternates, and official visitors joined 108 Lutheran delegates and alternates from other lands to constitute the largest confessional group in attendance. Lutherans were placed in many positions of responsibility including chairmanship of the Section on the Church and of the committees on nominations and on message. A Lutheran from America served as chairman of the credentials committee and another as a member of the steering committee, called the business committee. One of the six presidents of the Council was a Lutheran. The Assembly elected sixteen Lutherans, two from America, to the ninety-member Central Committee, and an American Lutheran was elected chairman of this policy-making body. In the course of the Assembly in study sections and business sessions, it became evident that the American Lutherans stood midway between the European churches, with their intense concentration on theology, and other American Protestants, with their equally emphatic stress on Christian activity. It became evident also that no church had a greater part in the new Council than the Lutheran.

The Assembly, with its 351 delegates and 238 alternates representing 147 member churches in 44 countries, voted unanimously in favor of the constitutional amendment proposed by the Provisional Committee. The principle of confessional representation was confirmed! Since this gratifying result enlisted the wholehearted participation of the greater portion of world Lutheranism in the World Council of Churches, it was the most important event of the past half century in the relation of Lutheran churches to the modern ecumenical movement.

The quality of American Lutheran participation in the modern ecumenical movement shows that after three centuries, they are no longer on the defensive for their evangelical positions. The Lutheran churches in America can accept responsibility for a clear and impressive testimony to Christ and the gospel, not only among American Christians but among Christians of the whole world.

Part VII

IN AN AGE OF PLURALISM AND ECUMENISM (1950-   )

CHAPTER 38

GENERAL BACKGROUND

In the latter half of the twentieth century, American Lutherans have become increasingly aware that they live in a radically altered world which is drastically changing the role of American Lutheranism.

It is one world, so that men must think in global terms. It is an increasingly secular world, so that everywhere large segments of society are virtually deaf to the traditional accents of the gospel. Global revolutionary ferment is producing new nationalisms, new secular aspirations, new bids for the loyalties of men. Great social movements like communism and fascism have forged huge collectivities that seek to be total in their control over human lives. Other religions have become resurgent, so that Christianity is but one among a handful of world religions vying for the exploding populations of the earth. During the same years in which Christians have been forming themselves into a meaningful worldwide fellowship in the ecumenical movement, they have come to realize that they are distinctly a minority group even in a West that was once called Christendom. For better or for worse, it is a post-Christendom era.

The churches, all of them, Protestant, Catholic, and Pentecostal or "third force," are beginning to sense their new position of challenge and insecurity. They have no place to hide from the jostling of gigantic threats, such as the universal disruptions of war, hot or cold, the massive pressure of the population explosion, the new thrust of non-Christian religions, the quiet infiltration of an alien morality through mass communications, the disruptive effect of mobility in every aspect of modern society, and the blighting results of urbanism in the modern metropolis and the approaching megalopolis.

The United States, thrust into world leadership, has been strongly shaped by all these modern trends. In religion and culture the impact has produced "pluralism." Pluralism is the social phenomenon of competing ideologies, religions, and institutions co-inhabiting the same nation under a set of fair-play ground rules and an indefinite common heritage called "the American way of life." A century ago America was broadly Protestant in its outlook and its cultural and moral assumptions. Today it is at the same time secular, Protestant, Catholic, Jewish, and what-have-you. This has proved disconcerting to a Protestantism that was for decades a predominating influence in, for example, public education, welfare services, Sunday observance, public oratory and ritual, and mores and folkways. Many Protestants feel challenged and insecure, while most thoughtful Americans are anxious to discern and to shape a viable future pattern for culture and the religious life of the nation.

These changes have thrust American Lutherans—like every other denomination—into a number of significant new relationships. In a global landscape, standing elbow-to-elbow with people of vastly different viewpoints, they have more quickly recognized other brands of Lutherans as their brethren and have entered more heartily into give-and-take and common action with fellow American Protestants. It is even suggested by some non-Lutheran historians that Lutherans are entering into a period of leadership among American Protestants.

Meanwhile wider relationships inevitably take on a tentative and exploratory nature—dialogues with Roman Catholics, encounters with pagans or adherents of other religions, experiments in penetrating culture or using mass communications. Despite temptation to withdraw into a new kind of sectarianism, responsible denominations continue to seek fresh ways to serve their communities and nation, and although large and powerful ecclesiastical organizations continue to grow, significant new life in American Christianity has begun to flow through small and mobile groups of Christians who raise up signs of Christ through new and radical forms of service to this secular and pluralistic modern age.

There were elements of urgency in the mid-century moves for union among Lutherans. A sense of insistence which came from the pressures of a non-Christian world and a non-Protestant America was supported by the multiplied contacts among all Christians, Protestants, Catholics and others, across denominational boundaries and on both the national and the international level. All major groups of American Christians having felt the pressure in varying degrees, they experienced an increased sense of belonging together. Some of the major developments in the broad areas of liturgy and hymnody, and some of the impressive undertakings in the field of social ministry, are outstanding examples of the spirit of the new age. Moreover, the multitude of conferences on the various levels of the ecumenical movement produced congenial personal fellowship that stretched across ecclesiastical boundaries and made it evident to everyone that genuine Christian faith dwells in men and women of all denominations and all sectors of the new Christian world.

At the close of the first half of the twentieth century, as we have seen in Chapter 36, two major steps in the direction of greater consolidation among the Lutheran forces in America were in prospect. Within a few years after 1950, it could be recorded that both of these steps had actually been taken. Eight of the independent Lutheran bodies in America had been organically merged into two large churches embracing more than two-thirds of all the Lutherans in the country. Moreover, within a decade these two large organizations had begun negotiations with the other third of Lutherans in America, looking towards association in the huge co-operative tasks that faced American Lutheranism in the age of ecumenism and pluralism.

CHAPTER 39

THE AMERICAN LUTHERAN CHURCH

The first of these significant mergers was consummated in 1960 and embraced the Evangelical (United Norwegian) Lutheran Church of 1917, the American (German) Lutheran Church of 1930, the United Evangelical (Danish) Lutheran Church of 1896, and ultimately the Lutheran Free (Norwegian) Church of 1897.

The initial step towards this merger was taken in 1949 when the United Evangelical Lutheran Church proposed organic union among all the bodies in the National Lutheran Council except the United Lutheran Church in America. After the Augustana Lutheran Church and the smaller Lutheran Free Church of 1897 had withdrawn from these negotiations, the three remaining bodies within the American Lutheran Conference continued to negotiate through a Joint Union Committee of the American Lutheran Conference (page 350). The first four meetings of the forty-five members of the Committee in 1951 brought forth a lengthy document called "United Testimony on Faith and Life" which set forth in detail what the Committee regarded as the Lutheran positions on Christian doctrine and practice. The three church bodies approved the United Testimony in 1952. In December, 1953, a second document on "Polity and Organization" appeared and was approved by all the negotiating bodies at their 1954 conventions. Two years later the conventions all adopted resolutions officially approving the merger.

But a number of unresolved problems delayed for several years the actual formation of the new church. Some of these were in the fields of higher education, administration, and social action. Some were in the field of external relations. Many people in the three bodies still hoped to include the Augustana Lutheran Church and some hoped to include the United Lutheran Church in the merger. A large number, also, which turned out to be a majority, wanted the new church to join the World Council of Churches. These and other problems were widely discussed and finally resolved by the Joint Union Committee in time to present the decisions to the national conventions of the bodies in 1958. These conventions ratified the Committee's decisions and adopted the Articles of Union, including the United Testimony, the constitutions, and the other basic documents. After much discussion they adopted the name The American Lutheran Church. They also set the date April, 1960, for the constituting convention of the new church and January 1, 1961, as the date for the new body to begin to function. The subsequent ratification of the Articles of Union by all thirteen districts of the American Lutheran Church assured the organic union of the three bodies.

The formal organization of The American Lutheran Church took place in Minneapolis on April 22, 1960. It climaxed more than ten years of negotiations. Under detailed terms previously approved, the constituent church bodies transferred all their properties and rights to the new church. The convention promptly elected officers: as president, Dr. Fredrik A. Schiotz, former president of the Evangelical Lutheran Church; as vice-president, Dr. Norman A. Menter, of the American Lutheran Church; and as secretary, Dr. William Larsen, former president of the United Evangelical Lutheran Church. All the boards and agencies that had been chosen by the Joint Union Committee and approved by the several bodies were now elected by the new church. The program of the church was committed to six divisions, American Missions, World Missions, Education, Publication, Charities, and Pensions; two commissions, one on Evangelism and one on Social Action; and three standing committees, Worship and Church Music, Relations to Lutheran Churches, and Public Relations.

The highest legislative agency in The American Lutheran Church is the biennial general convention. In the interim between conventions the supreme authority is vested in a Church Council with forty-six members, who are the president and vice-president of the church, the president and a layman from each of its nineteen districts, and six representatives at large. The constituting convention had a budget of $18,000,000 for 1961.

At its final session the convention elected a standing committee on relations with other Lutheran bodies and declared its willingness to "enter into discussions looking toward altar and pulpit fellowship with any and all Lutheran churches which confess their adherence to the Holy Scriptures as the Word of God in all matters of faith and life and subscribe to the Confessions of the Lutheran Church." It also voted to apply for membership in the National Lutheran Council, the Canadian Lutheran Council, the Lutheran World Federation, and the World Council of Churches.

The American Lutheran Church began to function January 1, 1961, with nearly 2,260,000 baptized members from about 5,000 congregations served by about 4,500 ministers. Of these numbers the American Lutheran Church of 1930 contributed about 51 per cent, the Evangelical Lutheran Church about 46 per cent, and the United Evangelical Lutheran Church about 3 per cent. It constituted the third largest Lutheran body in America and the tenth among Protestant bodies. At the second convention of The American Lutheran Church in 1962 it admitted to its membership the Lutheran Free Church, which had now, after two unsuccessful efforts, achieved a majority vote of its 83,000 members to merge with the other three bodies.

In one important respect this merger was unique and highly significant for the future. It was the first major breakthrough of Lutheran bodies across the lines of national origin, the Evangelical Lutheran Church and the Lutheran Free Church being mainly of Norwegian heritage, the American Lutheran Church of 1930 of German, and the United Evangelical of Danish. To the student of history this seems clearly to point to the eventual disappearance of all vestiges of historical variety and tradition among the Lutherans of America. It is a harbinger of Lutheran solidarity and ecumenism in America in response to an age of pluralism.

CHAPTER 40

THE LUTHERAN CHURCH IN AMERICA

The next step in the consolidation of American Lutheranism came in 1962. The two large bodies in the National Lutheran Council which had not joined in the negotiations leading to the formation of the new American Lutheran Church in 1960 were the United Lutheran Church in America of 1918 and the Augustana Lutheran Church of 1860. These two bodies, as we have seen, desired a more inclusive fellowship than The American Lutheran Church seemed to provide. Moreover, they had been reluctant to forego their opportunities for Lutheran witness in such general Christian movements as the World Council of Churches and the National Council of the Churches of Christ in the United States of America.

These two bodies, therefore, in 1956 joined with two smaller bodies, the American Evangelical (Danish) Lutheran Church of 1872 and the Suomi (Finnish) Synod of 1890, and set up their own Joint Commission on Lutheran Unity, known as the JCLU, which had forty-six members. Events took place in rapid succession. At the very first meeting of the JCLU in December, 1956, the conclusion was reached that "we have among us sufficient ground of agreement in the common confession of our faith to justify further procedure in seeking a basis for the organic union of our churches." This was a very large initial step for four independent Lutheran bodies to take at a single meeting, and it paved the way for rapid progress in the other seventeen meetings of the Commission during the following five and a half years. The Commission proceeded at once to prepare a Confession of Faith, to lay down general principles for the new organization, and to draft detailed constitutions and bylaws for the new church, for its synods, and for its congregations.

The JCLU worked with extraordinary speed. Early in 1960 both the Agreement of Consolidation, which included the general provisions for the merger, and the constitutions were ready to be presented to the four churches for adoption. During the year all four bodies approved the Agreement with almost complete unanimity. The constituting convention was held at Detroit from June 28 to July 1, 1962, when the church bodies participating in the merger held their final conventions and transferred all their interests to what was named the "Lutheran Church in America." The constituting convention elected as president Dr. Franklin Clark Fry, who had been president of the United Lutheran Church in America; as secretary Dr. Malvin H. Lundeen, who had been president of the Augustana Lutheran Church; and as treasurer Edmund F. Wagner, who had been treasurer of the United Lutheran Church in America. Boards and agencies were also elected and some of them began to operate immediately. The date of the official beginning of the full life of the new church was set for January 1, 1963.

The Lutheran Church in America is the largest Lutheran body in this country. It began to function with more than 3,200,000 baptized members, nearly 7,000 ordained ministers, and more than 6,000 congregations with combined assets of more than a billion dollars. Of these numbers nearly 80 per cent came from the United Lutheran Church in America, nearly 20 per cent from the Augustana Lutheran Church, a little more than one per cent from the Suomi Synod, and a little less than one per cent from the American Evangelical Lutheran Church.

In accord with the trends noted in Chapter 36 of this volume, the Lutheran Church in America did not undertake to make doctrinal declarations beyond the confessional writings of the Lutheran churches of four centuries. It announced no traditional "doctrinal basis" that might be understood as a legal code or standard of discipline, but issued instead a Confession of Faith. Although this new Confession of Faith was declared to be "the consensus of faith among those uniting to form the new church and those who will enter the fellowship at a later time," and "therefore the final and rightful test of the propriety of membership," nevertheless it was interpreted as primarily "an affirmation pointing to the fountain from which all the life and activities of the church flow." This document will probably constitute a landmark in Lutheran history. It recognizes that there is a confession of faith within and above and beyond the confessional writings, and that brotherhood and unity among Lutherans will not in the future be achieved by tedious arguments over phrases and nuances of meaning but by sincere subscription to the historic Lutheran confessions themselves, in their historic sense, rather than theological deductions from them or extra-confessional interpretations of them. It sets up the "Holy Scriptures as the norm for the faith and life of the Church . . . the divinely inspired record of God's redemptive act in Christ" through which "God still speaks . . . and realizes his redemptive purpose generation after generation." The Lutheran Church in America "acknowledges as one with it in faith and doctrine all churches that likewise accept the teachings of these symbols," i.e., the Unaltered Augsburg Confession and Luther's Small Catechism. It also accepts the three ecumenical creeds as true declarations of the church's faith and the other symbolical books of the Evangelical Lutheran Church as "further valid interpretations of the Confession of the Church."

As to the nature of the new church's structure, one observes that some elements were contributed by each of the merging bodies. In theory at least, the church is constituted not of the synods but of the congregations, though in practice the congregational powers of control over the church are rather remote, because a congregation must proceed through a district, and a synod, to a church convention, or the Executive Council, or the Court of Adjudication. Synods are less prominent in the structure of the new church than they were in the United Lutheran Church in America. Congregations belong primarily to the church-at-large, and synods are only the agents of the church in admitting congregations. The same applies to the ministers of the church. The synods are the agents of the church in admitting ministers, and the concurrence of both synod and church is necessary for the ordination of ministers. Ministers are finally subject to discipline by the synod, while congregations are responsible to the church-at-large. Synods and their officers are given a greater number of pastoral functions and fewer executive duties than they had in most of the constituency of the new church before the merger. Theological education is a responsibility of both synod and church. A board of theological education with wide powers of action nominates to the synods a minority percentage of the directors of their seminaries. Unusually large powers are delegated to the Executive Council of the church, which consists of its three officers, fifteen pastors, and fifteen laymen. It is given veto power on all actions and publications of boards, auxiliaries, and agencies; the power of assigning congregations to synods; the power to make pronouncement on social or moral issues in the name of the church; the power to appoint representatives to all interchurch associations; and many other powers.

In the new church the thirty-two synods of the former United Lutheran Church in America, the thirteen conferences of the former Augustana Lutheran Church, the seven conferences of the Suomi Synod, and the nine districts of the American Evangelical Lutheran Church, were merged and then rearranged into thirty-one synods of the Lutheran Church in America, each limited and designated by geographical boundaries except the Slovak Zion Synod. Three of the synods are in Canada. The thirty-one synods are delineated briefly in the 1963 Yearbook of the Lutheran Church in America (pages 9-14). For its first year the new church adopted a budget of $28,500,000.

The program of the church is carried out by eight boards, American Missions, World Missions, Parish Education, College Education and Church Vocations, Theological Education, Publication, Social Ministry, and Pensions; and six commissions, Worship, Stewardship, Evangelism, Church Papers, Youth Activities, and Church Architecture. The church is affiliated with the National Lutheran Council, the Lutheran World Federation, the National Council of the Churches of Christ in the United States of America, and the World Council of Churches.

This consolidation constituted the largest Lutheran body in America, the fourth in size among Protestants, and the fifth merger among the major units of American Lutheranism. It is in line with the formation of the Evangelical Lutheran Church in 1917, the United Lutheran Church in America in 1918, the American Lutheran Church in 1930, and The American Lutheran Church in 1960. Like the last-named church, the new Lutheran Church in America is significant in advancing the union of all Lutherans in the land, in that it combined churches of German, Swedish, Finnish, and Danish tradition. It was a large step forward, and with quickened pace, in the direction of Lutheran solidarity in a pluralistic society.

CHAPTER 41

THE LUTHERAN COUNCIL IN THE UNITED STATES

Another important development among Lutherans in America in recent years was the attempt to replace the National Lutheran Council with an agency of broader scope.

With the formation of The American Lutheran Church in 1960 and the Lutheran Church in America in 1962, the number of bodies participating in the National Lutheran Council was reduced from eight to two. The Council lost nothing in size. It continued to be a basis of manifold co-operation for the same constituency as previously. But the greater solidarity of its participating units gave it courage to seek still wider co-operation and for that purpose to have its member bodies seek further contacts among all Lutherans in this country. Both The American Lutheran Church and the Lutheran Church in America had closed their constituent conventions by extending their hands towards all other Lutheran churches in America.

It had been noted on all sides that the co-operation of the several Lutheran bodies through the National Lutheran Council, achieving distinguished results and promoting personal acquaintance and fellowship across synodical boundaries, had been one of the main elements in producing the climate conducive to organic mergers among those bodies. This was not an assigned responsibility of the Council but only a by-product. It encouraged the Council to go beyond its constitution and invite all Lutheran bodies to consultations concerning more extensive co-operative activities. This involved chiefly an approach to the bodies co-operating in the Synodical Conference of North America, of which The Lutheran Church—Missouri Synod was the chief constituent. The other major body in the Synodical Conference, the Wisconsin Synod, had been protesting against the "unionistic practices" of the Missouri Synod and in 1961 severed its relation with the Synodical Conference. The Wisconsin Synod promptly rejected the National Lutheran Council's invitation to a general consultation. Negative replies were received also from the six small independent groups of Lutherans.

The Lutheran Church—Missouri Synod, on the other hand, had been co-operating with the National Lutheran Council in several areas. It had for a time sought to establish pulpit and altar fellowship with the American Lutheran Church of 1930, but it did not participate in the merger negotiations that led to The American Lutheran Church of 1960. The Missouri Synod accepted the invitation of the National Lutheran Council and in July, 1960, the first general consultation was held. The discussion centered around Article VII of the Augsburg Confession: "And to the true unity of the Church it is enough to agree concerning the Doctrine of the Gospel and the administration of the Sacraments."

The first consultation was so encouraging in its general spirit and results that a second was held in November, 1960, when attention was centered on the significance of confessional subscription. Again the results were positive, and a third consultation was held in November, 1961, to answer the question "What kind of co-operation is possible in view of the discussions to date?" The result of the third consultation was a declaration that "sufficient consensus has been revealed to warrant the exploration of the feasibility of a new association to succeed the National Lutheran Council in which doctrinal studies and co-operative activities would be undertaken simultaneously." The proposal to form a new association to replace the National Lutheran Council was approved by all three of the Lutheran bodies at their national conventions, though not in identical terms.

When the group of consultants met in January, 1963, therefore, they came as representatives of their respective church bodies, not as representatives of the National Lutheran Council. The group now constituted itself the "Inter-Lutheran Consultation." The significance of the group can be measured by the fact that it consists of official representatives of the three major branches of Lutheranism in America, which include 95 per cent of the 8,600,000 Lutherans in the United States and Canada.

At the meeting in January, 1963, it was decided to "give careful attention to the nature and scope of current co-operative activities . . . to the purpose and objectives of the new inter-Lutheran agency, and to possible areas of work which properly could be undertaken by it." Much emphasis was laid on the necessity for continuing theological study both before and after the formation of a new inter-Lutheran agency. Six subcommittees of the Consultation were appointed to study the various aspects of a possible new agency and to report to the Consultation in October, 1963, and January, 1964. Hope was expressed that a constitution and, if necessary, additional rules of procedure for the proposed association for theological study and co-operative service might be submitted to the national church conventions by 1965.

In these consultations it was implicit and sometimes openly asserted that "co-operation can never be an end in itself: there should be a prime emphasis on deepening and broadening the existing consensus." Sometimes a federation of Lutheran churches was mentioned as a possibility. Frequently the work of the Inter-Lutheran Consultation was set in the context of the contemporary American scene. Pleas were made for a unified and "massive witness" of the Lutheran forces to the non-Christian culture now prevalent in American society. On all sides it was recognized that "Lutheran positions which had practical validity in situations obtaining in American Christendom in the nineteenth century must now be restated in the light of the revolutionary changes in American society which have taken place since World War I." A statement made by one of the secretaries of the Consultation brings into focus the primary motive that underlies this latest development in American Lutheranism: "The trend in American society, strongly influenced by contemporary world revolution, must evoke a Christian witness from a confessional family of more than 8,000,000 souls which is more commensurate with the potential influence God has given to Lutherans in this land."

As this volume goes to press (July, 1963) the Inter-Lutheran Consultation has completed arrangements for an agency to be called "The Lutheran Council in the United States of America." If the plans are ratified by the general bodies, the new Council will begin to function in 1967.

CHAPTER 42

EXTENDING SOCIAL MINISTRY

In The American Lutheran Church of 1960 and the Lutheran Church in America of 1962, all the avenues of social ministry opened by the several Lutheran churches in the preceding period (see Chapter 34) have been continued and their range has been expanded. The greater solidarity of the Lutheran forces in America has enabled their spokesmen to speak in higher places and with greater volume on all the issues that involve the application of the gospel to the massive problems of current American society.

Social activities have entered new areas that would have seemed unapproachable a generation earlier. Lutherans have concerned themselves with Christian citizenship, international affairs, diplomatic representation, the United Nations, interracial principles, tariff and international trade, alcohol, the conservation of food, federal relief to famine sufferers, social security for old age, universal military training and the atomic and hydrogen bombs. The influence of church groups is now regularly exerted upon law-making bodies.

Affirming the unity of all spheres of life and refusing to separate religious life from economics and politics, Lutheran theologians and church leaders in America set forth the fullness of the gospel, as Luther taught it and as Lutherans understand it, in every aspect of modern life.

Among the Lutheran bodies in America in 1963 there were more than 450 welfare agencies and institutions employing about 16,000 workers, with annual operating expenditures of more than $110,000,000 and property worth about $40,000,000. Periodic meetings at national, regional, and state levels bring together national groups in the National Lutheran Social Welfare Conference in America, an affiliate of the Council's Division of Welfare. The Conference is constituted of about

250 organizations for Christian welfare and social work and about 500 individuals interested in such work. In recent years regional meetings of the Social Welfare Conference have been held simultaneously with regional meetings of the Associated Charities of the Missouri Synod, and since 1953 there have been joint sessions of the two groups.

Conditions in this field change so rapidly and opportunities for service multiply so frequently that the Lutheran social agencies are in a constant state of flux both in objectives and in methods. In general it can be said that the social ministry of the Lutheran churches includes services to the aging, to unmarried mothers, to families, to the handicapped, to immigrants, and to seamen, in settlement centers, in hospitals and rehabilitation centers, and in institutional chaplaincies. Publications include the *Lutheran Health and Welfare Directory* and the *Lutheran Social Welfare Journal*.

A review of the major recent developments among Lutherans in the fields of social ministry suggests several definite trends in this new period of pluralism and ecumenism. First, it is recognized not only in the churches but also in government circles and among purely secular welfare agencies that the churches as such have a distinct responsibility for social action. Second, it is accepted among the churches that welfare services and social action programs are not optional but are an indispensable part of the church's life. Third, it is clear that the fulfillment of this social ministry cannot be left to private associations of individual Christians but must be embodied in every part of the church's own structure. And fourth, it is commonly agreed that the direct services of the church's social ministry must be adjusted to the welfare complex of governmental and non-church voluntary agencies.

As Lutherans of America move into the second half of the twentieth century, therefore, they are alert to the new responsibilities imposed on them by the great changes in society in general. They are solidifying their ranks in order to bear corporate witness to the power of the gospel as a leaven in social life. To the multitudes who are caught in the hard social conditions imposed by the industrial, economic, and political situation of this new age, such witness through social ministry may prove to be a more convincing witness than organic union or any other testimony that Lutherans might present. Certainly it has no less scriptural warrant.

CHAPTER 43

THE SERVICE BOOK AND HYMNAL

In the early 1940's, all the major bodies of Lutheranism were preparing to revise their service books and hymnals. To nearly all of them and at about the same time it occurred that this should be made a common project of American Lutherans. Several bodies took action looking towards co-operation in fashioning a common liturgy and a common collection of hymns. The Common Service Book Committee of the United Lutheran Church took the initiative and invited representatives of the other major bodies to meet in exploratory conferences. These gatherings began in 1945. That year a Joint Commission on a Common Hymnal was formed. The following year, at the urging of the Augustana Synod, these representatives organized the Joint Commission on a Common Liturgy. The eight churches co-operating in the National Lutheran Council all joined in the work of the Commissions.

The Commission on Liturgy decided to use the text of the Common Service of 1888 as the basis of its studies, but it declined to be bound by the rule that had governed the committee that prepared the Common Service, namely, "the common consent of the pure Lutheran liturgies of the sixteenth century." The Commission agreed "to study the important liturgies of the ecumenical church and to evaluate the rules of modern liturgical scholarship in all communions, particularly in matters relating to the worship of the Early Church."

By 1954 the work of the two Commissions had been approved by the Lutheran bodies authorizing the project. The new "Service Book and Hymnal of the Lutheran Church in America" was introduced into the congregations in 1958. The Missouri Synod did not co-operate in the project because it had recently published its own hymnal with a liturgy closely resembling the Common Service of 1888. It is estimated that by 1963 the new book was being used by about 90 per cent of all the congregations in the bodies of the National Lutheran Council.

The new service book and hymnal marked the high point of liturgical development among Lutherans in America during the three centuries of their history. It was both the offspring and the matrix of the process of Lutheran union. It was clear evidence of the large measure of unity that had been achieved in American Lutheranism, and it paved the way to further unity in the coming generations.

This happy culmination of a liturgical development that extended over more than a century and a half not only satisfied the longing for closer approach to common standards in devotional life and usages, but it also bore unmistakable witness to an inner girding of American Lutherans for life in a pluralistic society.

CHAPTER 44

SIGNIFICANT MOVES IN THE LUTHERAN WORLD FEDERATION

After the assembly of Hannover, the Executive Committee of the Lutheran World Federation combined a number of its commissions and appointed two new ones, one on Liturgy and one on Lutheran World Service. The number of the commissions was reduced from fifteen to nine. Their names indicate the broad range of the Federation's work at mid-century: Education, Inner Missions, Inter-Church Aid, International Affairs, World Service, Foreign Missions, Theology, Stewardship and Evangelism, and Liturgy. The Committee also set up a separate Department of Information, and a Committee on Latin America. The president of the Federation appointed Americans as chairmen of five of these agencies.

On invitation of the National Lutheran Council, the 1957 assembly of the Lutheran World Federation was scheduled to be held in America.

During the five years that followed the Hannover Assembly, the several commissions and national committees carried forward the work of the Federation with increased tempo, and when the third assembly was held at Minneapolis in 1957, a stately volume of high achievement could be set down in the record.

The central theme of the Minneapolis Assembly, held from August 15 to 25, 1957, was "Christ Frees and Unites." The 58 member churches registered 259 delegates. There were 215 official visitors, including 15 from The Lutheran Church—Missouri Synod. The new outreach of the Federation was indicated by the presence of official visitors from such world confessional groups as the Presbyterian, Baptist, Methodist, and Congregational ones, and from such ecumenical groups as the World Council of Churches, the International Missionary Council, the World Council of Christian Education, the United Bible Societies, the World Christian Federation, and the World Alliance of Young Men's Christian Associations.

In the elections at Minneapolis an American was chosen president of the Federation to succeed Bishop Hanns Lilje, who had presided since the Hannover assembly. The choice fell on Dr. Franklin Clark Fry, president of the United Lutheran Church in America. Dr. Carl Lund-Quist, of the Augustana Lutheran Church, who had become executive secretary in 1956 upon the death of Dr. Michelfelder, continued in that office. Shortly after the Minneapolis Assembly, however, his health began to fail, so that in 1961 he felt obliged to give up the work. He was succeeded by Dr. Kurt Schmidt-Claussen of Germany.

Unlike the procedure at previous assemblies, the central theme at Minneapolis was not subdivided for the several discussion groups; rather, the entire theme was assigned to all the groups. The results of the discussions were then condensed by a small committee into fifty-one brief theses under five heads: The Freedom We Have in Christ, The Unity of the Church in Christ, The Freedom to Reform the Church, Our Freedom for Service in the World, and Free and United in Hope. These theses were adopted by the Assembly and constituted the official report to the member churches.

Parallel with the group discussions and the plenary sessions of delegates and official visitors, there was a "visitors' program" that attracted about three thousand persons each day. The climax of a series of "public events" came at the closing festival service, when more than one-hundred fifteen thousand persons gathered on the approach to the state capitol in St. Paul, where they sang hymns led by a choir of three thousand and witnessed a dramatic presentation of the assembly theme and the core of the theses that had been adopted.

Several items in the reports of the departments and commissions are of importance to the history of the Federation. The Department of Theology reported that it had begun a series of national and international conferences of Lutheran theologians and pastors, including a congress on Luther research. It had begun an extensive program of international exchange of professors and students and pastors. It also proposed to give special attention to the great demand for Lutheran textbooks in Latin America and the younger churches. The Department of Theology, on the initiative of some delegates from Germany, was authorized to set up an Institute for Confessional Research, which would deal first of all with questions relating to Roman Catholic theology. The Commission on Theology was instructed to examine and clarify the nature, aims, and methods of the Federation, and to study the question whether the Lutheran confessions have validity in the actual life of the church today and in what way they are still binding on our churches.

The Department of World Service reported that it was spending annually about $1,500,000 to help refugees, emigrants, and needy churches in many part of the world. It proposed to enlarge its field by co-ordinating a global mission to Lutheran seamen. It reported increasing difficulties in many of the fields in the Far East, the growth of autonomy among the younger churches, and the need for continued support for those churches. Its report included extensive plans to establish a powerful radio station somewhere in East Africa to proclaim the gospel to the two and a half million radio receivers on the African continent.

The Minneapolis Assembly marked the tenth anniversary of the Lutheran World Federation. The spectacular growth of the young organization was strikingly manifest from the enthusiasm of the multitudes who flocked to its sessions and from the extent and depth of the work of its many departments, commissions, and committees, as reported and projected at Minneapolis. The Lutherans of the world are closer to unified intelligence and the consciousness of solidarity than they have ever been in the four centuries of their history. They have lifted their eyes above the limitations of language and nation and ecclesiastical organization. In the conscious efforts toward this end the Lutherans of America have had a leading part, and this has reacted in a wholesome manner upon their relations among themselves.

As this volume goes to press (July, 1963), Lutherans all over the world have turned their eyes to Helsinki, Finland, where the fourth assembly of the Federation is to be held July 30 to August 11, 1963. The general theme will be "Christ Today." There will be even greater emphasis than at Minneapolis on Bible study and worship. Besides the groups for the discussion of the main theme, there will be "sections" to deliberate on the actual programs and prospects of the several departments, commissions, and committees. In general, the program of the fourth assembly will follow the pattern of the third. A preliminary study document has been issued on "The Nature of the Lutheran World Federation." It will serve to guide a thorough discussion of the structure and function of the Federation in the light of changing conditions in every sector of the Christian church. Another study document has been prepared by the Commission on Theology. It deals with the present-day relevance of the doctrine of justification and attempts a new and practical interpretation of Articles I through VI of the Augsburg Confession.

In addition to the reports of broader range of effort and higher levels of achievement by the several departments and commissions, the Executive Committee will report the expansion of the confessional basis of the Federation as authorized at Minneapolis, recommendations of far-reaching changes in the structure of the Federation, the completion of the radio station in Ethiopia with a voice that reaches India as well as Africa, the progress of conversations with Roman Catholics through the Foundation for Inter-Confessional Research, and many other measures for furthering the Federation's work.

From this outline of the main events since 1950 it is clear that American Lutheranism has taken the initial steps into a new period of its history. In the context of pluralism and ecumenism, American Lutheranism has entered a period of consolidation among those within and of aggressive witness to those outside.

GENERAL BIBLIOGRAPHICAL NOTE

Few people would want to read all the details of every part of the history of the Lutheran church in America. Some want to know the particulars about a certain limited period or a certain small section of the church. But for most people it is sufficient to know the general course of events in times past and the main trends of today. Of course, these general trends can only be determined by one who has studied the details and knows how to interpret them in general terms.

Accordingly, there are two kinds of books that need to be considered by every student of our subject. The one kind consists of special works that deal with some particular aspect of the subject, some period of time, some section of territory, some local congregation, some individual person, some separate institution, some special phase of the church's life, or some special type of work. The other kind consists of general works that seek to cover the whole field, omitting details but pointing out the general course of events.

The first group of works is a very large one. I estimate that a complete list of the volumes and pamphlets dealing with the various aspects and details of the Lutheran church in America alone would embrace at least thirty thousand titles. And this would not include the much larger number of manuscripts which contain Lutheran history in our country but which have never been published. The collection of printed materials would include biographies, histories of congregations, conferences, synods, general bodies, institutions, and special lines of Christian work, minutes of synods, reports of agencies and proceedings of other organizations, periodicals, liturgies, catechisms, sermons, books of devotion, and special addresses, essays, and articles. These are found chiefly in the archives of synods, the libraries of seminaries and colleges, and the special collections of private individuals.

The quantity of these source materials is growing with increasing speed. Today we have better records of congregational life than formerly, and more of them are seeing the light of publication. The synods and church bodies keep more detailed and more accurate records of their proceedings and activities. The bulk of periodical literature on historical topics is steadily increasing and it reflects the growing sense of history among the Lutherans in America. Teachers of Lutheran church history are gratified to see the broadening stream of doctoral dissertations in Lutheran history that students are presenting for their degrees at the universities.

The second group of works is much smaller. These works are not concerned about setting forth details, but take the view of the whole in order to help the reader understand the situation in which he finds himself. In this kind of historical writing the author's personal point of view is important. His own position will help to determine what he regards as significant and so will color his narrative and his interpretation of the detailed facts. We may glance now at the titles of these volumes that seek to set forth the whole of the history of the Lutheran church in America. The list is not a long one. It embraces seven titles:

> Ernest L. Hazelius, *History of the American Lutheran Church, from its Commencement in the Year of Our Lord 1685, to the Year 1842.* Zanesville, O., 1846. 300 pages. 12 mo.

This little book is the first effort to review at any length the history of the whole Lutheran church in this country. Dr. Hazelius had been professor at Hartwick Seminary for fifteen years, professor of church history at Gettysburg for three years, and when he wrote his book was professor of theology at the theological seminary of the Synod of South Carolina at Lexington. In 1842 only a limited perspective of our history was possible. Dr. Hazelius in his history made the rounds of the several synods as they existed at that time and was chiefly concerned with calling the roll of the personalities who served the various pastorates.

> Edmund Jacob Wolf, *The Lutherans in America. A Story of Struggle, Progress, Influence and Marvelous Growth. With an Introduction by Henry Eyster Jacobs,* New York, 1889. 544 pages.

Dr. Wolf was professor of church history at the Gettysburg Seminary. His volume brings the narrative half the distance from Hazelius to our times. It is written with an objectivity and impartiality of judgment that was not very common at that time. It was intended for the general reader and is characterized chiefly by its readableness. The beauty of rhetoric and the eloquence of style carry the reader along from chapter to chapter and tend to fire him with enthusiasm for the Lutheran church as a whole. Dr. Wolf's volume proved to be a powerful factor in helping the several branches of Lutherans to know one another. The book is abundantly illustrated. Printed in large type, it still affords attractive reading for the elementary student or for one who wants to know how Lutheran history was conceived sixty-five years ago.

> A. L. Graebner, *Geschichte der Lutherischen Kirche in America. Erster Theil.* St. Louis, 1892. 726 pages.

The Missouri Synod commissioned Professor Graebner of the seminary at St. Louis to write the history of the Lutheran church in this country. He began his work with great industry and thoroughness. All parts of the field were visited and the original sources critically examined. Much new material was brought to light. Not only in gathering his materials but also in his presentation of them, Professor Graebner was more thorough and comprehensive than any other writer who tried to cover the whole field. Unfortunately he did not complete the work. The stately volume called the "First Part" brings the narrative down only to the founding of the General Synod in 1820. The other parts have never followed. Unfortunately, also, the book is in German and without table of contents or outline, so that it is not easily usable by the average Lutheran reader. Of course, the viewpoint is that of the Missouri Synod and the author finds much to criticize adversely not only in the patriarch Muhlenberg but also in all the Lutheranism of America before 1820. If the narrative could have been carried a century further, the author might have employed better perspective.

Henry Eyster Jacobs, *A History of the Evangelical Lutheran Church in the United States.* New York, 1893. 539 pages.

In the American Church History series this is Volume IV. It is scholarly, authoritative, and judicial. For many years it was the best work on the history of the Lutheran church in America up to sixty years ago and Dr. Jacobs was generally regarded as the outstanding authority on our subject. The developments of the past sixty years have given us a new perspective on many of the earlier events. All parts of Dr. Jacobs' book are covered by the bibliographies in our volume.

George J. Fritschel, *Geschichte der Lutherischen Kirche in Amerika. Erster Teil*, 1896. 432 pages. *Zweiter Teil*, 1897. 432 pages.

This is a German translation of Dr. Jacobs' book already mentioned, with additions concerning the development of the German Iowa Synod.

J. L. Neve, *A Brief History of the Lutheran Church in America.* First edition, 1903. Second revised and enlarged edition, 1916. 469 pages. Third revised edition, 1934. 399 pages. Burlington, Iowa.

Dr. Neve felt that Dr. Wolf's book sacrificed the real historical character of the work because it simply enumerated the leading events and co-ordinated them. He felt that Jacobs and Fritschel traced the development too much from the viewpoint of confessional progress and so confused the beginner. He therefore set about to present the materials "simply from the viewpoint of organization and growth." He divided his general subject into three parts: (1) origin of individual congregations, (2) congregations organized into synods, (3) synods organized into larger bodies.

Each of these parts constitutes a "period" of the history. The result is that the student gets a vivid impression of a multitude of parts and organizations in the Lutheran church in America but is in danger of failing to see any continuity of development or any relation to general history and culture. Attached to the several chapters are a number of biographical sketches.

F. Bente, *American Lutheranism.* Vol. I, Early History of American Lutheranism and the Tennessee Synod. St. Louis, 1919. 237 pages. Vol. II, The United Lutheran Church. St. Louis, 1919. 243 pages.

The first of these little volumes is taken mainly from Dr. Graebner's book mentioned above. Dr. Bente, like Dr. Graebner, was a professor in the Concordia Theological Seminary. The second volume is little more than a prolonged criticism of the theological positions of the former General Synod, General Council, and United Synod in the South. Volumes III and IV were to deal in similar fashion with other general bodies of Lutherans, but they have not appeared.

In the *Lutheran World Almanac* for 1931-33 (Vol. VII, pp. 108-137) is an essay by O. M. Norlie entitled "Outline History of the Lutherans of America." It is a series of thumbnail sketches covering 151 synods in alphabetical order. Among the annotations on these synods of past and present are a few bibliographical references in each case. This is a valuable reference work for the student of the complicated history of our synodical organizations in this country.

It would lead us too far afield if we should begin to list here the general sources of information on Lutheran history in this country, such as encyclopedias, periodicals, almanacs, and collections of source materials. We must content ourselves with a reference to the selected lists of books and articles for each chapter that are presented here.

In these bibliographies I have listed the corresponding parts of Wolf, Graebner, Jacobs, and Neve. I have also set down some of the special treatises which will furnish the student with more details on the subject of the chapter and at the same time will point to the documents containing the evidence for the facts set forth in the narrative. In a number of instances I have referred to more complete bibliographies along special lines. By following the lines thus indicated it would be possible for any student to pursue the study of American Lutheran history into almost infinite detail.

As this volume goes to press there is a project afoot to microfilm the doctoral dissertations on Lutheran history that have been written at various universities during the past few years. As this project proceeds it will make available to teachers and students a large body of source materials that research students have recently brought to light. The work is projected by the Lutheran Historical Conference and the dissertations are listed in the May, 1963, *News Letter* of that conference.

SELECTIVE BIBLIOGRAPHY

CHAPTER 1 — General Background (1625-1740)

Abrams, R. H. (Ed.). "Organized Religion in the United States," in the *Annals of the American Academy of Political and Social Science,* March, 1948.

Adams, J. T. *Provincial Society,* 1690-1763. 1928.

Andrews, C. M. *The Colonial Period of American History.* 2 vols., 1936.

Bacon, L. W. *A History of American Christianity.* 1897. Pp. 1-154.

Beard, Charles A. and Mary R. *The Rise of Civilization in America.* 1927. Vol. I, pp. 3-188.

——————. *A Basic History of the United States.* 1950. Pp. 1-101.

Cheney, E. P. *The European Background of American History.* 1907.

Dorchester, D. *Christianity in the United States.* 1888. Pp. 13-256.

Hall, Thomas C. *The Religious Background of American Culture.* 1930.

Jacobs, H. E. *The Lutheran Movement in England.* 1890.

Sweet, W. W. *The Story of Religion in America.* 1950. Pp. 1-154.

——————. *Religion in Colonial America,* 1942.

Wertenbaker, Thomas Jefferson. *The Founding of American Civilization: The Middle Colonies.* 1949.

CHAPTER 2 — New Netherland and New York

Clark, Delber W. *The World of Justus Falckner.* 1946.

Diffenderffer, F. R. *The German Exodus to England in* 1709. 1897.

Ecclesiastical Records of the State of New York. 6 vols., 1901-1905.

Evjen, J. O. *Scandinavian Immigrants in New York,* 1630-1674. 1916.

Finck, W. J. *Lutheran Landmarks and Pioneers in America.* 1913. Pp. 22-27.

Fiske, John. *The Dutch and Quaker Colonies in America.* 1899.

Graebner, A. L. *Geschichte der Lutherischen Kirche in America, Erster Theil.* 1892. Pp. 3-144; 165-232.

Jacobs, H. E. *A History of the Evangelical Lutheran Church in the United States.* 1893. Pp. 21-61; 110-132.

Kreider, J. H. *Lutheranism in Colonial New York.* 1942.

——————. *The Beginnings of Lutheranism in New York.* 1949.

——————————. *History of the United Lutheran Synod of New York and New England. Vol. I,* 1786-1860. 1954.

Mattice, P. B. (Ed.). *The Palatines of New York State.* 1953.

Nicum, J. *Geschichte des Evangelisch-Lutherischen Ministeriums vom Staate New York.* 1888. Pp. 1-32.

O'Callaghan, E. B. *The Documentary History of the State of New York.* 4 vols., 1849. Vol. III, pp. 101 ff.; 539-607; Vol. IV, p. 19.

——————————. *Documents Relating to the Colonial History of the State of New York.* 14 vols., 1856-1883.

Qualben, L. P. *The Lutheran Church in Colonial America.* 1940.

Reynolds, W. M. "The Lutheran Church in the New Netherlands and New York," in *The Evangelical Review,* Vol. VI, Jan., 1855, pp. 302-329.

Sachse, J. F. *Justus Falckner, Mystic and Scholar.* 1903.

Schmucker, B. M. "The Lutheran Church in the City of New York," in *The Lutheran Church Review,* Vol. III, July, Oct., 1884, pp. 203-222; 276-295.

Van Laer, Arnold J. H. (Trans.). *The Lutheran Church in New York,* 1649-1772.

——————————. *Records in the Lutheran Church Archives at Amsterdam, Holland.* 1946.

Wenner, G. U. *The Lutherans of New York,* 1648-1918. 1918.

Wolf, E. J. *The Lutherans in America.* 1889. Pp. 107-132.

CHAPTER 3 — New Sweden

Acrelius, Israel. *A History of New Sweden.* 1759. Trans. by W. M. Reynolds, 1876.

Benson, Adolph and Naboth Hedin. *Swedes in America.* 1938.

Bergendoff, Conrad. *Olavus Petri and the Ecclesiastical Transformation in Sweden.* 1928.

Campanius, Thomas. *The Province of New Sweden.* 1702. Trans. by P. S. DuPoneau. 1833.

Clay, J. C. *Annals of the Swedes on the Delaware.* 1834.

Dodge, T. A. *Gustavus Adolphus.* 1895.

Ferris, Benjamin. *History of the Original Settlements on the Delaware.* 1846.

Fletcher, C. R. L. *Gustavus Adolphus and the Struggle of Protestantism for Existence.* Revised ed., 1928.

Finck, W. J. *Lutheran Landmarks and Pioneers in America.* 1913. Pp. 28-80.

Fuhlbruegge, Irene. *The Swedes and Finns in New Jersey.* 1938.

Graebner, A. L. *Geschichte der Lutherischen Kirche in Amerika.* 1892. Pp. 3-37, 75-87, 117-144, 333-408.

Historical Society of Delaware Papers. II, III, VII, XXXVIII, XLIII.

Jacobs, H. E. *A History of the Evangelical Lutheran Church in the United States.* 1893. Pp. 62-110.

Johnson, Amandus. *The Swedish Settlements on the Delaware,* 1638-1664. 2 vols., 1911. (Including a complete bibliography.)

——————. *The Swedes on the Delaware.* 1913. (An abridgment of the preceding work).

——————. *The Instruction for Johan Printz.* 1930.

——————. *The Swedes and Finns in New Jersey.* 1938.

Louhi, E. A. *The Delaware Finns.* 1925.

Odhner, C. T. "The Founding of New Sweden, 1637-1642." 1876. Translated by G. B. Kenn. In *Pennsylvania Magazine of History and Biography,* vol. III, 1879, pp. 269-284, 395-411.

Reynolds, W. M. "The Swedish Churches on the Delaware." 1849. In *The Evangelical Review,* vol. I, Oct., 1849, pp. 161-199.

Richards, J. W. *Penn's Lutheran Forerunners and Friends.* 1926.

Rines, E. F. *Old Historic Churches of America.* 1936.

Schmauk, T. E. *A History of the Lutheran Church in Pennsylvania,* 1638-1820. 1903. Pp. 36-63.

Wallington, Nellie. *Historical Churches of America.* 1926.

Ward, Christopher. *The Dutch and Swedes on the Delaware,* 1609-64. 1930.

Wolf, E. J. *The Lutherans in America.* 1889. Pp. 133-168.

Wuorinen, John H. *The Finns on the Delaware,* 1638-1655. 1938.

CHAPTER 4 — Pennsylvania

(A complete bibliography on the German element in the United States would embrace more than ten thousand titles. The most extensive bibliography published is that in Faust's work listed below. A selective bibliography is found in Kuhns' volume listed below.)

Faust, A. B. *The German Element in the United States.* 2 vols., 1909. Vol. I, pp. 1-18.

Graebner, A. L. *Geschichte der Lutherischen Kirche in Amerika.* 1892. Pp. 242-252.

Hallesche Nachrichten. 1787. New edition, edited by Mann, Schmucker, and Germann, Vol. I, 1886, and Vol. II, 1895.

Jacobs, H. E. *A History of the Evangelical Lutheran Church in the United States.* 1893. Pp. 110-118, 133-149, 187-205.

Klees, Fredric. *The Pennsylvania Dutch.* 1951.

Kuhns, Oscar. *The German and Swiss Settlements of Colonial Pennsylvania.* 1901.

Mann, W. J. "Lutherans in America before Muhlenberg." 1887. In *The Lutheran Church Review,* Vol. VI, Oct., 1887, pp. 93-114.

Maurer, C. L. *Early Lutheran Education in Pennsylvania.* 1932.

Pennsylvania German Society, Proceedings of. Various volumes, especially VII-XII, XIX, XX, XXIX.

Qualben, L. P. *The Lutheran Church in Colonial America*. 1940.

Richards, J. W. *Penn's Lutheran Forerunners and Friends*. 1926.

Sachse, J. F. "The Influence of Halle Pietism in the Provincial Development of Pennsylvania." 1901. In *The Lutheran Quarterly*, Vol. 31, April, 1901, pp. 170-176.

————. "The Genesis of the German Lutheran Church in the Land of Penn." 1897. In *The Lutheran Church Review*. Vol. XVI, Jan., Apr., July, Oct., 1897, pp. 60-76, 283-301, 435-452, 521-539.

————. *The German Pietists of Provincial Pennsylvania*, 1694-1708. 1895.

————. *The German Sectarians of Pennsylvania*, 1708-1742. 1899.

————. *The German Sectarians of Pennsylvania*, 1742-1800. 1900.

Schmauk, T. E. *A History of the Lutheran Church in Pennsylvania*, 1638-1820. Pp. 64-576. (Only Vol. I appeared, 1903, which brings the narrative down to about 1750 and includes detailed bibliographies, references to original sources and profuse illustrations.)

Wentz, A. R. *The Beginnings of the German Element in York County, Pennsylvania*. 1916.

Wolf, E. J. *The Lutherans in America*. 1889. Pp. 169-187.

Wood, Ralph (Ed.). *The Pennsylvania Germans*. 1942.

CHAPTER 5 — From Maryland to Georgia

Bernheim, G. D. *History of the German Settlements and of the Lutheran Church in North and South Carolina*. 1872.

Finck, W. J. *Lutheran Landmarks and Pioneers in America*. 1913.

————. "The Orphan House in the Salzburg Colony." In *The Lutheran Church Review*, Vol. XXXIII, Jan., 1914, pp. 91-101.

Cassell, C. W., Finck, W. J., and Henkel, E. O. *History of the Lutheran Church in Virginia and East Tennessee*. 1930.

Gehrke, W. H. "The Beginnings of the Pennsylvania-German Element in Rowan and Cabarrus Counties, North Carolina." In the *Pennsylvania Magazine of History and Biography*, No. 4, 1934.

Gilbert, D. M. "Early History of the Lutheran Church in Georgia." 1897. In *The Lutheran Quarterly*, April, 1897, pp. 156-174.

Graebner, A. L. *Geschichte der Lutherischen Kirche in Amerika*. 1892. Pp. 156-162, 553-605.

Jacobs, H. E. *A History of the Evangelical Lutheran Church in the United States*. 1893. Pp. 150-186.

Morgan, J. L., Brown, B. S., and Hall, J. (Eds.). *History of the Lutheran Church in North Carolina*, 1803-1953. 1953.

Muhlenberg, H. M. "Journal of a Voyage from Philadelphia to Ebenezer in Georgia," 1774 and 1775. Trans. by J. W. Richards. In *The Evangelical Review*. Vol. I, Jan., Apr., 1850, pp. 390-419; 534-560; Vol. II, July, 1850, pp. 113-134; Vol. III, Oct., 1851, Jan., Apr., 1852, pp. 115-129, 418-435, 582-590; Vol. IV, Oct., 1852, pp. 172-203.

Ochsenford, S. E. "Salzburg and the Salzburg Lutherans." 1888. In *The Lutheran Church Review*, Vol. VII, July, 1888. Pp. 294-311.

Qualben, L. P. *The Lutheran Church in Colonial America.* 1940.

Stevens, W. B. *History of Georgia.* 1847.

Strobel, P. A. *The Salzburgers and their Descendants.* 1855.

Urlsperger, Samuel. *Die Salzburgischen Nachrichten.* In eighteen parts. 1735-1752.

Wentz, A. R. *History of the Maryland Synod,* 1820-1920. 1920.

Wolf, E. J. *The Lutherans in America.* 1889. Pp. 187-198.

CHAPTER 6 — The Religious Life of the Lutheran Colonies

In addition to the volumes and articles cited for previous chapters, reference is made to the following:

Beck, W. H. *Lutheran Elementary Schools in the United States.* 1939.

Faulkner, H. V. *American Political and Social History.* 5th ed. 1948.

Muhlenberg, H. M. *The Journals.* Three Volumes. Trans. by T. G. Tappert and J. W. Doberstein. 1942 ff.

Page, Evelyn. "The First Frontier. The Swedes and the Dutch." In *Pennsylvania History*, Oct., 1948.

Pennsylvania German Society Proceedings. 1891 ff.

Robacker, E. F. *Pennsylvania German Literature.* 1943.

Sessler, J. J. *Communal Pietism Among Early American Moravians.* 1933.

Shryock, R. H. "The Pennsylvania Germans in American History." In the *Pennsylvania Magazine of History and Biography.* July, 1939.

CHAPTER 7 — General Background (1740-1790)

Bacon, L. W. *A History of American Christianity.* 1897. Pp. 155-229.

Beard, Charles A. and Mary R., *The Rise of American Civilization.* 1927. Vol. I, pp. 189-296.

_____. *A Basic History of the United States.* 1950. Pp. 102-156.

Cobb, S. H. *Rise of Religious Liberty in America.* 1902.

Faulkner, H. V. *American Political and Social History.* 5th ed. 1948.

Humphrey, E. F. *Nationalism and Religion in America.* 1924.

Sweet, W. W. *The Story of Religion in America.* 1950. Pp. 155-204.

Turner, Frederick Jackson. *The Frontier in American History.* 1920.

CHAPTER 8 — Muhlenberg, the Organizer

Bernheim, G. D. *History of the German Settlements and of the Lutheran Church in North and South Carolina.* 1872.

Burgess, E. B. *Memorial History of the Pittsburgh Synod.* 1925. Pp. 13-63.

Cassell, Finck, and Henkel. *History of the Lutheran Church in Virginia and East Tennessee.* 1930.

Documentary History of the Lutheran Ministerium of Pennsylvania. 1898.

Faust, A. B. *The German Element in the United States.* 2 vols., 1909. Vol. I, pp. 53-285.

SELECTIVE BIBLIOGRAPHY

Finck, W. J. *Lutheran Landmarks and Pioneers in America.* 1913. Pp. 91-120.

Frick, W. K. *Henry Melchior Muhlenberg.* 1902.

Graebner, A. L. *Geschichte der Lutherischen Kirche in Amerika.* 1892 Pp. 235-330, 371-382, 473-522, 563-605.

Hallesche Nachrichten. 1787. New ed., edited by Mann, Schmucker, and Germann, Vol. I, 1886, and Vol. II, 1895.

Hiller, Alfred. "History of the Lutheran Church in New Jersey." In *The Lutheran Quarterly*, Vol. XXVIII, Jan., Apr., 1898, pp. 98-130, 165-196.

Jacobs, H. E. "The Confessional Problem in the Lutheran Church of America in 1742," in *The Lutheran Church Review.* Vol. XXXI, April, 1912, pp. 245-252.

—————. *A History of the Evangelical Lutheran Church in the United States.* 1893. Pp. 209-306.

Mann, W. J. "The Conservatism of Henry Melchior Muhlenberg," in *The Lutheran Church Review*, Vol. VII, Jan., 1888, pp. 18-46.

—————. *Life and Times of Henry Melchior Muhlenberg.* 1887.

Muhlenberg, H. A. *Life of Major-General Peter Muhlenberg.* 1849.

Muhlenberg, H. M. *Selbstbiographie,* 1711-1743. 1881.

Nicum, J. *Geschichte des Evangelisch-Lutherischen Ministeriums vom Staate New York.* 1888. Pp. 32-46.

Pohlman, H. N. "The German Colony and the Lutheran Church in Maine," in *The Evangelical Review*, Vol. XX, July, 1869, pp. 440-462.

Schaeffer, C. W. "Muhlenberg's Defense of Pietism." In *The Lutheran Church Review*, Vol. XII, Oct., 1893, pp. 349-375.

Schmauk, T. E. *A History of the Lutheran Church in Pennsylvania,* 1638-1820. 1903.

Schmucker, B. M. *The Organization of the Congregation in the Early Lutheran Churches in America.* 1887.

Stoever, M. L. *Life and Times of H. M. Muhlenberg.* 1856.

Tappert, T. G. and Doberstein, J. W. (trans.), *The Journals of Henry Melchior Muhlenberg. In Three Volumes.* 1942 ff.

Wallace, Paul A. W. *The Muhlenbergs of Pennsylvania.* 1950.

Wayland, J. W. *The German Element in the Valley of Virginia.* 1907.

Wolf, E. J. *The Lutherans in America.* 1889. Pp. 210-270.

CHAPTER 9 – The Lutheran Element
at the Birth of the Nation

Dorpalen, Andreas. "The Political Influence of the German Element in Colonial America." In *Pennsylvania History*, Vol. VI, 1939, pp. 147-239.

Knauss, James Owen, Jr. "Social Conditions Among the Pennsylvania Germans in the Eighteenth Century" (with extensive bibliography). In the *Proceedings of the Pennsylvania German Society*, Vol. XXIX, 1922.

Graeff, Arthur D. "Relations Between the Pennsylvania Germans and the British Authorities, 1750-1776" (with detailed bibliography). In the *Proceedings of the Pennsylvania German Society*, Vol. XLVII, 1939.

Keiser, Albert. *Lutheran Mission Work Among the American Indians.* 1922.

CHAPTER 10 — General Background (1790-1830)

Bacon, L. W. *A History of American Christianity.* 1897. Pp. 230-261.

Beard, Charles A. and Mary R. *The Rise of American Civilization.* 1927. Vol. I, pp. 297-506.

——————. *A Basic History of the United States.* 1950. Pp. 157-245.

Dorchester, D. *Christianity in the United States.* 1888. Pp. 259-558.

Elson, H. W. *History of the United States.* 1904. Pp. 342-508.

Krout, J. A. and D. R. Fox. *The Completion of Independence,* 1790-1830. 1944.

McMaster, J. B. *History of the People of the United States.* 1883 ff. Vols. I and II.

Mode, Peter G. *The Frontier Spirit in American Christianity.* 1923.

Sweet, W. W. *The Story of Religion in America.* 1950. Pp. 205-257.

Turner, F. J. *The Frontier in American History.* 1920. Pp. 1-38.

West, W. M. *American History and Government.* 1913. Pp. 378-463.

CHAPTER 11 — Westward Expansion and New Synods

Bernheim, G. D. *History of the German Settlements and of the Lutheran Church in North and South Carolina.* 1872. Pp. 274-401.

—————— and George H. Cox. *The History of the Evangelical Lutheran Synod and Ministerium of North Carolina.* 1902. Pp. 1-26, 35-57, 85-93.

Burgess, E. B. *Memorial History of the Pittsburgh Synod of the Evangelical Lutheran Church.* 1925. Pp. 1-63.

Cassell, Finck, and Henkel. *History of the Lutheran Church in Virginia and East Tennessee.* 1930. Pp. 1-151.

Fortenbaugh, Robert. *The Development of the Synodical Polity of the Lutheran Church in America to 1829.* 1926. Pp. 31-145 (with detailed bibliography).

Hallman, S. T. *History of the Evangelical Lutheran Synod of South Carolina.* 1924. Pp. 17-57.

Henkel, Socrates. *History of the Evangelical Lutheran Tennessee Synod.* 1890. Pp. 1-42.

Morgan, Brown, and Hall. *History of the Lutheran Church in North Carolina.* 1953. Pp. 41-89.

Nicum, J. *Geschichte des Evangelisch-Lutherischen Ministeriums vom Staate New York.* 1888. Pp. 47-123.

Peter, P. A. and William Schmidt. *Geschichte der Allgemeinen Evangelisch-Lutherischen Synode von Ohio und anderen Staaten.* 1900. Pp. 1-36.

Pershing, B. H. "Paul Henkel, Frontier Missionary." In *The Lutheran Church Quarterly*, April, 1934, pp. 125-151.

Sheatsley, C. V. *History of the Evangelical Lutheran Joint Synod of Ohio and other States.* 1918. Pp. 9-109.

Stump, A. and H. Anstadt. *History of the Evangelical Lutheran Synod of West Pennsylvania, 1825-1925.* 1925. Pp. 1-90.

Wentz, A. R. *History of the Evangelical Lutheran Synod of Maryland.* 1920. Pp. 33-81.

CHAPTER 12 — Problems of Faith and Language

Bernheim, G. D. *History of the German Settlements and of the Lutheran Church in North and South Carolina.* 1872.

Carson, James. *Trial of Frederick Eberle and Others.* 1817.

Giese, E. F. "The Chasm between the German and English in the General Synod." In *The Lutheran Quarterly*, Vol. VII, July, 1877, pp. 409-440.

Graebner, A. L. *Geschichte der Lutherischen Kirche in Amerika.* 1892. Pp. 525-550, 584-714.

Hull, William. "The Lutheran Church in the Courts." In *The Lutheran Church Review*, Vol. VI, Oct., 1887, pp. 296-324.

Jacobs, H. E. *A History of the Evangelical Lutheran Church in the United States.* 1893. Pp. 309-347.

Nicum, J. *Geschichte des Evangelisch-Lutherischen Ministeriums vom Staate New York.* 1888. Pp. 63-100.

Norlie, O. M. "A Study of Lutheran Losses." In *American Lutheran*, Oct., 1922, pp. 19-24.

Schmucker, B. M. "Luther's Small Catechism." In *Lutheran Church Review*, Vol. V, Apr., July, 1886. Pp. 87-113, 165-199.

Weng, A. G. "The Language Problem in the Lutheran Church in Pennsylvania, 1743-1820." In *Church History*, Dec., 1936, pp. 359-374.

Wolf, E. J. "The Lutheran Church in This Country One Hundred Years Ago." In *The Lutheran Quarterly*, Vol. XIX, April, 1889, pp. 242-280.
——————. *The Lutherans in America.* 1889. Pp. 271-321.

Yoder, Donald H. "Lutheran-Reformed Union Proposals, 1800-1850: An Experiment in Ecumenics." In the *Bulletin* of the Theological Seminary of the Evangelical and Reformed Church, Vol. XVII, No. 1, pp. 39-77, Jan., 1946.

CHAPTER 13 — A General Organization and a Seminary

Anstadt, P. *Life and Times of Rev. S. S. Schmucker, D.D.* 1896.

Conrad, F. W. "The Influence of the Theological Seminary of the General Synod." In *The Lutheran Quarterly*, Vol. XIV, July, 1884, pp. 435-448.

Documentary History of the General Council of the Evangelical Lutheran Church. 1912. Pp. 43-56.

Early, J. W. "The Ministerium of Pennsylvania and the Organization of the General Synod." In *The Lutheran Church Review*, Vol. XI, Jan., April, 1892, pp. 61-70, 172-186.

Fortenbaugh, Robert. *The Development of the Synodical Polity of the Lutheran Church in America to* 1829. 1926. Pp. 146-202 (with detailed bibliography).

Haussman, C. F. *Kunze's Seminarium.* 1917.

Hefelbower, S. G. *History of Gettysburg College.* 1932.

Jacobs, H. E. *A History of the Evangelical Lutheran Church in the United States.* 1893. Pp. 351-372.

Krauth, Charles Philip. "Our General Synod." In *The Evangelical Review,* Vol. V, Oct., 1853, pp. 239-280.

Kline, M. J. "The Genesis of the General Synod." In *The Lutheran Church Quarterly,* Vol. XLIX, Jan., 1919, pp. 44-60.

Memorial Volume of the Semi-Centennial Anniversary of Hartwick Seminary. 1866.

Morris, J. G. "History of the Theological Seminary of the General Synod of the Evangelical Lutheran Church." In *The Lutheran Quarterly,* Vol. VI, Oct., 1876, pp. 525-554.

Richard, J. W. "The Confessional History of the General Synod." In *The Lutheran Church Quarterly,* Vol. XXV, October, 1895, pp. 458-490.

Sparks, C. E. "The Development of the General Synod Lutheran Church in America." In *The Lutheran Quarterly,* Vol. XXXVI, Oct., 1906, pp. 566-584.

Wentz, A. R. *History of the Gettysburg Theological Seminary.* 1926. Pp. 1-156.

Wolf, E. J. "History of the General Synod." In *The Lutheran Quarterly,* Vol. XIX, July, 1889, pp. 420-458.

_____. *The Lutherans in America.* 1889. Pp. 322-348.

CHAPTER 14 — Lutheran People in the Youth of the Republic

Much of the material for this chapter is gathered from unpublished sources, such as letters and diaries of itinerant missionaries. Of special value are the journals of Paul Henkel. Some of the reports of these missionaries are published with the minutes of the synods in the East. Another source of information is the file of the early magazines mentioned in the text. The early histories of the Bible, tract, and missionary societies also help to portray the life of the people in this period. Some light is provided by the early parts of congregational and synodical histories. The social and cultural life of Lutherans is illuminated also by the studies of American life in general, such as the volumes by Wertenbaker and Faulkner, already referred to in connection with Chapters 1 and 7. In addition, we mention the following:

Cleveland, C. C. *The Great Revival in the West,* 1797-1805. 1916.

Paxson, F. L. *History of the American Frontier,* 1763-1893. 1924.

Riegel, R. E. *America Moves West.* 1949.

Schneider, Carl E. *The German Church on the American Frontier,* 1840-1860. 1939.

Speer, William. *The Great Revival of* 1800. 1892.

CHAPTER 15 — General Background (1830-1870)

Bacon, L. W. *A History of American Christianity.* 1897. Pp. 261-350.
Beard, Charles A. and Mary R. *The Rise of American Civilization.* 1927. Vol I, pp. 507-824; Vol. II, pp. 1-165.
⸻. *A Basic History of the United States.* 1950. Pp. 245-286.
Billington, R. A. *The Protestant Crusade,* 1800-1860—*A Study of the Origins of American Nativism.* 1953.
Denison, J. H. *Emotional Currents in American History.* 1932.
Dorchester, D. *Christianity in the United States.* 1888. Pp. 363-755.
Elson, H. W. *History of the United States.* 1914. Pp. 509-812.
Fish, C. R. *The Rise of the Common Man,* 1830-1850. Pp. 179-199.
McMaster, J. B. *History of the People of the United States.* 1883 ff. Vols. VI-VIII.
Maury, Reuben. *Wars of the Godly.* 1928.
Niebuhr, H. Richard. *Social Sources of Denominationalism.* 1929.
Sweet, W. W. *The Story of Religion in America.* 1950. Pp. 258-344.
Turner, F. J. *The Significance of Sectionalism in American History.* 1932.
West, W. M. *American History and Government.* 1913. Pp. 463-641.

CHAPTER 16 — Organized Benevolence

Anniversary Addresses. 1909. Pp. 11-24; 133-149; 273-280.
Breidenbaugh, E. S. *Pennsylvania College Book.* 1882.
Clark, G. G. *History of Wittenberg College.* 1887.
Diehl, M. *Biography of Rev. Ezra Keller, D.D.* 1859.
Drach, George and C. F. Kuder. *The Telugu Mission.* 1914.
Gerberding, G. H. *Life and Letters of W. A. Passavant, D.D.* 1906.
Gotwald, F. G. "Pioneer American Lutheran Journalism." In *The Lutheran Quarterly,* Vol. XLII, April, 1912, pp. 161-204.
Hunt, J. R. E. *Lutheran Home Missions.* 1913.
Hutter, E. W. *Eulogy on the Life and Character of Rev. Benjamin Kurtz, D.D., LL.D.* 1866.
Imhoff, A. J. *The Life of Rev. Morris Officer, A. M.* 1876.
Keiser, A. *Lutheran Mission Work Among the American Indians.* 1922. (With bibliography.)
Laury, P. A. *A History of Lutheran Missions.* 2nd ed., 1905.
Lewars, Elsie Singmaster. *The Story of Lutheran Missions.* 1917.
Ochsenford, S. E. *Muhlenberg College,* 1867-1892. 1892.
Philadelphia Seminary Biographical Record. 1923.
Wentz, A. R. *History of the Gettysburg Theological Seminary.* 1926. Pp. 187-190.
Wolf, L. B. *After Fifty Years, a Sketch of the Guntur Mission.* 1896.

For the missionary "societies" refer to the minutes of the General Synod. For the periodicals refer to the files of those mentioned in the chapter. For the beginnings of the new synods refer to the several synodical histories: the Alleghany by Carney (1918), the Pittsburgh by Burgess (1926), the Ohio by Mechling (1911), the Wittenberg by Ernsberger (1917), the East Pennsylvania by Hay (1892), the Virginia by Cassell, Finck, and Henkel (1930), the Kansas by Ott (1907), the Susquehanna by Manhart (1917), and the Maryland by Wentz (1920).

CHAPTER 17 — Immigration and Confessional Reaction

"Bibliography of the Saxon Immigration and the Early History of the Missouri Synod." (Mostly German) In the *Concordia Theological Monthly*, Dec., 1937. Pp. 934, 935.

Dau, W. H. T. (Ed.). *Ebenezer.* 1922.

Deindorfer, Johannes. *Geschichte der Evangel.-Luth. Synode von Iowa und anderen Staaten.* 1897.

Distinctive Doctrines and usages of the General Bodies of the Evangelical Lutherans in the United States. 4th ed. 1914. Chaps. III, V, and VII.

Flom, G. T. *A History of Norwegian Immigration to the United States to 1848.* 1909.

Forster, Walter O. *Zion on the Mississippi. The Settlement of the Saxon Lutherans in Missouri*, 1839-1841. 1953. (With complete bibliography.)

Gerberding, G. H. *Life and Letters of W. A. Passavant, D.D.* 1906. Pp. 194-221, 354-389.

Grabau, J. A. *Life of J. A. A. Grabau.* 1879.

Haapanen, Alfred. *Our Church. The Suomi Synod, the Finnish Evangelical Lutheran Church of America.* 1945.

Hall, P. F. *Immigration and its Effects upon the United States.* 1907.

Hansen, Marcus Lee. *The Atlantic Migration*, 1607-1860. *A History of the Continuing Settlement of the United States.* 1945.

———————. *The Immigrant in American History.* 1948.

Hochstetter, Chr. *Die Geschichte der Evangelisch-Lutherischen Missouri-Synode in Nord-Amerika.* 1885.

Jacobs, H. E. *A History of the Evangelical Lutheran Church in the United States.* 1893. Pp. 393-415.

Janson, Florence E. *The Background of Swedish Immigration*, 1840-1930. 1931.

Johnston, L. A. *The Augustana Synod. A Brief Review of its History*, 1860-1910. 1910.

Koehler, J. P. *Geschichte der Allgemeinen Evangelisch-Lutherischen Synode von Wisconsin und anderen Staaten.* 1925.

Kukkonen, Walter J. "Suomi Synod's Stream of Living Tradition." In *The Lutheran Quarterly*, 1958, pp. 26-54.

Mauelshagen, Carl. *American Lutheranism Surrenders to Forces of Conservatism.* 1936.

Norelius, E. "The Swedish Evangelical Lutheran Church in America." In *The Lutheran Church Review*, Vol. V, Jan., 1886, pp. 24-44.

Norlie, O. M. *History of the Norwegian People in America.* 1925.

Olson, Oscar N. *The Augustana Lutheran Church in America. Pioneer Period*, 1846 *to* 1860. 1950. (With detailed bibliography.)

Qualey, Carlton C. *Norwegian Settlement in the United States.* 1938.

Reynolds, W. M. "The Scandinavians in the Northwest." In *The Evangelical Review*, Vol. III, Jan., 1852, pp. 399-418.

Rohne, J. Magnus. *Norwegian American Lutheranism up to* 1872. 1926. (With detailed biblography.)

Rönnegärd, Sam. *Prairie Shepherd. Lars Paul Esbjörn and the Beginnings of the Augustana Lutheran Church.* 1952.

Steffens, D. H. *Doctor Carl Ferdinand Wilhelm Walther.* 1917.

Stephenson, G. M. *The Founding of the Augustana Synod, 1850-1860.* 1927. (With detailed bibliography.)

——————. *A History of American Immigration, 1820-1924.* 1926.

——————. *The Religious Aspects of Swedish Immigration.* 1932. Pp. 1-331. (With complete bibliography.)

Wolf, E. J. *The Lutherans in America.* 1889. Pp. 372-405.

Zeilinger, G. J. *A Missionary Synod with a Mission, 1854-1929.* (Iowa) 1929.

CHAPTER 18 — "American Lutheranism"

Anstadt, P. *Life and Times of Rev. S. S. Schmucker, D.D.* 1896. Pp. 296-360.

Bell, P. G. *Portraiture of the Life of Samuel Sprecher.* 1907.

Ferm, V. *The Crisis in American Lutheran Theology. A Study of The Issue between American Lutheranism and Old Lutheranism.* 1927. (With detailed bibliography and numerous quotations from minutes and periodical literature.)

Hay, Charles A. *Memoirs of Rev. Jacob Goering, Rev. George Lochman, D.D., and Benjamin Kurtz, D.D., LL.D.* 1887. Pp. 107-211.

Jacobs, H. E. *A History of the Evangelical Lutheran Church in the United States.* 1893. Pp. 415-433.

Mann, Emma T. *Memoir of the Life and Work of William Julius Mann.* 1893.

Richard, J. W. *The Confessional History of the Lutheran Church.* 1909. Pp. 601-623.

Spaeth, A. *Charles Porterfield Krauth, D.D., LL.D.* 2 Vols., 1898, 1900. Vol. I, pp. 316-413; Vol. II, pp. 77-126.

Strobel, P. A. *Memorial of the Hartwick Lutheran Synod.* 1881.

Wentz, A. R. *History of the Evangelical Lutheran Synod of Maryland.* 1920. Pp. 147-157, 165-168.

——————. *History of the Gettysburg Theological Seminary.* 1926.

——————. *Life of Samuel Simon Schmucker* (in preparation).

CHAPTER 19 — Disruption and Reconstruction

Bachman, C. L., *John Bachman, D.D., LL.D., Ph.D.* 1888.

Distinctive Doctrines and Usages of the Evangelical Lutheran Church in the United States. 4th ed., 1914.

Jacobs, H. E. *A History of the Evangelical Lutheran Church in the United States.* 1893. Pp. 445-475, 502-505.

Neve, J. L. *History of the Lutheran Church in America.* 3rd ed., 1934. Pp. 95-176.

Ochsenford, S. E. *Documentary History of the General Council.* 1912. Pp. 60-172.

Rohne, J. Magnus. *Norwegian American Lutheranism up to 1872.* 1926. Pp. 158-179, 202-243.

Spaeth, A. *Charles Porterfield Krauth, D.D., LL.D.* 2 Vols., 1898, 1909. Vol. II, pp. 127-249.

Stephenson, G. M. *The Founding of the Augustana Synod, 1850-1860.* 1927. Pp. 33-87.

Van Alstine, N. *Historical Review of the Franckean Synod of New York.* 1893.

Wentz, A. R. *History of the Gettysburg Theological Seminary.* 1926. Pp. 157-214.

Wolf, E. J. *The Lutherans in America.* 1889. Pp. 464-475.

The controversial literature of the period is enormous in bulk. It is found largely in the periodicals of the several bodies. Much of it is in German and the Scandinavian tongues. One large volume in English that might serve for orientation on the predestination controversy is that edited by G. H. Schodde in 1897, under the title *The Error of Modern Missouri: Its Inception, Development, and Refutation.*

CHAPTER 20 — In Civil Conflict

The materials for this chapter are gathered largely from the newspapers and periodicals mentioned in the text and from the minutes and proceedings of the Lutheran synods of that time. In addition we refer to the following volumes:

Andersen, A. W. *The Immigrant Takes His Stand. The Norwegian-American Press and Public Affairs, 1847-1872.* 1953.

Babcock, K. C. *The Scandinavian Element in the United States.* 1914. (With critical essay on materials and authorities.)

Blegen, T. C. *Norwegian Migration to America: The American Transition.* 1940.

Faust, A. B. *The German Element in the United States.* 2 vols., 1909. Vol. I, pp. 522-568.

Fortenbaugh, R. "American Lutheran Synods and Slavery, 1830-1860." In the *Journal of Religion*, Jan., 1933. Pp. 72-92.

_____. "The Representative Lutheran Periodical Press and Slavery, 1831-1860." In *The Lutheran Church Quarterly*, Vol. VIII, Apr., 1935, pp. 151-172.

Hansen, Marcus Lee. *The Immigrant in American History.* 1948.

Heathcote, C. W. *The Lutheran Church and the Civil War.* 1919.

Wentz, A. R. *The History of the Gettysburg Seminary.* 1926. Pp. 191-214.

CHAPTER 21 — General Background (1870-1910)

Abrams, Ray H. (Ed.). "Organized Religion in the United States." In the *Annals of the American Academy of Political Science.* March, 1948.

Bacon, L. W. *A History of American Christianity.* 1897. Pp. 351-373.

Beard, Charles A. and Mary R. *The Rise of American Civilization.* 1927. Vol. II, pp. 166-479.

——————. *A Basic History of the United States.* 1950. Pp. 287-426.

Douglas, H. P. and E. deS. Brunner. *The Church as a Social Institution.* 1935.

Elson, H. W. *History of the United States.* 1914. Pp. 813-911.

Hopkins, Charles H. *The Rise of the Social Gospel in American Protestantism,* 1865-1915. 1940.

Johnson, F. E. *The Social Gospel Re-Examined.* 1940.

May, H. F. *Protestant Churches and Industrial America.* 1949.

Nevins, Allan. *The Emergence of Modern America,* 1865-1878. 1927. Pp. 318-348.

Sweet, W. W. *The Story of Religion in America.* 1950. Pp. 495-523.

West, W. M. *American History and Government.* 1913. Pp. 642-748.

CHAPTER 22 — Growth in Numbers and Benevolence

Babcock, K. C. *The Scandinavian Element in the United States. A Study of Scandinavian Immigration and Its Results.* 1914. (With detailed bibliography.)

Bille, J. H. *A History of the Danes in America.* 1896.

Burgess, E. B. *Memorial History of the Pittsburgh Synod of the Evangelical Lutheran Church.* 1925. Pp. 121-164.

Dau, W. H. T. (Ed.). *Ebenezer.* 1922. Pp. 332-406.

Drach, G. (Ed.). *Our Church Abroad. The Foreign Missions of the Lutheran Church of America.* 1926.

Faust, A. B. *The German Element in the United States.* 1909. Vol. I, pp. 391-591.

Gerberding, G. H. *Life and Letters of W. A. Passavant, D.D.* 1906. Pp. 194-220, 354-388, 501-574.

——————. *Reminiscent Reflections of a Youthful Octogenarian.* 1928.

Nelson, O. N. *History of the Scandinavians and Successful Scandinavians in the United States.* 2 vols. 1900.

Nevins, Allan. *The Emergence of Modern America,* 1865-1878. 1927.

Parson, W. E. *Samuel Bacon Barnitz, Missionary and Western Secretary.* 1905.

Stephenson, G. M. *The Religious Aspects of Swedish Immigration.* 1932. Pp. 196-331.

Trabert, G. H. *English Lutheranism in the Northwest.* 1914.

Wenner, G. U. *The Lutherans of New York*. 1918. Pp. 41-69.

Wolf, L. B. (Ed.) *Missionary Heroes of the Lutheran Church*. 1911. Pp. 145-170, 199-246.

CHAPTER 23 — The Development of the Augustana Lutheran Church
Besides the periodicals of the Augustana Lutheran Church and the proceedings of its conventions, reference is made to the following:

Ander, O. F. *T. N. Hasselquist. The Career and Influence of a Swedish-American Clergyman, Journalist and Educator*. 1931. (With complete bibliography.)

Ander, O. F. and O. L. Nordstrom (Eds.) *The American Origin of the Augustana Synod. From Contemporary Lutheran Periodicals, 1851-1860*. Vol. IX of Augustana Historical Society Publications. 1942.

Arden, G. Everett. *A History of the Augustana Lutheran Church*. 1963.

Benson, Adolph B. and Naboth Hedin. *Americans from Sweden*. 1950.

Flom, George T. "Chapters on Scandinavian Immigration to Iowa." In the *Iowa Journal of History and Politics*. 1905 and 1906.

Forsander, Nils. "Religious Thought and Movements of the Church of Sweden during the 19th Century." In the *Augustana Theological Quarterly*, No. 2, 1900.

Jensson, J. C. *American Lutheran Biographies*. 1890.

Johnson, Amandus. *Swedish Contributions to America National Life, 1638-1921*. 1921.

Mattson, A. D. *Polity of the Augustana Synod*. 1941.

My Church. A Yearbook of the Lutheran Augustana Synod of North America. Edited by Ira O. Nothstein, 1915-1928; S. J. Sebelius, 1929-31; David Nystrom, 1932-37; Carl H. Sandgren, 1938.

Norelius, E. "The Swedish Evangelical Lutheran Church in America." In *The Lutheran Church Review*, Vol. V, Jan., 1886, pp. 27-44.

Olson, Oscar N. *The Augustana Lutheran Church in America. Pioneer Period, 1846 to 1860*. 1950. (With detailed bibliography.)

Olson, Oscar N. and George W. Wickstron. *A Century of Progress*. 1948.

Rönnegärd, Sam. "The Religious Movements in Northern Sweden a Hundred Years Ago and the Augustana Synod." In the *Augustana Quarterly*, Vol. XXVII. July, 1948.

Stephenson, G. M. *The Founding of the Augustana Synod, 1850-1860*. 1927. (With detailed bibliography.)

——————. *The Religious Aspects of Swedish Immigration*. 1932. Pp. 293-476. (With complete bibliography.)

Wentz, A. R. (Ed.) *Lutheran Churches of the World, 1952*. 1952.

Wolf, E. J. *The Lutherans in America*. 1889. Pp. 451-463.

CHAPTER 24 — Faith and Works in the Lutheran Church—Missouri Synod
Besides the periodicals of the Missouri Synod and the proceedings of its conventions, reference is made to the following:

SELECTIVE BIBLIOGRAPHY

Dau, W. H. T. (Ed.), *Ebenezer. Reviews of the Work of the Missouri Synod during Three Quarters of a Century.* 1922. Pp. 208-536.

Drewes, C. F. *Half a Century of Lutheranism among our Colored People.* 1927.

Fuerbringer, L., Th. Engelder, and P. E. Kretzmann. *Concordia Encyclopedia.* 1927. Pp. 485-515, 704, 804-806, 828-829, *et passim.*

Hochstetter, Chr. *Die Geschichte der Evangelisch-Lutherischen Missouri-Synode in Nord Amerika.* 1885.

Jacobs, H. E. *A History of the Evangelical Lutheran Church in the United States.* 1893. Pp. 498-505.

Koehler, J. P. *Geschichte der Allgemeinen Evangelisch-Lutherischen Synode von Wisconsin und anderen Staaten.* 1925.

Kuhn, A. *Geschichte der Minnesota Synode und ihrer einzelnen Gemeinden,* 1860-1910. 1910.

Kurzgefasste Geschichte der Evangelisch-Lutherischen Synode von Michigan und anderen Staaten. 1910.

Lueker, E. L. (Ed. in chief). *Lutheran Cyclopedia.* 1954. *Passim.*

Lutheran World Almanac and Encyclopedia. 1923. Pp. 41-45.

Mezger, G. (Ed.). *Denkstein zum fünfundsiebzigjährigen Jubiläum der Missourisynode.* 1922.

Mundinger, Carl. *Government in the Missouri Synod.* 1947.

Neve, J. L. *A History of the Lutheran Church in America.* 3rd ed., 1934. Pp. 177-250.

Steffens, D. H. *Doctor Carl Ferdinand Wilhelm Walther.* 1917.

Wentz, A. R. (Ed.). *The Lutheran Churches of the World,* 1952. 1952.

Wolf, E. J. *The Lutherans in America.* 1889. Pp. 406-431.

CHAPTER 25 — The Liturgical Development

Dickinson, Edward. *Music in the History of the Western Church.* 1902. Chaps. 7-9.

Horn, E. T. "The Common Service." Article in *Lutheran Encyclopedia,* 1899. Pp. 123, 124.

—————. "Lutheran Sources of the Common Service." In *The Lutheran Quarterly,* Vol. XXI, Apr., 1891, pp. 239-268.

—————. *Outlines of Liturgics.* 1912. (With bibliography.)

Jacobs, H. E. "The Common Hymnal" (historical). In *The Lutheran Church Review,* Vol. XXIX, Apr., 1910, pp. 250-275.

—————. *A History of the Evangelical Lutheran Church in the United States.* 1893. Pp. 505-510.

—————. *The Lutheran Movement in England.* 1890. Pp. 218-313.

Lewars, Elsie Singmaster. "The Common Service Book and Hymnal." In *The Lutheran Quarterly,* Vol. XLVIII, Jan., 1918, pp. 91-99.

"Liturgical Development within the Evangelical Lutheran Church in the United States" (each body treated by a separate writer). In *The Lutheran Church Review,* Vol. XXXVI, Oct., 1917, pp. 469-500.

Memoirs of the Lutheran Liturgical Association. Vols. I-VII, 1898-1907.

Ochsenford, S. E. *Documentary History of the General Council of the Evangelical Lutheran Church.* 1912. Pp. 410-457.

Reed, Luther D. *The Lutheran Liturgy. A Study of the Common Service of the Lutheran Church in America.* 1947. The first ten chapters are historical. Pp. 1-216. (Extensive bibliography.)

Reu, M. "The History of the Origin of the Lutheran Morning Service." In *The Lutheran Church Review,* Vol. XXIX, Jan., 1910, pp. 50-63.

Richard, J. W. and F. V. N. Painter. *Christian Worship: Its Principles and Forms.* 1892.

Schmucker, B. M. "The First Pennsylvania Liturgy." In *The Lutheran Church Review,* Vol. I, Jan., 1882, pp. 16-27. Vol. I, July, 1882, pp. 161-172.

―――――――――. *Preface to the Common Service.* 1888.

Smith, R. Morris. "The Liturgical Development of the General Synod of the Evangelical Lutheran Church in the United States." In *The Lutheran Quarterly,* Vol. XLVII, Oct., 1917, pp. 491-514; Vol. XLVIII, Jan., 1918, pp. 65-90.

Spaeth, A. "History of the Liturgical Development of the Ministerium of Pennsylvania." In *The Lutheran Church Review,* Vol. XVII, Jan., 1898, pp. 93-119.

CHAPTER 26 — Confessional Conservation

Baum, W. M. and J. A. Kunkleman (Eds.). *The Second Free Lutheran Diet in America,* 1878. *The Essays, Debates and Proceedings.* 1879.

Distinctive Doctrines and Usages of the Evangelical Lutheran Church. 4th ed. 1914.

Gotwald, L. A. *Trial of L. A. Gotwald, D.D.* 1893.

Jacobs, H. E. *A History of the Evangelical Lutheran Church in the United States.* 1893. Pp. 491-496, 505-514.

Jacobs, H. E. (Ed.). *The First Free Lutheran Diet in America, 1877. The Essays, Debates and Proceedings.* 1878.

―――――――― (Ed.). *The First General Conference of Lutherans in America,* 1898. *The Proceedings, Essays and Debates.* 1899.

―――――――― (Ed.). *The Second General Conference of Lutherans in America,* 1902. *The Proceedings, Essays and Debates.* 1904.

―――――――― (Ed.). *The Third General Conference of Lutherans in America,* 1904. *The Proceedings, Essays and Debates.* 1905.

Ochsenford, S. E. *Documentary History of the General Council of the Evangelical Lutheran Church.* 1912. Pp. 322-409.

Richard, J. W. "The Confessional History of the General Synod." In *The Lutheran Quarterly,* Vol. XXV, Oct., 1895, pp. 458-490.

―――――――――. *The Confessional History of the Lutheran Church.* 1909.

Sandt, G. W. *Theodore Emanuel Schmauk,* 1921. Pp. 117-281.

Schmauk, T. E. and C. Theodore Benze. *The Confessional Principle and the Confessions of the Lutheran Church.* 1911. Pp. 840-943. (Including in the table of contents a full bibliography and detailed references to the voluminous controversial literature in periodicals and special works.)

Spaeth, A. *Charles Porterfield Krauth, D.D., LL.D.,* Vol. II, 1909. Pp. 195-249.

Wolf, E. J. *The Lutherans in America.* 1889. Pp. 432-451.

CHAPTER 27 — General Background (1910-1950)

Bate, H. N. (Ed.). *Faith and Order, Proceedings of the World Conference at Lausanne.* 1927.

Beard, Charles A. and Mary R. *The Rise of American Civilization.* Vol. II, pp. 480-800.

──────────. *A Basic History of the United States.* 1950. Pp. 427-429.

Bell, G. K. A. (Ed.). *The Stockholm Conference on Life and Work,* 1925. *The Official Report.* 1926.

Brown, William Adams. *The Church in America.* 1922.

──────────. *Toward a United Church. Three Decades of Ecumenical Christianity.* 1946.

Carroll, H. K. *Religious Forces of the United States.* Revised ed. 1912.

Cavert, S. M. (Ed.). *Twenty Years of Church Federation.* 1929.

Clark, E. T. *The Small Sects in America.* 1949.

Committee on the War and the Religious Outlook, The (Editors). *Christian Unity: Its Principles and Possibilities.* 1921.

Douglass, H. Paul. *Protestant Co-operation in American Cities.* 1930.

──────────. *Christian Unity Movements in the United States.* 1934.

──────────. *A Decade of Objective Progress in Church Unity.* 1927-1936. 1937.

Fry, C. Luther. *The United States Looks at its Churches.* 1930.

Hodgson, L. (Ed.). *Faith and Order, Edinburgh,* 1937.

Hogg, W. R. *Ecumenical Foundations: A History of the International Missionary Council and its Nineteenth Century Background.* 1952.

Hutchison, John A. *We Are Not Divided. A Critical and Historical Study of the Federal Council of the Churches of Christ in America.* 1941.

Latourette, K. S. *A History of the Expansion of Christianity.* Vol. VII, *Advance Through Storm, A. D. 1914 and After.* 1945.

Macy, P. G. *The Story of the World Council of Churches.* 1947.

Oldham, J. H. *The Oxford Conference. The Official Report.* 1937.

Religious Bodies, 1926. **2** Vols. Published by the Federal Census Bureau 1926.

Religious Bodies, 1936. **2** Vols. Published by the Federal Census Bureau 1941.

Sanford, E. B. *Origin and History of the Federal Council of the Churches of Christ in America.* 1916.

Slosser, G. J. *Christian Unity: Its History and Challenge in All Communions in All Lands.* 1929.

Visser 't Hooft, W. A. *First Assembly of the World Council of Churches at Amsterdam,* 1948. 1949.

CHAPTER 28 — The Evangelical Lutheran Church

The definitive account of the formation of the Evangelical Lutheran Church is the doctoral dissertation of E. Clifford Nelson, presented to the faculty of Yale University in 1952. It is entitled *The Union Movement among Norwegian-American Lutherans from 1880 to 1917,* and it covers 673 pages. The information for the years since 1917 is gathered from the periodical publications and the convention proceedings of the Evangelical Lutheran Church. In addition we mention the following books in English:

Blegen, Theodore C. *Norwegian Migration to America, 1825-1860.* 1931.

——————. *Norwegian Migration to America. The American Transition.* 1940.

Carlsen, C. J. *The Years of our Church.* 1942.

Helland, Andreas. *Georg Sverdrup. The Man and His Message,* 1848-1907. 1947.

Hetle, Erik. *Lars Wilhelm Boe.* 1949.

Larsen, Karen. *Laur. Larsen. Pioneer College President.* 1936.

Lutheran World Almanac, The, 1921, pp. 98-105   1927-1928, pp. 24 f.
                               1922, pp. 63 f.   1929-1930, pp. 29 f.
                               1923, pp. 31 f.   1931-1933, pp. 56 f.
                               1924-1926, p. 31   1934-1937, pp. 51-53.

Melby, C. A. *St. Olaf College Through Fifty Years,* 1874-1924. 1925.

Nelson, E. Clifford, and Eugene L. Fevold. *The Lutheran Church among Norwegian-Americans.* 1960.

Neve, J. L. *A History of the Lutheran Church in America.* 1934. Pp. 288-314, 337-341.

Norlie, O. M. *History of the Norwegian People in America.* 1925. Pp. 302-510.

Rholl, Arthur (Ed.). *Red Wing Seminary. Fifty Years of Service.* 1930.

Rohne, J. M. *Norwegian American Lutheranism up to* 1872. 1926.

Swansen, H. F. *The Founder of St. Ansgar. The Life Story of Claus Laurits Clausen.* 1949.

Trabert, G. H. *English Lutheranism in the Northwest.* 1914.

Wentz, A. R. (Ed.). *The Lutheran Churches of the World,* 1952. 1952.

CHAPTER 29 — German Mergers in the Northwest

Engel. Otto. *Kurzgefasste Geschichte der Evangelisch-Lutherischen. Allgemeinen Synode von Wisconsin, Minnesota, Michigan und anderen Staaten.* 1915.

Everest, K. A. *Early Lutheran Immigration to Wisconsin.* Transactions of the Wisconsin Academy of Sciences, Arts, and Letters. Vol. 8, pp. 289-298.

Faust, A. B. *The German Element in the United States.* 1909. Vol. II, pp. 468-490. (With bibliography.)

Gerberding, G. H. *Life and Letters of W. A. Passavant, D.D.* 1906. Pp. 354-415.

Koehler, J. P. *Geschichte der Allgemeinen Evangelisch-Lutherischen Synode von Wisconsin und anderen Staaten.* Vol. I, 1925. (With bibliography.)

Kuhn, A. *Geschichte der Minnesota Synode.* 1910.

Neve, J. L. *A History of the Lutheran Church in America.* 1934. Pp. 222-287.

Thwaites, R. G. (Ed.). *Wisconsin Historical Collections.* 1892. Vols. V and XII.

Wentz, A. R. (Ed.). *The Lutheran Churches of the World,* 1952. 1952.

CHAPTER 30 – The United Lutheran Church in America

In addition to *The Lutheran Quarterly,* the periodical publications of The United Lutheran Church in America, and the minutes of the biennial conventions, reference is made to the following:

Burgess, E. B. *Memorial History of the Pittsburgh Synod of the Evangelical Lutheran Church.* 1925. Pp. 165-186.

Clutz, J. A. "The United Lutheran Church in America." In *The Lutheran Quarterly,* Vol. XLIX, Jan. and Apr., 1919, pp. 1-22, 313-329.

Eylands, V. J. *Lutherans in Canada.* 1945.

Hiller, A. "History of the First Ten Years of the Synod of New York." In *The Lutheran Quarterly,* Vol. XLIX, Apr., 1919, pp. 247-268.

Knubel, F. H. and M. G. G. Scherer (Eds.). *Our Church. An Official Study Book.* 1924.

Lentz, A. B. (Ed.). *Story of the Midwest Synod.* 1950.

Lutheran World Almanac, The, 1921, pp. 71-92, 117, 144-146
      1922, pp. 56 f., 60 f.
      1923, pp. 28-30
      1924-1926, pp. 28 f.
      1927-1928, p. 23
      1929-1930, p. 27
      1931-1933, pp. 51-53
      1934-1937, pp. 48 f.

Neve, J. L. *A History of the Lutheran Church in America.* 3rd ed. 1934. Pp. 342-356.

Proceedings of the Free Lutheran Diets (1877, 1878) and the General Conferences (1898, 1902, 1904) are listed under Chapter 26.

Schmauk, T. E. *Historical Report of the Merger,* 1918. Minutes of the U.L.C.A., 1918, pp. 37-42.

Smith, A. H. "The Synod of Ohio, 1920-1930." In *The Lutheran Church Quarterly*, Vol. IV, July, 1931, pp. 304-318.

Trexler, Samuel. *Crusaders of the Twentieth Century. A Lutheran Story in the Empire State.* 1926.

Voigt, G. P. *A. G. Voigt, Molder of Southern Lutheranism. ca.* 1949

Wentz, A. R. (Ed.). *The Lutheran Churches of the World,* 1952. 1952.

CHAPTER 31 — The American Lutheran Church (1930)

In addition to the periodical publications of the American Lutheran Church and the minutes of the Church's biennial conventions, reference is made to the following:

Deindörfer, Johannes. *Geschichte der Evangel-Luth. Synode von Iowa und Anderen Staaten.* 1897.

Distinctive Doctrines and Usages of the Evangelical Lutheran Church. (Composite.) 4th ed., 1914. Pp. 5-35, 69-92.

Lutheran Standard, The, and the *Lutherische Kirchenzeitung.* The files for 1930.

Lutheran World Almanac, The, 1931-1933, pp. 53-55
1934-1937, pp. 49 f.

Peter, P. A. and Wm. Schmidt. *Geschichte der Allgemeinen Evangelisch-Lutherischen Synode von Ohio und anderen Staaten.* 1900.

Sheatsley, C. V. *History of the Evangelical Lutheran Joint Synod of Ohio and Other States.* 1919.

_____. *The Story of the First Lutheran Seminary of the West,* 1830-1930. 1930.

Wachende Kirche, from June, 1920, to September, 1922. *Geschichte der Buffalo-Synode.*

Wentz, A. R. (Ed.). *The Lutheran Churches of the World,* 1952. 1952.

Zeilinger, G. J. *A Missionary Synod with a Mission* (Iowa). 1929.

CHAPTER 32 — The National Lutheran Council

In addition to the file of *The National Lutheran* and the minutes of the conventions of the several Lutheran bodies participating in the work of the Council, reference is made to the following:

Hauge, Osborne. *Lutherans Working Together. A History of the National Lutheran Council,* 1918-1943. With Supplementary Chapter, 1943-1945, by Ralph H. Long.

Lutheran World Almanac, The, 1921, pp. 492-515
1922, pp. 106-108
1923, pp. 38-40
1924-1926, pp. 35-39
1927-1928, pp. 28-30
1929-1930, pp. 35-38
1931-1933, pp. 66-68, 91, 285
1934-1937, pp. 61-63.

CHAPTER 33 — The American Lutheran Conference
and Independent Bodies

In addition to the file of *The Lutheran Outlook*, the reports of the biennial conventions of the Conference, and the minutes of the conventions of the several Lutheran bodies adhering to the Conference, see:

Lutheran World Almanac, The, 1931-1933, pp. 68-71; 1934-1937, pp. 63-65.

Wentz, A. R. (Ed.). *The Lutheran Churches of the World*, 1952. 1952. Pp. 370-372.

CHAPTER 34 — The Social Ministry of Lutherans

The most recent developments in social work among Lutherans are indicated by the reports of the various committees, commissions, and agencies set up by the several Lutheran bodies. These reports are found in the minutes of the conventions. Information about the work of the National Lutheran Council through its Division of Welfare may be gleaned from the file of the *National Lutheran*, from the proceedings of the national Lutheran Welfare Conference and its regional meetings, and from a large number of pamphlets and booklets dealing with individual phases of Lutheran social work. In addition we refer to the following books:

Anstadt, P. *Life and Times of Rev. S. S. Schmucker, D.D.* 1896.

Evjen, John O. *Life of J. H. W. Stuckenberg.* 1938.

Gerberding, G. *Life and Letters of W. A. Passavant, D.D.* 1906.

Hauge, Osborne. *Lutherans Working Together. A History of the National Lutheran Council*, 1918-1943. With Supplementary Chapter, 1943-1945, by Ralph H. Long.

Journals of Henry Melchior Muhlenberg, The. Trans. by Theodore G. Tappert and John W. Doberstein. In 3 vols. 1942 ff.

Mann, William J. *Life and Times of Henry Melchior Muhlenberg.* 1887.

CHAPTER 35 — The Lutheran World Federation

American Committee on Arrangements. *Lutheran World Convention. The Minutes, Addresses and Discussions of the Conference at Eisenach, Germany, August 19 to 26, 1923.*

Lund-Quist, Carl E. (Ed.). *Proceedings of the Second Assembly of the Lutheran World Federation, Hannover, Germany, 1952.* 1952.

Lutheran World Almanac, The, 1924-1926, pp. 26-28
1927-1928, pp. 21-23
1929-1930, pp. 17, 21-26, 112 f., 186
1931-1933, pp. 43-50, 91
1934-1937, pp. 31-38.

Marahrens, A. (Ed.). *Lutherischer Weltconvent zu Paris, 1935.* 1939.

Michelfelder, S. C. (Ed.). *Proceedings of the Lutheran World Federation Assembly, Lund, Sweden, 1947.* 1948.

Wentz, A. R. (Ed.). *The Second Lutheran World Convention. The Minutes, Addresses and Discussions of the Conference at Copenhagen, Denmark, June 26 to July 4, 1929.* 1930.
Wentz, A. R. (Ed.) *The Lutheran Churches of the World,* 1952. 1952.

CHAPTER 36 – Recent Moves Toward Lutheran Union

There has been no complete collection of the various documents that have been produced by recent efforts at Lutheran union. For the official text of the several declarations, sets of articles, chains of theses, statements, clarifications, and confessions, the student must turn to the minutes of the conventions of the Lutheran bodies concerned in each case. There also is the exact record of the action of each body. The details of the discussion are found in a very large number of articles in the periodical press of the various bodies, the weeklies, monthlies, and quarterlies. No books have recently been published on the subject. Nearly twenty years ago an essay on the history of Lutheran efforts at union was presented by the Missouri Synod historian, Theodore Graebner, in a book entitled *The Problem of Lutheran Union and Other Essays* (1935). The position of the Missouri Synod was presented more fully by Dr. Graebner and Dr. Paul E. Kretzmann in a book *Toward Lutheran Union* (1943). But our chief source of information on the process of Lutheran unification continues to be current periodical publications of the Lutheran church bodies.

CHAPTER 37 – Lutherans in the Modern Ecumenical Movement

Bate, H. N. (Ed.). *Faith and Order. Proceedings of the World Conference at Lausanne.* 1927.
Bell, G. K. A. (Ed.). *The Stockholm Conference on Life and Work,* 1925. *The Official Report.* 1926.
Hodgson, L. (Ed.). *Faith and Order, Edinburgh,* 1937.
Oldham, J. H. *The Oxford Conference. The Official Report.* 1937.
Visser 't Hooft, W. A. *First Assembly of the World Council of Churches at Amsterdam,* 1948. 1949.
Wentz, A. R. "Lutheran Churches and the Modern Ecumenical Movement." Pp. 391-417, in *World Lutheranism of Today, A Tribute to Anders Nygren.* 1950.

PART VII – In an Age of Pluralism and Ecumenism (1950-   )

From the multitude of materials in current periodicals and recent books that seek to analyze and interpret American culture in this new age, four are suggested as most direct and positive:

Herberg, Will. *Protestant, Catholic, Jew.* 1956.
Littell, Franklin H. *From State Church to Pluralism.* 1962.
Marty, Martin. *The New Shape of American Religion.* 1959.
West, Charles C. *Outside the Camp.* 1959.

For further details on the initial steps recorded in Part VII the reader is referred to the minutes of the past decade in the Lutheran bodies that have merged, to the reports of the Commissions on Liturgy and Hymnals and the reports of the National Lutheran Council as recorded in those minutes, to the Lutheran periodicals for the period, and to the following:

Lund-Quist, Carl E. (Ed.). *Proceedings of the Third Assembly of the Lutheran World Federation, Minneapolis, Minnesota, U.S.A., 1957.* 1958.

——————— (Ed.). *Lutheran Churches of the World.* Composite authorship. 1957.

INDEX

INDEX

Type, 10 on 13 and 9 on 11 Janson
Display, Garamond
Paper, Bright Natural Antique RRR